Storage Implementation in vSphere® 5.0

VMware Press is the official publisher of VMware books and training materials, which provide guidance on the critical topics facing today's technology professionals and students. Enterprises, as well as small- and medium-sized organizations, adopt virtualization as a more agile way of scaling IT to meet business needs. VMware Press provides proven, technically accurate information that will help them meet their goals for customizing, building, and maintaining their virtual environment.

With books, certification, study guides, video training, and learning tools produced by world-class architects and IT experts, VMware Press helps IT professionals master a diverse range of topics on virtualization and cloud computing and is the official source of reference materials for preparing for the VMware Certified Professional Examination.

VMware Press is also pleased to have localization partners that can publish its products into more than 42 languages, including, but not limited to, Chinese (Simplified), Chinese (Traditional), French, German, Greek, Hindi, Japanese, Korean, Polish, Russian, and Spanish.

For more information about VMware Press, please visit http://www.**vmware.com/go/vmwarepress**.

Storage Implementation in vSphere® 5.0

TECHNOLOGY DEEP DIVE

Mostafa Khalil, VCDX

vmware® PRESS

Upper Saddle River, NJ • Boston • Indianapolis • San Francisco
New York • Toronto • Montreal • London • Munich • Paris • Madrid
Capetown • Sydney • Tokyo • Singapore • Mexico City

STORAGE IMPLEMENTATION IN VSPHERE® 5.0

Published by VMware, Inc.

Publishing as VMware Press

ISBN-10: 0-321-79993-3

ISBN-10: 978-0-321-79993-7

Library of Congress Cataloging-in-Publication data is on file.

Printed in the United States of America

First Printing: August 2012

Warning and Disclaimer

Corporate and Government Sales

VMware Press offers excellent discounts on this book when ordered in quantity for bulk purchases or special sales, which may include electronic versions and/or custom covers and content particular to your business, training goals, marketing focus, and branding interests. For more information, please contact:

U.S. Corporate and Government Sales
(800) 382-3419
corpsales@pearsontechgroup.com

For sales outside the United States please contact:

International Sales
international@pearsoned.com

VMWARE PRESS PROGRAM MANAGER
Erik Ullanderson

ASSOCIATE PUBLISHER
David Dusthimer

EDITOR
Joan Murray

DEVELOPMENT EDITOR
Ellie Bru

MANAGING EDITOR
Sandra Schroeder

PROJECT EDITOR
Seth Kerney

COPY EDITOR
Charlotte Kughen

PROOFREADER
Megan Wade

EDITORIAL ASSISTANT
Vanessa Evans

BOOK DESIGNER
Gary Adair

COMPOSITOR
Studio Galou, LLC.

To my wife Gloria for her unconditional love and tireless efforts in helping make the time to complete this book.

Contents At A Glance

Contents

Preface

This first edition of *Storage Implementation in vSphere 5.0* is my first attempt to put all the practical experience I have acquired over the years supporting VMware products and drinking from the fountain of knowledge that is the VMware team. I share with you in-depth details of how things work so that you can identify problems if and when anything goes wrong. I originally planned to put everything in one book, but as I started writing the page count kept growing, partly due to the large number of illustrations and screenshots that I hope will make the picture clearer for you. As a result, I had to split this book into two volumes so that I don't have to sacrifice quality at the expense of page count. I hope you will find this content as useful as I intended it to be and that you'll watch for the second volume, which is coming down the pike.

The book starts with a brief introduction to the history of storage as I experienced it. It then provides details of the various storage connectivity choices and protocols supported by VMware: Fibre Channel (FC), Fibre Channel over Ethernet (FCoE), and Internet Small Computer System Interface (iSCSI). This transitions us to the foundation of vSphere storage, which is Pluggable Storage Architecture (PSA). From there I build upon this foundation with multipathing and failover (including third-party offerings) and ALUA. I then discuss storage virtual devices (SVDs) and VMDirectPath I/O architecture, implementation, and configuration. I also cover in intricate details Virtual Machine File System (VMFS) versions 3 and 5 and how this highly advanced clustered file system arbitrates concurrent access to virtual machine files as well as raw device mappings. I discuss the details of how distributed locks are handled as well as physical snapshots and virtual machines snapshots. Finally, I share with you vStorage APIs for Array Integration (VAAI) architecture and interactions with the relevant storage arrays.

Consider this volume as the first installment of more advanced content to come. I plan to update the content to vSphere 5.1, which will bear the name of *VMware Cloud Infrastructure Suite (CIS)*, and add more information geared toward design topics and performance optimization.

I would love to hear your opinions or suggestions for topics to cover. You can leave me a comment at my blog: http://vSphereStorage.com.

Thank you and God bless!

Mostafa Khalil, VCDX

Acknowledgments

I would like to acknowledge the endless support I got from my wife Gloria. I would also like to acknowledge the encouragement I got from Scot Bajtos, Senior VP of VMware Global Support Services, and Eric Wansong, VP of VMware Global Support Services (Americas).

I truly appreciate the feedback from those who took time out of their busy schedules to volunteer to review parts of the books:

Craig Risinger, Consulting Architect at VMware

Mike Panas, Senior Member of Technical Staff at VMware

Aboubacar Diar, HP Storage

Vaughn Stewart, NetApp

Jonathan Van Meter

A special thanks to Cormac Hogan, Senior Technical Marketing Architect at VMware, for permitting me to use some of his illustrations.

I also would like to acknowledge Pearson's technical reviewers, whom I knew only by their initials, and my editors Joan Murray and Ellie Bru for staying after me to get this book completed.

One last acknowledgement is to all who have taught and mentored me along the way throughout my journey. Their names are too many to count. You know who you are. Thank you all!

About the Author

Mostafa Khalil is a senior staff engineer at VMware. He is a senior member of VMware Global Support Services and has worked for VMware for more than 13 years. Prior to joining VMware, he worked at Lotus/IBM. A native of Egypt, Mostafa graduated from the Al-Azhar University's School of Medicine, and practiced medicine in Cairo. He became intrigued by the mini computer system used in his medical practice and began to educate himself about computing and networking technologies. After moving to the United States, Mostafa continued to focus on computing and acquired several professional certifications.

He is certified as VCDX (3, 4, & 5), VCAP (4 & 5)-DCD, VCAP4-DCA, VCP (2, 3, 4, & 5), MCSE, Master CNE, HP ASE, IBM CSE, and Lotus CLP.

As storage became a central element in the virtualization environment, Mostafa became an expert in this field and delivered several seminars and troubleshooting workshops at various VMware public events in the United States and around the world.

We Want to Hear from You!

As the reader of this book, *you* are our most important critic and commentator. We value your opinion and want to know what we're doing right, what we could do better, what areas you'd like to see us publish in, and any other words of wisdom you're willing to pass our way.

As an associate publisher for Pearson, I welcome your comments. You can email or write me directly to let me know what you did or didn't like about this book—as well as what we can do to make our books better.

Please note that I cannot help you with technical problems related to the topic of this book. We do have a User Services group, however, where I will forward specific technical questions related to the book.

When you write, please be sure to include this book's title and author as well as your name, email address, and phone number. I will carefully review your comments and share them with the author and editors who worked on the book.

Email: VMwarePress@vmware.com

Mail: David Dusthimer
         Associate Publisher
         Pearson
         800 East 96th Street
         Indianapolis, IN 46240 USA

Reader Services

Visit our website at www.informit.com/title/9780321799937 and register this book for convenient access to any updates, downloads, or errata that might be available for this book.

## Chapter 1

Storage Types

History of Storage

Historically, the concept of storage goes as far back as the Ancient Egyptians (my ancestors) who built silos to protect grains away from moisture and to store them for use when a famine hit. The well-known example of that is the story of Joseph when he oversaw the rationing and storage of grains as well as kept records of the stored amounts. This has evolved over the generations and nations to where we are now as we store data instead of dates (palm dates, that is)! Enough Ancient Egyptian history for now; let's get down to the wire or, in other words, the bits of computer storage history!

From a computing perspective, the smallest unit of data is a *bit* whose value is either a 0 or a 1. As you might already know, bits trace their roots back to the very early mini computer architecture in the form of toggle switches that can be in one of two positions: off (0) or on (1), which means it uses the so-called binary data. The number of bits that made up one character was 8; 8 bits are a *byte* of data.

Figure 1.1 shows an early model computer that utilized dip switches to program the bit digital values 0 or 1.

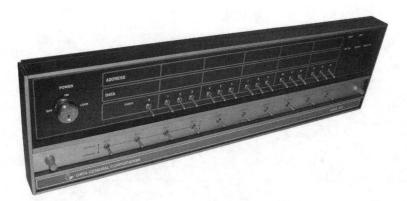

Figure 1.1   This photo of Data General's Nova 1200 Mini Computer shows a 16-bit design (16 toggle switches).

(Photo credit Arnold Reinhold, used under GNU free license)

(Trivia: Data General Corporation was the creator of EMC's CLARiiON® family of storage arrays.)

So, any data handled by a computer is simply a sequence of zeros and ones. I discuss the units of measuring data and address spaces in the "Units of Measuring Storage Capacity" section later in this chapter.

Data is stored on both volatile and permanent media forms.

Volatile data storage is also known as volatile memory or Random Access Memory (RAM). Reading data from RAM is a lot faster than reading it from most other forms of memory/storage because there are no moving parts. This type of memory/storage is used by computers to load programs and data for runtime use. Modified data in RAM is written to permanent storage at certain intervals and prior to shutting down the computer system.

Permanent data storage media types vary by the type of data to be stored or retrieved and the type of controllers to which they are attached. The earliest form of data storage was the *magnetic tape* used by mainframe computers. Data is written onto the tape in tracks more or less like the old 8-track audio tape format made popular by car stereo players in most American automobiles back in the 1970s. These tracks run parallel for the length of the tape and are read back by heads matching the number of tracks. Mainframe computers in the 1950s used 10.5" magnetic tape reels that were 0.5" wide. These have evolved into *quarter-inch* tape cartridges used with modern personal computers for the purpose of data backup.

Later forms of removable permanent data storage were the *floppy disks* that ranged from 8"
all the way down to 2". The surviving most popular form factors were 5.25" and then later
3.5" floppy disks.

(Trivia: DOS 1.0 [Disk Operating System] used by the first model of IBM PC was shipped
on both *compact cassette* as well as 5.25" floppy disks.)

IBM PC (model 5150) shipped with two 5.25" floppy drives (see Figure 1.2). Later models
(5160 or XT) shipped with a 10MB MFM hard disk. This hard disk's form factor was
5.25" full height (that is, it occupied the full slot) and replaced the second floppy disk
drive. I still have a couple of these systems in my collection, and I think there is one or
more on display at the Computer History Museum in Mountain View, California.

Figure 1.2 IBM PC (model 5150) shipped with two 5.25" floppy drives

Source: Wikipedia (retired document)

Birth of the Hard Disks

As programs and applications grew larger in size, the need arose for larger internal forms of permanent storage, which came to be known as *hard disks* or *hard disk drives*. The term *hard* was used because the disks were inflexible compared to floppy disks and tapes. They first appeared in the IBM PC/XT (Model 5160) mentioned in the previous section. It was a whopping 10MB in data size and 5.25" in diameter with an average 150 milliseconds seek time. This has been improved to 1/10 of the old seek time to about 15 milliseconds near the latter half of the 1980s.

The IBM PC/XT referenced in the previous paragraph was configured with an MFM (Modified Frequency Modulation) ST-506 interface. The Run Length Limited (RLL) ST-412 interface was also used in the late 1980s and early 1990s. The latter type required installing special software that provided a BIOS extension for expanding the Logical Block Addressing (LBA).

There were other forms of persistent storage and hard disk drives such as Enhanced Small Disk Interface (ESDI), which was rather common with early versions of AT&T UNIX and XENIX operating systems on Intel platforms in the late 1980s.

Along Comes SCSI

The need for larger, faster, and more disks in a PC begat the *Small Computer System Interface* or *SCSI* (pronounced *scuzzy*). This has proven to be the most successful and reliable interface and protocol to date. It became an industry standard for attaching all sorts of I/O devices including scanners; printers; tape drives; and storage devices, including large sets of disks in Disk Array Enclosures (DAEs). The most commonly used SCSI devices these days are disks and tape drives or libraries. The SCSI Protocol and standards are covered in the "SCSI Standards and Protocols" section of Chapter 2, "Fibre Channel Storage Connectivity"; Chapter 3, "FCoE Storage Connectivity"; and Chapter 4, "iSCSI Storage Connectivity."

SCSI disks, as well as their buffers, grew larger and faster. The interface also evolved from *parallel* to *serially attached SCSI (SAS)*. Here's an oversimplification of the SAS concept: Instead of daisy-chaining the disks between the controller and the power termination, they are now attached to dedicated channels on the controller or plugged into an external SAS disk enclosure connected to the computer's external SAS controller channels.

PATA and SATA—SCSI's Distant Cousins?

After the introduction of IBM PC/AT computers, disks commonly known as IDE disks were the next generation of disks to arrive. The Integrated Device Electronics (IDE) interface for these disks was actually AT Attachment (ATA) and AT Attachment Packet Interface (ATAPI), which was later renamed to Parallel ATA—PATA—to differentiate it from its new sibling, Serial ATA—or SATA.

PATA was limited to two drives per controller interface (master and slave), whereas SATA is limited by the number of channels provided by the controller.

The following are some differences between SAS and SATA:

- SCSI drives are more expensive and faster than SATA drives because of the design and performance achieved with this technology.

- SCSI uses a tagged command queuing implementation that allows many commands to be outstanding. This design provides significant performance gain for the drives/controllers to be able to reorder these commands in the most optimal execution manner possible.

- SCSI drives also use a processor for executing commands and handling the interface while a separate processor handles the head positioning through servos.

- SCSI disks certified for use with storage arrays include ECC (Error Checking and Correcting) buffers. This is critical for the integrity of the data especially in the vSphere environment.

- SATA 1.0 used Task Command Queuing (TCQ). This queuing technology was intended to help bridge the gap between SCSI and PATA/SATA drives; however, the overhead was fairly high and TCQ wasn't efficient enough. TCQ is also referred to as interrupt queuing.

- SATA 2.0 introduced Native Command Queuing (NCQ), which is very similar to the outstanding request queuing that SCSI uses. This technology drastically reduces the number of interrupts that TCQ uses due to the integrated first party Direct Memory Access (DMA) engine as well as the intelligent ordering of commands and interrupting when it is most optimal to do so.

- Buffer size has grown in newer SATA disks; however most do not provide ECC capability.

Table 1.1 lists various storage buses and their performance characteristics.

Table 1.1 Storage Interfaces Characteristics

Interface	Raw Bandwidth (Mbit/s)	Max Transfer Speed (MB/s)	Devices per Channel
SATA 3.0	6,000	600	1
SATA 2.0	3,000	300	
SATA 1.0	1,500	150	1 per line
PATA 133	1,064	133.5	2
SAS 600	6,000	600	1 (more than 65,000 with expanders)
SAS 300	3,000	300	
SAS 150	1,500	150	
SCSI Ultra-640	5,120	640	15 (plus the HBA)
SCSI Ultra-320	2,560	320	
Fibre Channel over fiber optic	10,520	2,000	126 $256^3 = 16,777,216$ (switched fabric)
Fibre Channel over copper cable	4,000	400	
InfiniBand	10,000	1,000	1 (point to point)
Quad Rate			Many (switched fabric)

Source http://en.wikipedia.org/wiki/Sata#Comparison_with_other_buses

Based on the varying performance characteristics of the various disk interfaces, capacity, and cost, storage can be grouped in tiers that meet relevant Service Level Agreements (SLAs).

Table 1.2 lists common storage tiers and their pros and cons.

Table 1.2 Examples of Storage Tiers

Tier	Storage Type	Pros	Cons
0	Solid State Drives (SSD)	Highest raw bandwidth and transfer speed. Fastest reads and writes both sequential and random. No moving parts.	Very expensive, lower capacity, life span is measured in write operations.

Tier	Storage Type	Pros	Cons
1	SCSI/SAS—Fibre	Higher raw bandwidth and transfer speed.	Expensive, lower capacity.
2	SCSI/SAS—Copper	Average transfer speed, less expensive than tier 1.	Somewhat expensive, lower capacity than tier 3.
3	SATA 2 or 3	Least expensive, higher capacity.	Slower transfer rate.

The concept of storage tiers plays an important role in Storage DRS feature introduced in vSphere 5.0.

Units of Measuring Storage Capacity

Storage capacity (binary) is measured in orders of magnitude of a bit where the smallest unit is 20 (1 bit) and a byte is 23. The next unit is 210 (kilobyte or KB), then 220 (megabyte or MB), and so on in the increment of 10 powers of base 2. The actual storage capacity is based on International Electrotechnical Commission (IEC), which is in increments of 1,000 when you count from a kilobyte onward. The former is commonly used to represent RAM capacity whereas the latter is used for disks.

Table 1.3 lists the units of storage capacity.

Table 1.3 Units of Storage Capacity

Unit	Abbreviation	Binary	Value	Disk Capacity
Bit	Bit	2^0	1 bit	1 bit
Byte	Byte	2^3	8 bits	8 bits
Kilobyte	KB	2^{10}	1,024 bytes	1,000 bytes
Megabyte	MB	2^{20}	1,024KB	1,000KB
Gigabyte	GB	2^{30}	1,024MB	1,000MB
Terabyte	TB	2^{40}	1,024GB	1,000GB
Petabyte	PB	2^{50}	1,024TB	1,000TB
Exabyte	EB	2^{60}	1,024PB	1,000PB

> **NOTE**
>
> The units of measuring bandwidth are based on bit count per second in increments of 1,024, and the abbreviation uses lowercase *b* to represent bits compared to uppercase *B* that represents bytes. For example, the bandwidth of 10 megabits per seconds is written as 10Mb/s or 10Mbps. It is a common oversight using *b* and *B* interchangeably. You must be careful to not specify the wrong naming convention or you might end up getting eight times less or more than you bargained for!

Permanent Storage Media Relevant to vSphere 5

ESXi 5 is installed on local disks, Storage Area Network (SAN)–presented LUNs, or iSCSI storage–presented LUNs (see Chapters 2 through 4).

(Trivia: Boot from iSCSI is not supported by ESX/ESXi releases prior to 4.1.)

Supported Local Storage Media

Supported local storage media can be the following types:

1. SCSI disks (parallel)

2. Serial SCSI disks (SAS)

3. Serial ATA disks (SATA)

4. SD flash drives and USB keys (This applies to versions as early as ESXi 3.5 embedded/installable configurations.)

5. Solid State Drives (SSD)

Shared Storage Devices

vSphere 5.0 requires shared storage for certain features to work—for example, High Availability (HA), Distributed Resource Scheduler (DRS), vMotion, Storage vMotion, Storage DRS, and so on.

Such shared storage, both Network Attached Storage (NAS) and block devices, must be on VMware's Hardware Compatibility List (HCL). Being listed there means that the devices have been tested and certified to meet minimum performance criteria, have capability of multipathing and failover, and also have possible support for certain VMware APIs such as vSphere Storage APIs for Array Integration (VAAI) and vSphere Storage APIs for Storage Awareness (VASA).

A typical block storage device meeting VMware's HCL requirement is comprised of the following:

1. One or more storage processors (SP)—also referred to as storage controllers.

2. Each SP has two or more ports of varying connectivity types and speed (for example, Fibre Channel, iSCSI). See Chapters 2 through 4 for further details.

3. Some EMC storage arrays provide multiple SPs (referred to as *directors*) with multiple ports on each director (for example, EMC DMX arrays provide multiple FA directors with four ports on each).

4. Back end of the SPs connect to one or more DAEs that house disks of various types listed in Table 1.2.

5. Some storage arrays connect the SPs to the DAEs via Fibre Channel Loop Switches.

Tips for Selecting Storage Devices

When you design a vSphere 5 environment, the choices you make for selecting storage components are crucial to successful design and implementation. The following guidelines and tips will help you make the right choices:

1. Identify the list of applications to be virtualized.

2. Identify the disk I/O criteria of these applications.

3. Identify the bandwidth requirements.

4. Calculate the disk capacity requirements for the applications' data.

5. Identify the SLAs for these applications.

Note that it is often more important to design for I/O peaks than for capacity. Inadequate storage architecture is one of the most common sources of performance problems for virtualized environments.

Summary

This chapter introduced you to storage, storage types in general, and storage used by vSphere ESXi 5. Further details are provided in the next few chapters.

## Chapter 2

Fibre Channel Storage Connectivity

In the field of diplomacy, protocols are defined as "the set of rules which guide how an activity should be performed." Comparably, protocols in the field of technology are not that far off; protocols in technology also guide how certain activities are performed!

This chapter provides an overview of Fibre Channel (FC) storage protocol and connectivity and the subsequent two chapters cover Fibre Channel over Ethernet (FCoE) and Internet Small Computer System Interface (iSCSI) protocols.

SCSI Standards and Protocols

SCSI (Small Computer System Interface) is a set of standards for physically connecting and transferring data between computers and SCSI peripheral devices. These standards define commands and protocols.

SCSI-2 and SCSI-3 Standards

SCSI-2 and SCSI-3 standards are governed by the *T10 Technical Committee* (see http://www.t10.org/drafts.htm).

SCSI-2 is the name given to the second-generation SCSI standard and SCSI-3 is the name for the third-generation SCSI Standard. However, the subsequent generations have dropped the number "-3" from the SCSI standard. When SCSI-3 Architecture Model (SAM) was revised, it became SCSI Architecture Model - 2 (SAM-2). In other words, there is no SCSI-4 standard. Rather, revisions of SAM are used and the subsequent generations are named SAM-2, SAM-4, and so on.

The chart in Figure 2.1 shows the SCSI Standards Architecture and related protocols.

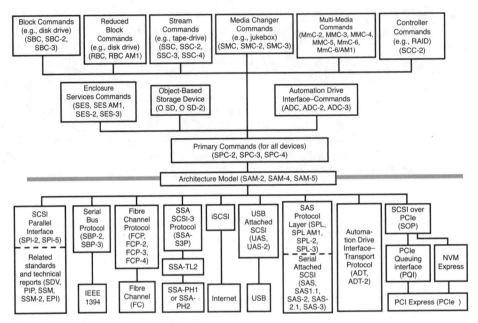

Figure 2.1   SCSI Standard Architecture

ESXi 5 mostly uses SCSI-2 standard. It also uses SCSI-3 with certain operations and configurations. I call out which standard is used with which vSphere 5 functions throughout this book.

Fibre Channel Protocol

Fibre Channel Protocol (FCP) is governed by the *T11 Technical Committee* (see http://www.t11.org/t11/stat.nsf/fcproj?OpenView&Count=70 for a list of current drafts).

FCP is used on Fibre Channel networks of varying line ratings (currently ranging between 1 and 8Gb/s, but higher ratings are in the works; for example, 16 and 20Gb/s). The basic element of a Fibre Channel connection is a *frame*. Figure 2.2 shows the structure of the FC frame. This is somewhat comparable to *Ethernet frames* or *IP packets*.

It is important to understand the FC frame structure as it aids you in interpreting storage-related messages listed in various vSphere logs discussed later in this book.

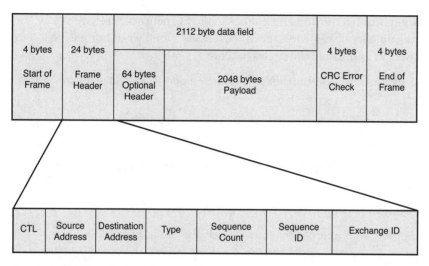

Figure 2.2 Fibre Channel frame architecture

Each frame contains 2KB of data being transmitted surrounded by fields that guarantee the integrity of the frame as well as information that helps the targets (that is, destinations) and initiators (that is, sources) reassemble the data at either ends of the connection. These fields are the following:

- Start of frame (4 bytes)
- End of frame (4 bytes)
- Frame header (24 bytes)

    - CTL (Control field)
    - Source Address
    - Destination Address
    - Type
    - Sequence Count
    - Sequence ID
    - Exchange ID

The communication between the different entities in the FC network is referred to as *exchange*, which is a number of sequences. Each sequence is a number of frames. To transfer information, FC protocol follows this process:

- Checks the address of the destination port (more on port types and addresses later in this chapter)

- Checks the possibility of connection between the *source* and *destination* ports using *logins*

- Breaks down protocol information (referred to as exchange) into information units (referred to as *sequences*)

- Break down sequences into parts small enough to fit into FC frames

- Labels each frame with (refer to the *frame header* diagram in Figure 2.2)

    - Source port address

    - Destination port address

    - Sequence number

    - Protocol

    - Exchange ID, and so on

- Moves sequences of frames to destination port

- At the destination it does the following:

    - Based on the frame labels, it reassembles the frames data to re-create the *information units* (also known as the sequences).

    - Based on the protocol, it puts the sequences together to re-create the protocol information (also known as the exchange).

The basic elements of storage can be grouped as *initiators*, *targets*, and the *network* that connects them. That network is also referred to as the *Fabric* in certain configurations. These elements vary based on the storage protocol in use.

This chapter covers Fibre Channel (FC) initiators, targets, and fabrics. Chapters 3 and 4 cover FCoE and iSCSI, respectively.

Fibre Channel (FC) Initiator

Initiators are the endpoints on the storage network that initiate SCSI sessions with the SCSI targets. Examples are SCSI HBA (Host Bus Adapter), FC-HBA, iSCSI Hardware Initiator, and iSCSI Software Initiator configured or installed in each vSphere host. I cover iSCSI initiators in Chapter 4.

FC initiators are the FC HBAs that are available in 1, 2, 4, and 8 Gbit/s port speeds and can be a single port or dual port. Higher speeds are planned as well but not released yet as of the date of this writing.

Some FC HBAs are in the form of mezzanine cards in blade servers. A variety of that is the Fibre Channel Flex-Connect technology from HP.

FC-Port Identifiers

FC Ports have unique identifiers referred to as World Wide Port Name (WWPN). It is an ID assigned that is guaranteed to be unique in the fabric and is based on an Organizationally Unique Identifier (OUI), which is assigned by the Institute for Electrical and Electronics Engineers (IEEE) registration authority. (See http://standards.ieee.org/develop/regauth/oui/public.html.) Each FC HBA manufacturer registers its own OUI and generates the WWPN based on that OUI.

```
Sample WWPN: 21:00:00:1b:32:17:34:c9
```

The bytes highlighted are the OUI.

To identify the registered owner of the OUI, search for that OUI (without the colons) at the IEEE URL—for example, you could search for 001b32.

FC-Node Identifiers

FC Nodes have unique identifiers referred to as World Wide Node Name (WWNN). These IDs are generated by the HBA manufacturer using their unique OUIs in the same fashion described in WWPN in the previous section.

Sample initiator WWNN: `20:00:00:1b:32:17:34:c9`

This sample was taken from the same HBA used in the WWPN example in the previous section. Notice that the OUI is identical. In this example, the HBA is QLogic QLE2462 model.

Sample Target WWNN: `50:06:01:60:c1:e0:65:22`

This sample was taken from a CLARiiON SP port. Notice that the target OUI bits are in a different position than in the WWNN.

Locating HBA's WWPN and WWNN in vSphere 5 Hosts

In the process of troubleshooting storage area network (SAN) connectivity or mapping out an existing vSphere 5.0 host's SAN connectivity, you need to identify the installed HBAs' WWPNs and WWNNs. In this section I show you how to do that via the user interface (UI) as well as the command-line interface (CLI).

Procedure Using the UI

To locate HBA's WWPN and WWNN, you may use this procedure:

1. Log on to the vSphere 5.0 host directly or to the vCenter server that manages the host using the VMware vSphere 5.0 Client as a user with Administrator privileges.

2. While in the Inventory — Hosts and Clusters view, locate the vSphere 5.0 host in the inventory tree and select it.

3. Navigate to the Configuration tab.

4. Under the Hardware section, select the **Storage Adapters** option.

5. Locate the HBAs with the Type column showing Fibre Channel.

6. Select one HBA at a time and in the Details pane locate the WWN field. There, you see the WWNN followed by the WWPN listed, separated by a space.

See Figure 2.3 for an example.

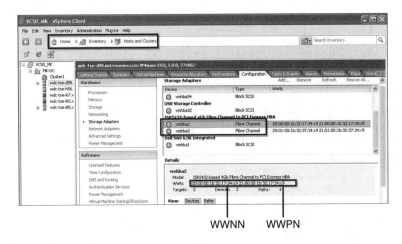

Figure 2.3   Locating HBAs' WWNN and WWPN using the UI

Procedures Using the CLI

Storage adapter properties can also be identified via the CLI. The CLI is available via multiple facilities:

- **SSH**—SSH access to the host is disabled by default. To enable it, you may follow the procedure in the "Enabling SSH Host Access" section. If you do not wish to do so, follow one of the next two options: vMA or vShpere CLI (vCLI).

- **vMA**—vSphere Management Assistant version 5.0 is a SuSE Linux Enterprise Server 11 Virtual Appliance that is preinstalled with all you need to remotely manage one or more ESXi 5.0 hosts including vCLI. For more information see http://www.vmware.com/go/vma.

- **vCLI**—vCLI is available for both Windows and Linux. You can install it on your management workstation. The syntax for using the Linux version is the same as that for the Windows version. Keep in mind that additional OS-specific commands and tools available on Linux might not be available on Windows. I cover the Linux version only, and you may apply the same procedure on Windows substituting non-ESXCLI commands with relevant ones that are available on Windows. For example, on Linux I might infrequently use sed and awk, which are not available on Windows by default. You might get a Windows version of sed from http://gnuwin32.sourceforge.net/packages/sed.htm and awk from http://gnuwin32.sourceforge.net/packages/gawk.htm.

Enabling SSH Host Access

Access to the ESXi 5.0 host is not enabled by default. To enable it, follow this procedure:

1. Log on to the vSphere 5.0 host directly or to the vCenter server 5.0 that manages the host using the VMware vSphere 5.0 Client as a user with Administrator privileges.

2. While in the Inventory—Hosts and Clusters view, locate the vSphere 5.0 host in the inventory tree and select it.

3. Navigate to the Configuration tab.

4. Under the Software section, select the **Security Profile** option, as shown in Figure 2.4.

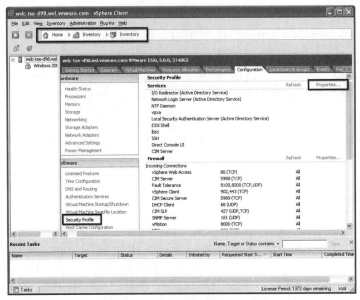

Figure 2.4   Modifying the security profile

5. Click **Properties** in the Services section in the right-hand side pane. The dialog shown in Figure 2.5 displays.

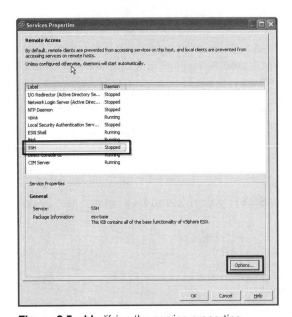

Figure 2.5   Modifying the service properties

6. Click **SSH** under the list of services displayed in the resulting dialog.

7. Click **Options** at the lower-right corner of the dialog. The dialog shown in Figure 2.6 displays.

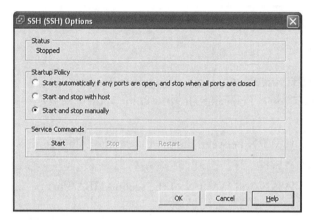

Figure 2.6 SSH options

8. If you want to temporarily enable SSH access to the host, the radio button **Start and stop manually** is selected by default; click the **Start** button, click **OK**, and then click **OK** again and stop here. If you want to permanently enable SSH access to the host, proceed to the next step.

9. Select the **Start and stop with host** option.

10. If you want to enable SSH access to the host when the SSH port is enabled, on the ESXi Firewall, without having to manually start the SSH service, select the **Start automatically if any ports are open, and stop when all ports are closed** option.

Procedure Using SSH

To locate HBA's WWPN and WWNN using SSH, you may follow this procedure:

1. Connect to the vSphere 5.0 host using an SSH client.

2. If root SSH access is disabled, log on using the user account assigned to you; then use *su* to elevate your privileges to *root*. Notice that your shell prompt changes from $ to #. (Note that sudo is no longer available in ESXi 5.)

3. Run the following command if you are using QLogic FC-HBAs:

```
grep adapter- /proc/scsi/qla2xxx/*
```

This returns an output similar to Figure 2.7.

```
wdc-tse-d98.wsl.vmware.com - PuTTY
~ # grep adapter- /proc/scsi/qla2xxx/*
/proc/scsi/qla2xxx/7:scsi-qla0-adapter-node=2000001b321734c9:080600:0;
/proc/scsi/qla2xxx/7:scsi-qla0-adapter-port=2100001b321734c9:080600:0;
/proc/scsi/qla2xxx/8:scsi-qla1-adapter-node=2001001b323734c9:391700:0;
/proc/scsi/qla2xxx/8:scsi-qla1-adapter-port=2101001b323734c9:391700:0;
~ #
```

Figure 2.7 Locating WWPN/WWNN via the CLI

The first line shows the first HBA's WWNN between `node=` and the colon. In this example, the WWNN is 2000001b321734c9. The value after the colon is the *Port ID*, which I discuss later in this chapter.

The second line shows the first HBA's WWPN between the `port=` and the colon. In this example, the WWPN is 2100001b321734c9.

The third and fourth lines show the WWNN and WWPN of the second HBA/Port respectively.

If you are using Emulex HBAs, substitute `qla2xxx` with the node relevant to your HBA's driver — for example, lpfc820 — but the command that searches for the string `Port` instead of `adapter-` is a bit different, as listed here:

```
# fgrep Port lpfc820/5
Portname: 10:00:00:00:c9:6a:ff:ac   Nodename: 20:00:00:00:c9:6a:ff:ac
```

In this example, the WWPN and the WWNN are listed on the same line as Portname and Nodename, respectively. Alternatively, you may run this command (output shown in Figure 2.8):

```
esxcfg-mpath -b |grep WWNN |sed 's/.*fc //;s/Target.*$//'
```

```
wdc-tse-d98.wsl.vmware.com - PuTTY
~ # esxcfg-mpath -b |grep WWNN |sed 's/.*fc //;s/Target.*$//'
Adapter: WWNN: 20:01:00:1b:32:37:34:c9 WWPN: 21:01:00:1b:32:37:34:c9
Adapter: WWNN: 20:01:00:1b:32:37:34:c9 WWPN: 21:01:00:1b:32:37:34:c9
Adapter: WWNN: 20:00:00:1b:32:17:34:c9 WWPN: 21:00:00:1b:32:17:34:c9
Adapter: WWNN: 20:00:00:1b:32:17:34:c9 WWPN: 21:00:00:1b:32:17:34:c9
Adapter: WWNN: 20:01:00:1b:32:37:34:c9 WWPN: 21:01:00:1b:32:37:34:c9
Adapter: WWNN: 20:01:00:1b:32:37:34:c9 WWPN: 21:01:00:1b:32:37:34:c9
Adapter: WWNN: 20:00:00:1b:32:17:34:c9 WWPN: 21:00:00:1b:32:17:34:c9
Adapter: WWNN: 20:00:00:1b:32:17:34:c9 WWPN: 21:00:00:1b:32:17:34:c9
~ #
~ #
```

Figure 2.8 Alternative command to identify HBAs WWPN and WWNN

This truncates the output up to the first occurrence of the string `fc` and removes the trailing text starting with `Target`. I discuss identifying the targets IDs in the next section.

The output shows the HBAs' (Adapters) WWNN and WWPN associated with all paths to the attached storage devices (read more about paths and multipathing in Chapter 7, "Multipathing and Failover").

In this example, we have two HBAs with the following names:

First HBA:

> WWNN: 20:01:00:1b:32:37:34:c9
>
> WWPN: 21:01:00:1b:32:37:34:c9

Second HBA:

> WWNN: 20:00:00:1b:32:17:34:c9
>
> WWPN: 21:00:00:1b:32:17:34:c9

Procedure Using vMA (vSphere Management Assistant) 5.0

This procedure assumes that you have already installed and configured vMA 5.0 as outlined in documentations available at http://www.vmware.com/go/vma where you can also find the link to download it:

1. Log on to vMA as vi-admin or a user that can use *sudo* (that is, added to the **sudoers** file using visudo editor).

2. The first time you use vMA after a fresh installation, you need to add each ESXi host you plan to manage via this appliance (Figure 2.9).

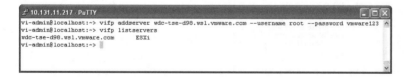

Figure 2.9   Adding a managed host

3. The command to add a managed host is

   ```
   vifp addserver <ESXi host name> --username root --password <root's
   password>
   ```

4. Verify that the host has been successfully added

   ```
   vifp listservers
   ```

   You should see the host name you just added listed along with its host type being ESXi (Figure 2.9).

5. Repeat steps 2 and 3 for each host you want to manage via this vMA. Set the ESXi server as the current managed target host (see Figure 2.10).

Figure 2.10   Setting the target managed host

The command to accomplish that is

```
vifptarget -s <ESXi host name>
```

Notice that the prompt changes to include the managed target ESXi Host name.

From this point on, all subsequent commands apply to that host without the need to specify the host name with each command. You may repeat this command using another host name later when you want to manage a different host.

You can use the CLI to locate the HBA's WWPN and WWNN as shown in Figure 2.11.

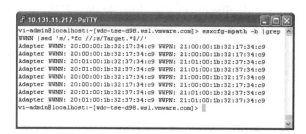

Figure 2.11   Locating the HBA's WWPN and WWNN using CLI

6. To locate the HBA's WWPN and WWNN, run the following command:

```
esxcfg-mpath -b |grep WWNN |sed 's/.*fc //;s/Target.*$//'
```

> **NOTE**
>
> You cannot use the procedure listing the proc node for the HBAs because these nodes are not available remotely.

Procedure Using Linux vCLI

Using vCLI is similar to using vMA but without fast-pass (FP) facility, which provides *vifp* and *vifptarget* commands. This means that you have to provide the host's credentials with each command, which include `--server`, `--username`, and `--password` in addition to the rest of the command options used in section "Procedure Using vMA 5.0."

For example, the command would be

```
esxcfg-mpath -b --server <host name> --username root --password <password>
|grep WWNN |sed 's/.*fc //;s/Target.*$//'
```

TIP

You may use the `--credstore` option (variable VI_CREDSTORE) to avoid providing the credentials details with every command you run against the ESXi hosts.

The name of the credential store file defaults to **<HOME>/.vmware/credstore/ vicredentials.xml** on Linux and **<APPDATA>/VMware/credstore/vicredentials.xml** on Windows.

See the vMA 5.0 user guide for additional details.

FC Targets

Targets are the SCSI endpoints that wait for the initiators commands and provide the required input/output (I/O) data transfer to/from them. This is where LUNs (Logical Units) are defined and presented to the initiators.

Examples of SCSI targets are Storage Arrays' Controllers (also known as Processors) ports. These ports can be FC, iSCSI, FCoE, or Serial Attached Storage (SAS) ports. I discuss FC targets in this chapter and cover FCoE and iSCSI targets in Chapters 3 and 4, respectively.

FC targets are the FC ports on one or more Storage Array Controllers/Processors (SPs). These ports have globally unique identifiers like those we discussed in the "FC Initiator" section. In most configurations, a given Storage Array uses a single WWNN whereas each SP port has a unique WWPN.

Most storage vendors Original Equipment Manufacturer (OEM) the FC ports from an original manufacturer and the former assign WWNN and WWPN using their own registered OUI in a similar fashion as those assigned to FC HBAs discussed in the "FC Initiators" section.

Storage array vendors have different algorithms for generating the WWPNs of their SP ports. Table 2.1 lists some of the patterns that I have identified over the years of reading through hundreds of vSphere logs and with help from storage partners. The table lists the WWPNs of the SP ports where the nonsignificant bytes are replaced with the letter *X* leaving the relevant bytes to show the pattern (with the exception of IBM DS4000 family where I masked the nonsignificant bytes as zeros).

Table 2.1   Identifying SP Port Association with Each SP

Array Family	SP Port ID	WWPN
EMC CLARiiON CX	SPA0	xx:xx:xx:**60**:xx:xx:xx:xx
	SPA1	xx:xx:xx:**61**:xx:xx:xx:xx
	SPA2	xx:xx:xx:**62**:xx:xx:xx:xx
	SPA3	xx:xx:xx:**63**:xx:xx:xx:xx
	SPA4	xx:xx:xx:**64**:xx:xx:xx:xx
	SPA5	xx:xx:xx:**65**:xx:xx:xx:xx
	SPA6	xx:xx:xx:**66**:xx:xx:xx:xx
	SPA7	xx:xx:xx:**67**:xx:xx:xx:xx
	SPB0	xx:xx:xx:**68**:xx:xx:xx:xx
	SPB1	xx:xx:xx:**69**:xx:xx:xx:xx
	SPB2	xx:xx:xx:**6A**:xx:xx:xx:xx
	SPB3	xx:xx:xx:**6B**:xx:xx:xx:xx
	SPB4	xx:xx:xx:**6C**:xx:xx:xx:xx
	SPB5	xx:xx:xx:**6D**:xx:xx:xx:xx
	SPB6	xx:xx:xx:**6E**:xx:xx:xx:xx
	SPB7	xx:xx:xx:**6F**:xx:xx:xx:xx

Array Family	SP Port ID	WWPN
HDS Lightning (95XXv)	SP0A	xx:xx:xx:xx:xx:xx:xx:90
	SP0B	xx:xx:xx:xx:xx:xx:xx:91
	SP0C	xx:xx:xx:xx:xx:xx:xx:92
	SP0D	xx:xx:xx:xx:xx:xx:xx:93
	SP1A	xx:xx:xx:xx:xx:xx:xx:94
	SP1B	xx:xx:xx:xx:xx:xx:xx:95
	SP1C	xx:xx:xx:xx:xx:xx:xx:96
	SP1D	xx:xx:xx:xx:xx:xx:xx:97
HP EVA	SPA1	xx:xx:xx:xx:xx:xx:xx:x9
	SPA2	xx:xx:xx:xx:xx:xx:xx:x8
	SPB1	xx:xx:xx:xx:xx:xx:xx:xD
	SPB2	xx:xx:xx:xx:xx:xx:xx:xC
IBM FAStT/DS4000 family	See note	20:0X:00:00:00:00:xx
	See note	20:0Z:00:00:00:00:zz

Compare the X and Y where the lower value indicates the primary SP and the higher one indicates the secondary SP. Also, Compare xx and zz where the higher the value, the higher SP port number.

Decoding EMC Symmetrix WWPN

To decode the EMC Symmetrix/DMX WWPN is a bit tricky. Figure 2.12 helps explain this process.

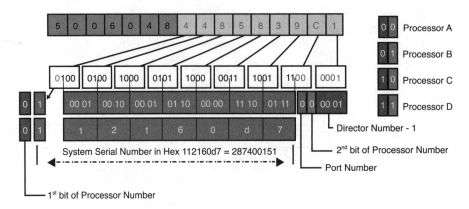

Figure 2.12   Decoding EMC Symmetrix WWPN

The Symmetrix/DMX FA Director port WWPN begins with 5006048 (because EMC's OUI is 006048). Each word in the diagram is converted from hex to decimal in the box directly connected to it. For example, the first word after the OUI has a value of "0x4" hex which translates to "0100" binary.

The first bit combined with the bit labeled "2nd bit of Processor Number" is used to identify which processor it is on the FA Director.

> **NOTE**
>
> FA Director Boards have two sides with two processors on each making total of four processors per Director Board (labeled processors A, B, C, and D in Figure 2.12).
>
> The number of FA Ports is four or eight depending on the options ordered with the array.

When the first bit (or first half) of the processor number is not set (the value is 0), the processor ID is A or B, and when it is set (the value is 1) the ID is C or D. The second bit differentiates which processor of the pair it is.

The identification of the processors is shown in Figure 2.12 and is also listed in Table 2.2.

Table 2.2 Calculating FA Director Processor Number

First Bit (First Half of ID)	Second Bit (Second Half of ID)	Processor Number
0	0	Processor A
0	1	Processor B
1	0	Processor C
1	1	Processor D

Locating Targets' WWNN and WWPN Seen by vSphere 5 Hosts

Targets' WWPNs and WWNNs can be located using similar approaches to what's covered in the "Locating HBA's WWPN and WWNN in vSphere 5 Hosts" section.

Procedure Using the UI

To locate targets' WWNN and WWPN using the UI, you may follow this procedure:

1. Log on to the vSphere 5.0 host directly or to the vCenter server that manages the host using the VMware vSphere 5.0 Client as a user with Administrator privileges.

2. While in the Inventory — Hosts and Clusters view, locate the vSphere 5.0 host in the inventory tree and select it.

3. Navigate to the Configuration tab.

4. Under the Hardware section, select the **Storage Adapters** option.

5. Select one of the HBAs whose Type column is Fibre Channel.

6. Under the Details pane, click the **Paths** button.

7. Click the **LUN** column to sort by the LUN number.

8. The UI should look similar to Figure 2.13:

   a. The target column shows the WWNN and WWPN separated by a space.

   b. Each row lists the target ID for a separate path from the selected HBA to a LUN.

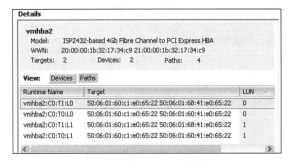

Figure 2.13   Locating targets' WWPN and WWNN

9. Repeat steps 5 through 8 for each HBA.

An Alternative Procedure Using the UI

To list all targets accessible by all HBAs in the vSphere 5.0 host, you may use the following procedure, which lists all paths to a given LUN and then identifies the target IDs:

1. Log on to the vSphere 5.0 host directly or to the vCenter server that manages the host using the VMware vSphere 5.0 Client as a user with Administrator privileges.

2. While in the Inventory — Hosts and Clusters view, locate the vSphere 5.0 host in the inventory tree and select it.

3. Navigate to the Configuration tab.

4. Under the Hardware section, select the **Storage** option.

5. Under the View field, click the **Devices** button.

6. Under the Devices pane, select one of the SAN LUNs (see Figure 2.14). In this example, its name starts with **DGC Fibre Channel Disk**.

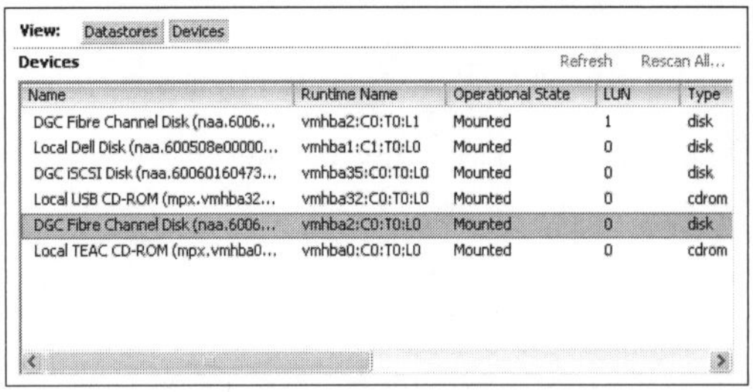

Name	Runtime Name	Operational State	LUN	Type
DGC Fibre Channel Disk (naa.6006...	vmhba2:C0:T0:L1	Mounted	1	disk
Local Dell Disk (naa.600508e00000...	vmhba1:C1:T0:L0	Mounted	0	disk
DGC iSCSI Disk (naa.60060160473...	vmhba35:C0:T0:L0	Mounted	0	disk
Local USB CD-ROM (mpx.vmhba32...	vmhba32:C0:T0:L0	Mounted	0	cdrom
DGC Fibre Channel Disk (naa.6006...	vmhba2:C0:T0:L0	Mounted	0	disk
Local TEAC CD-ROM (mpx.vmhba0...	vmhba0:C0:T0:L0	Mounted	0	cdrom

Figure 2.14   Listing datastores

7. Select **Manage Paths** in the Device Details pane.

8. Figure 2.15 shows the LUN details. In this example, I sorted on the Runtime Name field in ascending order:

   ■ The Paths section shows all available paths to the LUN in the format.

   ■ Runtime Name: vmhbaX:C0:Ty:Lz where X is the HBA number, y is the target number, and z is the LUN number. More on that later in this chapter.

   ■ Target: Both the WWNN followed by the WWPN of the target separated by a space.

9. You can also select one of the paths at a time. The path details displays in the lower pane in the Fibre Channel field:

   ■ Adapter: the HBA's WWNN then WWPN separated by a space

   ■ Target: The SP WWNN then WWPN.

Figure 2.15 Listing paths to the SAN LUN

In this example, the targets have the IDs listed in Table 2.3.

Table 2.3 List of Target IDs

HBA Number	Target Number	Target WWNN	Target WWPN
2	0	50:06:01:60:c1:e0:65:22	50:06:01:60:c1:e0:65:22
2	1	50:06:01:60:c1:e0:65:22	50:06:01:68:41:e0:65:22
3	0	50:06:01:60:c1:e0:65:22	50:06:01:61:41:e0:65:22
3	1	50:06:01:60:c1:e0:65:22	50:06:01:69:41:e0:65:22

Notice that in this example the WWNN is the same for all targets whereas the WWPNs are unique.

Using Table 2.1, we can identify which WWPN belongs to which SP port on the array as listed in Table 2.4.

Table 2.4 Mapping Targets to the SP Ports

HBA Number	Target Number	SP Number	Port Number
2	0	A	0
2	1	B	0
3	0	A	1
3	1	B	1

SAN Topology

SAN Topology is a term that refers to how objects are connected in the Storage Area Network.

Fibre Channel (FC)

FC is the infrastructure and the medium that connects storage devices utilizing FC Protocol.

FC Layers

Fibre Channel is comprised of five layers as shown in Figure 2.16 .

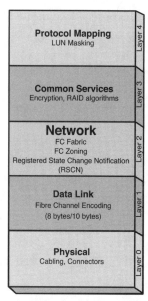

Figure 2.16 Fibre channel layers

FC Ports

FC ports vary based on their function in the FC network. They can be one of the types listed in Table 2.5.

Table 2.5 FC Port Types

FC Port Type	Expanded Name	Description
N-Port	Node Port	Node port that connects nodes with each other using Point-to-Point topology and also connects nodes to the fabric via FC switch ports
NL-Port	Node Loop Port	Node ports when they connect via Arbitrated Loop (FC-AL) topology
F-Port	Fabric Port	Switch port that connects to Nodes N-Port in a Point-to-Point topology
FL-Port	Fabric Loop Port	Switch port that connects to Nodes NL-Port in an Arbitrated Loop Topology
E-Port	Expansion Port	Switch port that connects FC switches forming an ISL (Inter-Switch Link)
TE-Port	Trunking E-Port	Only on Cisco switches; connects FC switches and routes between VSANs

FC network connects ports with or without FC switches. The way the ports are connected with each other is defined by the *topology*.

FC Topology

FC topologies describe how the various ports are connected together. There are three major FC topologies: Point-to-Point (FC-P2P), Arbitrated Loop (FC-AL), and Switched Fabric (FC-SW).

FC-P2P (Point-to-Point)

FC Point-to-Point topology is where two devices are connected directly to each other as shown in Figure 2.17.

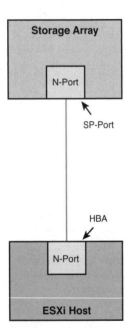

Figure 2.17   Point-to-Point topology

An example of FC-P2P topology is connecting an ESXi host's FC HBA directly to a Storage Array's SP port. Some storage arrays are supported by VMware with this topology. Check the HCL for the Array Test Configuration option **FC Direct Attached**.

When you configure FC-HBA BIOS, this is the setting to select regardless of using this topology or Switched Fabric.

FC-AL (Arbitrated Loop)

Arbitrated Loop topology is similar to the Token Ring networking where all devices are connected in a loop or a ring, as shown in Figure 2.18.

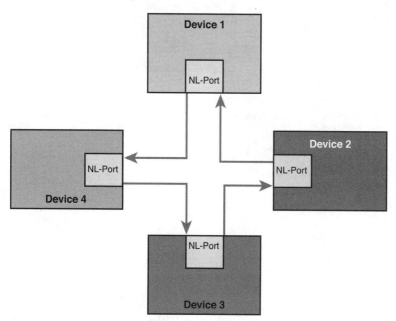

Figure 2.18   FC-AL topology

Adding or removing any device breaks the ring, and all devices are affected. This topology is not supported by VMware.

Some models of HP EVA arrays use FC Loop Switches to connect the SPs to the Disk Array Enclosures (DAEs), as shown in Figure 2.19.

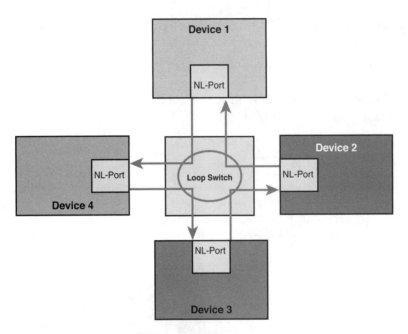

Figure 2.19   FC Loop Switch

This solution helps avoid breaking the loop when adding or removing devices.

Switched Fabric

Switched Fabric configuration is when nodes (N-port or NL-Port) connect to FC switches (see Figure 2.20).

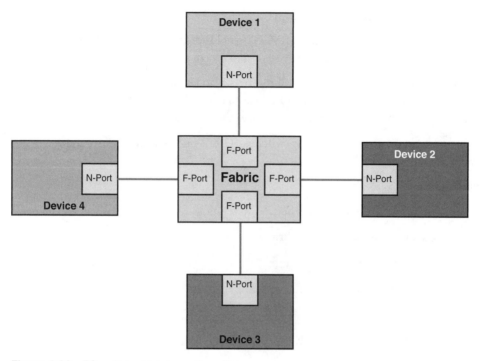

Figure 2.20   FC switched fabric configuration

In this configuration, switches are connected to each other via Inter-Switch-Links (ISLs) to form a *Fabric*. Design decisions for switch connectivity are covered later in the "Designing Storage with No Single Points of Failure" section.

Fabric Switches

The FC Fabric is composed of one or more interconnected FC switches that share a set of services provided by the switches' fabric OS. Some of these services are Name Services, RSCN, FDMI, and FLOGI.

Name Service

Maintains a list of attributes of all hosts and storage devices currently connected to the fabric, or that were connected to it sometime in the past, and that have successfully registered their own port information.

Examples of attributes maintained by the name service are WWPN, WWNN, and Port Aliases.

Registered State Change Notification

Registered State Change Notification (RSCN) is a Fibre Channel service that informs hosts about changes in the fabric.

State Change Notifications are sent to all registered nodes (within the same zone) and reachable fabric switches in case of major fabric changes. This refreshes the nodes' knowledge of the fabric so that they may react to these changes.

RSCNs are implemented on the fabric switches. This is part of *Layer 2* of the Fibre Channel model (Network Layer).

Events triggering RSCNs are

- Nodes joining or leaving the fabric

- Switches joining or leaving the fabric

- Switch name change

- New zone enforcement

- Switch IP address change

- Disks joining or leaving the fabric

Fabric-Device Management Interface

Fabric-Device Management Interface (FDMI) is a Fibre Channel service that enables management of devices such as Fibre Channel HBAs through in-band (via the storage network) communications. This service complements name service and management service functions of the Fabric Switch. This service extracts information from connected nodes and stores it in a persistent database.

Examples of extracted information are

- Manufacturer, model, and serial number

- Node name and node symbolic name

- Hardware, driver, and firmware versions

- Host operating system (OS) name and version number

Fabric Login

The Fabric Login (FLOGI) service receives and executes login requests from nodes connected to the fabric.

FC Zoning

FC Fabric can experience large numbers of events that can be disruptive to entities not involved in these events. In addition, a certain level of security must be considered while designing the FC SAN (Storage Area Network). Main elements of FC SAN security are *Zoning* and *LUN Masking*.

Zoning enables you to partition the FC Fabric into a smaller subset for better security and easier management. In addition, fabric events occurring on one zone are isolated to that zone only and the rest of the zones are spared the noise.

Zone Types

Zoning is available in two types: Soft Zoning and Hard Zoning. Zoning combines the following attributes:

- **Name**—The name given to the zone
- **Port**—The initiator, target, or switch port that is a member of this zone

Fabric switches group multiple zone definitions into one or more *ZoneSets*. However, only one ZoneSet can be active at a time. Figure 2.21 shows a logical representation of two zones with separate members. In this example, Node 1 and Node 2 can only access SPA on the storage array whereas Node 3 and Node 4 can only access SPB of the same storage array. Depending on the entities that make up the zone definition, zone types can be classified as soft or hard zones.

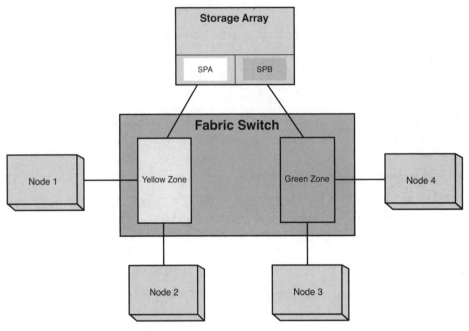

Figure 2.21 Zoning logical diagram

Soft Zoning

The fabric name service allows each device to query the addresses of all other devices. Soft zoning restricts the fabric name service so that it shows only an allowed subset of devices. Effectively, when a node that is a member of a soft zone looks at the content of the fabric, it only sees the devices that belong to that soft zone.

The addresses listed in the soft zone are any of the following:

- Initiators' WWPN.

- Targets' WWPN.

- Aliases of the initiators' or targets' WWPNs.

- Using aliases simplifies identification of the various WWPNs by providing descriptive names to the complex WWPNs and makes it easier for SAN admins to select the correct members of the zones.

In the event of a switch port failure, reconnecting the affected node to another port in the switch or the fabric allows the node to reconnect to the rest of the zone members.

However, if the node's HBA fails, replacing it requires a zone modification to use the new HBA's WWPN instead of that of the failed one. Figure 2.22 shows a logical representation of soft zones. Here, you see the members of the zone are defined by the aliases assigned to the initiators ports and the target ports.

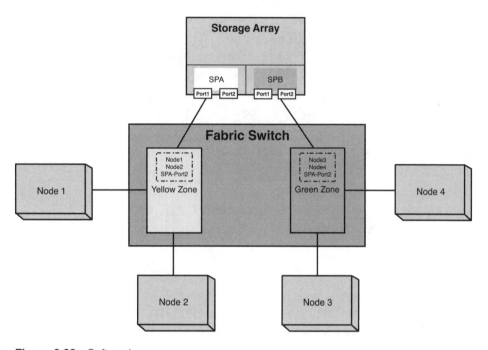

Figure 2.22 Soft zoning

Hard Zoning

Hard zoning is a similar concept to soft zoning with the difference that switch ports are used as members of the zones instead of the nodes' WWPNs. This means that whichever node connected to a switch port in a given zone can access devices connected to any of the ports in that are members of that zone. Disconnecting that node from the switch port and connecting a different node to that port permits the latter node to access all ports in that zone without any zone modifications.

Figure 2.23 shows a logical representation of hard zones. Here, you see the members of the zone are defined by the physical switch ports to which the initiators and targets ports are connected.

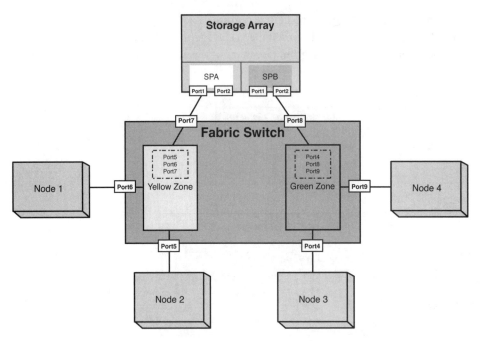

Figure 2.23 Hard zoning

Multi Initiator Zoning Versus Single Initiator Zoning

Based on the entities included in a zone configuration the can be grouped as

- **Single Initiator—Single Target Zones** —This type includes two nodes only: an initiator and a target. It is the most restrictive type and requires more administrative efforts. The advantage of this type is limiting the RSCNs to a single target and a single initiator and the fabric in between. It results in less disruption to other initiators due to event originating from members of the zone. This is recommended by most of VMware's storage partners.

- **Single Initiator—Multiple Target Zones** —This is similar to the previous type but with more targets in the zone. This is recommended by some of VMware's storage partners.

- **Multi-Initiator Zones** —This type includes multiple initiators and multiple targets. This is not recommended by VMware as it exposes all nodes in the zone to RSCNs and other events originating from any of the nodes in the zone. Although this has the least effect on administrative efforts, it is the most disruptive configuration and must be avoided in production environments.

NOTE

VMware recommends single initiator zoning but single-initiator—multi-target zoning is also acceptable unless the storage vendor does not support it.

Designing Storage with No Single Points of Failure

Storage is a critical element of vSphere 5.0 environment. If it becomes unavailable, all virtual machines residing on it suffer outages that can be very costly to your business. In order to avoid unplanned outages, you must design your storage without single points of failure.

Additional aspects of Business Continuity/Disaster Recovery (BC/DR) are covered later in this book.

SAN Design Guidelines

The basic Fibre Channel SAN design elements include

- FC Host Bus Adapters
- FC Cables
- Fabric Switches
- Storage Arrays and Storage Processors

I share some sample design choices over the next few pages and point out the points of failure in a gradual fashion until we build the best environment possible.

Design Scenario 1

In this scenario, each ESX host has a single HBA with a single port and one port from one of the two SPs are all connected to a single Fabric Switch (see Figure 2.24).

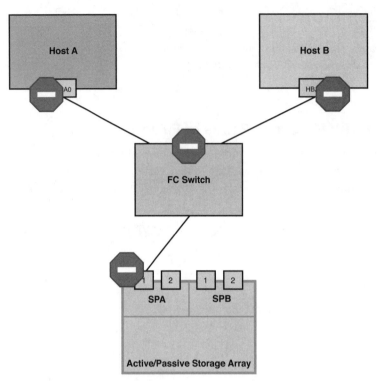

Figure 2.24   Design 1—All points

This is the worst design that can possibly exist. Every element in the design is a single point of failure. In other words, I would call this *All Points of Failure!*

The points of failure include

- If the FC switch fails, both hosts lose access to the Storage Array.
- If the HBA in one of the hosts or its cable fail, that host loses access to the Storage Array.
- If the cable connecting SPA Port 1 to the FC switch fails, both hosts lose access to the Storage Array.
- If any of the connected ports on the FC switch fails, the node connected to that port loses access to the FC switch.
- If SPA fails, both hosts lose access to the Storage Array.

Design Scenario 2

The same as Design 1 (see Figure 2.24) with the addition of a link between SPA port 2 and the FC switch. (See Figure 2.25.)

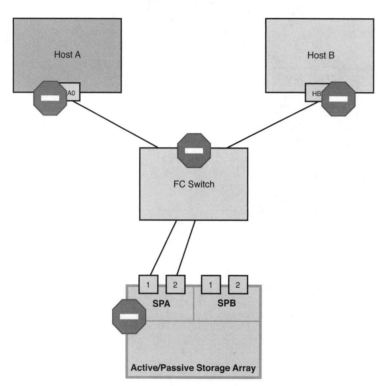

Figure 2.25   Design 2—Multiple points of failure

There are redundant connections to the fabric switch from SPA. However, SPA itself is a point of failure. All other components are still points of failure as described in Design 1.

Design Scenario 3

In this scenario, the storage array is no longer a point of failure because there is a link from each SP to the fabric switch. The remaining elements are still points of failure.

Each host now has a path to each SP with a total of two paths (see Figure 2.26).

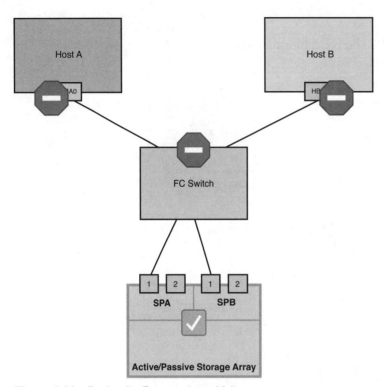

Figure 2.26   Design 3—Fewer points of failure

Design Scenario 4

In this scenario, each host has a dual port HBA but everything else remained the same. Even though on the HBA port level there is redundancy, the HBA itself can still fail and with it both HBA ports would fail leaving the host with no SAN connectivity. The fabric switch is still a point of failure. (See Figure 2.27.)

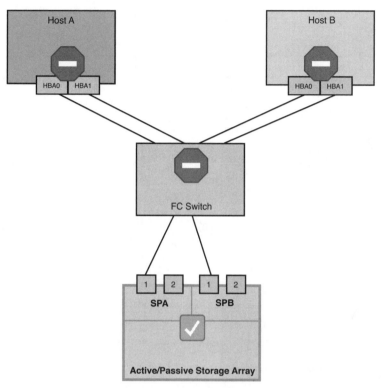

Figure 2.27   Design 4—Still a few points of failure

Design Scenario 5

Now, each host has two separate single port HBAs (see Figure 2.28). This eliminates the HBAs and the Storage Array's SPs as points of failure, leaving us with the fabric switch as the only remaining point of failure.

Each host still has four paths to the storage array because each HBA can access SPA1 and SPB1.

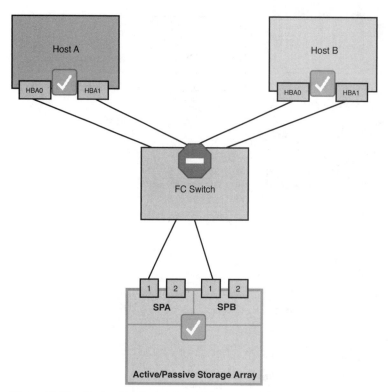

Figure 2.28   Design 5—One point of failure remaining

Design Scenario 6

Now, we have fully redundant fabric by adding a second FC switch (see Figure 2.29). Each host still has four paths to the storage array. However, these paths have no single points of failure.

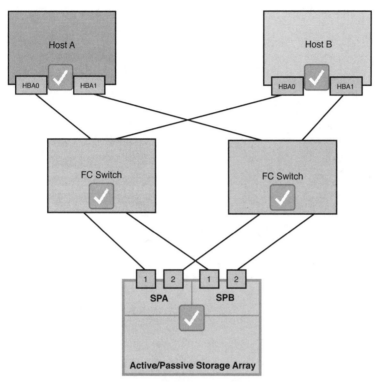

Figure 2.29   Design 6—Fully redundant fabric

The Design Scenarios 1–6 are overly simplified for the purpose of illustrating the various combinations. Actual FC fabric design would include multiple FC switches connected to form two separate fabrics. Furthermore, switches in each fabric would be connected as edge switches and core switches.

Summary

vSphere 5.0 utilizes SCSI-2 and SCSI-3 standards and supports block storage protocols FC, iSCSI, and FCoE. This chapter dealt with FC protocol and FC SAN. I discussed how to design Fibre Channel connectivity without single points of failure. I also explained in detail FC initiators and targets and how to identify each. The next two chapters cover FCoE and iSCSI protocols, respectively.

## Chapter 3

FCoE Storage Connectivity

FCoE (Fibre Channel over Ethernet)

Fiber Channel over Ethernet, or FCoE (pronounced Ef-See-Oh-Ee), is an encapsulation of FC frames over Ethernet networks. The spec is governed by the T11 committee, which is part of the INCITS (InterNational Committee for Information Technology Standards). It is defined in T11 FC-BB-5 standard (Fibre Channel BackBone — 5) available at http://www.t11.org/ftp/t11/pub/fc/bb-5/09-056v5.pdf (later revisions might exist by the time this book is published).

FCoE maps FC directly over Ethernet but is independent of the Ethernet forwarding scheme. The spec replaces layers 0 and 1 of the FC stack (see Chapter 2, "Fibre Channel Storage Connectivity"), which are the *Physical* and the *Data Link* layers, with Ethernet. Simply put, FCoE utilizes Ethernet (10GigE or faster) as a backbone for FC. It provides a loss-less transport over Ethernet even though Ethernet itself is prone to errors and dropped frames.

The FCoE encapsulation (see Figure 3.1) is somewhat like the childhood toy you may have had which is a figurine nested within another which is in turn nested within a third one. Here, the FC frame is encapsulated within the FCoE frame. The latter is encapsulated within an Ethernet frame.

The encapsulated FC frame architecture is unmodified from what I covered in Chapter 2.

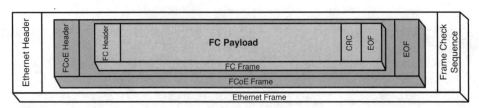

Figure 3.1 FCoE encapsulation

Figure 3.2 shows the architecture of the FCoE frame within an Ethernet frame with the following structure:

It starts with the Destination and Source MAC address fields followed by IEE 802.1Q tag (more on VLAN requirements later). Then an Ethernet Type field with a value of FCoE (hex value is 0x8906) followed by the Version field. The start of the Frame (SOF) field follows some reserved space, then the Encapsulated FC Frame and the End of Frame (EOF) field. The Ethernet FCS (Frame Check Sequence) is at the end of the FCoE frame.

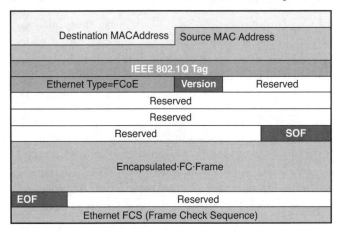

Figure 3.2 FCoE frame architecture

Because the encapsulated FC frame payload can be as large as 2.2 KB, the Ethernet frame has to be larger than 1500 bytes. As a result, Ethernet mini Jumbo Frames (2240 bytes) are used for FCoE encapsulation.

> **NOTE**
>
> FCoE runs directly on Ethernet (not on top of TCP or IP like iSCSI) as a Layer 3 protocol and cannot be routed. Based on this fact, both initiators and targets (native FCoE targets) must be on the same network.
>
> If native FC targets are accessible via FCoE switches, the latter must be on the same network as the FCoE initiators.

FCoE Initialization Protocol

FCoE Initialization Protocol (FIP) is an integral part of the FCoE protocol. It is used to discover FCoE-capable devices connected to an Ethernet network and to negotiate their capabilities and MAC addresses for use for further transactions.

The FIP header has its own Ethernet Type FIP (0x8914) as well as an encapsulated FIP operation (for example, Discovery, Advertise). This is different from the FCoE Ether Type listed earlier. Compared to FCoE frames, FIP frames describe a new set of protocols that do not exist in native Fibre Channel whereas FCoE frames encapsulate native FC payloads.

There are two types of FCoE endpoints:

- **End-Nodes (ENodes)** — FCoE Adapters are the FCoE endpoints on the hosts' side. I expand on this further in the "FCoE Initiators" section.

- **FCoE Forwarders (FCF)** — As shown in Figure 3.3, FCoE Forwarders are Dual Stack Switches (understand both FC and Ethernet). These switches connect to FC switches using an E_Port type (Expansion Port), which is an ISL (Inter-Switch-Link). In addition, they connect to other Ethernet switches and routers natively.

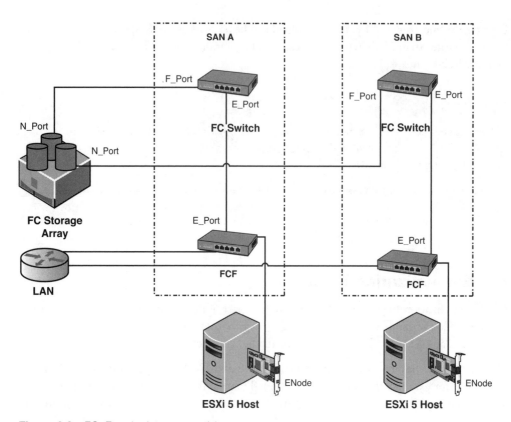

Figure 3.3   FCoE endpoints connectivity

FIP as a control protocol is designed to establish and maintain virtual links between pairs of FCoE devices: ENodes (FCoE Initiators) and FCFs (Dual Stack Switches).

The process of establishing these virtual links is outlined in the following steps and is illustrated in Figure 3.4.

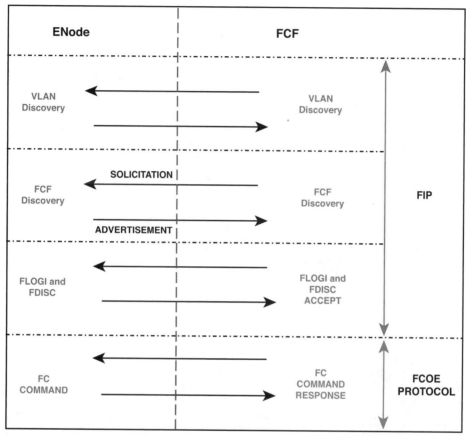

Figure 3.4   Establishing virtual links
(Image courtesy http://www.cisco.com/en/US/prod/collateral/switches/ps9441/ps9670/white_paper_c11-560403.html)

1. FIP discovers FCoE VLANs and remote virtual FC Interfaces.

2. FIP performs virtual link initialization functions (similar to native FC equivalents):

    a. FLOGI: Fabric Login

    b. FDISC: Fabric Discovery

    c. ELP: Exchange Link Parameters

After establishing the virtual link, FC payloads can be exchanged on that link. FIP remains in the background to perform virtual link maintenance functions. It continuously verifies reachability between the two virtual FC interfaces on the Ethernet network. It also offers primitives to delete the virtual link in response to administrative actions.

FCoE Initiators

To use FCoE, your vSphere host should have an FCoE Initiator. These initiators are of two types: Hardware and Software FCoE Initiators.

Hardware FCoE Adapter

An I/O card that is usually available as a CNA (Converged Network Adapter). This class of adapters combines different types of I/O cards that utilize Ethernet as a backbone; for example, Network Interface Card (NIC) and iSCSI initiator or FC HBA (using FCoE). An example of such CNAs is Emulex OneConnect OCe10102 (which is rebranded by HP as NC551i).

Figure 3.5 clarifies how FCoE and CNAs fit in vSphere 5.0 configurations.

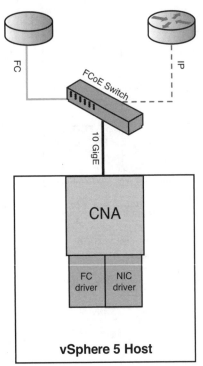

Figure 3.5   FCoE and Converged Network Adapters (CNAs)

This diagram shows an FC driver and a NIC driver both loaded for the CNA. The latter connects to an FCoE switch via a 10GigE connection. The FCoE switch unencapsulates the FC frames and sends them via the FC connection to the Storage fabric. The switch also receives regular Ethernet frames sent by the NIC driver and sends them to the Ethernet network unmodified.

Software FCoE Adapter

You can also use Software FCoE Adapter if your ESXi 5 host is equipped with a Software FCoE Enabled NIC that is certified for use with on vSphere 5. An example of such NICs is Intel 82599 10 Gigabit Adapter. Several NICs on VMware HCL are based on Intel 82599 chipset such as Cisco M61-KR, Dell X520, and IBM X520.

TIP

To search VMware HCL for 10GbE NICs supported for use with Software FCoE Adapter, use the *Search Compatibility Guide* field instead of the search criteria. The text you use is *Software FCoE Enabled*, and you get matches to the footnotes of the device listing.

The Software FCoE Adapter in ESXi 5 is based on Intel's Open FCoE Software. Figure 3.6 shows how SW FCoE Adapter runs on top of the NIC driver side-by-side with TCP/IP.

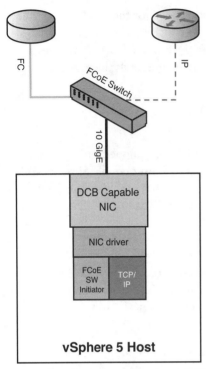

Figure 3.6   Software FCoE and a DCB-capable NIC

The transmit and receive queues of the NIC are split between the stacks sharing the NIC.

Overcoming Ethernet Limitations

For Fibre Channel to work reliably over Ethernet, several limitations of the latter must be overcome first:

1. **Packets/Frames loss** — Making sure that no packets are dropped is the most critical aspect of using FCoE. If the traffic were TCP/IP, retransmits would have taken care of this. However, FCoE does not run over TCP/IP and it has to ensure that it is *lossless*!

2. **Congestion** — As you might have noticed in Figure 3.5, the FCoE interface and the Ethernet interface share a 10GigE link. In some blades, there might be a single CNA in each blade. This means that FCoE, VM, vMotion, Management, and FT traffic share the same 10GigE link, which might result in congestion (I/O bottleneck).

3. **Bandwidth** — Sharing a 10GigE pipe with everything else might necessitate dividing that pipe among the various types of traffic. However, this is not generally doable without specialized technology like HP Virtual Connect Flex-10 and similar technologies from other vendors.

Flow Control in FCoE

Fibre Channel has Flow control using Buffer-to-Buffer Credits (BBC), which represents the number of frames a given port can store. Every time a port transmits a frame, the port's BBC is decremented by one. Conversely, for each R-RDY received, the port's BBC is incremented by one. If the BBC reaches Zero, the port cannot transmit until at least an R-RDY is received back.

However, Ethernet does not have such a function. So, FCoE required an enhancement in Ethernet so that it supports flow control. When this is accomplished, it prevents packet loss.

Such a flow control also helps Ethernet handle congestion and avoid packet drop that would have resulted from such congestion.

So, the solution was to implement a flow control PAUSE mechanism to be used by FCoE. This PAUSE mechanism works in a fashion similar to FC's BBC I mentioned previously by "telling" the sender to hold off sending frames until the receiver's buffer is cleared.

Considering the fact that the PAUSE mechanism does not have the same intelligence provided by FC's BBC, the QoS priority bit in the VLAN tag (refer to Figure 3.2) is used to ensure that the most important data is delivered to its destination first and not be affected by congestion. Utilizing this mechanism, Ethernet is divided to eight virtual lanes according to the QoS priority bit in the VLAN tag. Each of these virtual lanes can be subject to different policies such as *Lossless-ness*, *Bandwidth Allocation*, and *Congestion Control*. This mechanism is referred to as *Priority based Flow Control (PFC)*.

Protocols Required for FCoE

FCoE depends on a set of extension protocols that enhance Ethernet for use to bridge datacenters. This set of protocols is referred to as Data Center Bridging (DCB).

DCB is a standard body term that Cisco refers to as Data Center Ethernet (DCE) and IBM refers to as Converged Enhanced Ethernet (CEE).

vSphere 5 supports the DCB set of protocols for FCoE that are described in the following sections.

Priority-Based Flow Control

Priority-based Flow Control (PFC) is an extension of the current Ethernet pause mechanism, sometimes called Per-Priority PAUSE. To emulate *lossless-ness*, per priority pause frames are used. This way it can pause traffic with a specific priority and allow all other traffic to flow (for example, pause FCoE traffic while allowing other network traffic to flow).

As mentioned in the previous section, PFC creates eight separate virtual links on the physical link and allows any of these links to be paused and restarted independently from each other based on the flow control mechanism applied to each of these virtual links. This allows multiple traffic types to share the same 10GigE link with separate flow control mechanisms. Based on that, it is advantageous to have different types of traffic classes with PFC (for example, FCoE, vMotion, and VM traffic) because vMotion is not used most of the time; the virtual link it uses is available until vMotion traffic starts again. When needed, some of the traffic on other virtual links may be paused if there is congestion and the QoS priority for one of the virtual links is higher than the rest. See the "802.1p tag" section for further details on how QoS priority tags work.

Enhanced Transmission Selection

Enhanced Transmission Selection (ETS) provides a means to allocate bandwidth to traffic that has a particular priority. The protocol supports changing the bandwidth dynamically. So, PFC creates eight different lanes with different traffic classes/priorities and ETS allocates the bandwidth according to the assigned priorities.

ETS is the means to providing traffic differentiation so that multiple traffic classes can share the same consolidated Ethernet link without impacting each other.

Data Center Bridging Exchange

Data Center Bridging Exchange (DCBX) exchanges the PFC and ETS information with the link peers before an FCoE link is established. This is the management protocol and uses specific Type Length Values (TLV) in the Link Layer Discovery Protocol (LLDP) to negotiate values.

DCBX has the following functions:

1. **Discovery of DCB capability**: DCB-capable devices can discover and identify capabilities of DCB peers and identify non-DCB capable legacy devices.

2. **Identification of misconfigured DCB features**: Discover misconfiguration of features between DCB peers. Some DCB features can be configured differently on each end of a link. Other features must match on both sides to be effective. This allows detection of configuration errors for these symmetric features

3. **Configuration of peers**: DCBX passes configuration information to DCB peer. A DCB-capable switch can pass PFC information to the Converged Network Adapter (CNA) to ensure FCoE traffic is appropriately tagged and that PAUSE is enabled on the appropriate traffic class.

DCBX relies on LLDP in order to pass this configuration information. LLDP is an industry standard version of Cisco Discovery Protocol (CDP).

NOTE

Any link supporting DCBX must have LLDP enabled on both ends of the link for Transmit/Receive (Tx/Rx). If LLDP to be disabled on a port for either Rx or Tx; DCBX TLV within received LLDP frames are ignored.

That is the reason why the NIC must be bound to a vSwitch. Frames are forwarded to the Datacenter Bridging Daemon (DCBD) to DCBX via the CDP vmkernel module. The latter does both CDP and LLDP. I discuss DCBD later in this chapter.

10GigE — A Large Pipeline

The bandwidth provided by 10Gb/s Ethernet accommodates several types and classes of traffic (see Figure 3.7).

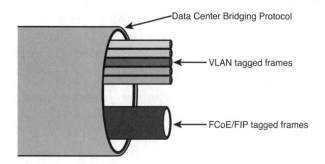

Figure 3.7   10GigE pipeline
(Image courtesy http://nickapedia.com/2011/01/22/the-vce-model-yes-it-is-different/#more-1446)

For example, Voice over IP (VoIP), Video, Messaging, and Storage can travel over a common Ethernet infrastructure. With faster Ethernet being under development at the time of writing this, 100GigE is eminent, which makes for even better convergence of these various types of traffic.

802.1p Tag

802.1p priority is carried in the VLAN tags defined in IEEE 802.1q/p (802.1p).

A field in the 802.1q tag carries one of eight priority values (3 bits in length), which is recognized by Layer 2 devices on the network. This priority tag determines the service level that packets receive when crossing an 802.1p-enabled network.

Figure 3.8 shows the structure of a frame tagged with 802.1p tag for Ethernet frames.

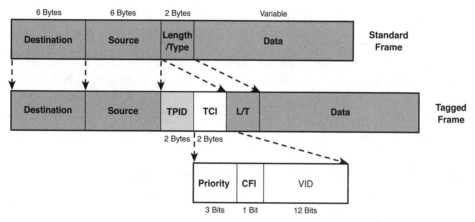

Figure 3.8 802.1p tag

The fields in the tag are

- **TPID** — Tag Protocol Identifier: 2 bytes long and carries the IEEE 802.1Q/802.1P tag when the frame has "EtherType" value of 0x8100

- **TC I** — Tag Control Information: 2 bytes long and includes User Priority (3 bits), Canonical Format Indicator "CFI" (1bit), and VLAN ID "VID" (12 bits)

The value in the Priority field defines the class of service as shown in Table 3.1.

Table 3.1 QoS Priority Levels

Priority	Traffic Characteristics
0 (Lowest)	Background
1	Best Effort
2	Excellent Effort
3	Critical Application
4	Video, < 100 ms Latency
5	Voice, < 10 ms Latency
6	Internetwork Control
7 (Highest)	Network Control

Hardware FCoE Adapters

Hardware (HW) FCoE Adapters are CNAs that are capable of fully offloading FCoE processing and network connectivity. Although physically we see the CNA as one card, to the ESXi environment, they just show up in the UI as two separate adapters: a Network Adapter and an FC Adapter. You can identify them by *FCoE* listed in the physical CNA's name. Figure 3.9 shows an example of how HW FCoE adapters are listed in the user interface (UI).

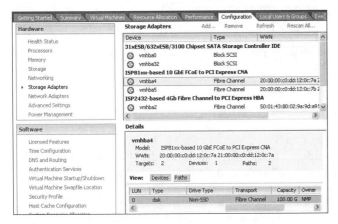

Figure 3.9   UI listing of HW FCoE adapters (CNA)

Figure 3.9 shows a dual-port 10GbE CNA based on an ISP81XX adapter. Its FCoE part shows up as Fibre Channel type and is given the names vmhba4 and vmhba5.

If you look closely at the attached LUNs, you notice that the Transport used is also Fibre Channel. However, the Details section shows the Model as ISP81xx-based 10 GbE FCoE to PCI Express CNA.

How SW FCoE Is Implemented in ESXi 5

Software FCoE adapter is a VMware-provided component on vSphere 5 that performs some FCoE processing. You can use it with a number of network cards (NICs) that support partial FCoE offload. The vSphere Administrator needs to manually enable this adapter before it can be configured and used. Software FCoE is based on Open FCoE stack, which was created by Intel and is licensed under GPL. It is loaded as a vmkernel module that you can list using this command:

```
vmkload_mod -l |grep 'Name\|fc'
Name                   Used Size (kb)
libfc                   2    112
libfcoe                 1    28
fcoe                    3    32
```

Notice that there are three modules: libfc, libfcoe, and fcoe. The latter is the FCoE stack kernel module and the former two are VMware common libraries that provide APIs used by FCoE driver as well as third-party drivers.

The mechanism through which FCoE works on ESXi 5 is as follows:

- The NICs that support partial FCoE offloading create a pseudo netdev interface for use by vmklinux. The former is a Linux network device interface, and the latter is the ESXi facility that allows drivers ported from Linux to run on ESXi.

- FCoE transport module is registered with vmklinux.

- Each NIC (or CNA capable of FCoE) is made visible to the user via vSphere Client. From there, the user can enable and configure software FCoE. Once configured, vmklinux performs the discovery.

- DCBD, which is located in /sbin/dcbd and its init script is in /etc/init.d/dcbd, is then started on the ESXi host.

- FCoE module registers one adapter with the ESXi Storage stack. I cover the latter in Chapter 5, "VMware Pluggable Storage Architecture (PSA)."

- FCoE Adapter information is stored in /etc/vmware/esx.conf file. This ensures that the configuration and information persist across host reboots. Do not change any of the content of esx.conf file directly. You should use esxcli command-line options to make FCoE changes. I cover the esxcli options where relevant throughout this chapter.

NOTE

FIP, Jumbo frame (actually baby jumbo frames, which are configured on the physical switch, are used to accommodate the FC frame payload which is 2112 bytes long), FCoE, and DCBX modules are enabled in ESXi 5 Software FCoE initiator by default.

Configuring FCoE Network Connections

NICs ports, used with SW FCoE Adapters, should be connected to switch ports configured as follows:

- Spanning Tree Protocol(STP): **Disabled**

  If this is not done, FIP (See the "FIP" section earlier in this chapter) response at the switch can experience excessive delays which, in turn, result in an All Paths down (APD) state (see Chapter 7, "Multipathing and Failover," for more information about APD).

- LLDP: **Enabled**.

- PFC: **AUTO**.

- VLAN ID: Specify a VLAN dedicated to FCoE traffic. Do not mix FCoE traffic with other storage or data traffic because you need to take advantage of PFC.

> **NOTE**
>
> VMware recommends the following switch firmware minimum versions:
>
> Cisco Nexus 5000: version 4.1(3)N2
>
> Brocade FCoE Switch: version 6.3.1

In contrast to HW FCoE Adapters, which do not require special ESXi network configuration, the NIC, on which you configure SW FCoE Adapter, must be bound to a vmkernel Standard Virtual Switch. To do so, follow this procedure:

1. Connect to the ESXi 5 host using the vSphere 5.0 client as a user with root privileges, or connect to the vCenter server that manages that host as a user with Administrator privileges.

2. If logged into vCenter, navigate to the Inventory — Hosts and Clusters view and then locate the vSphere 5.0 host in the inventory tree and select it. Otherwise, skip to the next step.

3. Navigate to the **Configuration** tab.

4. Under the Networking section, select the **Add Networking** link (see Figure 3.10).

Figure 3.10   Network configuration tab — vSphere 5.0 Client

5. Select **VMkernel** connection type and then click **Next** (see Figure 3.11).

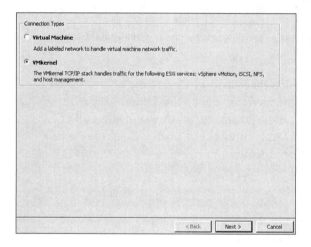

Figure 3.11   Creating a VMkernel port group — Connection Type — vSphere 5.0 Client

6. Select **Create a vSphere standard switch,** select the vmnic that supports FCoE, and then click **Next**. (See Figure 3.12.)

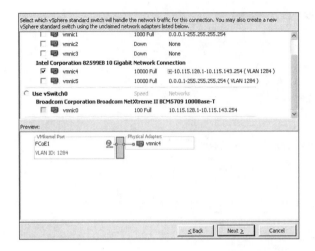

Figure 3.12   Creating a VMkernel port group — creating a vSwitch — vSphere 5.0 Client

7. You might be tempted to add all ports that support FCoE to the newly created vSwitch. However, it is not recommended that you do that because any changes you make to the vSwitch in the future can be disruptive, which would affect all FCoE traffic. This might result in an APD state. It would be a better design to create a separate vSwitch for each SW FCoE Adapter.

NOTE

You can configure up to four SW FCoE adapters on a single vSphere 5 host.

8. Enter the port group name (for example, FCoE1, FCoE2, and so on).

9. Enter the VLAN ID configured on the physical switch for FCoE traffic. Leave all checkboxes unchecked and then click **Next** (see Figure 3.13).

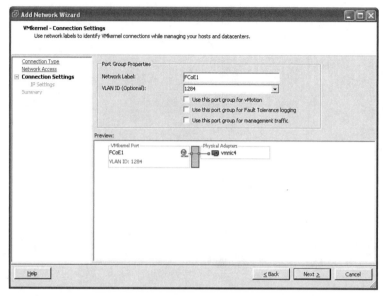

Figure 3.13 Configuring port group properties

10. Enter the IP configuration shown in Figure 3.14, and then click **Next**.

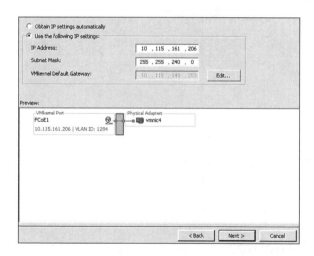

Figure 3.14 Configuring port group IP address

11. Click **Finish** (see Figure 3.15).

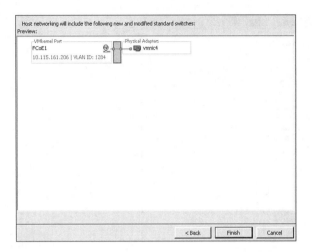

Figure 3.15 Completed FCoE virtual switch configuration

Figure 3.16 shows the host's network configuration after adding the FCoE port group and its Standard Virtual Switch.

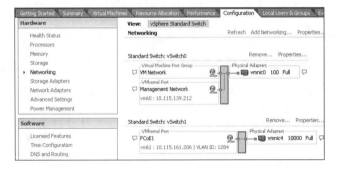

Figure 3.16 ESXi host networking after adding port group and its Standard Virtual Switch

Enabling Software FCoE Adapter

To enable Software FCoE Adapter after completing Steps 1–11 in the previous section, continue with Step 12:

12. In the **Hardware** section, select the **Storage Adapters** link.

13. Next to the Storage Adapters section heading, select the **Add** link or right-click any empty space below the last adapter listed. (See Figure 3.17.)

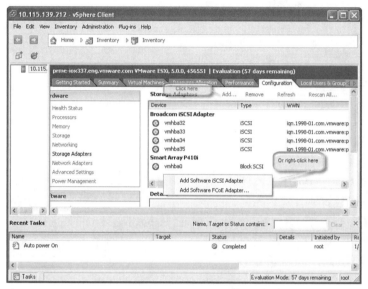

Figure 3.17   Adding a software FCoE initiator — Step 1 — vSphere 5.0 Client

14. Select the **Add Software FCoE Adapter** menu option or radio button, and then click **OK** (see Figure 3.18).

Figure 3.18   Adding a software FCoE adapter — Step 2 — vSphere 5.0 Client

15. In the resulting dialog (see Figure 3.19), select the vmnic that you bound earlier to the vSwitch in Step 7.

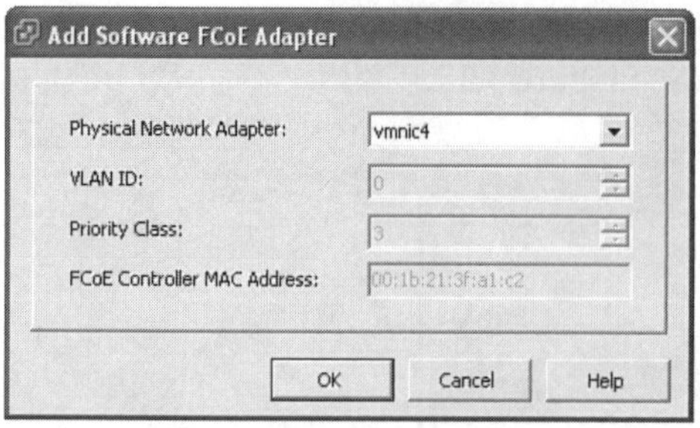

Add Software FCoE Adapter

Physical Network Adapter:	vmnic4
VLAN ID:	0
Priority Class:	3
FCoE Controller MAC Address:	00:1b:21:3F:a1:c2

OK   Cancel   Help

Figure 3.19   Adding a software FCoE adapter — Step 4 — vSphere 5.0 Client

NOTE

The VLAN ID is not selectable in this dialog. However, it was discovered automatically via FIP VLAN discovery process.

Notice that the Priority Class, which is set to 3, is also not selectable. Based on Table 3.1, this means that the priority is set to Critical Application.

16. Click **OK**.

The SW FCoE Adapter should appear in the UI now as a vmhba; in this example it is vmhba33. Figure 3.20 shows the FCoE Adapter identified by arrows.

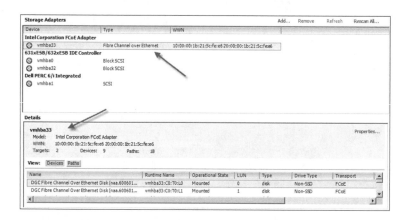

Figure 3.20   Software FCoE adapter added

> **TIP**
>
> The number assigned to the vmhba is a hint to whether it is Hardware or Software FCoE Adapter. vmhba numbers lower than 32 are assigned to Hardware (SCSI-related) Adapters, for example, SCSI HBA, RAID Controller, FC HBA, HW FCoE, and HW iSCSI HBAs. vmhba numbers 32 and higher are assigned to Software Adapters and non-SCSI Adapters; for example, SW FCoE, SW iSCSI Adapters, IDE, SATA, and USB storage controllers.

Notice that the new vmhba has been assigned an FC WWN. Also, the targets and LUNs have been discovered without the need to rescan.

At this point let's compare Figure 3.20 to Figure 3.9. The HBA type in Figure 3.20 (the top red arrow) is Fibre Channel over Ethernet because this is a software FCoE Adapter. In contrast, Figure 3.9 shows the type Fibre Channel because it is a hardware FCoE Adapter.

Removing or Disabling a Software FCoE Adapter

You may remove a Software FCoE Adapter via the UI or the CLI.

Using the UI to Remove the SW FCoE Adapter

To remove the Software FCoE Adapter via the UI, follow this procedure:

1. While logged into vCenter Server and after selecting the ESXi 5 host that you want to modify, select the configuration tab and then select the Storage Adapters option. The UI should look like Figure 3.20.

2. Click the vmhba representing the SW FCoE Adapter you want to remove.

3. Select the **Remove** menu option or right-click the vmhba in the list, and then click **Remove** (see Figure 3.21).

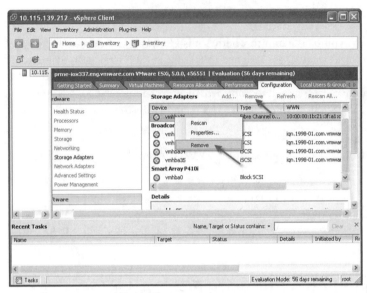

Figure 3.21   Removing SW FCoE adapter

4. Confirm the removal when prompted (see Figure 3.22).

Figure 3.22   Confirming SW FCoE adapter removal

5. The adapter has been disabled in the ESXi host configuration and is removed when the host is rebooted.

Using the CLI to Remove the SW FCoE Adapter

To remove the Software FCoE Adapter via the CLI, follow this procedure:

1. Access vMA, vCLI, or SSH, or directly access the ESXi host's CLI. See the "Locating HBA's WWPN and WWNN in vSphere 5 Hosts" section in Chapter 2 for details.

2. Run the following command to identify which vmnic is used by the FCoE Adapter:

```
esxcli fcoe adapter list
vmhba36
    Source MAC: 00:1b:21:3f:a1:c2
    FCF MAC: 00:0d:ec:6d:a7:40
    VNPort MAC: 0e:fc:00:1b:00:0a
    Physical NIC: vmnic4
    User Priority: 3
    VLAN id: 123
```

The field named `Physical NIC` lists the vmnic you use in the next step. In this example, it is `vmnic4`.

3. To remove the SW FCoE Adapter, disable the vmnic it is using by running this command:

```
esxcli fcoe nic disable --nic-name=vmnic4
Discovery on device 'vmnic4' will be disabled on the next reboot
```

If the operation is successful, you should get the following prompt: Discovery on device 'vmnic4' will be disabled on the next reboot.

4. To complete the procedure, reboot the ESXi host.

Troubleshooting FCoE

To troubleshoot and manage FCoE, there are two facilities to help you: ESXCLI commands and DCBD logs.

ESXCLI

ESXCLI provides a dedicated Software FCoE namespace, which you can list using the command shown in Figure 3.23:

```
esxcli fcoe
```

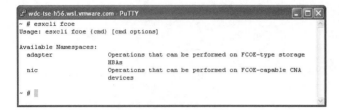

Figure 3.23   ESXCLI FCoE namespace

The next level is adapter or nic.

Running the following returns the output shown in Figure 3.24:

```
esxcli fcoe adapter
```

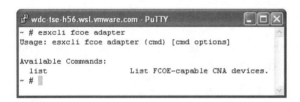

Figure 3.24   ESXCLI FCoE adapter namespace

If you run the `list` command, it lists the SW FCoE adapters and their configurations:

```
~ # esxcli fcoe adapter list
vmhba33
    Source MAC: 00:1b:21:5c:fe:e6
    FCF MAC: 00:0d:ec:6d:a7:40
    VNPort MAC: 0e:fc:00:1b:00:0a
    Physical NIC: vmnic2
    User Priority: 3
    VLAN id: 123
```

NOTE

This output shows FCF MAC, which is the physical switch port MAC (FCF stands for FCoE Forwarder).

See the "FIP" section for more information.

On the other hand, the nic namespace works directly on the physical NIC (vmnic) and provides disable, discover, and list options.

The disable option is used to disable rediscovery of FCoE storage on behalf of a specific vmnic, that is FCoE capable, upon the next boot. The command option example is

```
esxcli fcoe nic disable --nic-name=vmnic2
```

The discover option is used to initiate FCoE adapter discovery on behalf of an FCoE-capable vmnic. The command-line syntax is similar to the disable option (this time I am using the -n option, which is shorthand for the --nic-name option):

```
esxcli fcoe nic discover -n vmnic2
```

Sample outputs of this command in various configurations are listed here:

In this example, vmnic2 was successfully enabled for discovery:

```
~ # esxcli fcoe nic discover -n vmnic2
Discovery enabled on device 'vmnic2'
```

In the following example, vmnic0 is bound to a vmkernel port group on a standard vSwitch but the NIC is not DCB-capable (Data Center Bridging), which means it is not FCoE-capable:

```
~ # esxcli fcoe nic discover -n vmnic0
PNIC "vmnic0" is not DCB-capable
```

In this example, the vmnic was not bound to a vmkernel port on a standard vSwitch. You cannot enable the vmnic for discovery until it is bound as such:

```
~ # esxcli fcoe nic discover -n vmnic5
Error: Failed to obtain the port for vmnic5. This adapter must be bound to
a switch uplink port for activation.
```

Figure 3.25 shows a similar message when using the vSphere Client to add a Software FCoE Adapter for a vmnic that is not bound to a vSwitch uplink port.

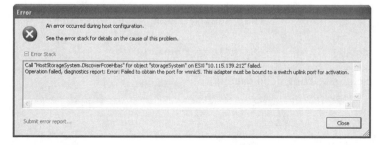

Figure 3.25   Error adding a software FCoE adaptor to an unbound vmnic

Finally, the list option is used to list all FCoE-capable vmnics:

```
~ # esxcli fcoe nic list
vmnic2
    User Priority: 3
    Source MAC: 00:1b:21:5c:fe:e6
    Active: true
    Priority Settable: false
    Source MAC Settable: false
    VLAN Range Settable: false
vmnic3
    User Priority: 3
    Source MAC: 00:1b:21:5c:fe:e7
    Active: false
    Priority Settable: false
    Source MAC Settable: false
    VLAN Range Settable: false
```

In this example vmnic2 was already configured with FCoE whereas vmnic3 was not but is FCoE capable.

FCoE-Related Logs

FCoE discovery- and communication-related events generated by DCBD are logged to /var/log/syslog.log and the events are prefixed with dcbd.

This listing shows a sample log entry from /var/log/syslog.log:

```
2011-10-08T06:00:25Z root: init Running dcbd start
2011-10-08T06:00:25Z watchdog-dcbd: [2936] Begin '/usr/sbin/dcbd
++group=net-daemons', min-uptime = 60, max-quick-failures = 1, max-total-
failures = 5, bg_pid_file = ''
2011-10-08T06:00:25Z watchdog-dcbd: Executing '/usr/sbin/dcbd ++group=net-
daemons'
2011-10-08T06:00:25Z dcbd: [info]     Not adding inactive FCOE adapter:
"vmnic2"
2011-10-08T06:00:26Z dcbd: [info]     Not adding inactive FCOE adapter:
"vmnic3"
2011-10-08T06:00:26Z dcbd: [info]     Main loop running.
```

The first line shows the event of starting dcbd daemon.

The second line shows the watchdog for dcbd daemon startup parameter. They are as follows:

- group is `net-daemons`, which means that the watchdog monitors the status of this daemon in the group with that name.

- `min-uptime` is `60` seconds. It is the minimum time the daemon should be up. If it runs for less than that time, the watchdog considers it a *quick-failure* (see next parameter).

- `max-quick-failures` is `1`, which means that the watchdog gives up on restarting the daemon if it runs for less than 60 seconds. If it stays up for 60 seconds or more, it reloads it. If this value were 2, the daemon would have to die quickly two times in a row before the watchdog gives up. Consider the following sequence of events:

  The daemon could stay up for 40 seconds, gets restarted, stays up for 70 seconds (not a `quick failure`), gets restarted, stays up for 30 seconds, gets restarted, stays up for 55 seconds, and then crashes.

  In this sequence of events, the daemon stays down because there were two quick failures in a row.

- `max-total-failures` is `5` which is the total number of times the daemon fails to run over any length of time before the watchdog gives up on reloading the daemon. For example, after the dcbd daemon fails five times since the ESXi host booted, the watchdog no longer restarts it.

- `bg_pid_file` is set to null, which means that no background process ID file is created.

> **NOTE**
>
> The Watchdog is a script that manages VMware services and is located in /sbin/watchdog.sh.
>
> It launches the specified process and respawns it after it exits.
>
> It gives up after recording the specified number of quick failures in succession or after recording a specified total number of failures (over any length of time).

The third line is the execution of loading the watchdog.

The fourth and fifth lines indicate that vmnic2 and vmnic3 are not activated as FCoE adapters.

The last line shows that the daemon is now running.

The log snippet in Listing 3.1 shows events related to adding vmnic2 as an FCoE adapter:

Listing 3.1   /var/log/syslog.log Listing of addinc vmnic as an FCoE Adapter

```
2011-03-08T06:06:33Z dcbd: [info]    add_adapter (vmnic2)
2011-03-08T06:06:33Z dcbd: [info]      dcbx subtype = 2
2011-03-08T06:06:33Z dcbd: [info]    get_dcb_capabilities for "vmnic2"
2011-03-08T06:06:33Z dcbd: [info]    get_dcb_numtcs for "vmnic2"
2011-03-08T06:06:33Z dcbd: [info]    Reconciled device numTCs (PG 4, PFC
4)
2011-03-08T06:06:33Z dcbd: [info]    Set Syncd to 0 [3682]
2011-03-08T06:06:33Z dcbd: [info]    Feature state machine (flags 1)
2011-03-08T06:06:33Z dcbd: [info]      Local change: PG
2011-03-08T06:06:33Z dcbd: [info]    Set Syncd to 0 [3682]
2011-03-08T06:06:33Z dcbd: [info]    Feature state machine (flags 2)
2011-03-08T06:06:33Z dcbd: [info]      Local change:  PFC
2011-03-08T06:06:33Z dcbd: [info]      CopyConfigToOper vmnic2
2011-03-08T06:06:33Z dcbd: [info]    set_pfc_cfg for "vmnic2", operMode: 0
2011-03-08T06:06:33Z dcbd: [info]    set_pfc_state for "vmnic2", pfc_
state: FALSE
2011-03-08T06:06:33Z dcbd: [info]    Set Syncd to 0 [3682]
2011-03-08T06:06:33Z dcbd: [info]    Feature state machine (flags 4)
2011-03-08T06:06:33Z dcbd: [info]      Local change:   APP
2011-03-08T06:06:33Z dcbd: [info]    DCB Ctrl in LISTEN
2011-03-08T06:06:33Z dcbd: [info]      Local change detected: PG PFC APP
2011-03-08T06:06:33Z dcbd: [info]      Local SeqNo == Local AckNo
2011-03-08T06:06:33Z dcbd: [info]      *** Sending packet -- SeqNo = 1
AckNo = 0
2011-03-08T06:06:33Z dcbd: [info]    Set portset name for "vmnic2" :
"vSwitch1"
2011-03-08T06:06:33Z dcbd: [info]    Added adapter "vmnic2" via IPC
2011-03-08T06:06:35Z dcbd: [info]      *** Received a DCB_CONTROL_TLV: --
SeqNo=1, AckNo=1 ID(37) MSG_INFO_PG_OPER: vmnic2
```

After the adapter vmnic2 was added, it is identified as a dcbx subtype 2. This means that it is a Converged Enhanced Ethernet (CEE) port that supports FCoE. In other words, the I/O card represented by vmnic2 is FCoE-capable.

FCoE device and path claiming events are logged to the ESXi syslog.log file which is located in /var/log directory. A sample syslog.log file is shown in Listing 3.2.

Listing 3.2   /var/log/syslog.log Snippet Showing Device and Path Claiming Events

```
dcbd: [info] Connect event for vmnic2, portset name: "vSwitch1"

storageDeviceInfo.plugStoreTopology.adapter["key-vim.host.
PlugStoreTopology.Adapter-vmhba33"].path["key-vim.host.PlugStoreTopology.
Path-fcoe.1000001b215cfee6:2000001b215cfee6-fcoe.500601609020fd54:500601611
020fd54-naa.60060160d1911400a3878ec1656edf11"]

storageDeviceInfo.plugStoreTopology.path["key-vim.host.PlugStoreTopology.
Path-fcoe.1000001b215cfee6:2000001b215cfee6-fcoe.500601609020fd54:500601611
020fd54-naa.60060160d1911400a3878ec1656edf11"],

storageDeviceInfo.plugStoreTopology.target["key-vim.host.PlugStoreTopology.
Target-fcoe.500601609020fd54:500601611020fd54"],

storageDeviceInfo.plugStoreTopology.device["key-vim.host.PlugStoreTopology.
Device-020008000060060160d1911400a3878ec1656edf11524149442030"],

storageDeviceInfo.plugStoreTopology.plugin["key-vim.host.PlugStoreTopology.
Plugin-NMP"].device["key-vim.host.PlugStoreTopology.Device-
020008000060060160d1911400a3878ec1656edf11524149442030"],

storageDeviceInfo.plugStoreTopology.plugin["key-vim.host.PlugStoreTopology.
Plugin-NMP"].claimedPath["key-vim.host.PlugStoreTopology.Path-fcoe.1000001b
215cfee6:2000001b215cfee6-fcoe.500601609020fd54:500601611020fd54-"],
```

In the log snippet shown in Listing 3.2, I removed the time stamp and added a blank line between log entries for readability.

The first line shows a Connect event for the FCoE port that is on vmnic2 (what was bound on vSwitch1).

The second line shows the connection topology as follows:

- The FCoE adapter name (as seen in the UI) is vmhba33.

- The Adapter's WWNN:WWPN combination is 1000001b215cfee6:2000001b21 5cfee6.

- The Storage Processor Port WWNN:WWPN combination is 500601609020fd54:5 00601611020fd54.

- Based on Table 2.1 in Chapter 2, the SP WWPN translates to SPA-Port 1 of a CLARiiON CX Storage Array.

- The LUN visible on this path has NAA ID 60060160d1911400a3878ec1656edf11.

The third line identifies the path details, which is the combination of the information listed in bullets 2 through 4.

The fourth line identifies the target, which is the WWNN:WWPN combination listed in the second bullet.

The fifth line shows the device ID. This is similar to the vml device ID seen in /vmfs/devices/disks but without the prefix vml.

NOTE

vml is a **vm**kernel **l**ist link that points to the corresponding device ID, for example, NAA ID. This is for backward compatibility with earlier releases prior to introducing the use of device IDs. I provide more details on this in Chapter 13, "Virtual Disks and RDMs."

This command lists the *vml* IDs and the device IDs to which they link:

```
ls -al /vmfs/devices/disks/

733909245952 Jan 22 06:05 naa.600508b10010373839414243444450400

36 Jan 22 06:05 vml.0200000000600508b1001037383941424344504004c
4f47494341 -> naa.600508b10010373839414243444450400
```

I truncated the permissions and owners from the output and added a blank line between outputs for readability.

The sixth line shows that the Native Multipathing Plugin (NMP) has claimed the device identified in the previous line. I discuss NMP later in Chapter 5.

The last line shows that NMP has claimed the path that begins with the FCoE adapter's WWNN:WWPN combination going through the SPA-Port1 I explained previously.

NOTE

The reference to `plugStoreTopology` refers to Pluggable Storage Architecture (PSA), which I discuss later in Chapter 5.

I also discuss the definition of path and multipathing in Chapter 7.

The log snippet shown in Listing 3.3 is a continuation of the previous log sample.

Listing 3.3   Continuation of /var/log/syslog.log

```
storageDeviceInfo.hostBusAdapter["key-vim.host.FibreChannelOverEthernetHba-
vmhba33"].status,

storageDeviceInfo.hostBusAdapter["key-vim.host.FibreChannelOverEthernetHba-
vmhba33"].linkInfo.vnportMac,

storageDeviceInfo.hostBusAdapter["key-vim.host.FibreChannelOverEthernetHba-
vmhba33"].linkInfo.fcfMac,

storageDeviceInfo.hostBusAdapter["key-vim.host.FibreChannelOverEthernetHba-
vmhba33"].linkInfo.vlanId]

storageDeviceInfo.scsiTopology.adapter["key-vim.host.ScsiTopology.
Interface-vmhba33"].target["key-vim.host.ScsiTopology.Target-vmhba33:0:0"].
lun["key-vim.host.ScsiTopology.Lun-0200010000060060160d19114008de22dbb5e5e
df11524149442035"],
```

It continues on to request the (vmhba33) HBA status on line 1.

On lines 2, 3, and 4 it requests the link information of the following entities:

1. `linkInfo.vnportMac` — VN_Port is the FCoE equivalent of the FC's N_Port, which is the type of port for the FCoE Adapters.

2. `linkInfo.fcfMac` — FCF is the FCoE Forwarder, which is the switch port's MAC.

3. `linkInfo.vlanId` is the VLAN ID.

The three entities make up the FCoE link.

The last line shows the canonical name of the path (see Chapter 7) with the exception that the LUN is identified by its "vml" name I mentioned previously. This is composed of the combination of the Adapter:Channel:Target:LUN. The channel number is always "0" except for direct attached storages via a dual-channel HBA (for example, a RAID Adapter with an internal channel and an external one) where it would use 0 for the internal channel and 1 for the external one — for example, vmhba2:0:0 and vmhba2:1:0. However, because this does not apply to FCoE Adapters, the channel number is always 0. So, the canonical name here is "vmhba33:0:0:<LUN>".

These connection properties are also displayed in the FCoE Adapter's properties via the UI. Figure 3.26 shows these properties in addition to the physical NIC's vmnic name as well as the Priority class, which is discussed in Table 3.1.

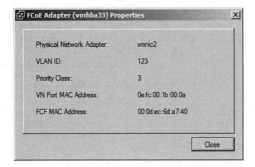

Figure 3.26   FCoE adapter properties

Parting Tips

Consider the following scenario:

A vSphere administrator configures FCoE on an ESXi 5 host. The linked vmnic is connected to a 10GigE network and from there to an FCoE switch, which in turn connects to the storage array via a 4Gig FC fabric. Because the FCoE traffic would not benefit from more than the bandwidth provided by the FC SAN, the administrator attempts to guarantee it 4Gbps bandwidth by configuring network I/O control and assigns the FCoE 40% of the total bandwidth. So, effectively, the FCoE traffic gets assigned a priority on the networking stream after it has already assigned that priority via the protocol itself. However, the administrator notices that FCoE is not getting the bandwidth dedicated to it.

As a famous TV detective says, "I solved the case! Here is what happened":

FCoE uses 802.1p User Priority for dedicated bandwidth (Enhanced Transmission Selection — ETS).

Network I/O Control feature of vSphere 5 also uses 802.1p User Priority for Quality of Service (QoS).

The bandwidth split happens at a "Priority Group" (PG) level between the NIC/CNA and the switch. Each PG consists of multiple priorities, and most administrators typically configure FCoE in a separate PG.

The switch sees multiple streams of data: FCoE and L2 Network (which happen to be both for the same FCoE traffic). If the combined capacity exceeds the 40% allocated to FCoE traffic, the switch would try to throttle the rate by sending a PFC on the FCoE priority. This effectively stops the FCoE traffic.

The moral of the story: Don't get overzealous and attempt to guarantee FCoE bandwidth using Network I/O Control because it is already assigned the appropriate priority via the FCoE protocol. Doing so results in a negative effect and the FCoE traffic is stopped instead.

Summary

This chapter covered the details of the FCoE protocol and its architecture and how it is implemented in vSphere 5. It also provided details of configuring SW FCoE Adapters on vSphere 5. I shared some sample logs and familiarized you with how to interpret them. Finally, I discussed a potential *gotcha* if using Network I/O Control and FCoE.

iSCSI Storage Connectivity

iSCSI Protocol

IETF (Internet Engineering Task Force) is responsible for the iSCSI protocol. (See RFC 3720 at http://tools.ietf.org/html/rfc3720.)

iSCSI (Internet Small Computer System Interface) is an IP (Internet protocol)-based storage standard that connects iSCSI initiators to iSCSI targets over IP networks. To put it simply, the SCSI packets are encapsulated in IP packets and sent over a standard IP network where the initiators and targets reassemble the packets and interpret the commands carried by these packets.

This standard takes advantage of existing IP infrastructure unlike FC (Fibre Channel), which requires special cables and switches.

Overview of iSCSI Connectivity

The main elements of iSCSI connectivity are initiators, targets, portals, sessions, and connections. I'm starting first with iSCSI Sessions as a high-level connectivity overview, and then I cover the remaining elements in later sections of this chapter.

iSCSI Sessions

Each iSCSI Initiator establishes a single session with each iSCSI target server via TCP (Transmission Control Protocol). Within that session, there can be one or more connections between initiators and portals on the target server. (See Figure 4.1.)

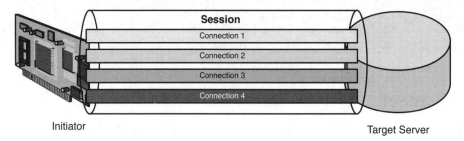

Figure 4.1   iSCSI sessions

A portal is an IP address and TCP port combination. (Find out more details on portals in the next section, "iSCSI Portals.") The default TCP port is 3260.

Figure 4.2 shows an example of an ESXi 5.0 host with two iSCSI initiators (vmhba2 and vmhba3) connected to an iSCSI storage array.

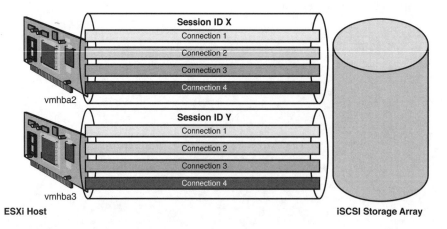

Figure 4.2   iSCSI sessions from multiple initiators

vmhba2 established session X with the storage array and has four connections within that session.

In the same fashion, vmhba3 established session Y with the same iSCSI storage array and also has four connections within that session.

To understand this better, examine Listing 4.1 with output collected from the ESXi host used in this example. I truncated some of the lines in the output, leaving the lines relevant to this section.

Listing 4.1 Listing iSCSI Sessions

```
~ # esxcli iscsi session list

vmhba2,iqn.1992-04.com.emc:cx.apm00064000064.a0,00c0dd09b6c3
    Adapter: vmhba2
    Target: iqn.1992-04.com.emc:cx.apm00064000064.a0
    ISID: 00c0dd09b6c3
    TargetPortalGroupTag: 1

vmhba2,iqn.1992-04.com.emc:cx.apm00064000064.a1,00c0dd09b6c3
    Adapter: vmhba2
    Target: iqn.1992-04.com.emc:cx.apm00064000064.a1
    ISID: 00c0dd09b6c3
    TargetPortalGroupTag: 2

vmhba2,iqn.1992-04.com.emc:cx.apm00064000064.b0,00c0dd09b6c3
    Adapter: vmhba2
    Target: iqn.1992-04.com.emc:cx.apm00064000064.b0
    ISID: 00c0dd09b6c3
    TargetPortalGroupTag: 3

vmhba2,iqn.1992-04.com.emc:cx.apm00064000064.b1,00c0dd09b6c3
    Adapter: vmhba2
    Target: iqn.1992-04.com.emc:cx.apm00064000064.b1
    ISID: 00c0dd09b6c3
    TargetPortalGroupTag: 4

vmhba3,iqn.1992-04.com.emc:cx.apm00064000064.a0,00c0dd09b6c5
    Adapter: vmhba3
    Target: iqn.1992-04.com.emc:cx.apm00064000064.a0
    ISID: 00c0dd09b6c5
```

```
   TargetPortalGroupTag: 1

vmhba3,iqn.1992-04.com.emc:cx.apm00064000064.a1,00c0dd09b6c5
   Adapter: vmhba3
   Target: iqn.1992-04.com.emc:cx.apm00064000064.a1
   ISID: 00c0dd09b6c5
   TargetPortalGroupTag: 2

vmhba3,iqn.1992-04.com.emc:cx.apm00064000064.b0,00c0dd09b6c5
   Adapter: vmhba3
   Target: iqn.1992-04.com.emc:cx.apm00064000064.b0
   ISID: 00c0dd09b6c5
   TargetPortalGroupTag: 3

vmhba3,iqn.1992-04.com.emc:cx.apm00064000064.b1,00c0dd09b6c5
   Adapter: vmhba3
   Target: iqn.1992-04.com.emc:cx.apm00064000064.b1
   ISID: 00c0dd09b6c5
   TargetPortalGroupTag: 4
```

In Listing 4.1, I removed some of the output content to highlight the portions relevant to this section. Notice the ISID value, which is the iSCSI Session ID. Each HBA is associated with one session ID to four targets.

The correlation between initiators, targets, sessions, and connections in this example are shown in Table 4.1.

Table 4.1 Correlating Initiators, Targets, Sessions, and Connections

Target IQN	Session ID	Target Portal Group Tag	Notes
vmhba2			
iqn.1992-04.com.emc:cx. apm00064000064.a0	00c0dd09b6c3	1	SPA Port 0
iqn.1992-04.com.emc:cx. apm00064000064.a1	00c0dd09b6c3	2	SPA Port 1
iqn.1992-04.com.emc:cx. apm00064000064.b0	00c0dd09b6c3	3	SPB Port 0
iqn.1992-04.com.emc:cx. apm00064000064.b1	00c0dd09b6c3	4	SPB Port 1

Target IQN	Session ID	Target Portal Group Tag	Notes
vmhba3			
iqn.1992-04.com.emc:cx. apm00064000064.a0	00c0dd09b6c5	1	SPA Port 0
iqn.1992-04.com.emc:cx. apm00064000064.a1	00c0dd09b6c5	2	SPA Port 1
iqn.1992-04.com.emc:cx. apm00064000064.b0	00c0dd09b6c5	3	SPB Port 0
iqn.1992-04.com.emc:cx. apm00064000064.b1	00c0dd09b6c5	4	SPB Port 1

Table 4.1 shows that vmhba2 and vmhba3 are connected to the same targets. The latter are two ports on each Storage Processor (SP). Notice the SP-Port combination is part of the target's IQN (which is explained further in the "iSCSI Targets" section).

You can also list Active Target Sessions information for a given HBA using the following command:

```
vmkiscsi-tool -C <hba-name>
```

Or using esxcli:

```
esxcli storage iscsi session list --adapter=<hba-name>
```

The following is the shorthand version of this command:

```
esxcli storage iscsi session list -A <hba-name>
```

Example:

```
vmkiscsi-tool -C vmhba2
```

Or

```
esxcli storage iscsi session list -A vmhba2
```

To list the same information for one target, you can instead use the following command:

```
vmkiscsi-tool -C -t <target iqn> <hba-name>
```

Or

```
esxcli storage iscsi session list --name <iSCSI Target Name>
```

The shorthand version of this command is

```
esxcli storage iscsi session list --n <iSCSI Target Name>
```

Example:

```
vmkiscsi-tool -C -t iqn.1992-04.com.emc:cx.apm00064000064.a0 vmhba2
```

Or

```
esxcli storage iscsi session list --name iqn.1992-04.com.emc:cx.
apm00064000064.a0
```

Listing 4.2 is a sample output of the first command using vmkiscsi-tool.

Listing 4.2   Listing iSCSI Sessions with a Specific Target Using vmkiscsi-tool

```
vmkiscsi-tool -C -t iqn.1992-04.com.emc:cx.apm00064000064.a0 vmhba3
------ Target [iqn.1992-04.com.emc:cx.apm00064000064.a0] info ------
NAME                               : iqn.1992-04.com.emc:cx.apm00064000064.a0
ALIAS                              : 0064.a0
DISCOVERY METHOD FLAGS             : 8
SEND TARGETS DISCOVERY SETTABLE    : 0
SEND TARGETS DISCOVERY ENABLED     : 1
Portal 0                           : 10.23.1.30:3260


------------------------------------------
    Session info [isid:00:c0:dd:09:b6:c5]:
     - authMethod:              NONE
     - dataPduInOrder:          YES
     - dataSequenceInOrder:     YES
     - defaultTime2Retain:      0
     - errorRecoveryLevel:      0
     - firstBurstLength:        128
     - immediateData:           NO
     - initialR2T:              YES
     - isid:                    00:c0:dd:09:b6:c5
     - maxBurstLength:          512
     - maxConnections:          1
     - maxOutstandingR2T:       1
     - targetPortalGroupTag:    1
    Connection info [id:0]:
     - connectionId:                 0
     - dataDigest:                   NONE
```

```
- headerDigest:                    NONE
- ifMarker:                        NO
- ifMarkInt:                       0
- maxRecvDataSegmentLength:        128
- maxTransmitDataSegmentLength:    128
- ofMarker:                        NO
- ofMarkInt:                       0
- Initial Remote Address:          10.23.1.30
- Current Remote Address:          10.23.1.30
- Current Local Address:           10.23.1.215
- Session Created at:              Not Available
- Connection Created at:           Not Available
- Connection Started at:           Not Available
- State:                           LOGGED_IN
```

In Listing 4.2, the iSCSI Session ID (ISID) is listed with colons separating the bytes. Listing 4.3 is a sample of the output from the second command using esxcli.

Listing 4.3 Listing Active iSCSI Sessions with a Specific Target Using esxli

```
esxcli iscsi session list -n iqn.1992-04.com.emc:cx.apm00064000064.a0

vmhba3,iqn.1992-04.com.emc:cx.apm00064000064.a0,00c0dd09b6c5
    Adapter: vmhba3
    Target: iqn.1992-04.com.emc:cx.apm00064000064.a0
    ISID: 00c0dd09b6c5
    TargetPortalGroupTag: 1
    AuthenticationMethod: none
    DataPduInOrder: true
    DataSequenceInOrder: true
    DefaultTime2Retain: 0
    DefaultTime2Wait: 2
    ErrorRecoveryLevel: 0
    FirstBurstLength: Irrelevant
    ImmediateData: false
    InitialR2T: true
    MaxBurstLength: 512
    MaxConnections: 1
    MaxOutstandingR2T: 1
    TSIH: 0
```

Notice that the esxcli output does not include connection information. You can obtain a list of connections within the same iSCSI session using the following esxcli command:

```
esxcli iscsi session connection list --isid=<session-id>
```

The shorthand version for this command is

```
esxcli iscsi session connection list -s <session-id>
```

Example:

```
esxcli iscsi session connection list -s 00c0dd09b6c5
```

The output is shown in Listing 4.4.

Listing 4.4   Listing iSCSI Session's Connection Information

```
vmhba3,iqn.1992-04.com.emc:cx.apm00064000064.a0,00c0dd09b6c5,0
   Adapter: vmhba3
   Target: iqn.1992-04.com.emc:cx.apm00064000064.a0
   ISID: 00c0dd09b6c5
   CID: 0
   DataDigest: NONE
   HeaderDigest: NONE
   IFMarker: false
   IFMarkerInterval: 0
   MaxRecvDataSegmentLength: 128
   MaxTransmitDataSegmentLength: 128
   OFMarker: false
   OFMarkerInterval: 0
   ConnectionAddress: 10.23.1.30
   RemoteAddress: 10.23.1.30
   LocalAddress: 10.23.1.215
   SessionCreateTime: Not Available
   ConnectionCreateTime: Not Available
   ConnectionStartTime: Not Available
   State: logged_in
```

```
vmhba3,iqn.1992-04.com.emc:cx.apm00064000064.b0,00c0dd09b6c5,0
    Adapter: vmhba3
    Target: iqn.1992-04.com.emc:cx.apm00064000064.b0
    ISID: 00c0dd09b6c5
    CID: 0
    DataDigest: NONE
    HeaderDigest: NONE
    IFMarker: false
    IFMarkerInterval: 0
    MaxRecvDataSegmentLength: 128
    MaxTransmitDataSegmentLength: 16
    OFMarker: false
    OFMarkerInterval: 0
    ConnectionAddress: 10.23.2.30
    RemoteAddress: 10.23.2.30
    LocalAddress: 10.23.1.215
    SessionCreateTime: Not Available
    ConnectionCreateTime: Not Available
    ConnectionStartTime: Not Available
    State: free
```

I truncated the output in Listing 4.4 to show two connections. Note in the listing that the two connections are between the same HBA *vmhba3* and the same remote address *10.23.1.30*. This is an example of multiple connections within the same session. Also note that the first connection shows the state is `logged_in`, whereas the second one shows the state is *free*. This means that the first one is an active connection, but the second one is not.

iSCSI Portals

A *portal* is defined as a component of a network entity that has a TCP/IP network address and may be used by an iSCSI node within that network entity for the connection within one of its iSCSI sessions.

A portal in an initiator is identified by its IP address.

A portal in a target is identified by its IP address and its listening TCP port. The default port is 3260. Figure 4.3 shows network portals on an iSCSI Server listening on port 3260. On the host's side, two iSCSI initiators also have network portals associated with the initiators' IP addresses.

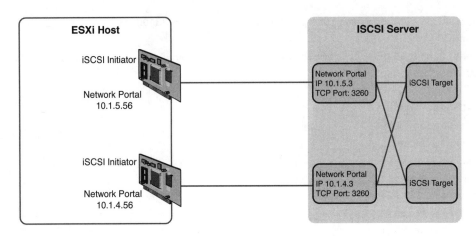

Figure 4.3   iSCSI portals

Using SSH, vMA, or ESXCLI (I cover details about using these facilities later in this chapter), you can list the iSCSI target portals using esxcli commands. The commands shown in Listings 4.5 and 4.6 return the target portals for HW Initiators and SW Initiators, respectively.

Listing 4.5   Listing iSCSI Target Portals—HW Initiators

```
~ # esxcli iscsi adapter target portal list
Adapter Target                                    IP          Port  Tpgt
------- --------------------------------------    ---------   ----  ----
vmhba2  iqn.1992-04.com.emc:cx.apm00064000064.a0  10.23.1.30  3260  1
vmhba2  iqn.1992-04.com.emc:cx.apm00064000064.a1  10.23.1.31  3260  2
vmhba2  iqn.1992-04.com.emc:cx.apm00064000064.b0  10.23.2.30  3260  3
vmhba2  iqn.1992-04.com.emc:cx.apm00064000064.b1  10.23.2.31  3260  4

vmhba3  iqn.1992-04.com.emc:cx.apm00064000064.a0  10.23.1.30  3260  1
vmhba3  iqn.1992-04.com.emc:cx.apm00064000064.a1  10.23.1.31  3260  2
vmhba3  iqn.1992-04.com.emc:cx.apm00064000064.b0  10.23.2.30  3260  3
vmhba3  iqn.1992-04.com.emc:cx.apm00064000064.b1  10.23.2.31  3260  4
```

NOTE

I added a blank line between HBAs for readability.

Listing 4.6   Listing iSCSI Target Portals—SW Initiators

```
~ # esxcli iscsi adapter target portal list

Adapter Target                                          IP            Port Tpgt
------- -------------------------------------------- ------------ ---- ----
vmhba34 iqn.1992-04.com.emc:cx.apm00071501971.a0 10.131.7.179 3260 1
vmhba34 iqn.1992-04.com.emc:cx.apm00071501971.b0 10.131.7.180 3260 2
```

The main difference between HW and SW Initiators outputs is the vmhba enumeration. I provide more details on this fact in the "iSCSI Initiators" section later in this chapter.

You may use an alternative command using vmkiscsi-tool, which might be deprecated in a future release. It is also not available remotely via vMA or vCLI. This command is shown in Listings 4.7 and 4.8.

Listing 4.7   Alternative Method for Listing iSCSI Target Portals—HW Initiators

```
~ # vmkiscsi-tool -T -l vmhba3 |awk '/iqn/||/Portal/{print}'

------ Target [iqn.1992-04.com.emc:cx.apm00064000064.a0] info ------
NAME         : iqn.1992-04.com.emc:cx.apm00064000064.a0
Portal 0     : 10.23.1.30:3260
------ Target [iqn.1992-04.com.emc:cx.apm00064000064.a1] info ------
NAME         : iqn.1992-04.com.emc:cx.apm00064000064.a1
Portal 0     : 10.23.1.31:3260
```

Listing 4.8   Alternative Method for Listing iSCSI Target Portals—SW Initiators

```
~ # vmkiscsi-tool -T -l vmhba34 |awk '/iqn/||/Portal/{print}'

------ Target [iqn.1992-04.com.emc:cx.apm00071501971.a0] info ------
NAME         : iqn.1992-04.com.emc:cx.apm00071501971.a0
Portal 0     : 10.131.7.179:3260
------ Target [iqn.1992-04.com.emc:cx.apm00071501971.b0] info ------
NAME         : iqn.1992-04.com.emc:cx.apm00071501971.b0
Portal 0     : 10.131.7.180:3260
```

The main difference between the outputs from HW and SW Initiator is the vmhba number used. The next section, "iSCSI Initiators," provides details about the differences between these initiators.

iSCSI Initiators

iSCSI Initiators are used to connect hosts to iSCSI storage arrays over an Ethernet network. vSphere 5 supports two types of iSCSI initiators:

- Hardware Initiators, which are available in two classes:

    - Dependent—These are physical adapters that depend on ESXi for network stack, initiator configuration, and management. The adapter offloads iSCSI processing from the host using TOE or TCP Offload Engine. It requires a vmkernel port group configured and linked to the adapter.

    - Independent—These are physical adapters that offload iSCSI and network processing from the host. They provide their own management capabilities via their firmware. However, you can still configure them via vSphere Client.

- Software initiator—This is a software implementation of the iSCSI Initiator. ESXi includes this software as a vmkernel component. It requires a vmkernel port group configured and linked to physical network interface cards (NICs) in the ESXi host.

iSCSI Names and Addresses

According to RFC 3721 (http://tools.ietf.org/html/rfc3721):

"The main addressable, discoverable entity in iSCSI is an iSCSI Node. An iSCSI node can be an initiator, a target, or both. The rules for constructing an iSCSI name are specified in RFC3720."

iSCSI nodes, initiators, and targets require special names for the purpose of identification. These names can be in one of the following formats:

- IQN (iSCSI Qualified Name)
- EUI (Extended Unique Identifier)
- NAA (T11 Network Address Authority)
- Alias

IQN

IQN is an iSCSI naming scheme constructed to give an organizational naming authority the flexibility to further subdivide the responsibility for name creation to subordinate naming authorities.

This is the commonly used identifier among HBA and array vendors. The IQN format is defined in RFC 372. The example in Figure 4.4 shows a Hardware Initiator's IQN.

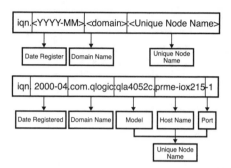

Figure 4.4   HW Initiators—anatomy of iqn

The following items are the breakdown of the IQN:

1. The string iqn.

2. <YYYY-MM>: A date code specifying the year and month in which the organization registered the domain or subdomain name used as the naming authority string.

3. <domain>: The organizational naming authority string, which consists of a valid, reversed DNS domain or subdomain name.

4. <Node Identifier>: A unique identifier for each node which is assigned by the Organizational Naming Authority stated in item 3 (in this example it is qlogic.com), or you can manually assign it during configuration. A colon ":" separates this from the previous strings.

In Figure 4.4, the node name is based on the HBA's model (qla4052c) in addition to other strings assigned during the HBA configuration. In this case, it is the ESXi relative DNS host name (FQDN without the domain name). The -1 at the end of the name in this case is a port identifier of a dualport HBA. The second port of this HBA would be named

```
iqn.2000-04.com.qlogic:qla4052c.prme-iox215-2
```

A similar approach is used for software initiators as illustrated in Figure 4.5 with the difference that the Naming Authority is com.vmware. The unique node name is a combination of the host name and a unique string.

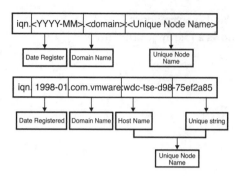

Figure 4.5   SW Initiators—anatomy of iqn

iSCSI EUI

The iSCSI EUI naming format allows a naming authority to use IEEE EUI-64 identifiers in constructing iSCSI names. The details of constructing EUI-64 identifiers are specified by the IEEE Registration Authority (see http://standards.ieee.org/develop/regauth/tut/eui64.pdf). I discuss this further in Chapter 5, "VMware Pluggable Storage Architecture (PSA)."

EUI is not commonly used by HBA vendors. However, you might see some LUNs using this ID format regardless of being iSCSI based, but the ID is usually longer than the following example:

```
eui.02004567A425678D
```

NAA ID

I discuss NAA IDs in Chapter 5 in the context of identifying LUNs.

Alias

iSCSI alias is used to simplify identification of initiators or targets. The alias is not used as part of the authentication credentials. It is ignored by arrays that do not use it.

Here is an example from an alias table from a storage array configuration:

```
+--Connected-To-These-Targets---------------------
|
|  Alias           Target Name
|
|  ESXi1 HBA1      iqn.1995-04.com.example:sn.5551212.target.450
|  ESXi1 HBA2      iqn.1995-04.com.example:sn.5551212.target.489
|  Exchange 2      iqn.1995-04.com.example:sn.8675309
|
+-------------------------------------------------
```

Locating iSCSI Initiators' IQN in vSphere 5 Hosts

In the process of troubleshooting iSCSI connectivity or mapping out an existing vSphere 5.0 host's iSCSI connectivity, you need to identify the installed initiators' IQNs. In this section I show you how to do that via the user interface (UI) as well as the command-line interface (CLI).

Procedure Using the UI

To locate the iSCSI Initiators' IQN using the UI, you may follow this procedure:

1. Log on to the vSphere 5.0 host directly or to the vCenter server that manages the host using the VMware vSphere 5.0 Client as a user with Administrator privileges.

2. While in the Inventory—Hosts and Clusters view, locate the vSphere 5.0 host in the inventory tree and select it.

3. Navigate to the Configuration tab.

4. Under the Hardware section, select the **Storage Adapters** option.

5. Locate the HBAs with the Type column showing iSCSI type.

6. The next column in the UI is WWN, which is where you can locate the IQN for each iSCSI type adapter. Alternatively, select one HBA at a time and in the Details pane locate the iSCSI Name field. There, you also see the IQN.

Figure 4.6 shows an example of Hardware (HW) Initiators.

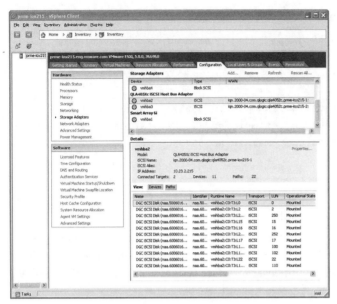

Figure 4.6   Example of HW Initiators—vSphere 5.0 Client UI

Observe that, in the Storage Adapters pane, the HBAs are grouped under the heading QLA405Xc iSCSI Host Bus Adapter, which is the HBA's model. You can see this model also listed in the Details pane in the field Model.

The WWN column values here are

```
iqn.2000-04.com.qlogic:qla4052c.prme-iox215-1
iqn.2000-04.com.qlogic:qla4052c.prme-iox215-2
```

These are the IQNs used as examples in IQN subsection of the "iSCSI Names and Addresses" section. Figure 4.7 shows an example of Software (SW) Initiators.

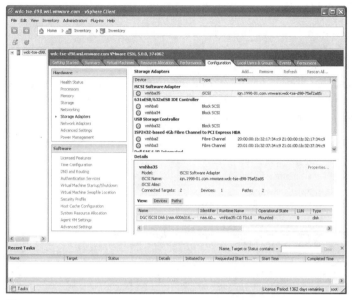

Figure 4.7   Example of SW Initiators—vSphere 5.0 Client UI

Observe that, in the Storage Adapters pane, the HBAs are grouped under the heading iSCSI Software Adapter, which is the HBA's type. You can also see this listed in the Details pane in the Model field.

The WWN column value here is

```
iqn.1998-01.com.vmware:wdc-tse-d98-75ef2a85
```

Using what was discussed in the previous sections, you can identify this IQN as follows:

1. The Naming Authority is registered to vmware.com.

2. The intiator name is wdc-tse-d98.

3. The port ID/Unique string is 75ef2a85.

> **NOTE**
>
> An ESXi host can have only one SW Initiator, which can be connected to more than one vmnic (Uplink). (See more about port-binding later in this chapter.)
>
> In contrast, the ESXi host can have more than one HW Initiator, which are dedicated to one physical port each. More on that in the next section, "Configuring iSCSI Initiators."

Procedure Using SSH

To list the iSCSI Initiators using the CLI, you may follow this procedure:

1. Connect to the vSphere 5.0 host using an SSH client.

2. If root SSH access is disabled, log on with the user account assigned to you and then use su to elevate your privileges to root. Notice that your shell prompt changes from $ to #. You need to provide root's password when prompted.

3. You may use the following command to list all iSCSI initators in the ESXi host:

   ```
   esxcli iscsi adapter list
   ```

   The output for SW Initiators is similar to Figure 4.8.

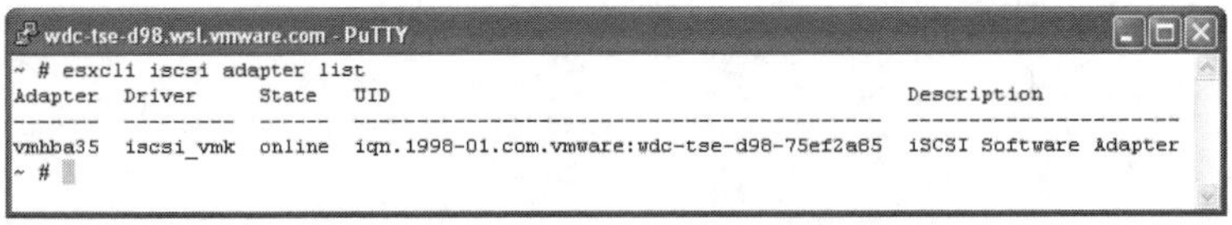

Figure 4.8   Listing SW Initiator—SSH

In this example, the initiator has the attributes listed in Table 4.2.

Table 4.2   Attributes of an iSCSI Initiator

Attribute	Value
Adapter (name)	vmhba35
Driver	iscsi_vmk
State	Online
UID	iqn.1998-01.com.vmware:wdc-tse-d98-75ef2a85
Description	iSCSI Software Adapter

The output for HW Initiators is similar to Figure 4.9.

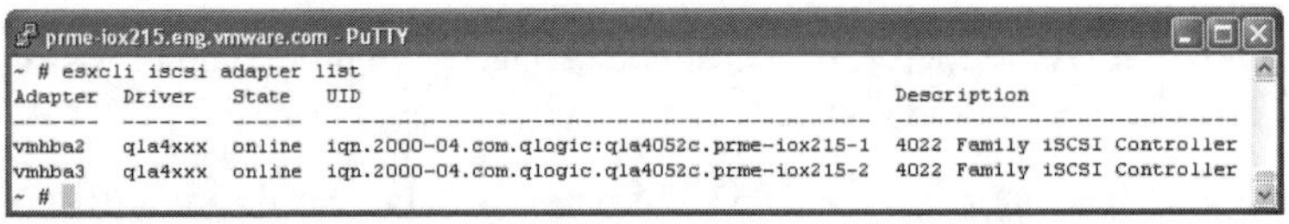

Figure 4.9   Listing HW Initiators—SSH

In this example, the initiator (vmhba2) has the attributes listed in Table 4.3.

Table 4.3 Attributes of an iSCSI HW Initiator

Attribute	Value
Adapter (name)	Vmhba2
Driver	qla4xxx
State	Online
UID	iqn.2000-04.com.qlogic:qla4052c.prme-iox215-1
Description	4022 Family iSCSI Controller

From the last two examples, the initiator type is clearly stated in the description column of the output.

An Alternative Approach to Listing iSCSI Initiators Using the CLI

For an alternative approach to listing the iSCSI Initiators using the CLI, you may follow this procedure:

1. Follow Steps 1 and 2 in the "Procedure Using SSH" section.

2. Run the following command if you are using QLogic HW Initiators:

   ```
   grep -i "iscsi name" /proc/scsi/qla4xxx/*
   ```

   If you are using a different brand/model, substitute qla4xxx with the HBA's relevant proc node. Output similar to Figure 4.10 returns.

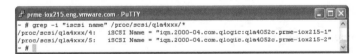

Figure 4.10 Alternative method for listing HW Initiators—SSH

In this example, the ESXi host has two QLogic HW iSCSI Initiators. Observe that both adapters share the same name but have two different port IDs—-1 and -2—which might indicate that this is a dual port HBA.

You can verify the number of adapters by checking the PCI Hardware information using the following command:

```
lspci | grep -i qla4
```

Output similar to Figure 4.11 is returned.

```
prme-iox215.eng.vmware.com - PuTTY                                    _ □ X
~ # lspci | grep -i qla4
000:005:07.1 Network controller: QLogic Corp QLA405Xc iSCSI Host Bus Adapter [vmhba2]
000:005:07.3 Network controller: QLogic Corp QLA405Xc iSCSI Host Bus Adapter [vmhba3]
~ #
```

Figure 4.11   Locating PCI location of iSCSI HW Initiators—SSH

The first column shows the location of the adapter on the PCI bus in the format

```
ddd:BBB:DD:F
```

where

```
ddd: PCI Domain number (this is usually 000)
BBB: PCI Bus number
DD: PCI Device number
F: PCI Function number
```

In this example, the adapters are at the following PCI location:

```
Bus 5: Device 7: Function 0
Bus 5: Device 7: Function 1
```

which means that it is a single adapter with two functions (that is, ports).

This is due to the adapter not having a PCI-to-PCI bridge; otherwise, each adapder would have a different device number and a single PCI function.

Notice that the output also lists the assigned vmhba number: vmhba2 and vmhba3. You can match this with what you see in the UI.

3. Run the following command if you have a SW Initiator:

```
esxcfg-mpath --list-paths |grep -i iqn |sed 's/Target.*$//'
```

You may also run the shorthand version of the command:

```
esxcfg-mpath -b |grep -i iqn |sed 's/Target.*$//'
```

The output of the shorthand version looks like Figure 4.12.

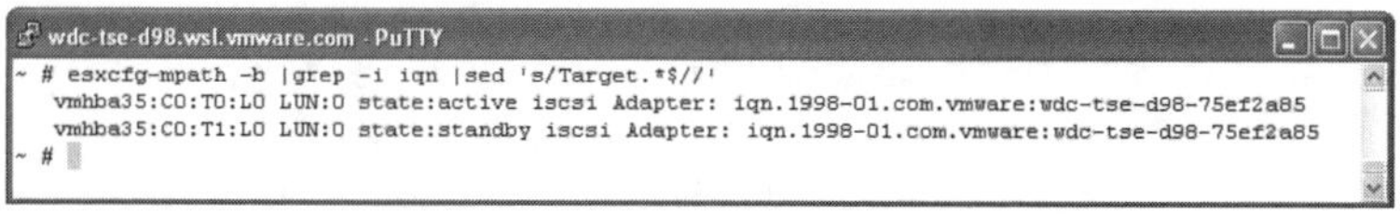

Figure 4.12 Alternative method for listing iSCSI SW Initiators

In this example the SW Initiator is vmhba35 with WWN:

```
iqn.1998-01.com.vmware:wdc-tse-d98-75ef2a85
```

NOTE

The same procedure can be used for HW Initiators.

You can tell the difference from the IQN; if it has "com.vmware" as the naming authority, it is a SW Initiator. Otherwise, it is an HW Initiator.

Procedure Using vMA 5.0

If you have already used "Procedure Using vMA 5.0" under FC Initiators earlier in Chapter 2, "Fibre Channel Storage Connectivity," skip to Step 5.

The following procedure assumes that you have already installed and configured vMA 5.0 as outlined in the VMA Guide available at: http://www.vmware.com/go/vma, which is also where you can download the appliance:

1. Log on to vMA as vi-admin or a user that can use sudo (that is, added to the sudoers file using visudo editor).

2. Add each ESXi host you plan to manage via this appliance.

```
vifp addserver <ESXi host name> --username root --password <root's
password>
```

3. Verify that the host has been successfully added.

```
vifp listservers
```

NOTE

If you omit the –password parameter, you are prompted to enter it as shown in Figure 4.13.

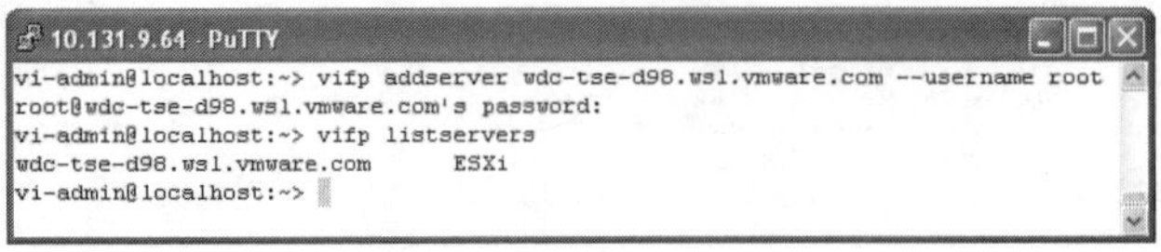

Figure 4.13   Adding a managed host

4. Repeat Steps 2 and 3 for each host you want to manage via this vMA.

5. Set the ESXi server as the target for subsequent commands:

```
vifptarget --set <ESXi host name>
```

You may also use the shorthand version of the command:

```
vifptarget -s <ESXi host name>
```

The output of the shorthand version of the command is shown in Figure 4.14.

Figure 4.14   Setting the target managed host

Notice that the prompt changes to include the ESXi host name.

6. Run the following command to list iSCSI initiators:

```
esxcli iscsi adapter list
```

The output is similar to Figure 4.15.

Figure 4.15   Listing iSCSI SW Initiators—vMA 5.0

In this example, the initiator has the attributes listed in Table 4.4.

Table 4.4 Attributes of an iSCSI Initiator

Attribute	Value
Adapter (name)	vmhba35
Driver	Iscsi_vmk
State	Online
UID	iqn.1998-01.com.vmware:wdc-tse-d98-75ef2a85
Description	iSCSI Software Adapter

The output for HW Initiators is similar to Figure 4.16.

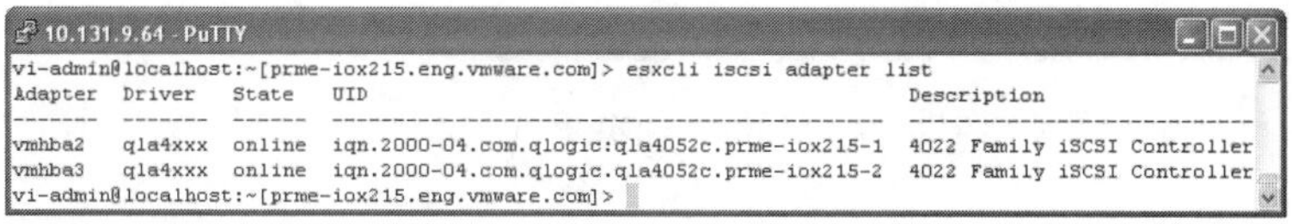

Figure 4.16 Listing iSCSI HW Initiators—vMA 5.0

In this example, the initiator (vmhba2) has the attributes listed in Table 4.5.

Table 4.5 Attributes of an iSCSI HW Initiator

Attribute	Value
Adapter (name)	Vmhba2
Driver	qla4xxx
State	Online
UID	iqn.2000-04.com.qlogic:qla4052c.prme-iox215-1
Description	4022 Family iSCSI Controller

From the last two examples, the initiator type is clearly stated in the description column of the output.

An Alternative Command to List iSCSI Initiators Using vMA 5.0

You may use the following command to list all iSCSI initators in an ESXi host:

```
esxcfg-mpath --list-paths |grep -i iqn |sed 's/Target.*$//'
```

You may also use the shorthand version of the command:

```
esxcfg-mpath -b |grep -i iqn |sed 's/Target.*$//'
```

This lists the output lines (see Figure 4.17) that include iqn and then truncates the rest of the lines starting with the word `Target`.

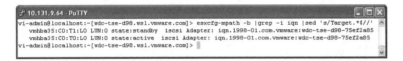

Figure 4.17   Alternative method to list iSCSI SW Initiators—vMA 5.0

In this example, the iSCSI initiator is a software initiator because the naming authority is com.vmware. It is listed twice because it is associated with two different targets. For more details on Targets, see the "iSCSI Sessions" section earlier in this chapter.

Notice that the host name is part of the node name listed after the colon.

Procedure Using Linux vCLI

Using vCLI is similar to using vMA but without fast-pass facility (FP), which provides vifp and vifptarget commands. This means that you have to provide the host's credentials with each command, which include `--server`, `--username`, and `--password` in addition to the rest of the command options used in the "Procedure Using vMA 5.0" section. For example, the commands would be

```
esxcli --server <host name> --username root --password <password> iscsi
adapter list
```

and

```
esxcfg-mpath --list-paths --server <host name> --username root --password
<password> |grep iqn |sed 's/Target.*$//'
```

The shorthand version is

```
esxcfg-mpath -b --server <host name> --username root --password <password>
|grep iqn |sed 's/Target.*$//'
```

TIP

You may use the --credstore option (variable VI_CREDSTORE) to avoid providing the credentials details with every command you run against the ESXi hosts.

The name of the credential store file defaults to <HOME>/.vmware/credstore/vicredentials.xml on Linux and <APPDATA>/VMware/credstore/vicredentials.xml on Windows.

See the vMA 5.0 user guide for additional details.

NOTE

The syntax for using the Windows version is the same as that for the Linux version of vCLI. Keep in mind that additional OS-specific commands/tools available on Linux might not be available on Windows. I covered the Linux version only, and you may apply the same procedure on Windows substituting non-ESXCLI commands with relevant commands that are available on Windows. For example, on Linux I infrequently use sed and awk, which are not available on Windows by default. You may get a Windows version of sed from http://gnuwin32.sourceforge.net/packages/sed.htm and awk from http://gnuwin32.sourceforge.net/packages/gawk.htm.

Configuring iSCSI Initiators

Configuring iSCSI initiators for HW Initiators is somewhat different from configuring SW Initiators. Before diving into the details of each, make sure to review the "iSCSI Connectivity" section at the beginning of this chapter.

Configuring Independent HW Initiator

You can configure hardware initiators via their own firmware, and you can modify them using the vSphere client.

Configuring HW iSCSI Initiator via HBA's BIOS

Using QLA405x Dual Port HBA as an example, here are the steps to configure the HBA using its BIOS:

1. Boot the host and, when prompted, press the key combination to access the HBA's BIOS. In this example, the hotkey for the QLogic HBA is Ctrl-Q. (See Figure 4.18.)

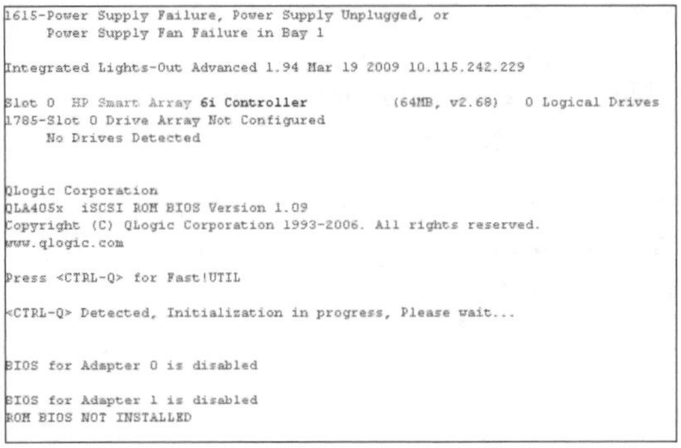

1615-Power Supply Failure, Power Supply Unplugged, or
Power Supply Fan Failure in Bay 1
Integrated Lights-Out Advanced 1.94 Mar 19 2009 10.115.242.229
Slot 0 HP Smart Array 6i Controller (64MB, v2.68) 0 Logical Drives
1785-Slot 0 Drive Array Not Configured
No Drives Detected
QLogic Corporation
QLA405x iSCSI ROM BIOS Version 1.09
Copyright (C) QLogic Corporation 1993-2006. All rights reserved.
www.qlogic.com
Press <CTRL-Q> for Fast!UTIL
<CTRL-Q> Detected, Initialization in progress, Please wait...
BIOS for Adapter 0 is disabled
BIOS for Adapter 1 is disabled
ROM BIOS NOT INSTALLED

Figure 4.18 Accessing the QLogic HBA's BIOS

2. If you have more than one HBA installed, select the HBA you want to configure and then press **Enter**.

3. The QLogic Fast1UTIL menu is displayed. Select the **Configuration Settings** option then press **Enter**. (See Figure 4.19.)

QLogic Fast!UTIL
Selected Adapter
Adapter Boot Mode I/O Address Slot Bus Device Function MAC Address
QLA405x Disable 6400 01 05 07 1 00-C0-DD-09-B6-C3
Fast!UTIL Options
Configuration Settings
Scan iSCSI Devices
iSCSI Disk Utility
Ping Utility
Loopback Test
Reinit Adapter
Select Host Adapter
Exit Fast!UTIL
Use <Arrow keys> to move cursor, <Enter> to select option, <Esc> to backup
RC4 Secured (128 Bit)

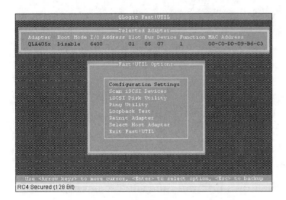

Figure 4.19 QLogic Fast! UTIL Options menu

4. Select the **Host Adapter Settings** option then press **Enter**. (See Figure 4.20.)

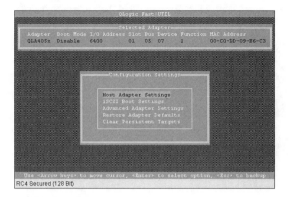

Figure 4.20   Accessing the Host Adapter Settings menu

5. Enter the HBA's IP settings by selecting each field and then pressing **Enter**. Fill in the corresponding address/subnet mask. When done entering each field's value, press **Enter** to go back to the Host Adapter Settings menu. (See Figure 4.21.)

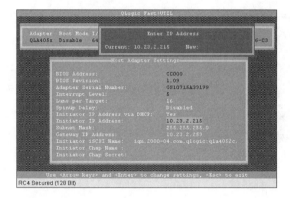

Figure 4.21   Host adapter settings menu

6. Press **Esc** *twice*.

7. When prompted, select **Save Changes** and then press **Enter**. (See Figure 4.22.)

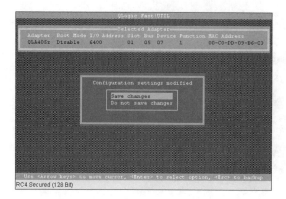

Figure 4.22   Saving adapter configuration changes

8. To configure a second port on the HBA or on another QLogic iSCSI HBA, at the Fast!UTIL Options menu, scroll down to the **Select Host Adapter** and then press **Enter**. (See Figure 4.23.)

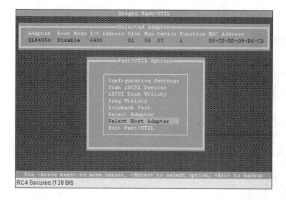

Figure 4.23   Accessing Host Adapter selection menu

9. Select the adapter from the displayed list and then press **Enter**. (See Figure 4.24.)

Figure 4.24 Selecting Host Adapter

10. Repeat Steps 2 through 7.

11. When done configuring all the HBAs' ports, press **Esc** *twice* at the Fast!UTIL Options menu.

12. When prompted, select **Reboot System**. (See Figure 4.25.)

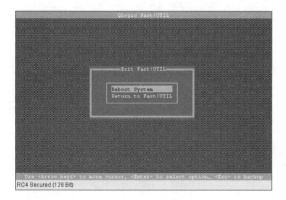

Figure 4.25 Exiting Fast!UTIL and rebooting the system

Modifying Independent HW iSCSI Initiator's Configuration via vSphere 5 Client

There is no virtual network configuration required for this class of initiators. The following steps cover using vSphere client to configure or to make configuration changes to Independent HW Initiators:

1. Install the HBA into an available PCI slot matching the adapter's PCI standard and clock speed.

2. Connect the HBA to the iSCSI network and configure the VLAN if the design calls for it. (Read more about design decisions later in this chapter.)

3. Power on the ESXi host and use the vSphere 5.0 client to connect to it as a user with root privileges or connect to the vCenter server that manages that host as a user with Administrator privileges.

4. If logged into vCenter, navigate to the Inventory—Hosts and Clusters view and then locate the vSphere 5.0 host in the inventory tree and select it. Otherwise, proceed to the next step.

5. Navigate to the Configuration tab.

6. Under the Hardware section, select **Storage Adapters**.

7. Locate the HBA with the model name or HBA family name matching the HBA you are configuring and select it. In this example it is a QLA405xc family and the HBA name is vmhba2. (See Figure 4.26.)

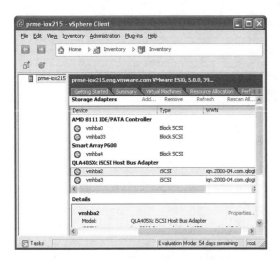

Figure 4.26   Selecting the iSCSI HW Initiator—vSphere 5.0 Client

8. In the Details pane, click **Properties** to view the dialog shown in Figure 4.27.

Figure 4.27   Viewing iSCSI HW Initiator configuration properties—vSphere 5.0 Client

9. Click the **Configure** button. (Figure 4.27 was actually collected from an HBA that was already configured.)

10. In the resulting dialog (shown in Figure 4.28), the iSCSI Name is populated with the vendor's Name Authority and the device name. You may modify the latter part, if the design calls for it.

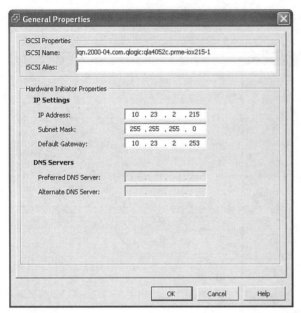

Figure 4.28   Configuring or modifying iSCSI HW Initiator's iSCSI properties and IP settings

11. Type an alias, if you want to assign one to this HBA.

12. Under the **Hardware Initiator Properties,** fill in the IP settings with the IP address you want to assign to this HBA. DNS servers are optional.

13. Click **OK**. You return to the dialog shown previously in Figure 4.27.

14. If your storage array requires the CHAP (Challenge-Handshake Authentication Protocol) authentication method, click the **CHAP** button to configure it. You should see the dialog shown in Figure 4.29.

15. Select **Use CHAP unless prohibited by target** option from the pull-down menu.

16. Check the **Use initiator name** box unless you want to manually enter the IQN here. It is easier to use the checkbox to avoid any typographical errors.

17. In the Secret field, enter the password assigned by the storage array to this initiator.

18. Click **OK**.

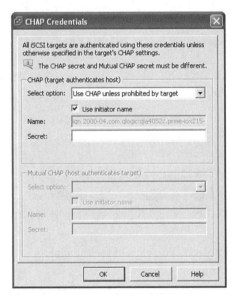

Figure 4.29   Configuring CHAP credentials—vSphere 5.0 Client

HW Initiators provide Static Discovery as well as Dynamic Discovery of iSCSI targets. SW Initiators also support both Static Discovery and Dynamic Discovery as early as ESX 4.0. However, with certain iSCSI storage arrays that present each LUN on a separate target, using static discovery can be impractical.

Figure 4.30 shows the list of discovered targets on this host.

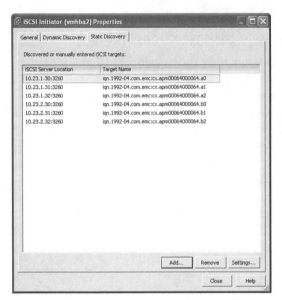

Figure 4.30   Adding iSCSI HW Initiator's static discovery address—Step 1—vSphere 5.0 Client

19. To add Static Discovery targets, click the **Add** button. You should see the dialog shown in Figure 4.31.

Figure 4.31   Adding iSCSI HW Initiator's static discovery address—Step 2—vSphere 5.0 Client

20. In the Add Static Target Server dialog, enter

    a. iSCSI Server IP address.

    b. iSCSI port (default is 3260).

    c. iSCSI Target Name—This is the IQN of one of the iSCSI ports on the storage array. You can obtain this from the array management utility.

Configuring Dependent HW Initiators

Configuring dependent HW initiators is identical to the steps in the "Configuring Independent HW Initiators" section. The only differences are that you can only configure them via the vSphere UI whereas independent HW initiators can be configured via the HBA's firmware as well. You also must create a vmkernel port group to assign to the dependent HW Initiator HBA.

Configuring SW iSCSI Initiator

Configuring the SW initiator is identical to the steps outlined in the "Configuring Independent HW Initiators" section. The only differences are that you can only configure it via the vSphere UI and that you cannot configure Static Discovery of iSCSI targets. You also must create a vmkernel port group to assign to the SW Initiator.

To create and configure an SW Initiator, use the following steps:

1. Install one or more Ethernet NIC (1Gb/s or preferably 10Gb/s) into an available PCI slot matching the adapter's PCI standard and clock speed.

2. Connect the NIC to the iSCSI network and configure the VLAN if the design calls for it. (Read more about design decisions later in this chapter.)

3. Power on the ESXi host, and connect to it using the vSphere 5.0 client as a user with root privileges or connect to the vCenter server that manages that host as a user with Administrator privileges.

4. If logged into vCenter, navigate to the Inventory—Hosts and Clusters view, and then locate the vSphere 5.0 host in the inventory tree and select it. Otherwise, skip to the next step.

5. Navigate to the Configuration tab.

6. In the Networking section, select the **Add Networking** link (see Figure 4.32).

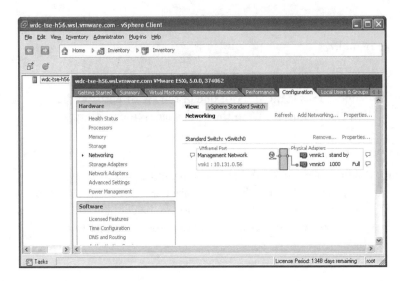

Figure 4.32   Network configuration tab—vSphere 5.0 Client

7. Select **VMkernel** as the connection type and then click **Next**. (See Figure 4.33.)

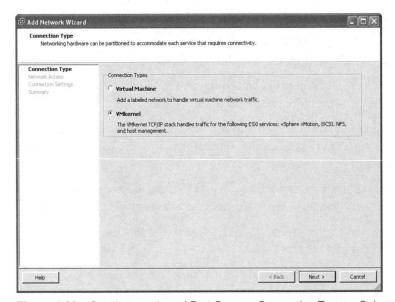

Figure 4.33   Creating a vmkernel Port Group—Connection Type—vSphere 5.0 Client

8. Select the **Use vSwitch0** (if you're using a standard vSwitch) or the **Use dvSwtich0** (if you're using a vNetwork Distributed Switch vDS) radio button if you want to add this port group to the existing vSwitch/vDS. Otherwise, select the **Create a vSphere standard switch** radio button as shown in Figure 4.34. I cover the detailed network design choices later in this chapter.

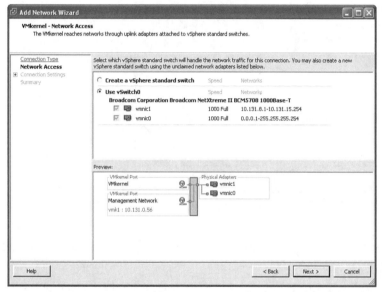

Figure 4.34   Creating a Vmkernel Port Group—Selecting vSwitch—vSphere 5.0 Client

9. Select the vmnics to which you want to link this port group. In this example, I only have two NICs available for storage in this host. I use one of the NICs for iSCSI and share it as a standby NIC with the Management Network.

10. Click **Next**.

11. Type the name you selected for the port group Network Label. In this example I am using iSCSI Network.

12. Select the **VLAN ID** if your design calls for it. Make sure to match the VLAN to which the iSCSI storage array is connected.

13. Leave all checkboxes unchecked as shown in Figure 4.35. Click **Next**.

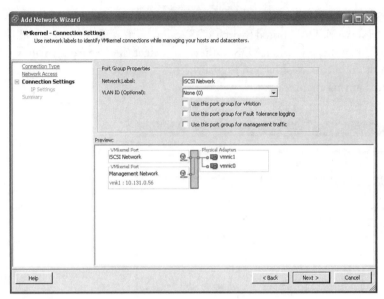

Figure 4.35   Creating a Vmkernel Port Group—Entering port group properties—vSphere 5.0 Client

14. Select the **Use the following IP settings** radio button and then enter the IP settings you allocated for this port group.

15. If the iSCSI network has a default gateway that is different from the VMkernel Port group, click the **Edit** button and enter the iSCSI default gateway (see Figure 4.36).

16. Click **Next**.

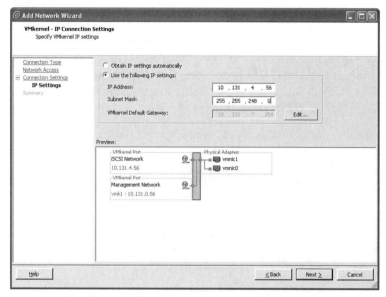

Figure 4.36 Creating a Vmkernel Port Group—IP settings—vSphere 5.0 Client

17. Review the information in the preview screen and, if you have no corrections to make, click the **Finish** button. (See Figure 4.37.)

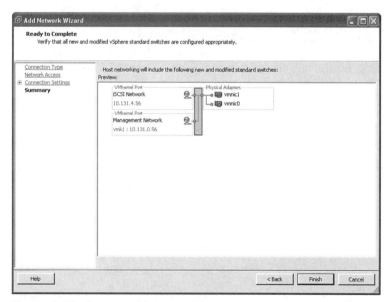

Figure 4.37 Creating a Vmkernel port group—summary—vSphere 5.0 Client

18. Figure 4.38 shows the network configuration after the previous changes.

Notice that both Management Network and iSCSI Network are using vmnic0 as the active uplink (vmnic1 shows as stand by). You need to change the NIC teaming configuration so that the iSCSI port group uses vmnic1 as the active uplink and vmnic0 as unused. I discuss NIC teaming design choices later in this chapter.

19. Select the **Properties** link under the Standard Switch: vSwitch0 section.

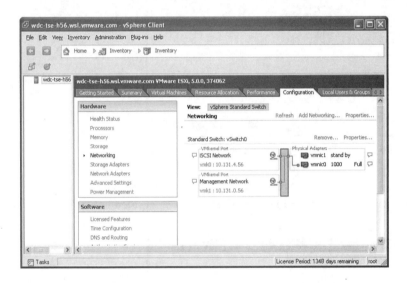

Figure 4.38   Networking configuration tab after adding port group—vSphere 5.0 Client

20. Select the iSCSI Network port group and then click the **Edit** button. (See Figure 4.39.)

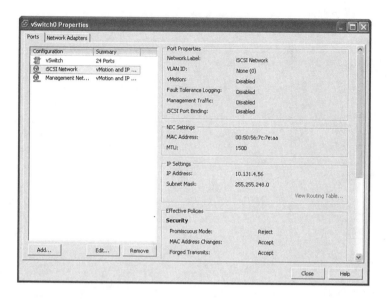

Figure 4.39   Editing iSCSI Port Group—vSphere 5.0 Client

The Software Initiator does not support Active/Active or Active/Standby NIC teaming on vSphere 5. So, if your current configuration looks like Figure 4.40, proceed with the Step 21. Otherwise, if you have no NIC teaming configured, your Network Property should look like Figure 4.41 and you may skip to Step 27.

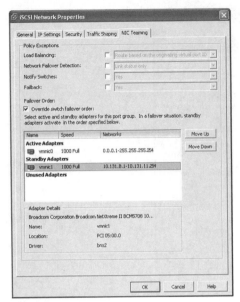

Figure 4.40　Editing iSCSI Port Group—modifying failover order—vSphere 5.0 Client

21. Select the **NIC Teaming** tab and then check the **Override switch failover order** checkbox.

22. Select **vmnic1** and click the **Move Up** button *twice* to place it in the top of the Active Adapters.

23. Select the **vmnic0** and then click the **Move Down** button *twice* to place it in the Unused Adapters section.

24. The failover order should look similar to Figure 4.41.

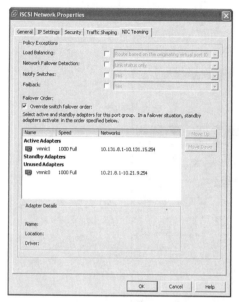

Figure 4.41 Editing iSCSI Port Group—failover order after modifications—vSphere 5.0 Client

25. Click **OK** and then click **Close**.

26. To verify the failover order changes, click the bubble icon to the left side of the iSCSI Network port group. You should see a box similar to Figure 4.42. Notice that the Active Adapter is now vmnic1 and that vmnic0 is unused.

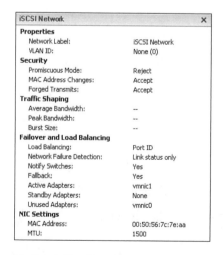

Figure 4.42 Displaying the iSCSI Network Port Group Failover Order—vSphere 5.0 Client

27. Add the SW Initiator. In the Hardware Section, select the **Storage Adapters** link, shown in Figure 4.43.

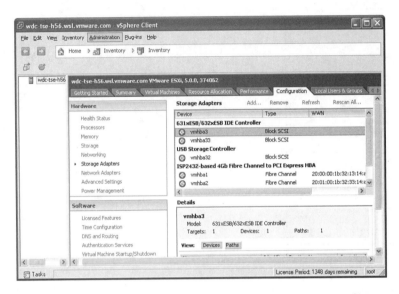

Figure 4.43   Adding an iSCSI SW Initiator—Step 1—vSphere 5.0 Client

28. Next to the Storage Adapters section heading, select the **Add** link. The Add Storage Adapter dialog displays as shown in Figure 4.44.

Figure 4.44   Adding an iSCSI SW Initiator—Step 2—vSphere 5.0 Client

29. Select the **Add Software iSCSI Adapter** radio button and then click **OK**.

30. Acknowledge the displayed message (see Figure 4.45) by clicking **OK**.

Figure 4.45 Adding an iSCSI SW Initiator—Step 3—vSphere 5.0 Client

31. You should now see the SW Initiator listed in the Storage Adapters section as shown in Figure 4.46.

NOTE

The number assigned to the SW Initiator name (for example, vmhba34 or vmhba35) is based on the next available vmhba number. In this example, the next number is vmhba34 since the IDE adapter was assigned vmhba33. The reason for the high vmhba numbers is that the numbers lower than 32 are reserved for physical SCSI, FC, and Independent FCoE/iSCSI HBAs.

32. Under the Details section, select **Properties**. (See Figure 4.46.)

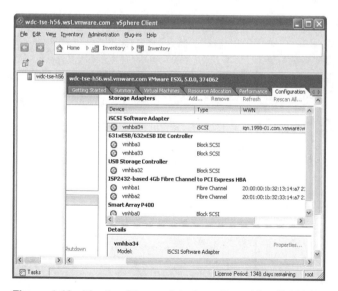

Figure 4.46 Viewing Storage Adapters after adding iSCSI SW Initiator

33. Select the Network Configuration tab; then click **Add.** (See Figure 4.47.)

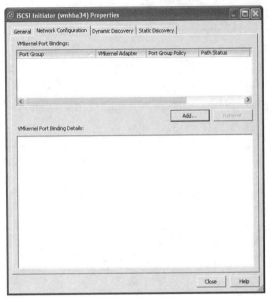

Figure 4.47   iSCSI initiator properties—displaying Network Configuration tab—vSphere 5.0 Client

34. Select the iSCSI Network Port Group (vmk0 VMkernel Adapter) and then click **OK.** (See Figure 4.48.)

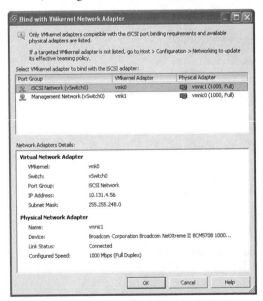

Figure 4.48   Selecting VMkernel port group to bind with iSCSI SW Initiator—vSphere 5.0 Client

35. Repeat Steps 33 and 34 to bind the Management Network with the iSCSI Adapter. If you have enough NICs to dedicate to iSCSI storage, select the corresponding port group instead. This provides an alternative NIC (the active NIC used by the Management Network port group, in this example vmnic0) for availability.

> **NOTE**
>
> If you had not changed the NIC Teaming failover order so that the iSCSI Network Port Group has one active NIC and no standby NICs, you would have received a message similar to Figure 4.49 which states the following:
>
> "The selected physical network adapter is not associated with VMkernel with compliant teaming and failover policy. VMkernel network adapter must have exactly one active uplink and no standby uplinks to be eligible for binding to the iSCSI HBA."
>
> All bound ports must be connected to the same network as the targets because Software iSCSI Initiators traffic is not routable in this release. This may change in a future release, though.

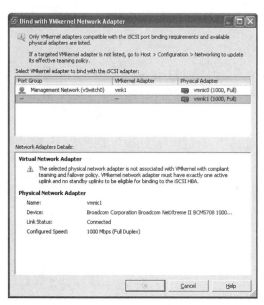

Figure 4.49   What you see if Failover Order was not set correctly—vSphere 5.0 Client

36. A successful addition should look similar to Figure 4.50.

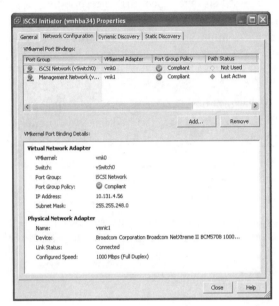

Figure 4.50   iSCSI SW Initiator after Port Groups binding—vSphere 5.0 Client

37. Click the **Dynamic Discovery** tab; then click the **Add** button. Figure 4.51 shows a blank Dynamic Discovery list because this is the first time you have configured iSCSI Initiator.

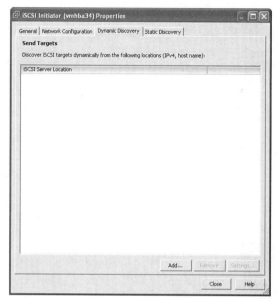

Figure 4.51   iSCSI SW Initiator—adding dynamic discovery—Step 1—vSphere 5.0 Client

38. Enter the iSCSI Server's IP Address and then click **OK**. (See Figure 4.52.)

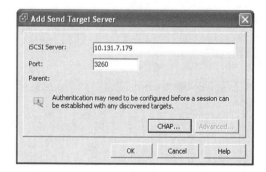

Figure 4.52   iSCSI SW Initiator—adding dynamic discovery—Step 2—vSphere 5.0 Client

39. Repeat for each iSCSI Server's IP address.

40. The target should look similar to Figure 4.53. Click **Close**.

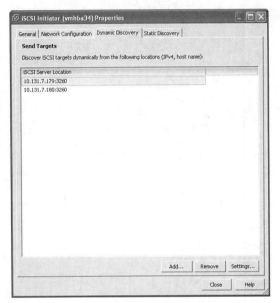

Figure 4.53   iSCSI software initiator—dynamic discovery address added—vSphere 5.0 Client

41. When you receive the dialog in Figure 4.54, click **OK** to rescan.

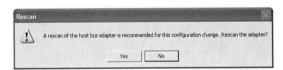

Figure 4.54   iSCSI SW Initiator—accepting "Rescan" dialog—vSphere 5.0 Client

42. To verify the discovered targets, examine the Details section of the iSCSI Software Adapter. The example exhibited in Figure 4.55 shows that there are two connected targets, one device, and two paths.

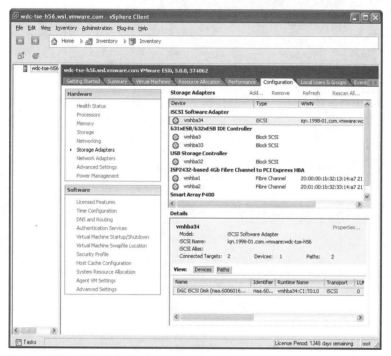

Figure 4.55 iSCSI SW Initiator—configuration detail upon completion

43. To display the list of paths, click the **Paths** button. You should see something similar to Figure 4.56.

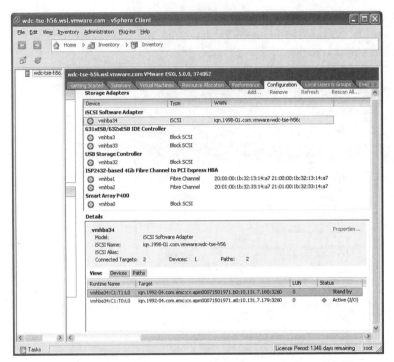

Figure 4.56   iSCSI SW Initiator—displaying paths—vSphere 5.0 Client

In this example, two paths to the device are available; one of them is Active (I/O) and the other is Stand by. I discuss this further in Chapter 7, "Multipathing and Failover."

TIP

The iSCSI initiator configuration is facilitated by iSCSI "Plug-ins" installed on the ESXi host. To identify these plug-ins, run the following command:

```
esxcli iscsi plugin list
```

You should get an output similar to Figure 4.57.

In this example, there are two plug-ins: VMware and QLogic. For more information on IMA iSCSI Management API, see the "iSCSI Architecture" section later in this chapter. Also, see the SNIA white paper at http://www.snia.org/sites/default/files/iSCSI_Management_API_SNIA_White_Paper.pdf.

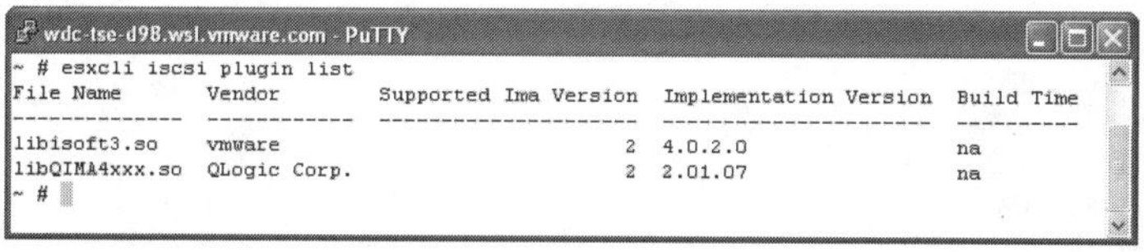

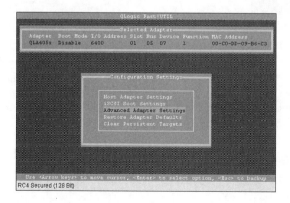

Figure 4.57   Listing iSCSI Plug-ins installed on ESXi 5.0 host—SSH

Configuring Independent HW iSCSI Initiator with Jumbo Frames

To configure Jumbo Frames on Independent HW iSCSI initiators, you can use the HBA's BIOS directly. The following is only the procedure for doing that:

1. Boot the host and, when prompted, press the key combination to access the HBA's BIOS. In this example, the hotkey for the QLogic HBA is Ctrl-Q. (Refer to Figure 4.18 earlier in this chapter.)

2. If you have more than one HBA installed, select the HBA you want to configure and then press **Enter**.

3. The QLogic **Fast1UTIL Options** menu is displayed. Select the **Configuration Settings** option and then press **Enter**. (Refer to Figure 4.19 earlier in this chapter.)

4. Scroll down to **Advanced Adapter Settings** and then press **Enter**. (See Figure 4.58.)

Figure 4.58   Selecting Advanced Adapter Settings

5. Select the MTU field and press **Enter**—as shown in Figure 4.59—and then select the value **9000**. Press **Enter**.

Figure 4.59   Modifying the MTU size

6. Press **Esc** to return to the previous menu. When prompted, select **Save changes** as shown in Figure 4.60 and press **Enter**.

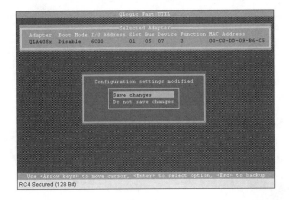

Figure 4.60   Saving MTU changes

7. To configure a second port on the HBA or on another QLogic iSCSI HBA, at the Fast!UTIL Options menu, scroll down to **Select Host Adapter**; then press **Enter**.

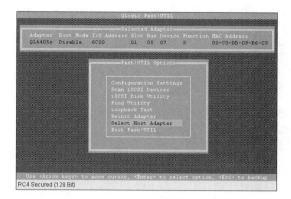

Figure 4.61   Preparing to select the host adapter

8. Select the adapter from the displayed list and then press **Enter**. (See Figure 4.62.)

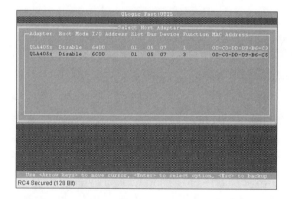

Figure 4.62   Selecting the host adapter

9. Repeat Steps 1 through 3 in this procedure.

10. At the Fast!UTIL Options menu, press **Esc** again.

11. Select **Reboot System**. (See Figure 4.63.)

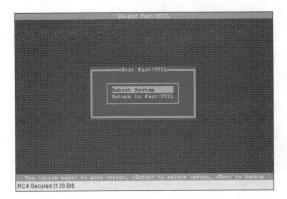

Figure 4.63   Exiting the Fast!UTIL menu and rebooting the system

Configuring SW Initiator with Jumbo Frame

To compensate for lack of offloading capabilities of the iSCSI SW Initiator, enabling Jumbo Frame can significantly improve I/O throughput.

Here I'm covering the procedure of enabling Jumbo Frame assuming that your design meets the requirements:

1. Connect to the ESXi host using the vSphere 5.0 client as a user with root privileges, or connect to the vCenter server that manages that host as a user with Administrator privileges.

2. If logged into vCenter, navigate to the Inventory—Hosts and Clusters view, locate the vSphere 5.0 host in the inventory tree, and select it. Otherwise, skip to the next step.

3. Navigate to the Configuration tab and then select **Networking** under the Hardware section.

4. Select the **Properties** link under the Standard Switch: vSwitch0 section (see Figure 4.64). Your vSwitch number might vary depending on your design.

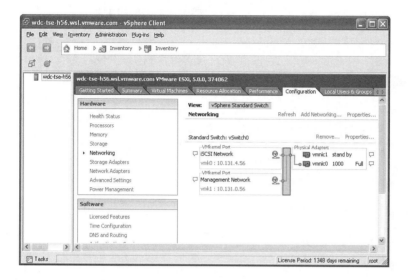

Figure 4.64   Navigating to the Networking configuration—vSphere 5.0 Client

5. Select vSwitch; then click the **Edit** button as shown in Figure 4.65.

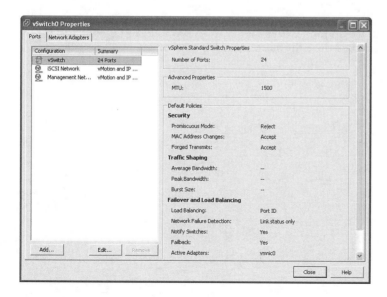

Figure 4.65   Editing vSwitch properties

6. Under the General Tab, enter the value **9000** in the MTU field and then click **OK** (see Figure 4.66).

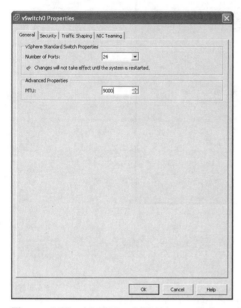

Figure 4.66   Modifying MTU size—vSphere 5.0 Client

7. Select the port group you bound to the iSCSI SW Initiator (in this example, it is iSCSI Network); then click the **Edit** button (see Figure 4.67).

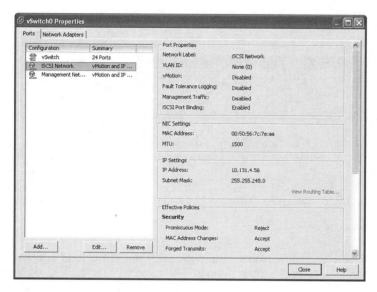

Figure 4.67   Editing the iSCSI port group—vSphere 5.0 Client

8. Under the General tab, enter the value **9000** in the MTU field and then click **OK**, as shown in Figure 4.68.

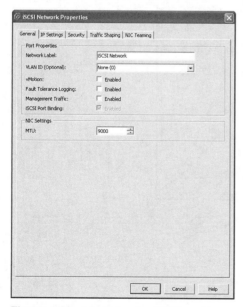

Figure 4.68   Modifying the iSCSI port group properties—vSphere 5.0 Client

9. Acknowledge the resulting warning dialog (see Figure 4.69) by clicking **Yes**.

Figure 4.69   Possible iSCSI connection disruption warning dialog

10. Repeat Steps 7 through 9 for each port group you bound to the iSCSI SW Initiator.

11. Click the **Close** button.

If you compare Figure 4.70 to Figure 4.67, you should notice that the MTU field under the NIC Settings section has changed from 1500 to 9000.

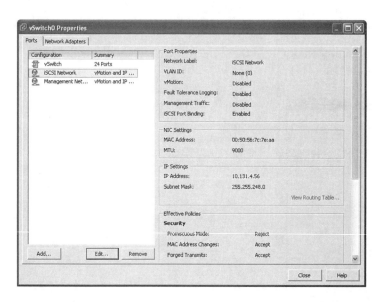

Figure 4.70   vSwitch Properties after portgroup changes

iSCSI Targets

On most iSCSI storage arrays, targets are represented by Storage Processor Ports. However, there are some exceptions, such as Dell Equallogic, where each iSCSI LUN has a unique target. For the former type of iSCSI array, you can use the following procedure to identify iSCSI targets from vSphere 5.0 hosts. You can run one command to check for iSCSI targets for HW and SW Initiators:

```
esxcli iscsi adapter target list
```

The output looks similar to Figure 4.71 for SW Initiators and Figure 4.72 for HW Initiators.

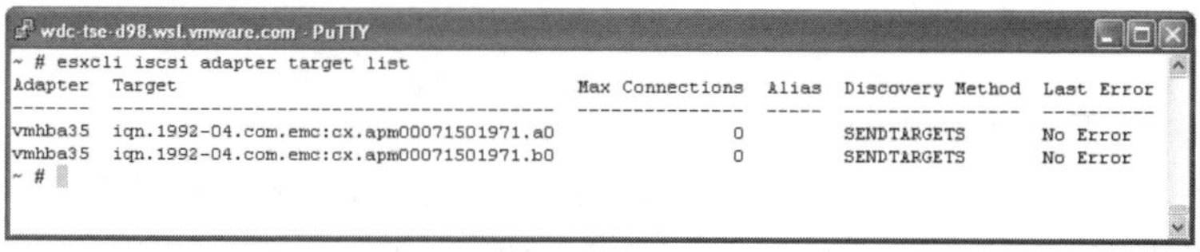

Figure 4.71 SW Initiator—listing iSCSI targets—SSH

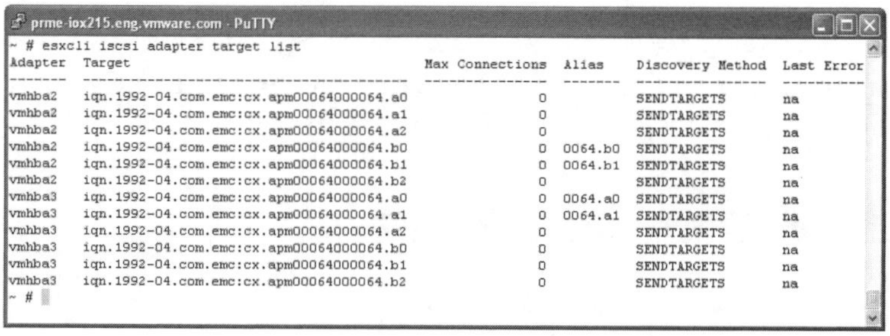

Figure 4.72 HW Initiators—listing iSCSI targets—SSH

NOTE

In these two examples, the initiators' IQNs do not show by using this command. However, you might recognize the SW Initiators from the Adapter name, which by default is of a high adapter number (for example, vmhba35) whereas the HW Initiator is assigned the next available adapter number after the local SCSI and other HBAs (for example, vmhba2 or vmhba3).

Also note that Figure 4.57 shows an example of using iSCSI aliases (discussed earlier in the "iSCSI Initiators" section). In this case the aliases are as shown in Table 4.6.

Table 4.6   iSCSI Alias Examples

Target IQN	Alias	Comment
iqn.1992-04.com.emc:cx.apm00064000064.b0	0064.b0	SPB Port 0
iqn.1992-04.com.emc:cx.apm00064000064.b1	0064.b1	SPB Port 1
iqn.1992-04.com.emc:cx.apm00064000064.a0	0064.a0	SPA Port 0
iqn.1992-04.com.emc:cx.apm00064000064.a1	0064.a1	SPA Port 1

Dissecting SW Initiator's Configuration

Assuming that you have access to the ESXi host via the CLI, you may identify the SW Initiator's various configurations and obtain enough information to create a logical diagram of the virtual network configuration. The following is a step-by-step process and gradual build-up of that logical diagram.

1. Identify the Virtual Adapter name (for example vmhbaX) assigned to the SW Initiator.

   The command output shown in Figure 4.73 shows that the iSCSI Adapter is vmhba34 and that the initiator type is iSCSI Software Adapter.

Figure 4.73   Identifying the SW Initiator's adapter name

2. Identify the vmknic (also known as the vmkernel port) connected to the Virtual Adapter identified in Step 1.

   The command output shown in Figure 4.74 shows that vmhba34 connects to two vmkernel ports (vmknics) named vmk0 and vmk1. The latter two have been assigned a VMware MAC address each (the Organizationally Unique Identifier (OUI) is 00:50:56).

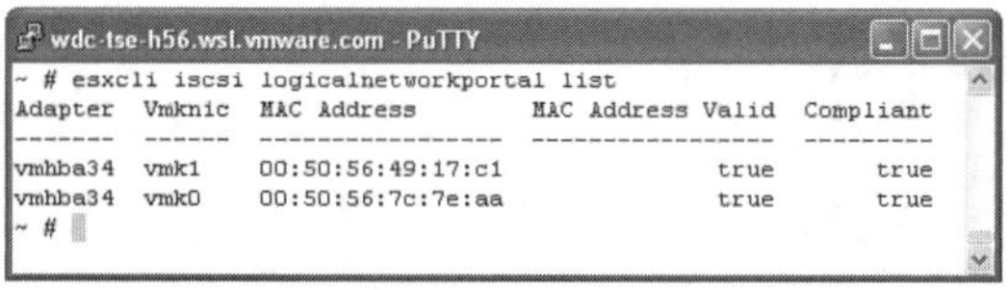

wdc-tse-h56.wsl.vmware.com - PuTTY
~ # esxcli iscsi logicalnetworkportal list
Adapter Vmknic MAC Address MAC Address Valid Compliant
------- ------ ----------------- ----------------- ---------
vmhba34 vmk1 00:50:56:49:17:c1 true true
vmhba34 vmk0 00:50:56:7c:7e:aa true true
~ #

Figure 4.74 Identifying SW Initiator's vmkernel ports

We can depict the details from the last two steps (apart from the MAC addresses) as shown in Figure 4.75.

Host A
SW Initiator
vmhba34
vmknic
vmk0
vmk1
Virtual

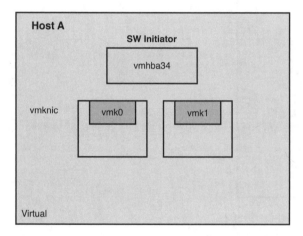

Figure 4.75 SW Initiator virtual network build-up Step 1

3. Identify the Port Group name to which the vmkernel ports are attached:

```
# esxcfg-vmknic --list
```

You may also use the shorthand version of the command:

```
# esxcfg-vmknic -l
```

The output of the shorthand version of the command is shown in Figure 4.76. It lists the vmkernel port names and associated Port Groups in addition to these ports' IP configurations.

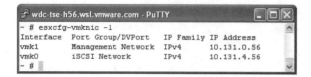

Figure 4.76 Listing port groups associated with vmkernel ports

The Logical Diagram now appears like Figure 4.77.

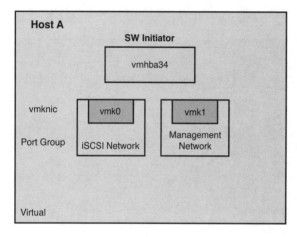

Figure 4.77 SW Initiator virtual network build-up Step 2

Figure 4.77 shows the logical relations between Adapter Name, vmkernel Ports, and vSwitch Port Groups.

4. Find the name of the Virtual Switch using the following command (the output is shown in Figure 4.78):

```
# esxcli network vswitch standard portgroup list
```

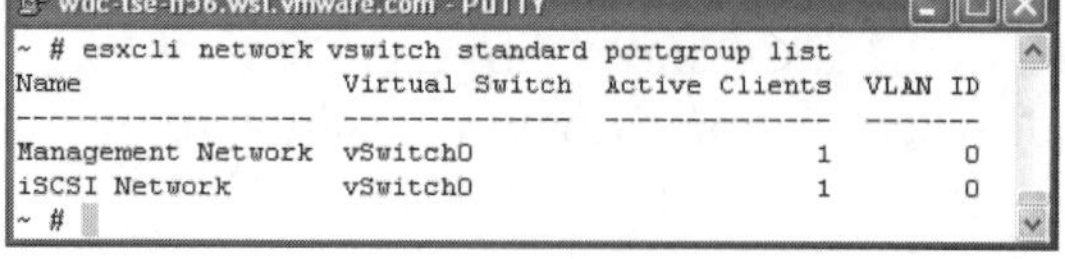

Figure 4.78 Identifying the vSwitch name

From the output in Figure 4.78, both Port Groups connect to vSwitch0.

Let's add this to the Logical Network diagram as well, which results in Figure 4.79.

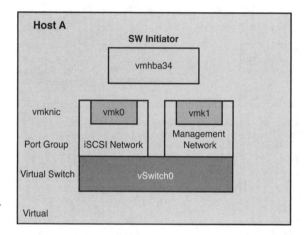

Figure 4.79 SW Initiator virtual network build-up Step 3

5. Find out the uplinks:

```
# esxcfg-vswitch  --list
```

You may also use the shorthand version of the command:

```
# esxcfg-vswitch  -l
```

This command lists the Virtual Switch's properties, as shown in Figure 4.80.

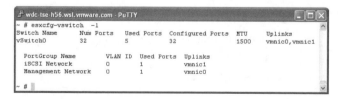

Figure 4.80   Listing vSwitch uplinks

Figure 4.80 shows that vSwitch0 has two uplinks: vmnic0 and vmnic1. It also shows that iSCSI Network port group is connected to vmnic1 and Management Network is connected to vmnic0.

Based on Steps 1 through 5, Figure 4.81 shows the final Logical Network diagram.

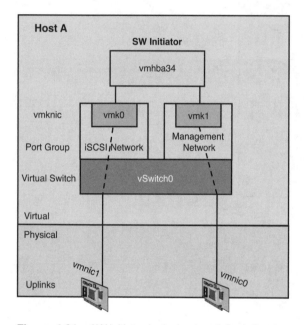

Figure 4.81   AW initiator logical network final diagram

To list all these parameters—excluding vmnics—using a single command, you may run:

```
# esxcli iscsi networkportal list
```

The output is shown in Listing 4.7. The relevant parameters are highlighted.

Listing 4.7   iSCSI Portal Parameters to Identify the iSCSI Logical Network

```
vmhba34
   Adapter: vmhba34
   Vmknic: vmk0
   MAC Address: 00:1f:29:e0:4d:50
   MAC Address Valid: true
   IPv4: 10.131.4.56
```

```
IPv4 Subnet Mask: 255.255.248.0
IPv6:
MTU: 1500
Vlan Supported: true
Vlan ID: 0
Reserved Ports: 63488~65536
TOE: false
TSO: true
TCP Checksum: false
Link Up: true
Current Speed: 1000
Rx Packets: 25341947
Tx Packets: 134
NIC Driver: bnx2
NIC Driver Version: 2.0.15g.v50.11-4vmw
NIC Firmware Version: bc 1.9.6
Compliant Status: compliant
NonCompliant Message:
NonCompliant Remedy:
Vswitch: vSwitch0
PortGroup: iSCSI Network
VswitchUuid:
PortGroupKey:
PortKey:
Duplex:
Path Status: unused


vmhba34
Adapter: vmhba34
Vmknic: vmk1
MAC Address: 00:1f:29:e0:4d:52
MAC Address Valid: true
IPv4: 10.131.0.56
IPv4 Subnet Mask: 255.255.248.0
IPv6:
MTU: 1500
Vlan Supported: true
Vlan ID: 0
Reserved Ports: 63488~65536
TOE: false
```

```
TSO: true
TCP Checksum: false
Link Up: true
Current Speed: 1000
Rx Packets: 8451953
Tx Packets: 1399744
NIC Driver: bnx2
NIC Driver Version: 2.0.15g.v50.11-4vmw
NIC Firmware Version: bc 1.9.6
Compliant Status: compliant
NonCompliant Message:
NonCompliant Remedy:
Vswitch: vSwitch0
PortGroup: Management Network
VswitchUuid:
PortGroupKey:
PortKey:
Duplex:
Path Status: last path
```

NOTE

The command producing the output in Listing 4.7 works for SW Initiators only. Running it with HW Initiators just returns a blank output. In the same listing you might also check the MTU size to verify if Jumbo Frames (discussed in the previous section) is enabled. In this example the MTU value is 1500, which means no jumbo frames.

Dissecting HW Initiator's Configuration

Compared to SW Initiator's configuration, HW Initiator's configuration, both dependent and independent, is fairly simple.

The following command identifies the configured HW Initiators on this host:

```
# esxcli iscsi adapter list
```

Figure 4.82 shows the output.

```
prme-iox215.eng.vmware.com - PuTTY                                                    _ □ X
~ # esxcli iscsi adapter list
Adapter  Driver    State    UID                                          Description
-------  -------   ------   -------------------------------------------  ----------------------------
vmhba2   qla4xxx   online   iqn.2000-04.com.qlogic:qla4052c.prme-iox215-1  4022 Family iSCSI Controller
vmhba3   qla4xxx   online   iqn.2000-04.com.qlogic:qla4052c.prme-iox215-2  4022 Family iSCSI Controller
~ #
```

Figure 4.82   Listing configured HW Initiators

Figure 4.82 shows that this host is configured with two QLogic 4022 Family HW Initiators. They have been assigned vmhba2 and vmhba3 Adapter Names respectively.

Listing the network portals for these HW Initiators is done by listing the Physical Network Portals in contrast to the SW Initiators, which have Logical Network Portals only.

The following command lists the HW Initiators' Physical Network Portals.

```
# esxcli iscsi physicalnetworkportal list
```

Figure 4.83 shows the output.

```
prme-iox215.eng.vmware.com - PuTTY                                                    _ □ X
~ # esxcli iscsi physicalnetworkportal list
Adapter  Vmnic  MAC Address        MAC Address Valid  Current Speed  Max Speed  Max Frame Size
-------  -----  -----------------  -----------------  -------------  ---------  --------------
vmhba2          00:c0:dd:09:b6:c3             true            1024       1024             1500
vmhba3          00:c0:dd:09:b6:c5             true            1024       1024             1500
~ #
```

Figure 4.83   Listing HW Initiators' physical network portals

You can conclude from Figure 4.83 that the HW Initiators named vmhba2 and vmhba3 have QLogic assigned MAC addresses (OUI 00:c0:dd). It also shows that Jumbo Frame is not configured because the MTU size is 1500.

iSCSI Adapter Parameters

Occasionally you might need to identify the current iSCSI Adapter's parameters for the purpose of troubleshooting or managing your vSphere 5 storage.

You can accomplish that via the UI or the CLI.

Using the UI to List and Modify iSCSI Adapter Parameters

The iSCSI Adapter Parameters are available via the advanced options of the iSCSI Initiator Properties. Use the following steps to access these properties:

1. Use the vSphere 5.0 client to connect to the ESXi host as a user with "root" privileges or connect to the vCenter server that manages that host as a user with Administrator privileges.

2. If logged into vCenter, navigate to the Inventory—Hosts and Clusters view, locate the vSphere 5.0 host in the inventory tree, and select it. Otherwise, proceed to the next step.

3. Navigate to the Configuration tab.

4. Under the Hardware section, select **Storage Adapters**.

5. Locate the HBAs with the model name or HBA family name matching the Dependent HW iSCSI HBA or *iSCSI Software Adapter* you are configuring and select it.

6. Click the **Properties** link on the upper-right corner of the *Details* pane. You see a dialog similar to Figure 4.84.

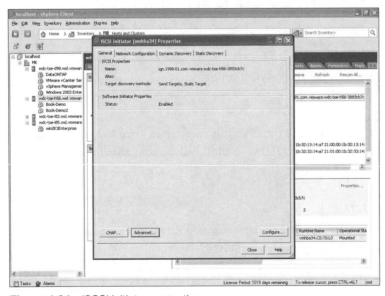

Figure 4.84   iSCSI initiator properties

7. Click the **Advanced** button. You see a dialog similar to Figure 4.85.

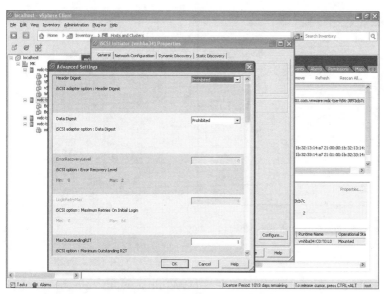

Figure 4.85   iSCSI adapter parameter list

8. Scroll down to locate the parameter you would like the list to modify. If the parameter's value is grayed out, then it is not *settable*. The parameters descriptions as well as the minimum and maximum values are listed below each parameter.

9. Make the changes you want, and then click **OK** and then **Close**.

Using the CLI to List and Modify iSCSI Adapter Parameters

In releases prior to vSphere 5, you used to list the iSCSI Adapter Parameters via *vmkiscsi-tool*. This tool is still available in vSphere 5. However, because *vmkiscsi-tool* is not available remotely via vMA or vCLI, vSphere 5 provides the same capability via an *esxcli* namespace that is available locally or remotely:

```
esxcli iscsi adapter param get --adapter=<iSCSi-Adapter-Name>
```

Example:

```
esxcli iscsi adapter param get --adapter=vmhba34
```

You may also use the shorthand version of this command using `-A` instead of `--Adapter=`:

```
esxcli iscsi adapter param get -A vmhba35
```

Figure 4.86 shows the output of the shorthand version of the command.

```
wdc-tse-d98.wsl.vmware.com - PuTTY
~ # esxcli iscsi adapter param get -A vmhba35
Name                  Current     Default     Min  Max       Settable  Inherit
--------------------  ----------  ----------  ---  --------  --------  -------
ErrorRecoveryLevel    0           0           0    2            false    false
InitialLoginRetryMax  4           4           0    64           false    false
InitialR2T            false       false       na   na           false    false
FirstBurstLength      262144      262144      512  16777215      true    false
MaxBurstLength        262144      262144      512  16777215      true    false
MaxRecvDataSegment    131072      131072      512  16777215      true    false
MaxOutstandingR2T     1           1           1    8             true    false
MaxCmds               128         128         2    2048         false    false
ImmediateData         true        true        na   na           false    false
DefaultTime2Retain    0           0           0    60           false    false
DefaultTime2Wait      2           2           0    60           false    false
LoginTimeout          5           5           0    60           false    false
LogoutTimeout         15          15          0    60           false    false
NoopOutInterval       15          15          1    60            true    false
NoopOutTimeout        10          10          10   30            true    false
RecoveryTimeout       10          10          1    120           true    false
DelayedAck            true        true        na   na            true    false
HeaderDigest          prohibited  prohibited  na   na            true    false
DataDigest            prohibited  prohibited  na   na            true    false
~ #
```

Figure 4.86 Listing iSCSI adapter parameters (software initiator)

This command applies to both software and dependent HW Initiators, though the output values from the latter might be different (see Figure 4.87). The main difference is that these values are not *Settable* while some of the SW Initiator's parameters are.

```
prme-iox215.eng.vmware.com - PuTTY
~ # esxcli iscsi adapter param get -A vmhba3
Name                  Current     Default     Min  Max    Settable  Inherit
--------------------  ----------  ----------  ---  -----  --------  -------
ErrorRecoveryLevel    na          na          na   na        false    false
InitialLoginRetryMax  na          na          na   na        false    false
InitialR2T            false       false       na   na        false    false
FirstBurstLength      256         0           1    65535     false    false
MaxBurstLength        512         0           1    65535     false    false
MaxRecvDataSegment    128         0           1    65535     false    false
MaxOutstandingR2T     1           0           1    65535     false    false
MaxCmds               64          0           0    65535     false    false
ImmediateData         false       false       na   na        false    false
DefaultTime2Retain    20          0           0    65535     false    false
DefaultTime2Wait      2           0           0    0         false    false
LoginTimeout          na          na          na   na        false    false
LogoutTimeout         na          na          na   na        false    false
NoopOutInterval       14          0           0    65535     false    false
NoopOutTimeout        14          0           0    65535     false    false
RecoveryTimeout       na          na          na   na        false    false
DelayedAck            true        false       na   na        false    false
HeaderDigest          prohibited  prohibited  na   na        false    false
DataDigest            prohibited  prohibited  na   na        false    false
~ #
```

Figure 4.87 Listing iSCSI adapter parameters (independent HW Initiator)

Options with the value of `true` in the `Settable` column can be modified using the `set` option.

Example:

To set the `NoopOutTimeout` value to 15, use the following:

```
esxcli iscsi adapter param set --adapter vmhba34 --key NoopOutTimeout
--value 15
```

You may also use the shorthand version:

```
esxcli iscsi adapter param set -A vmhba34 -k NoopOutTimeout -v 15
```

These commands do not provide any feedback if successful. Otherwise, an error would be returned. To verify the outcome, you may run the `get` command. Compare the output to that in Figure 4.87. The value in the Current column should reflect changed value.

To reset the value back to default, which is the value listed in the Default column, run this command:

```
esxcli iscsi adapter param set -adapter vmhba34 --default --key
NoopOutTimeout
```

You may also use the shorthand version:

```
esxcli iscsi adapter param set -A vmhba34 -D -k NoopOutTimeout
```

Should You Change iSCSI Adapter Parameters?

The default settings of the iSCSI Adapter parameters are the best practice, and you should not change them. I take one exception to that: The `LoginTimeout` should be settable, but it is currently not! However, this may change in a future release.

vSphere 5 iSCSI Architecture

iSCSI architecture is depicted in Figure 4.88, which spans vmkernel modules, user-level daemons, and software components.

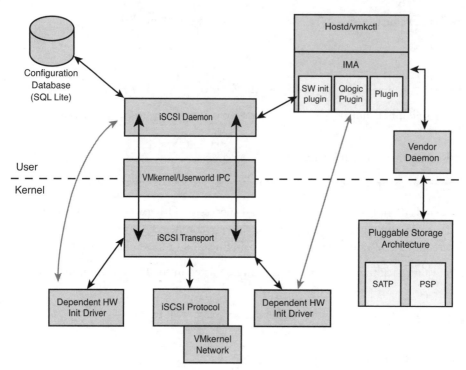

Figure 4.88   vSphere 5 iSCSI architecture

vSphere 5 iSCSI architecture is comprised of the following components, which I discuss in subsequent sections:

- iSCSI database
- iSCSI daemon
- IMA (iSCSI Management API)
- iSCSI transport module
- iSCSI protocol module
- Dependent iSCSI initiator modules
- Independent iSCSI HBA modules

iSCSI Database

iSCSI configuration and iSCSI runtime environment are stored in an SQL Lite database. Changes to the database persist between ESXi host reboots. The configuration is restored whenever the host is rebooted or the iSCSI daemon (vmkiscsid) is restarted. You can dump the database using the following:

```
vmkiscsid --dump-db=<file-name>
```

From the database dump, you can easily locate various iSCSI configuration properties details. For example, the dump includes the following sections:

- ISID: iSCSI Session ID information

- InitiatorNodes: iSCSI Initiators information

- Targets: iSCSI Targets information

- discovery: Target Discovery information

- ifaces: The iSCSI Network configuration including the vmnic and vmknic names

iSCSI Daemon

The ESXi iSCSI daemon is vmkiscsid, which runs on any vSphere host with iSCSI enabled as a User World process. This means that it is not a vmkernel module and runs like other applications/daemons on top of vmkernel. vmkiscsid is started at boot time; if it finds a valid configuration or if iBFT (iSCSI Boot Firmware Table) is enabled in the NIC's BIOS, it continues to run. (iBFT is used for Boot-From-iSCSI configurations.) It is also run whenever an iSCSI management command is run from the command line or via hostd. If it finds no valid iSCSI configuration, it stops.

The iSCSI daemon does the following tasks:

- Dynamic and static iSCSI targets discovery

- Authentication of iSCSI targets

- Maintains information about vmknics, ports, and so on for iSCSI use (see database dump)

- Establishes connections to iSCSI targets

- Reconnects to iSCSI targets if sessions get disconnected

- Updates the iSCSI configuration database based on sessions establishment or tear down

- Updates the iSCSI configuration database based on administrative input

- Listens for connections from IMA plug-ins (more on IMA in the next section)

- Communicates with iSCSI kernel components on connection events and session establishment

IMA (iSCSI Management API)

IMA is used to manage and configure iSCSI on the host. It is standardized by SNIA (see the white paper at http://www.snia.org/sites/default/files/iSCSI_Management_API_SNIA_White_Paper.pdf).

IMA provides interfaces to

- Configure the iSCSI adapter, including network and iSCSI parameters

- Enter and examine iSCSI discovery information

- Enter and examine authentication types and credentials

- View target, LU, session, and connection information

- Allocate and free lists for IMA consumers

The implementation on ESXi 5 includes four components: IMA common Library, ESX IMA plug-in, third-party vendors' IMA plug-ins, and storage vendor daemons.

IMA Common Library

The IMA common library is mostly a shim interface to the IMA plug-ins. It is also responsible for serializing the commands to the IMA plug-ins among other programmatic functions.

ESX IMA Plug-in

The ESX IMA plug-in is called by the IMA common library and used to configure and manage the ESX Software iSCSI initiator and any dependent HW iSCSI initiators.

If vmkiscsid is not running when the ESX IMA plugin is called, the plug-in starts vmkiscsid. This ensures any iSCSI configuration on the system is returned any time an IMA call is made.

Vendor IMA Plug-ins

Third-party independent HW iSCSI Initiator vendors are required to deliver an IMA plug-in to manage their adapters and driver. These plug-ins present the standard IMA interfaces to the IMA common library and use vendor-specific methods to communicate with the associated driver and hardware. For example, the Qlogic plug-in communicates with the qla4xxx driver to accomplish management functions.

Storage Vendor Daemons

Storage vendors may deliver session management daemons that make IMA library calls. The daemons are delivered as CIM (Common Information Model) providers, running in an unmanaged "daemon" mode, and they are used to manage sessions for a storage vendor's multipath software, delivered via PSA (Pluggable Storage Architecture). For more information about PSA refer to Chapter 5. The CIM provider uses vendor-specific communication methods to coordinate and interact with their PSA components. CIM is an industry standard management API that is used by VMware Partners to monitor and manage systems' health as well as communicate with and manage software components on ESXi.

iSCSI Transport Module

The iSCSI transport module, iscsi_trans, is a VMware-provided module that facilitates communications between the iSCSI daemon (vmkiscsid) and any iSCSI media modules, such as the ESX SW iSCSI initiator or HW iSCSI initiators drivers.

iscsi_trans presents a set vmkernel API that facilitates the following:

- Gather and set configuration parameters in the ESX iSCSI module and any other vmkernel modules that might later consume these interfaces

- Pass network configuration information to dependent HW iSCSI initiators because they depend on vmkernel for networking

iSCSI Protocol Module

The iSCSI protocol (or media) module, iscsi_vmk , is the VMware-provided module that implements the iSCSI protocol for the ESX software iSCSI initiator. This module packages SCSI commands in iSCSI PDUs and passes them to the vmkernel networking stack through a socket interface. Iscsi_vmk accepts management calls from iscsi_trans, SCSI commands and data from the SCSI midlayer, and network transition information via its socket connections.

Dependent iSCSI Initiator Modules

Dependent iSCSI Initiator modules are vmklinux drivers delivered by third-party vendors. (vmklinux is the ESXi facility that enables drivers ported from Linux to run on ESXi.) These modules utilize vmklinux driver interfaces and several vmkernel API interfaces to get the network configuration. Dependent iSCSI HBA drivers get their network configuration from a vmknic, including IP address information, MTU, and VLAN. (I covered these details in the "Configuring Dependent HW Initiators" section.) Configuration management is handled by the ESX IMA plug-in.

The ESX IMA plug-in sends configuration information to the iSCSI daemon, which uses this configuration information to discover and authenticate targets and then establish and tear down sessions.

Independent iSCSI HBA Modules

Independent iSCSI HBA modules are vmklinux modules delivered by third-party vendors. They utilize vmklinux driver interfaces for storage and iSCSI path information. They also rely on communication with IMA plug-ins supplied by the vendor for configuration and management. IMA plug-ins are used to provide discovery and authentication information and session management.

TIP

To list the vmkernel modules mentioned in the previous sections, you may run these commands from the ESXi Shell:

```
~# vmkload_mod --list |grep iscsi
iscsi_trans              8      52
iscsi_linux              1      16
iscsi_vmk                4     204

~ # ps |grep iscsi
2670        iscsi_trans_vmklink
2693        iscsivmk-log
5891 5891 vmkiscsid                /usr/sbin/vmkiscsid
5892 5891 vmkiscsid                /usr/sbin/vmkiscsid
```

You may also run the short-hand version of the first command using -l instead of --list. These commands apply to both Software and HW iSCSI Initiators with slight differences in the outputs.

The first command lists the loaded vmkernel modules, which shows iscsi_trans and iscsi_vmk. The middle module, iscsi_linux, is a module that allows third-party vendors to port Linux iSCSI drivers with minimal changes.

The second command shows the running processes which include two vmkiscsid processes, iscsi_trans_vmklink (see Step 6 under Software iSCSI initiators). The process called iscsivmk-log is the process used by the iSCSI stack to log events into the vmkernel logs.

Flow of Communication Through the iSCSI Architecture

To put things in perspective, let me share with you the logical flow of communication through the vSphere iSCSI architecture for the purpose of target discovery.

Software iSCSI Initiators

1. Socket is open on a port or set of ports, connecting to an iSCSI target.

2. iSCSI target returns a list of targets via a Send Target payload.

3. iSCSI Configuration Database is populated with the returned target list.

4. vmkiscsid (iSCSI Daemon) logs into iSCSI targets.

5. vmkiscsid exchanges authentication parameters with the target and, if configured, performs a Challenge-Handshake authentication.

6. vmkiscsid, which is on the user side, communicates with iscsi_trans (iSCSI Transport), on the kernel side, via a Userworld-VMkernel IPC socket (IPC stands for Inter-Process Communication). This link is also known as vmklink.

7. After the session with the target is established, an open socket descriptor is passed on to the SW iSCSI initiator module. The latter builds iSCSI Protocol Data Units (PDUs) to transport SCSI commands and data to the iSCSI target.

8. vmkiscsid updates the iSCSI configuration database with:

   - Target information

   - ESX port information

   - Session parameters

Dependent HW iSCSI Initiators

Dependent HW iSCSI Initiators are driven by vmkscsid. So, a similar flow would be the following:

1. vmkscsid passes the connection establishment commands to the dependent HW iSCSI Initiator via the iSCSI Transport (iscsi_trans).

2. After the connection with the target is established, vmkscsid constructs PDUs to discover, authenticate, and establish sessions with the iSCSI target (like Steps 2 through 6 in the previous section).

3. The dependent HW iSCSI Initiator builds iSCSI PDUs to transport SCSI commands and data to the iSCSI target (hardware offloading).

4. If the connection is lost, the dependent HW Initiator driver informs vmkscsid via iSCSI Transport. vmkscsid directs session reestablishment.

5. vmkiscsid updates the iSCSI configuration database similar to what is listed in Step 8 in the "Software Initiators" section.

Independent HW iSCSI Initiators

Independent HW iSCSI Initiators communicate directly with iSCSI Transport and handle their own connections and sessions establishment as well as constructing their own iSCSI PDUs to transport SCSI commands and data to iSCSI target.

Summary

In this chapter I provided details of the iSCSI protocol, connectivity, and its implementation on vSphere 5. I also covered iSCSI initiators (both HW and SW) as well as iSCSI targets and how to identify them. I walked you through gradually building up the logical iSCSI network diagram based on commands available on ESXi 5. Finally, I provided details of iSCSI Architecture and the flow of communication between its components.

Chapter 5

vSphere Pluggable Storage Architecture (PSA)

vSphere 5.0 continues to utilize the Pluggable Storage Architecture (PSA) which was introduced with ESX 3.5. The move to this architecture modularizes the storage stack, which makes it easier to maintain and to open the doors for storage partners to develop their own proprietary components that plug into this architecture.

Availability is critical, so redundant paths to storage are essential. One of the key functions of the storage component in vSphere is to provide multipathing (if there are multiple paths, which path should a given I/O use) and failover (when a path goes down, I/O failovers to using another path).

VMware, by default, provides a generic Multipathing Plugin (MPP) called Native Multipathing (NMP).

Native Multipathing

To understand how the pieces of PSA fit together, Figures 5.1, 5.2, 5.4, and 5.6 build up the PSA gradually.

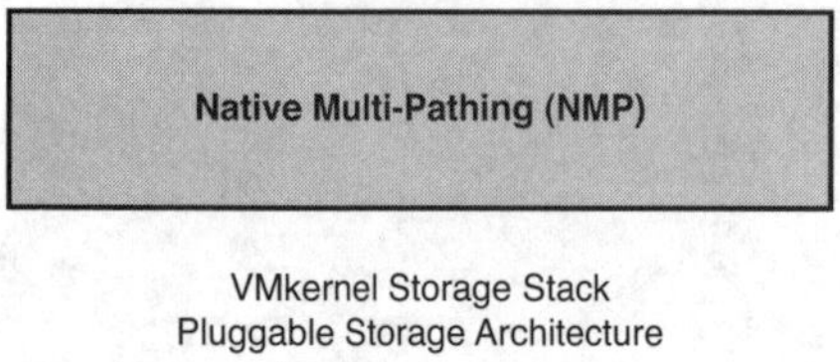

```
┌─────────────────────────────────────┐
│                                     │
│       Native Multi-Pathing (NMP)    │
│                                     │
└─────────────────────────────────────┘

         VMkernel Storage Stack
       Pluggable Storage Architecture
```

Figure 5.1   Native MPP

NMP is the component of vSphere 5 vmkernel that handles multipathing and failover. It exports two APIs: Storage Array Type Plugin (SATP) and Path Selection Plugin (PSP), which are implemented as plug-ins.

NMP performs the following functions (some done with help from SATPs and PSPs):

- Registers logical devices with the PSA framework

- Receives input/output (I/O) requests for logical devices it registered with the PSA framework

- Completes the I/Os and posts completion of the SCSI command block with the PSA framework, which includes the following operations:

  - Selects the physical path to which it sends the I/O requests

  - Handles failure conditions encountered by the I/O requests

- Handles task management operations—for example, Aborts/Resets

PSA communicates with NMP for the following operations:

- Open/close logical devices.

- Start I/O to logical devices.

- Abort an I/O to logical devices.

- Get the name of the physical paths to logical devices.

- Get the SCSI inquiry information for logical devices.

Storage Array Type Plug-in (SATP)

Figure 5.2 depicts the relationship between SATP and NMP.

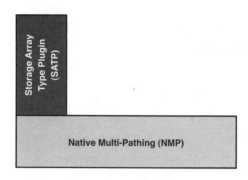

VMkernel Storage Stack
Pluggable Storage Architecture

Figure 5.2   SATP

SATPs are PSA plug-ins specific to certain storage arrays or storage array families. Some are generic for certain array classes—for example, Active/Passive, Active/Active, or ALUA-capable arrays.

SATPs handle the following operations:

- Monitor the hardware state of the physical paths to the storage array

- Determine when a hardware component of a physical path has failed

- Switch physical paths to the array when a path has failed

NMP communicates with SATPs for the following operations:

- Set up a new logical device—claim a physical path

- Update the hardware states of the physical paths (for example, Active, Standby, Dead)

- Activate the standby physical paths of an active/passive array (when Active paths state is dead or unavailable)

- Notify the plug-in that an I/O is about to be issued on a given path

- Analyze the cause of an I/O failure on a given path (based on errors returned by the array)

Examples of SATPs are listed in Table 5.1:

Table 5.1   Examples of SATPs

SATP	Description
VMW_SATP_CX	Supports EMC CX that do not use the ALUA protocol
VMW_SATP_ALUA_CX	Supports EMC CX that use the ALUA protocol
VMW_SATP_SYMM	Supports EMC Symmetrix array family
VMW_SATP_INV	Supports EMC Invista array family
VMW_SATP_EVA	Supports HP EVA arrays
VMW_SATP_MSA	Supports HP MSA arrays
VMW_SATP_EQL	Supports Dell Equalogic arrays
VMW_SATP_SVC	Supports IBM SVC arrays
VMW_SATP_LSI	Supports LSI arrays and others OEMed from it (for example, DS4000 family)
VMW_SATP_ALUA	Supports non-specific arrays that support ALUA protocol
VMW_SATP_DEFAULT_AA	Supports non-specific active/active arrays
VMW_SATP_DEFAULT_AP	Supports non-specific active/passive arrays
VMW_SATP_LOCAL	Supports direct attached devices

How to List SATPs on an ESXi 5 Host

To obtain a list of SATPs on a given ESXi 5 host, you may run the following command directly on the host or remotely via an SSH session, a vMA appliance, or ESXCLI:

```
# esxcli storage nmp satp list
```

An example of the output is shown in Figure 5.3.

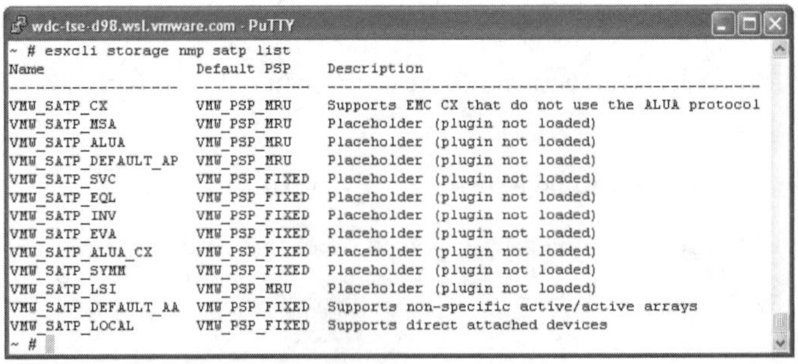

Figure 5.3   Listing SATPs

Notice that each SATP is listed in association with a specific PSP. The output shows the default configuration of a freshly installed ESXi 5 host. To modify these associations, refer to the "Modifying PSA Plug-in Configurations Using the UI" section later in this chapter.

If you installed third-party SATPs, they are listed along with the SATPs shown in Table 5.1.

NOTE

ESXi 5 only loads the SATPs matching detected storage arrays based on the corresponding claim rules. See the "Claim Rules" section later in this chapter for more about claim rules. Otherwise, you see them listed as (Plugin not loaded) similar to the output shown in Figure 5.3.

Path Selection Plugin (PSP)

Figure 5.4 depicts the relationship between SATP, PSP, and NMP.

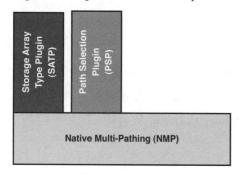

VMkernel Storage Stack
Pluggable Storage Architecture

Figure 5.4   PSP

PSPs are PSA plug-ins that handle path selection policies and are replacements of failover policies used by the Legacy-MP (or Legacy Multipathing) used in releases prior to vSphere 4.x.

PSPs handle the following operations:

- Determine on which physical path to issue I/O requests being sent to a given storage device. Each PSP has access to a group of paths to the given storage device and has knowledge of the paths' states—for example, Active, Standby, Dead, as well as Asymmetric Logical Unit Access (ALUA), Asymmetric Access States (AAS) such as Active optimized Active non-optimized, and so on. This knowledge is obtained from what SATPs report to NMP. Refer to Chapter 6, "ALUA," for additional details about ALUA.

- Determine which path to activate next if the currently working physical path to storage device fails.

> **NOTE**
>
> PSPs do not need to know the actual storage array type (this function is provided by SATPs). However, a storage vendor developing a PSP may choose to do so (see Chapter 8, "Third-Party Multipathing I/O Plug-ins").

NMP communicates with PSPs for the following operations:

- Set up a new logical storage device and claim the physical paths to that device.
- Get the set of active physical paths currently used for path selection.
- Select a physical path on which to issue I/O requests for a given device.
- Select a physical path to activate when a path failure condition exists.

How to List PSPs on an ESXi 5 Host

To obtain a list of PSPs on a given ESXi 5 host, you may run the following command directly on the host or remotely via an SSH session, a vMA appliance, or ESXCLI:

```
# esxcli storage nmp psp list
```

An example of the output is shown in Figure 5.5.

Figure 5.5   Listing PSPs

The output shows the default configuration of a freshly installed ESXi 5 host. If you installed third-party PSPs, they are also listed.

Third-Party Plug-ins

Figure 5.6 depicts the relationship between third-party plug-ins, NMP, and PSA.

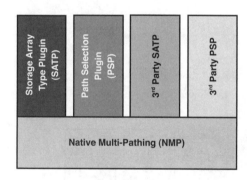

VMkernel Storage Stack
Pluggable Storage Architecture

Figure 5.6   Third-party plug-ins

Because PSA is a modular architecture, VMware provided APIs to its storage partners to develop their own plug-ins. These plug-ins can be SATPs, PSPs, or MPPs.

Third-party SATPs and PSPs can run side by side with VMware-provided SATPs and PSPs.

The third-party SATPs and PSPs providers can implement their own proprietary functions relevant to each plug-in that are specific to their storage arrays. Some partners implement only multipathing and failover algorithms, whereas others implement load balancing and I/O optimization as well.

Examples of such plug-ins in vSphere 4.x that are also planned for vSphere 5 are

- **DELL_PSP_EQL_ROUTED**—Dell EqualLogic PSP that provides the following enhancements:
  - Automatic connection management
  - Automatic load balancing across multiple active paths
  - Increased bandwidth
  - Reduced network latency

- **HTI_SATP_HDLM**—Hitachi ported their HDLM MPIO (Multipathing I/O) management software to an SATP. It is currently certified for vSphere 4.1 with most of the USP family of arrays from Hitachi and HDS. A version is planned for vSphere 5 as well for the same set of arrays. Check with VMware HCL for the current list of certified arrays for vSphere 5 with this plug-in.

See Chapter 8 for further details.

Multipathing Plugins (MPPs)

Figure 5.7 depicts the relationship between MPPs, NMP, and PSA.

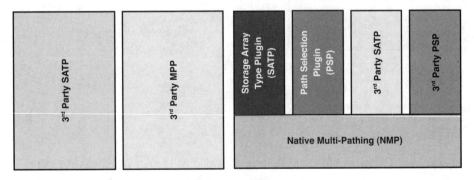

VMkernel Storage Stack
Pluggable Storage Architecture

Figure 5.7   MPPs, including third-party plug-ins

MPPs that are not implemented as SATPs or PSPs can be implemented as MPPs instead. MPPs run side by side with NMP. An example of that is EMC PowerPath/VE. It is certified with vSphere 4.x and is planned for vSphere 5.

See Chapter 8 for further details.

Anatomy of PSA Components

Figure 5.8 is a block diagram showing the components of PSA framework.

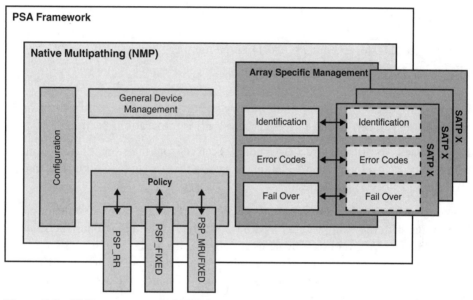

Figure 5.8   NMP components of PSA framework

Now that we covered the individual components of PSA framework, let's put its pieces together. Figure 5.8 shows the NMP component of the PSA framework. NMP provides facilities for configuration, general device management, array-specific management, and path selection policies.

The configuration of NMP-related components can be done via ESXCLI or the user interface (UI) provided by vSphere Client. Read more on this topic in the "Modifying PSA Plug-in Configurations Using the UI" section later in this chapter.

Multipathing and failover policy is set by NMP with the aid of PSPs. For details on how to configure the PSP for a given array, see the "Modifying PSA Plug-in Configurations Using the UI" section later in this chapter.

Arrray-specific functions are handled by NMP via the following functions:

- **Identification**—This is done by interpreting the response data to various inquiry commands (Standard Inquiry and Vital Product Data (VPD) received from the array/storage. This provides details of device identification which include the following:

  - Vendor

  - Model

  - LUN number

  - Device ID—for example, NAA ID, serial number

  - Supported mode pages—for example, page 80 or 83

  I cover more detail and examples of inquiry strings in Chapter 7, "Multipathing and Failover" in, the "LUN Discovery and Path Enumeration" section.

- **Error Codes**—NMP interprets error codes received from the storage arrays with help from the corresponding SATPs and acts upon these errors. For example, an SATP can identify a path as dead.

- **Failover**—After NMP interprets the error codes, it reacts in response to them. Continuing with the example, after a path is identified as dead, NMP instructs the relevant SATP to activate standby paths and then instructs the relevant PSP to issue the I/O on one of the activated paths. In this example, there are no active paths remaining, which results in activating standby paths (which is the case for Active/Passive arrays).

I/O Flow Through PSA and NMP

In order to understand how I/O sent to storage devices flows through the ESXi storage stack, you first need to understand some of the terminology relevant to this chapter.

Classification of Arrays Based on How They Handle I/O

Arrays can be one of the following types:

- **Active/Active**—This type of array would have more than one Storage Processor (SP) (also known as Storage Controller) that can process I/O concurrently on all SPs (and SP ports) with similar performance metrics. This type of array has no concept of logical unit number (LUN) ownership because I/O can be done on any LUN via any SP port from initiators given access to such LUNs.

- **Active/Passive**—This type of array would have two SPs. LUNs are distributed across both SPs in a fashion referred to as LUN ownership in which one of the SPs owns some of the LUNs and the other SP owns the remaining LUNs. The array accepts I/O to given LUN via ports on that SP that "owns" it. I/O sent to the non-owner SPs (also known as Passive SP) is rejected with a SCSI check condition and a sense code that translates to ILLEGAL REQUEST. Think of this like the No Entry sign you see at the entrance of a one-way street in the direction opposite to the traffic. For more details on sense codes, see Chapter 7 's "LUN Discovery and Path Enumeration" section.

> **NOTE**
>
> Some older firmware versions of certain arrays, such as HP MSA, are a variety of this type where one SP is active and the other is standby. The difference is that all LUNs are owned by the active SP and the standby SP is only used when the active SP fails. The standby SP still responds with a similar sense code to that returned from the passive SP described earlier.

- **Asymmetric Active/Active or AAA (AKA Pseudo Active/Active)**—LUNs on this type of arrays are owned by either SP similarly to the Active/Passive Arrays concept of LUN ownership. However, the array would allow concurrent I/O on a given LUN via ports on both SPs but with different I/O performance metrics as I/O is sent via proxy from the non-owner SP to the owner SP. In this case, the SP providing the lower performance metric accepts I/O to that LUN without returning a check condition. You may think of this as a hybrid between Active/Passive and Active/Active types. This can result in poor I/O performance of all paths to the owner SP that are dead, either due to poor design or LUN owner SP hardware failure.

- **Asymmetrical Logical Unit Access (ALUA)**—This type of array is an enhanced version of the Asymmetric Active/Active arrays and also the newer generation of some of the Active/Passive arrays. This technology allows initiators to identify the ports on the owner SP as one group and the ports on the non-owner SP as a different group. This is referred to as Target Port Group Support (TPGS). The port group on the owner SP is identified as Active Optimized port group with the other group identified as Active Non-Optimized port group. NMP would send the I/O to a given LUN via a port in the ALUA optimized port group only as long as they are available. If all ports in that group are identified as dead, I/O is then sent to a port on the ALUA non-optimized port group. When sustained I/O is sent to the ALUA non-optimized port group, the array can transfer the LUN ownership to the non-owner SP and then transition the ports on that SP to ALUA optimized state. For more details on ALUA see Chapter 6.

Paths and Path States

From a storage perspective, the possible routes to a given LUN through which the I/O may travel is referred to as *paths*. A path consists of multiple points that start from the initiator port and end at the LUN.

A path can be in one of the states listed in Table 5.2.

Table 5.2   Path States

Path State	Description
Active	A path via an Active SP. I/O can be sent to any path in this state.
Standby	A path via a Passive or Standby SP. I/O is not sent via such a path.
Disabled	A path that is disabled usually by the vSphere Administrator.
Dead	A path that lost connectivity to the storage network. This can be due to an HBA (Host Bus Adapter), Fabric or Ethernet switch, or SP port connectivity loss. It can also be due to HBA or SP hardware failure.
Unknown	The state could not be determined by the relevant SATP.

Preferred Path Setting

A preferred path is a setting that NMP honors for devices claimed by VMW_PSP_FIXED PSP only. All I/O to a given device is sent over the path configured as the Preferred Path for that device. When the preferred path is unavailable, I/O is sent via one of the surviving paths. When the preferred path becomes available, I/O fails back to that path. By default, the first path discovered and claimed by the PSP is set as the preferred path. To change the preferred path setting, refer to the "Modifying PSA Plug-in Configurations Using the UI" section later in this chapter.

Figure 5.9 shows an example of a path to LUN 1 from host A (interrupted line) and Host B (interrupted line with dots and dashes). This path goes through HBA0 to target 1 on SPA.

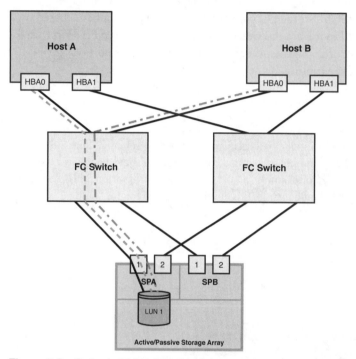

Figure 5.9   Paths to LUN1 from two hosts

Such a path is represented by the following Runtime Name naming convention. (Runtime Name is formerly known as Canonical Name.) It is in the format of HBAx:Cn:Ty:Lz—for example, vmhba0:C0:T0:L1—which reads as follows:

vmhba0, Channel 0, Target 0, LUN1

It represents the path to LUN 0 broken down as the following:

- **HBA0**—First HBA in this host. The vmhba number may vary based on the number of storage adapters installed in the host. For example, if the host has two RAID controllers installed which assume vmhba0 and vmhba1 names, the first FC HBA would be named vmhba2.

- **Channel 0**—Channel number is mostly zero for Fiber Channel (FC)- and Internet Small Computer System Interface (iSCSI)-attached devices to target 0, which is the first target. If the HBA were a SCSI adapter with two channels (for example, internal connections and an external port for direct attached devices), the channel numbers would be 0 and 1.

- **Target 0**—The target definition was covered in Chapters 3, "FCoE Storage Connectivity," and 4, "iSCSI Storage Connectivity." The target number is based on the order in which the SP ports are discovered by PSA. In this case, SPA-Port1 was discovered before SPA-Port2 and the other ports on SPB. So, that port was given "target 0" as the part of the runtime name.

NOTE

Runtime Name, as the name indicates, does not persist between host reboots. This is due to the possibility that any of the components that make up that name may change due to hardware or connectivity changes. For example, a host might have an additional HBA added or another HBA removed, which would change the number assumed by the HBA.

Flow of I/O Through NMP

Figure 5.10 shows the flow of I/O through NMP.

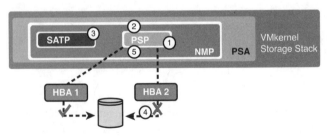

Figure 5.10   I/O flow through NMP

The numbers in the figure represent the following steps:

1. NMP calls the PSP assigned to the given logical device.

2. The PSP selects an appropriate physical path on which to send the I/O. If the PSP is VMW_PSP_RR, it load balances the I/O over paths whose states are Active or, for ALUA devices, paths via a target port group whose AAS is Active/Optimized.

3. If the array returns I/O error, NMP calls the relevant SATP.

4. The SATP interprets the error codes, activates inactive paths, and then fails over to the new active path.

5. PSP selects new active path to which it sends the I/O.

Listing Multipath Details

There are two ways by which you can display the list of paths to a given LUN, each of which are discussed in this section:

- Listing paths to a LUN using the UI

- Listing paths to a LUN using the CLI

Listing Paths to a LUN Using the UI

To list all paths to a given LUN in the vSphere 5.0 host, you may follow this procedure, which is similar to the procedure for listing all targets discussed earlier in Chapter 2, "Fibre Channel Storage Connectivity" Chapter 3 and Chapter 4:

1. Log on to the vSphere 5.0 host directly or to the vCenter server that manages the host using the VMware vSphere 5.0 Client as a user with Administrator privileges.

2. While in the Inventory—Hosts and Clusters view, locate the vSphere 5.0 host in the inventory tree and select it.

3. Navigate to the **Configuration** tab.

4. Under the Hardware section, select the **Storage** option.

5. Under the **View** field, click the **Devices** button.

6. Under the Devices pane, select one of the SAN LUNs (see Figure 5.11). In this example, the device name starts with DGC Fibre Channel Disk.

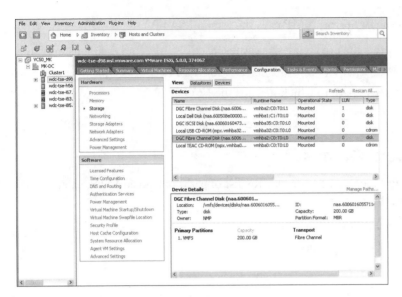

Figure 5.11   Listing storage devices

7. Select **Manage Paths** in the **Device Details** pane.

8. Figure 5.12 shows details for an FC-attached LUN. In this example, I sorted on the Runtime Name column in ascending order. The **Paths** section shows all available paths to the LUN in the format:

   ■ **Runtime Name**—vmhbaX:C0:Ty:Lz where X is the HBA number, y is the target number, and z is the LUN number. More on that in the "Preferred Path Setting" section later in this chapter.

   ■ **Target**—The WWNN followed by the WWPN of the target (separated by a space).

   ■ **LUN**—The LUN number that can be reached via the listed paths.

   ■ **Status**—This is the path state for each listed path.

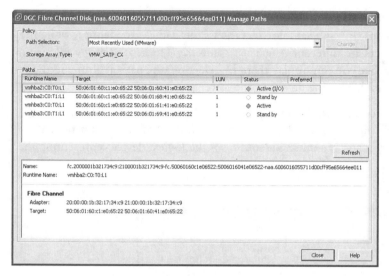

Figure 5.12   Listing paths to an FC-attached LUN

9. The Name field in the lower pane is a permanent one compared to the Runtime
    Name listed right below it. It is made up of three parts: HBA name, Target Name,
    and the LUN's device ID separated by dashes (for FC devices) or commas (for iSCSI
    devices). The HBA and Target names differ by the protocol used to access the LUN.

    Figure 5.12 shows the FC-based path Name, which is comprised of

    - **Initiator Name**—Made up from the letters FC followed by a period and then
      the HBA's WWNN and WWPN. The latter two are separated by a colon
      (these are discussed in Chapter 3).

    - **Target Name**—Made up from the target's WWNN and WWPN separated
      by a colon.

    - **LUN's Device ID**—In this example the NAA ID is naa.6006016055711d0
      0cff95e65664ee011, which is based on the Network Address Authority nam-
      ing convention and is a unique identifier of the logical device representing the
      LUN.

    Figure 5.13 shows the iSCSI-based path Name which is comprised of

    - **Initiator Name**—This is the iSCSI iqn name discussed in Chapter 4.

- **Target Name**—Made up from the target's iqn name and target number separated by colons. In this example, the target's iqn names are identical while the target numbers are different—such as t,1 and t,2. The second target info is not shown here, but you can display them by selecting one path at a time in the paths, pane to display the details in the lower pane.

- **LUN's Device ID**—In this example the NAA ID is naa.6006016047301a00 eaed23f5884ee011, which is based on the Network Address Authority naming convention and is a unique identifier of the logical device representing the LUN.

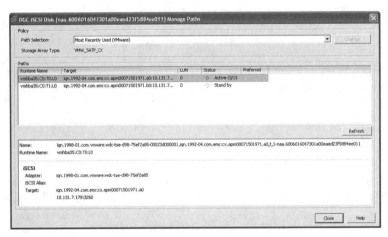

Figure 5.13 Listing paths to an iSCSI-attached LUN

Figure 5.14 shows a Fibre Channel over Ethernet (FCoE)-based path name, which is identical to the FC-based pathnames. The only difference is that fcoe is used in place of fc throughout the name.

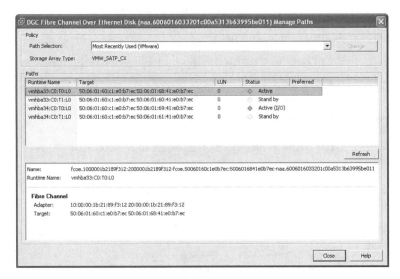

Figure 5.14   Listing paths to an FCoE-attached LUN

Listing Paths to a LUN Using the Command-Line Interface (CLI)

ESXCLI provides similar details to what is covered in the preceding section. For details about the various facilities that provide access to ESXCLI, refer to the "Locating HBA's WWPN and WWNN in vSphere 5 Hosts" section in Chapter 2.

The namespace of ESXCLI in vSphere 5.0 is fairly intuitive! Simply start with esxcli followed by the area of vSphere you want to manage—for example, esxcli network, esxcli software, esxcli storage—which enables you to manage Network, ESXi Software, and Storage, respectively. For more available options just run `esxcli -help`. Now, let's move on to the available commands:

Figure 5.15 shows the `esxcli storage nmp` namespace.

```
~ # esxcli storage nmp
Usage: esxcli storage nmp {cmd} [cmd options]

Available Namespaces:
  psp       Operations pertaining to the Path Selection Policy Plugins for the VMware Native Multipath Plugin.
  satp      Operations pertaining to the Storage Array Type Plugins for the VMware Native Multipath Plugin.
  device    Operations pertaining to the devices currently claimed by the VMware Native Multipath Plugin.
  path      Operations pertaining to the paths currently claimed by the VMware Native Multipath Plugin.

~ #
```

Figure 5.15   esxcli storage nmp namespace

The namespace of `esxcli storage nmp` is for all operations pertaining to native multipathing, which include psp, satp, device, and path.

I cover all these namespaces in detail later in the "Modifying PSA Plug-in Configurations Using the UI" section. The relevant operations for this section are

- `esxcli storage nmp path list`
- `esxcli storage nmp path list -d <device ID e.g. NAA ID>`

The first command provides a list of paths to *all* devices regardless of how they are attached to the host or which protocol is used.

The second command lists the paths to the device specified by the device ID (for example, NAA ID) by using the `-d` option.

The command in this example is

```
esxcli storage nmp path list -d naa.6006016055711d00cff95e65664ee011
```

You may also use the verbose command option `--device` instead of `-d`.

You can identify the NAA ID of the device you want to list by running a command like this:

```
esxcfg-mpath -b |grep -B1 "fc Adapter"| grep -v -e "--" |sed 's/
Adapter.*//'
```

You may also use the verbose command option `--list-paths` instead of `-b`.

The output of this command is shown in Figure 5.16.

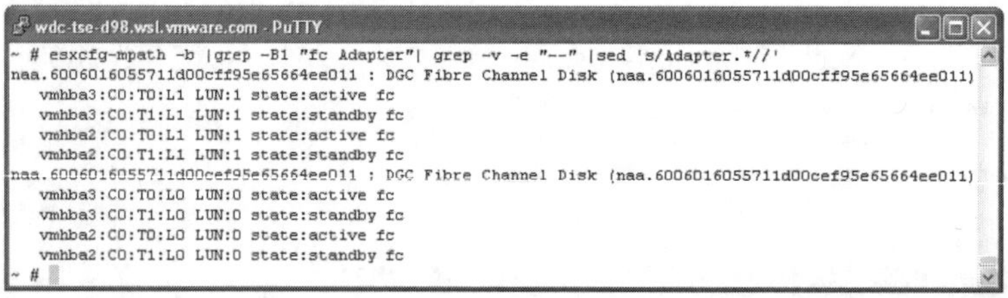

Figure 5.16   Listing paths to an FC-attached LUN via the CLI

This output shows all FC-attached devices. The Device Display Name of each device is listed followed immediately by the Runtime Name (for example, vmhba3:C0:T0:L1) of all paths to that device. This output is somewhat similar to the legacy multipathing outputs you might have seen with ESX server release 3.5 and older.

The Device Display Name is actually listed after the device NAA ID and a colon.

From the runtime name you can identify the LUN number and the HBA through which they can be accessed. The HBA number is the first part of the Runtime Name, and the LUN number is the last part of that name.

All block devices conforming to the SCSI-3 standard have an NAA device ID assigned, which is listed at the beginning and the end of the Device Display Name line in the preceding output.

In this example, FC-attached LUN 1 has NAA ID `naa.6006016055711d00cff95e65 664ee011` and that of LUN0 is `naa.6006016055711d00cef95e65664ee011`. I use the device ID for LUN 1 in the output shown in Figure 5.17.

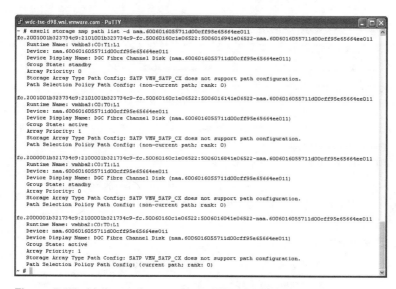

Figure 5.17 Listing pathnames to an FC-attached device

You may use the verbose version of the command shown in Figure 5.17 by using `--device` instead of `-d`.

From the outputs of Figure 5.16 and 5.17, LUN 1 has four paths.

Using the Runtime Name, the list of paths to LUN1 is

- `vmhba3:C0:T1:L1`

- `vmhba3:C0:T0:L1`

- `vmhba2:C0:T1:L1`

- `vmhba2:C0:T0:L1`

This translates to the list shown in Figure 5.18 based on the physical pathnames. This output was collected using this command:

```
esxcli storage nmp path list -d naa.6006016055711d00cff95e65664ee011 |grep
fc
```

Or the verbose option using the following:

```
esxcli storage nmp path list --device naa.6006016055711d00cff95e65664ee011
|grep fc
```

Figure 5.18 Listing physical pathnames of an FC-attached LUN

This output is similar to the aggregate of all paths that would have been identified using the corresponding UI procedure earlier in this section.

Using Table 2.1, "Identifying SP port association with each SP," in Chapter 2, we can translate the targets listed in the four paths as shown in Table 5.3:

Table 5.3 Identifying SP Port for LUN Paths

Runtime Name	Target WWPN	Sp Port Association
vmhba3:C0:T1:L1	5006016941e06522	SPB1
vmhba3:C0:T0:L1	5006016141e06522	SPA1
vmhba2:C0:T1:L1	5006016841e06522	SPB0
vmhba2:C0:T0:L1	5006016041e06522	SPA0

Identifying Path States and on Which Path the I/O Is Sent—FC

Still using the FC example (refer to Figure 5.17), two fields are relevant to the task of identifying the path states and the I/O path: Group State and Path Selection Policy Path Config. Table 5.4 shows the values of these fields and their meanings.

Table 5.4 Path State Related Fields

Runtime Name	Group State	PSP Path Config	Meaning
vmhba3:C0:T1:L1	Standby	non-current path; rank: 0	Passive SP—no I/O
vmhba3:C0:T0:L1	Active	non-current path; rank: 0	Active-SP—no I/O
vmhba2:C0:T1:L1	Standby	non-current path; rank: 0	Passive SP—no I/O
vmhba2:C0:T0:L1	Active	current path; rank: 0	Active SP—I/O

Combining the last two tables, we can extrapolate the following:

- The LUN is currently owned by SPA (therefore the state is Active).
- The I/O to the LUN is sent via the path to SPA Port 0.

> **NOTE**
>
> This information is provided by the PSP path configuration because its function is to "Determine on which physical path to issue I/O requests being sent to a given storage device" as stated under the PSP section.
>
> The rank configuration listed here shows the value of 0. I discuss the ranked I/O in Chapter 7.

Example of Listing Paths to an iSCSI-Attached Device

To list paths to a specific iSCSI-attached LUN, try a different approach for locating the device ID:

```
esxcfg-mpath -m |grep iqn
```

You can also use the verbose command option:

```
esxcfg-mpath --list-map |grep iqn
```

The output for this command is shown in Figure 5.19.

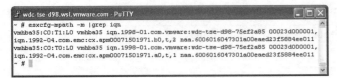

Figure 5.19   Listing paths to an iSCSI-attached LUN via the CLI

In the output, the lines wrapped. Each line actually begins with vmhba35 for readability. From this ouput, we have the information listed in Table 5.5.

Table 5.5   Matching Runtime Names with Their NAA IDs

Runtime Name	NAA ID
vmhba35:C0:T1:L0	naa.6006016047301a00eaed23f5884ee011
vmhba35:C0:T0:L0	naa.6006016047301a00eaed23f5884ee011

This means that these two paths are to the same LUN 0 and the NAA ID is naa.6006016 047301a00eaed23f5884ee011.

Now, get the pathnames for this LUN. The command is the same as what you used for listing the FC device:

```
esxcli storage nmp path list -d naa.6006016047301a00eaed23f5884ee011
```

You may also use the verbose version of this command:

```
esxcli storage nmp path list --device naa.6006016047301a00eaed23f5884ee011
```

The output is shown in Figure 5.20.

Figure 5.20 Listing paths to an iSCSI-attached LUN via CLI

Note that the path name was wrapped for readability.

Similar to what you observed with the FC-attached devices, the output is identical except for the actual path name. Here, it starts with iqn instead of fc.

The Group State and Path Selection Policy Path Config shows similar content as well. Based on that, I built Table 5.6.

Table 5.6 Matching Runtime Names with Their Target IDs and SP Ports

Runtime Name	Target IQN	Sp Port Association
vmhba35:C0:T1:L0	iqn.1992-04.com.emc:cx.apm00071501971.b0	SPB0
vmhba35:C0:T0:L0	iqn.1992-04.com.emc:cx.apm00071501971.a0	SPA0

To list only the pathnames in the output shown in Figure 5.20, you may append |grep iqn to the command.

The output of the command is listed in Figure 5.21 and was wrapped for readability. Each path name starts with iqn:

```
esxcli storage nmp path list --device naa.6006016047301a00eaed23f5884ee011
|grep iqn
```

Figure 5.21 Listing pathnames of iSCSI-attached LUNs

Identifying Path States and on Which Path the I/O Is Sent—iSCSI

The process of identifying path states and I/O path for iSCSI protocol is identical to that of the FC protocol listed in the preceding section.

Example of Listing Paths to an FCoE-Attached Device

The process of listing paths to FCoE-attached devices is identical to the process for FC except that the string you use is `fcoe Adapter` instead of `fc Adapter`.

A sample output from an FCoE configuration is shown in Figure 5.22.

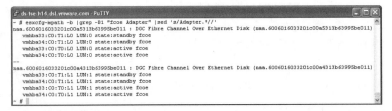

Figure 5.22   List of runtime paths of FCoE-attached LUNs via CLI

The command used is the following:

```
esxcfg-mpath -b |grep -B1 "fcoe Adapter" |sed 's/Adapter.*//'
```

You may also use the verbose command:

```
esxcfg-mpath --list-paths |grep -B1 "fcoe Adapter" |sed 's/Adapter.*//'
```

Using the NAA ID for LUN 1, the list of pathnames is shown in Figure 5.23.

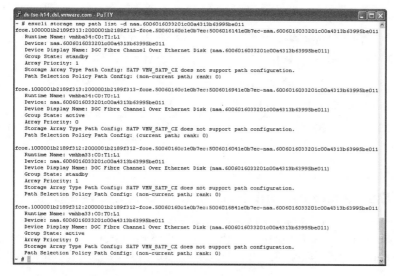

Figure 5.23   List of pathnames of an FCoE-attached LUN

You may also use the verbose version of the command shown in Figure 5.23 by using `--device` instead of `-d`.

This translates to the physical pathnames shown in Figure 5.24.

Figure 5.24   List of paths names of an FCoE LUN

The command used to collect the ouput shown in Figure 5.24 is

```
esxcli storage nmp path list -d 6006016033201c00a4313b63995be011 |grep fcoe
```

Using Table 2.1, "Identifying SP Port Association with Each SP," in Chapter 2, you can translate the targets listed in the returned four paths as shown in Table 5.7.

Table 5.7   Translation of FCoE Targets

Runtime Name	Target WWPN	SP Port Association
vmhba34:C0:T1:L1	5006016141e0b7ec	SPA1
vmhba34:C0:T0:L1	5006016941e0b7ec	SPB1
vmhba33:C0:T1:L1	5006016041e0b7ec	SPA0
vmhba33:C0:T0:L1	5006016841e0b7ec	SPB0

Identifying Path States and on Which Path the I/O Is Sent—FC

Still following the process as you did with the FC example (refer to Figure 5.17), two fields are relevant to the task of identifying the path states and the I/O path: Group State and Path Selection Policy Path Config. Table 5.8 shows the values of these fields and their meaning.

Table 5.8   Interpreting Path States—FCoE

Runtime Name	Group State	PSP Path Config	Meaning
vmhba34:C0:T1:L1	Standby	non-current path; rank: 0	Passive SP — no I/O
vmhba34:C0:T0:L1	Active	current path; rank: 0	Active-SP — I/O
vmhba33:C0:T1:L1	Standby	non-current path; rank: 0	Passive SP — no I/O
vmhba33:C0:T0:L1	Active	non-current path; rank: 0	Active SP — no I/O

Combining the last two tables, we can extrapolate the following:

- The LUN is currently "owned" by SPB (hence the state is Active).
- The I/O to the LUN is sent via the path to SPB Port 1.

Claim Rules

Each storage device is managed by one of the PSA plug-ins at any given time. In other words, a device cannot be managed by more than one PSA plug-in.

For example, a host that has a third-party MPP installed alongside with NMP, devices managed by the third-party MPP cannot be managed by NMP unless the configuration is changed to assign these devices to NMP. The process of associating certain devices with certain PSA plug-ins is referred to as *claiming* and is defined by Claim Rules. These rules define the correlation between a device and NMP or MPP. NMP has additional association between the claimed device and a specific SATP and PSP.

This section shows you how to list the various claim rules. The next section discusses how to change these rules.

Claim rules can be defined based on one or a combination of the following:

- **Vendor String**—In response to the standard inquiry command, the arrays return the standard inquiry response, which includes the Vendor string. This can be used in the definition of a claim rule based on the exact match. A partial match or a string with padded spaces does not work.

- **Model String**—Similar to the Vendor string, the Model string is returned as part of the standard inquiry response. Similar to the Vendor string, a claim rule can be defined using the exact match of the Model string and padded spaces are not supported here.

- **Transport**—Defining a claim rule based on the transport type, Transport facilitates claiming of all devices that use that transport. Valid transport types are block, fc, iscsi, iscsivendor, ide, sas, sata, usb, parallel, and unknown.

- **Driver**—Specifying a driver name as one of the criteria for a claim rule definition allows all devices accessible via such a driver to be claimed. An example of that is a claim rule to mask all paths to devices attached to an HBA that uses mptscsi driver.

MP Claim Rules

The first set of claim rules defines which MPP claims which devices. Figure 5.25 shows the default MP claim rules.

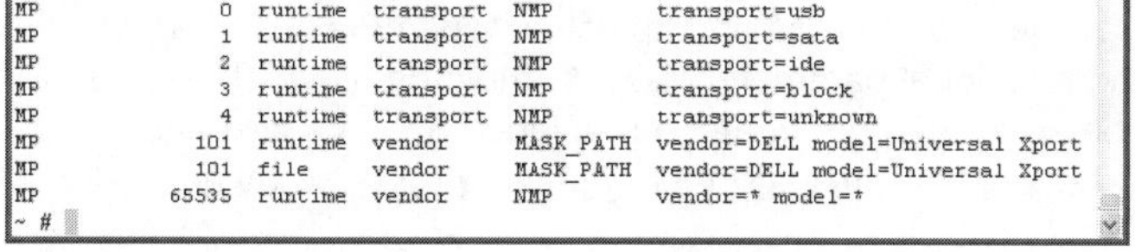

Figure 5.25   Listing MP Claim Rules

The command to list these rules is

```
esxcli storage core claimrule list
```

The namespace here is for the Core Storage because the MPP definition is done on the PSA level. The output shows that this rule class is MP, which indicates that these rules define the devices' association to a specific multipathing plug-in.

There are two plugins specified here: NMP and MASK_PATH. I have already discussed NMP in the previous sections. The MASK_PATH plug-in is used for masking paths to specific devices and is a replacement for the deprecated Legacy Multipathing LUN Masking vmkernel parameter. I provide some examples in the "Modifying PSA Plug-in Configurations Using the UI" section.

Table 5.9 lists each column name in the ouput along with an explanation of each column.

Table 5.9   Explanation of Claim Rules Fields

Column Name	Explanation
Rule Class	The plugin class for which this claim rule set is defined. This can be MP, Filter, or VAAI.
Rule	The rule number. This defines the order the rules are loaded. Similar to firewall rules, the first match is used and supersedes rules with larger numbers.
Class	The value can be `runtime` or `file`. A value of `file` means that the rule definitions were stored to the configuration files (more on this later in this section). A value of `Runtime` means that the rule was read from the configuration files and loaded into memory. In other words, it means that the rule is active. If a rule is listed as `file` only and no `runtime`, the rule was just created but has not been loaded yet. Find out more about loading rules in the next section.
Type	The type can be `vendor`, `model`, `transport`, or `driver`. See the explanation in the "Claim Rules" section.
Plugin	The name of the plug-in for which this rule was defined.
Matches	This is the most important field in the rule definition. This column shows the "Type" specified for the rule and its value. When the specified type is `vendor`, an additional parameter, `model`, must be used. The `model` string must be an exact string match or include an * as a wild card. You may use a ^ as "begins with" and then the string followed by an *—for example, `^OPEN-*`.

The highest rule number in any claim rules set is 65535. It is assigned here to a Catch-All rule that claims devices from "any" vendor with "any" model string. It is placed as the last rule in the set to allow for lower numbered rules to claim their specified devices. If the attached devices have no specific rules defined, they get claimed by NMP.

Figure 5.26 is an example of third-party MP plug-in claim rules.

```
wdc-tse-d98.wsl.vmware.com - PuTTY
~ # esxcli storage core claimrule list
Rule Class   Rule  Class     Type       Plugin      Matches
----------   ----- -------   ---------  ---------   ------------------------------------------
MP              0   runtime  transport   NMP         transport=usb
MP              1   runtime  transport   NMP         transport=sata
MP              2   runtime  transport   NMP         transport=ide
MP              3   runtime  transport   NMP         transport=block
MP              4   runtime  transport   NMP         transport=unknown
MP            101   runtime  vendor      MASK_PATH   vendor=DELL model=Universal Xport
MP            101   file     vendor      MASK_PATH   vendor=DELL model=Universal Xport
MP            230   runtime  vendor      NMP         vendor=HITACHI model=*
MP            230   file     vendor      NMP         vendor=HITACHI model=*
MP            240   runtime  location    NMP         adapter=vmhba2 channel=* target=* lun=1
MP            240   file     location    NMP         adapter=vmhba2 channel=* target=* lun=1
MP            250   runtime  vendor      PowerPath   vendor=DGC model=*
MP            250   file     vendor      PowerPath   vendor=DGC model=*
MP            260   runtime  vendor      PowerPath   vendor=EMC model=SYMMETRIX
MP            260   file     vendor      PowerPath   vendor=EMC model=SYMMETRIX
MP            270   runtime  vendor      PowerPath   vendor=EMC model=Invista
MP            270   file     vendor      PowerPath   vendor=EMC model=Invista
MP            280   file     vendor      PowerPath   vendor=HITACHI model=*
MP            290   runtime  vendor      PowerPath   vendor=HP model=*
MP            290   file     vendor      PowerPath   vendor=HP model=*
MP            300   runtime  vendor      PowerPath   vendor=COMPAQ model=HSV111 (C)COMPAQ
MP            300   file     vendor      PowerPath   vendor=COMPAQ model=HSV111 (C)COMPAQ
MP            310   runtime  vendor      PowerPath   vendor=EMC model=Celerra
MP            310   file     vendor      PowerPath   vendor=EMC model=Celerra
MP            320   runtime  vendor      PowerPath   vendor=IBM model=2107900
MP            320   file     vendor      PowerPath   vendor=IBM model=2107900
MP          65535   runtime  vendor      NMP         vendor=* model=*
~ #
```

Figure 5.26 Listing EMC PowerPath/VE claim rules.

Here you see that rules number 250 through 320 were added by PowerPath/VE, which allows PowerPath plug-in to claim all the devices listed in Table 5.10.

Table 5.10 Arrays Claimed by PowerPath

Storage Array	Vendor	Model
EMC CLARiiON Family	DGC	Any (* is a wild card)
EMC Symmetrix Family	EMC	SYMMETRIX
EMC Invista	EMC	Invista
HITACHI	HITACHI	Any
HP	HP	Any
HP EVA HSV111 family (Compaq Branded)	HP	HSV111 (C) COMPAQ
EMC Celerra	EMC	Celerra
IBM DS8000 family	IBM	2107900

NOTE

There is currently a known limitation with claim rules that use a partial match on the model string. So, older versions of PowerPath/VE that used to have rules stating model=OPEN may not claim the devices whose model string is something such as OPEN-V, OPEN-10, and so on. As evident from Figure 5.26, version 5.7 no longer uses partial matches. Instead, partial matches have been replaced with an *.

Plug-in Registration

New to vSphere 5 is the concept of *plug-in registration*. Actually this existed in 4.x but was not exposed to the end user. When a PSA plug-in is installed, it gets registered with the PSA framework along with their dependencies, if any, similar to the output in Figure 5.27.

```
~ # esxcli storage core plugin registration list
Module Name          Plugin Name          Plugin Class  Dependencies                       Full Path
-------------------  -------------------  ------------  --------------------------------  ---------
mask_path_plugin     MASK_PATH            MP
nmp                  NMP                  MP
vmw_satp_symm        VMW_SATP_SYMM        SATP
vmw_satp_svc         VMW_SATP_SVC         SATP
vmw_satp_msa         VMW_SATP_MSA         SATP
vmw_satp_lsi         VMW_SATP_LSI         SATP
vmw_satp_inv         VMW_SATP_INV         SATP          vmw_satp_lib_cx
vmw_satp_eva         VMW_SATP_EVA         SATP
vmw_satp_eql         VMW_SATP_EQL         SATP
vmw_satp_cx          VMW_SATP_CX          SATP          vmw_satp_lib_cx
vmw_satp_alua_cx     VMW_SATP_ALUA_CX     SATP          vmw_satp_alua,vmw_satp_lib_cx
vmw_satp_lib_cx      None                 SATP
vmw_satp_alua        VMW_SATP_ALUA        SATP
vmw_satp_default_ap  VMW_SATP_DEFAULT_AP  SATP
vmw_satp_default_aa  VMW_SATP_DEFAULT_AA  SATP
vmw_satp_local       VMW_SATP_LOCAL       SATP
vmw_psp_lib          None                 PSP
vmw_psp_mru          VMW_PSP_MRU          PSP           vmw_psp_lib
vmw_psp_rr           VMW_PSP_RR           PSP           vmw_psp_lib
vmw_psp_fixed        VMW_PSP_FIXED        PSP           vmw_psp_lib
vmw_vaaip_emc        None                 VAAI
vmw_vaaip_mask       VMW_VAAIP_MASK       VAAI
vmw_vaaip_symm       VMW_VAAIP_SYMM       VAAI          vmw_vaaip_emc
vmw_vaaip_netapp     VMW_VAAIP_NETAPP     VAAI
vmw_vaaip_lhn        VMW_VAAIP_LHN        VAAI
vmw_vaaip_hds        VMW_VAAIP_HDS        VAAI
vmw_vaaip_eql        VMW_VAAIP_EQL        VAAI
vmw_vaaip_cx         VMW_VAAIP_CX         VAAI          vmw_vaaip_emc,vmw_satp_lib_cx
vaai_filter          VAAI_FILTER          Filter
~ #
```

Figure 5.27 Listing PSA plug-in registration

This output shows the following:

- **Module Name**—The name of the plug-in kernel module; this is the actual plug-in software binary as well as required libraries, if any, that get plugged into vmkernel.

- **Plugin Name**—This is the name by which the plug-in is identified. This is the exact name to use when creating or modifying claim rules.

- **Plugin class**—This is the name of the class to which the plug-in belongs. For example, the previous section covered the MP class of plug-ins. The next sections discuss SATP and PSP plug-ins and later chapters cover VAAI and VAAI_Filter classes.

- **Dependencies**—These are the libraries and other plug-ins which the registered plug-ins require to operate.

- **Full Path**—This is the full path to the files, libraries, or binaries that are specific to the registered plug-in. This is mostly blank in the default registration.

SATP Claim Rules

Now that you understand how NMP plugs into PSA, it's time to examine how SATP plugs into NMP.

Each SATP is associated with a default PSP. The defaults can be overridden using SATP claim rules. Before I show you how to list these rules, first review the default settings.

The command used to list the default PSP assignment to each SATP is

```
esxcli storage nmp satp list
```

The output of this command is shown in Figure 5.28.

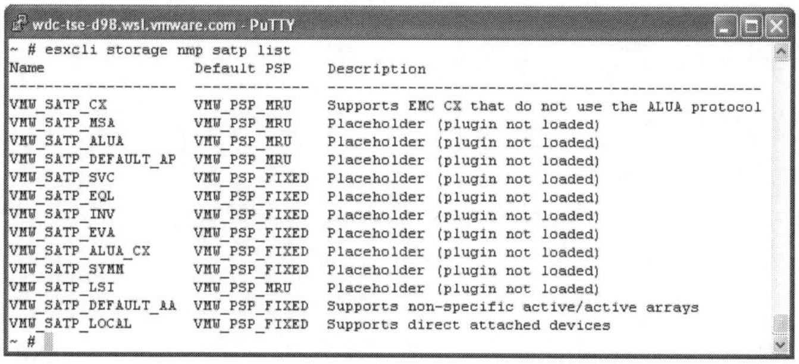

Figure 5.28 Listing SATPs and their default PSPs

The name space is Storage, NMP, and finally SATP.

NOTE

VMW_SATP_ALUA_CX plug-in is associated with VMW_PSP_FIXED. Starting with vSphere 5.0, the functionality of VMW_PSP_FIXED_AP has been rolled into VMW_PSP_FIXED. This facilitates the use of the Preferred Path option with ALUA arrays while still handling failover triggering events in a similar fashion to Active/Passive arrays. Read more on this in Chapter 6.

Knowing which PSP is the default policy for which SATP is half the story. NMP needs to know which SATP it will use with which storage device. This is done via SATP claim rules that associate a given SATP with a storage device based on matches to Vendor, Model, Driver, and/or Transport.

To list the SATP rule, run the following:

```
esxcli storage nmp satp rule list
```

The output of the command is too long and too wide to capture in one screenshot. I have divided the output to a set of images in which I list a partial output then list the text of the full output in a subsequent table. Figures 5.29, 5.30, 5.31, and 5.32 show the four quadrants of the output.

TIP

To format the output of the preceding command so that the text is arranged better for readability, you can pipe the output to `less -S`. This truncates the long lines and aligns the text under their corresponding columns.

So, the command would look like this:

```
esxcli storage nmp satp list | less -S
```

Name	Device	Vendor	Model	Driver	Transport	Options	Rule Group	Claim Options
VMW_SATP_CX		DGC					system	tpgs_off
VMW_SATP_MSA			MSA1000 VOLUME				system	
VMW_SATP_ALUA		NETAPP					system	tpgs_on
VMW_SATP_ALUA		IBM	2810XIV				system	tpgs_on
VMW_SATP_ALUA							system	tpgs_on
VMW_SATP_ALUA		IBM	2107900			reset_on_attempted_reserve	system	
VMW_SATP_DEFAULT_AP		DEC	HSG80				system	
VMW_SATP_DEFAULT_AP			HSVX700				system	tpgs_off
VMW_SATP_DEFAULT_AP			HSV100				system	
VMW_SATP_DEFAULT_AP			HSV110				system	
VMW_SATP_SVC		IBM	2145				system	
VMW_SATP_EQL		EQLOGIC					system	
VMW_SATP_INV		EMC	Invista				system	
VMW_SATP_INV		EMC	LUNZ				system	
VMW_SATP_EVA			HSV200				system	tpgs_off
VMW_SATP_EVA			HSV210				system	tpgs_off
VMW_SATP_EVA			HSVX740				system	tpgs_off
VMW_SATP_EVA			HSV101				system	tpgs_off
VMW_SATP_EVA			HSV111				system	tpgs_off
VMW_SATP_EVA			HSV300				system	tpgs_off
VMW_SATP_EVA			HSV400				system	tpgs_off
VMW_SATP_EVA			HSV450				system	tpgs_off
VMW_SATP_ALUA_CX		DGC					system	tpgs_on
VMW_SATP_SYMM		EMC	SYMMETRIX				system	
VMW_SATP_LSI		IBM	^1742*				system	
VMW_SATP_LSI		IBM	^3542*				system	
VMW_SATP_LSI		IBM	^3552*				system	
VMW_SATP_LSI		IBM	^1722*				system	
VMW_SATP_LSI		IBM	^1815*				system	
VMW_SATP_LSI		IBM	^1724*				system	
VMW_SATP_LSI		IBM	^1726-*				system	
VMW_SATP_LSI		IBM	^1814*				system	
VMW_SATP_LSI		IBM	^1818*				system	
VMW_SATP_LSI			Universal Xport				system	

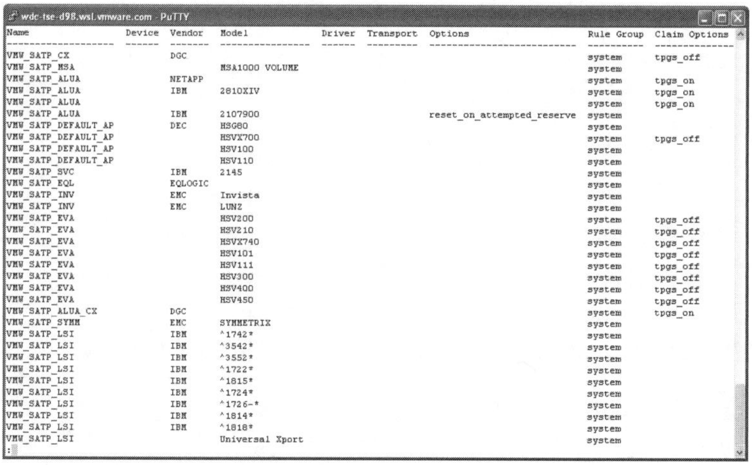

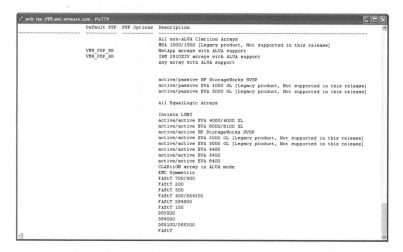

Figure 5.29 Listing SATP claim rules—top-left quadrant of output.

Default PSP	PSP Options	Description
		All non-ALUA Clariion Arrays
		MSA 1000/1500 [Legacy product, Not supported in this release]
VMW_PSP_RR		NetApp arrays with ALUA support
VMW_PSP_RR		IBM 2810XIV arrays with ALUA support
		Any array with ALUA support
		active/passive HP StorageWorks SVSP
		active/passive EVA 3000 GL [Legacy product, Not supported in this release]
		active/passive EVA 5000 GL [Legacy product, Not supported in this release]
		All EqualLogic Arrays
		Invista LUNZ
		active/active EVA 4000/6000 XL
		active/active EVA 8000/8100 XL
		active/active HP StorageWorks SVSP
		active/active EVA 3000 GL [Legacy product, Not supported in this release]
		active/active EVA 5000 GL [Legacy product, Not supported in this release]
		active/active EVA 4400
		active/active EVA 6400
		active/active EVA 8400
		CLARiiON array in ALUA mode
		EMC Symmetrix
		FAStT 700/900
		FAStT 200
		FAStT 500
		FAStT 600/DS4300
		FAStT DS4800
		FAStT 100
		DS3X00
		DS4000
		DS5100/DS5300
		FAStT

Figure 5.30 Listing SATP claim rules—top-right quadrant of output.

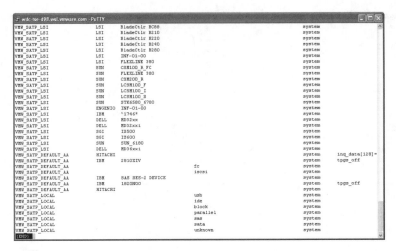

Figure 5.31   Listing SATP claim rules—bottom-left quadrant of output

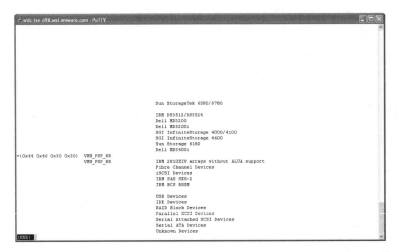

Figure 5.32   Listing SATP claim rules—bottom-right quadrant of output

To make things a bit clearer, let's take a couple of lines from the output and explain what they mean.

Figure 5.33 shows the relevant rules for CLARiiON arrays both non-ALUA and ALUA capable. I removed three blank columns (Driver, Transport, and Options) to fit the content on the lines.

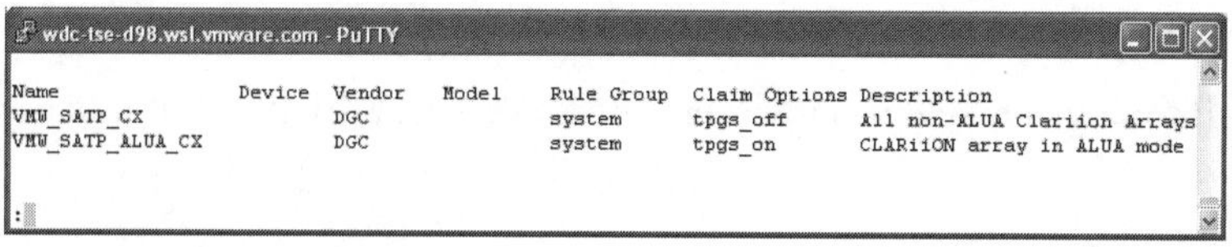

Figure 5.33   CLARiiON Non-ALUA and ALUA Rules

The two lines show the claim rules for EMC CLARiiON CX family. Using this rule, NMP identifies the array as CLARiiON CX when the Vendor string is DGC. If NMP stopped at this, it would have used VMW_SATP_CX as the SATP for this array. However, this family of arrays can support more than one configuration. That is the reason the value `Claim Options` column comes in handy! So, if that option is `tpgs_off`, NMP uses the VMW_SATP_CX plug-in, and if the option is `tpgs_on`, NMP uses VMW_SATP_ALUA_CX. I explain what these options mean in Chapter 6.

Figure 5.34 shows another example that utilizes additional options. I removed the Device column to fit the content to the display.

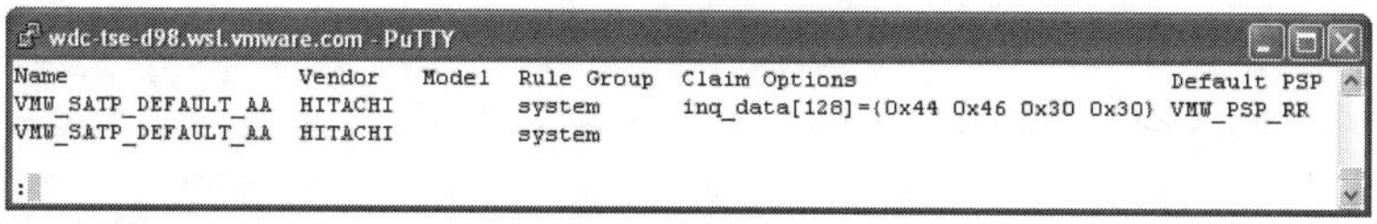

Figure 5.34   Claim rule that uses Claim Options

In this example, NMP uses VMW_SATP_DEFAULT_AA SATP with all arrays returning `HITACHI` as a model string. However, the default PSP is selected based on the values listed in the Claim Options column:

- If the column is blank, the default PSP (which is VMW_PSP_FIXED and is based on the list shown earlier in this section in Figure 5.28) is used. In that list, you see that VMW_SATP_DEFAULT_AA is assigned the default PSP named VMW_PSP_FIXED.

- If the column shows `inq_data[128]={0x44 0x46 0x30 0x30}`, which is part of the data reported from the array via the Inquiry String, NMP overrides the default PSP configuration and uses VMW_PSP_RR instead.

Modifying PSA Plug-in Configurations Using the UI

You can modify PSA plug-ins' configuration using the CLI and, to a limited extent, the UI. Because the UI provides far fewer options for modification, let me address that first to get it out of the way!

Which PSA Configurations Can Be Modified Using the UI?

You can change the PSP for a given device. However, this is done on a LUN level rather than the array.

Are you wondering why you would want to do that?

Think of the following scenario:

You have Microsoft Clustering Service (MSCS) cluster nodes in Virtual Machines (VMs) in your environment. The cluster's shared storage is Physical Mode Raw Device Mappings (RDMs), which are also referred to as (Passthrough RDMs). Your storage vendor recommends using Round-Robin Path Selection Policy (VMW_PSP_RR). However, VMware does not support using that policy with the MSCS clusters in shared RDMs.

The best approach is to follow your storage vendor's recommendations for most of the LUNs, but follow the procedure listed here to change just the RDM LUNs' PSP to their default PSPs.

Procedure to Change PSP via UI

1. Use the vSphere client to navigate to the MSCS node VM and right-click the VM in the inventory pane. Select **Edit Settings** (see Figure 5.35).

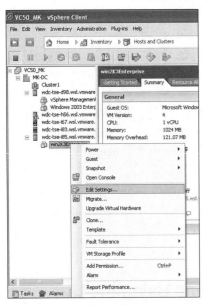

Figure 5.35   Editing VM's settings via the UI

The resulting dialog is shown in Figure 5.36.

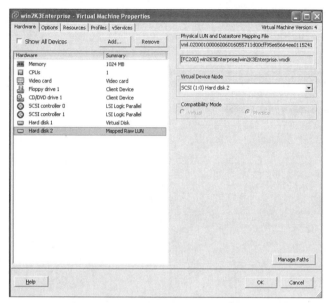

Figure 5.36   Virtual Machine Properties dialog

2. Locate the RDM listed in the Hardware tab. You can identify this by the summary column showing Mapped Raw LUN. On the top right-hand side you can locate the Logical Device Name, which is prefixed with vml in the field labeled Physical LUN and Datastore Mapping File.

3. Double-click the text in that field. Right-click the selected text and click **Copy** (see Figure 5.37).

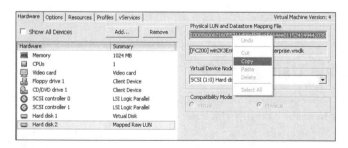

Figure 5.37   Copying RDM's VML ID (Logical Device Name) via the UI

4. I use the copied text to follow Steps 4 and 5 of doing the same task via the CLI in the next section. However, for this section, click the **Manage Paths** button in the dialog shown in Figure 5.37.

The resulting Manage Paths dialog is shown in Figure 5.38.

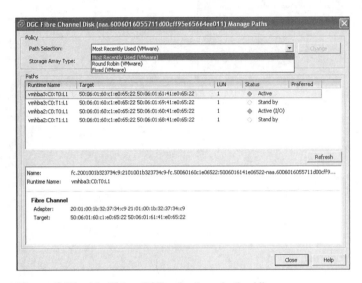

Figure 5.38   Modifying PSP selection via the UI

5. Click the pull-down menu next to the Path Selection field and change it from Round Robin (VMware) to the default PSP for your array. Click the **Change** button. To locate which PSP is the default, check VMware HCL. If the PSP listed there is Round Robin, follow the examples listed in the previous section, "SATP Claim Rules," to identify which PSP to select.

6. Click **Close**.

Modifying PSA Plug-ins Using the CLI

The CLI provides a range of options to configure, customize, and modify PSA plug-in settings. I provide the various configurable options and their use cases as we go.

Available CLI Tools and Their Options

New to vSphere 5.0 is the expansion of using esxcli as the main CLI utility for managing ESXi 5.0. The same binary is used whether you log on to the host locally or remotely via

SSH. It is also used by vMA or vCLI. This simplifies administrative tasks and improves portability of scripts written to use esxcli.

TIP

The only difference between the tools used locally or via SSH compared to those used in vMA and Remote CLI is that the latter two require providing the server name and the user's credentials on the command line. Refer to Chapter 3 in which I covered using the FastPass (fp) facility of vMA and how to add the users' credentials to the CREDSTORE environment variable on vCLI.

Assuming that the server name and user credentials are set in the environment, the command-line syntax in all the examples in this book is identical regardless of where you use them.

ESXCLI Namespace

Figure 5.39 shows the command-line help for esxcli.

Figure 5.39   Listing esxcli namespace

The relevant namespace for this chapter is `storage`. This is what most of the examples use. Figure 5.40 shows the command-line help for the `storage` namespace:

```
esxcli storage
```

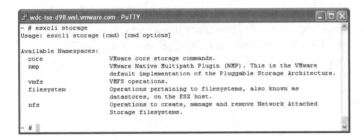

Figure 5.40   Listing esxcli `storage` namespace

Table 5.11 lists ESXCLI namespaces and their usage.

Table 5.11   Available Namespaces in the `storage` Namespace

Name Space	Usage
core	Use this for anything on the PSA level like other MPPs, PSA claim rules, and so on.
nmp	Use this for NMP and its "children," such as SATP and PSP.
vmfs	Use this for handling VMFS volumes on snapshot LUNs, managing extents, and upgrading VMFS manually.
filesystem	Use this for listing, mounting, and unmounting supported datastores.
nfs	Use this to mount, unmount, and list NFS datastores.

Adding a PSA Claim Rule

PSA claim rules can be for MP, Filter, and VAAI classes. I cover the latter two in Chapter 6.

Following are a few examples of claim rules for the MP class.

Adding a Rule to Change Certain LUNs to Be Claimed by a Different MPP

In general, most arrays function properly using the default PSA claim rules. In certain configurations, you might need to specify a different PSA MPP.

A good example is the following scenario:

You installed PowerPath/VE on your ESXi 5.0 host but then later realized that you have some MSCS cluster nodes running on that host and these nodes use Passthrough RDMs (Physical compatibility mode RDM). Because VMware does not support third-party MPPs with MSCS, you must exclude the LUNs from being managed by PowerPath/VE.

You need to identify the device ID (NAA ID) of each of the RDM LUNs and then identify the paths to each LUN. You use these paths to create the claim rule.

Here is the full procedure:

1. Power off one of the MSCS cluster nodes and locate its home directory. If you cannot power off the VM, skip to Step 6.

   Assuming that the cluster node is located on Clusters_Datastore in a directory named node1, the command and its output would look like Listing 5.1.

Listing 5.1   Locating the RDM Filename

```
#cd /vmfs/volumes/Clusters_datastore/node1

#fgrep scsi1 *.vmx |grep fileName

scsi1:0.fileName = "/vmfs/volumes/4d8008a2-9940968c-04df-001e4f1fbf2a/
node1/quorum.vmdk"

scsi1:1.fileName = "/vmfs/volumes/4d8008a2-9940968c-04df-001e4f1fbf2a/
node1/data.vmdk"
```

   The last two lines are the output of the command. They show the RDM filenames for the node's shared storage, which are attached to the virtual SCSI adapter named `scsi1`.

2. Using the RDM filenames, including the path to the datastore, you can identify the logical device name to which each RDM maps as shown in Listing 5.2.

Listing 5.2   Identifying RDM's Logical Device Name Using the RDM Filename

```
#vmkfstools --queryrdm /vmfs/volumes/4d8008a2-9940968c-04df-001e4f1fbf2a/
node1/quorum.vmdk

Disk /vmfs/volumes/4d8008a2-9940968c-04df-001e4f1fbf2a/node1/quorum.vmdk is
a Passthrough Raw Device Mapping
Maps to: vml.02000100006006016055711d00cff95e65664ee011524149442035
```

You may also use the shorthand version using -q instead of --queryrdm.

This example is for the `quorum.vmdk`. Repeat the same process for the remaining RDMs. The device name is prefixed with vml and is highlighted.

3. Identify the NAA ID using the vml ID as shown in Listing 5.3.

Listing 5.3 Identifying NAA ID Using the Device vml ID

```
#esxcfg-scsidevs --list --device vml.02000100006006016055711d00cff95e65664
ee011524149442035 |grep Display


Display Name: DGC Fibre Channel Disk (naa.6006016055711d00cff95e65664ee011)
```

You may also use the shorthand version:

```
#esxcfg-scsidevs -l -d vml.02000100006006016055711d00cff95e65664
ee011524149442035 |grep Display
```

4. Now, use the NAA ID (highlighted in Listing 5.3) to identify the paths to the RDM LUN.

Figure 5.41 shows the output of command:

```
esxcfg-mpath -m |grep naa.6006016055711d00cff95e65664ee011 | sed 's/
fc.*//'
```

Figure 5.41 Listing runtime pathnames to an RDM LUN

You may also use the verbose version of the command:

```
esxcfg-mpath --list-map |grep naa.6006016055711d00cff95e65664ee011 |
sed 's/fc.*//'
```

This truncates the output beginning with "fc" to the end of the line on each line. If the protocol in use is not FC, replace that with "iqn" for iSCSI or "fcoe" for FCoE.

The output shows that the LUN with the identified NAA ID is LUN 1 and has four paths shown in Listing 5.4.

Listing 5.4   RDM LUN's Paths

```
vmhba3:C0:T1:L1
vmhba3:C0:T0:L1
vmhba2:C0:T1:L1
vmhba2:C0:T0:L1
```

If you cannot power off the VMs to run Steps 1–5, you may use the UI instead.

5. Use the vSphere client to navigate to the MSCS node VM. Right-click the VM in the inventory pane and then select **Edit Settings** (see Figure 5.42).

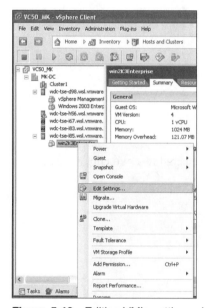

Figure 5.42   Editing VM's settings via the UI

6. In the resulting dialog (see Figure 5.43), locate the RDM listed in the Hardware tab. You can identify this by the summary column showing Mapped Raw LUN. On the top right-hand side you can locate the Logical Device Name, which is prefixed with vml in the field labeled Physical LUN and Datastore Mapping File.

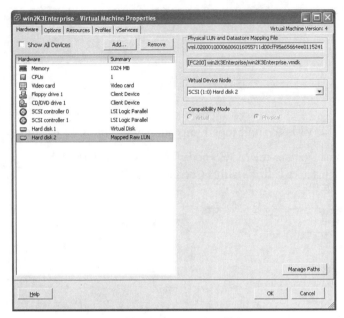

Figure 5.43   Virtual machine properties dialog

7. Double-click the text in that field. Right-click the selected text and click **Copy** as shown in Figure 5.44.

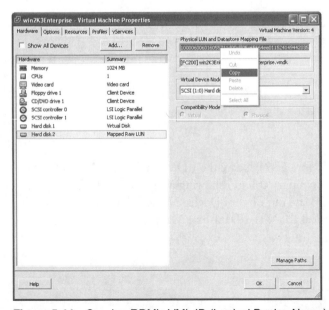

Figure 5.44   Copying RDM's VML ID (Logical Device Name) via the UI

8. You may use the copied text to follow Steps 4 and 5. Otherwise, you may instead get the list of paths to the LUN using the **Manage Paths** button in the dialog shown in Figure 5.44.

9. In the Manage Paths dialog (see Figure 5.45), click the Runtime Name column to sort it. Write down the list of paths shown there.

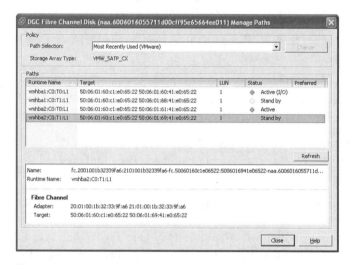

Figure 5.45   Listing the runtime pathnames via the UI

10. The list of paths shown in Figure 5.45 are

```
vmhba1:C0:T0:L1
vmhba1:C0:T1:L1
vmhba2:C0:T0:L1
vmhba2:C0:T1:L1
```

NOTE

Notice that the list of paths in the UI is different from that obtained from the command line. The reason can be easily explained; I used two different hosts for obtaining the list of paths. If your servers were configured identically, the path list should be identical as well.

However, this is not critical because the LUN's NAA ID is the same regardless of paths used to access it. This is what makes NAA ID the most unique element of any LUN, and that is the reason ESXi utilizes it for uniquely identifying the LUNs. I cover more on that topic later in Chapter 7.

11. Create the claim rule.

I use the list of paths obtained in Step 5 for creating the rule from the ESXi host from which it was obtained.

The Ground Rules for Creating the Rule

- The rule number must be lower than any of the rules created by PowerPath/VE installation. By default, they are assigned rules 250–320 (refer to Figure 5.26 for the list of PowerPath claim rules).

- The rule number must be higher than 101 because this is used by the Dell Mask Path rule. This prevents claiming devices masked by that rule.

- If you created other claim rules in the past on this host, use a rule number that is different from what you created in a fashion that the new rules you are creating now do not conflict with the earlier rules.

- If you must place the new rules in an order earlier than an existing rule but there are no rule numbers available, you may have to move one of the lower-numbered rules higher by the number of rules you plan on creating.

  For example, you have previously created rules numbered 102–110 and that rule 109 cannot be listed prior to the new rules you are creating. If the new rules count is four, you need to assign them rule numbers 109–112. To do that, you need to move rules 109 and 110 to numbers 113 and 114. To avoid having to do this in the future, consider leaving gaps in the rule numbers among sections.

  An example of moving a rule is

  ```
  esxcli storage core claimrule move --rule 109 --new-rule 113
  esxcli storage core claimrule move --rule 110 --new-rule 114
  ```

  You may also use the shorthand version:

  ```
  esxcli storage core claimrule move -r 109 -n 113
  esxcli storage core claimrule move -r 110 -n 114
  ```

Now, let's proceed with adding the new claim rules:

1. The set of four commands shown in Figure 5.46 create rules numbered 102–105. The rules criteria are

   - The claim rule type is "location" (`-t location`).

   - The location is specified using each path to the same LUN in the format:

     - `-A` or `--adapter vmhba(x)` where X is the vmhba number associated with the path.

- -C or --channel (Y) where Y is the channel number associated with the path.

- -T or --target (Z) where Z is the target number associated with the path.

- -L or --lun (n) where n is the LUN number.

- The plug-in name is NMP, which means that this claim rule is for NMP to claim the paths listed in each rule created.

NOTE

It would have been easier to create a single rule using the LUN's NAA ID by using the --type device option and then using --device <NAA ID>. However, the use of device as a rule type is not supported with MP class plug-ins.

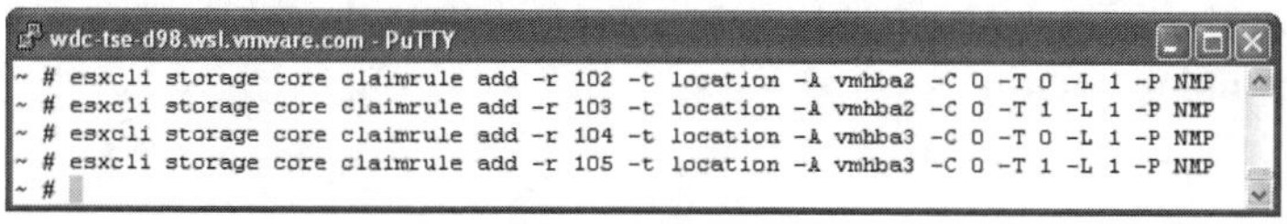

```
wdc-tse-d98.wsl.vmware.com - PuTTY
~ # esxcli storage core claimrule add -r 102 -t location -A vmhba2 -C 0 -T 0 -L 1 -P NMP
~ # esxcli storage core claimrule add -r 103 -t location -A vmhba2 -C 0 -T 1 -L 1 -P NMP
~ # esxcli storage core claimrule add -r 104 -t location -A vmhba3 -C 0 -T 0 -L 1 -P NMP
~ # esxcli storage core claimrule add -r 105 -t location -A vmhba3 -C 0 -T 1 -L 1 -P NMP
~ #
```

Figure 5.46   Adding new MP claim rules

2. Repeat Step 1 for each LUN you want to reconfigure.

3. Verify that the rules were added successfully. To list the current set of claim rules, run the command shown in Figure 5.47:

   ```
   esxcli storage core claimrule list.
   ```

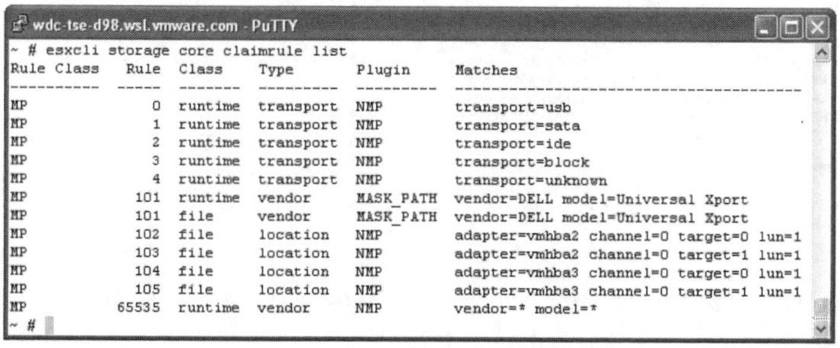

```
wdc-tse-d98.wsl.vmware.com - PuTTY
~ # esxcli storage core claimrule list
Rule Class   Rule   Class     Type        Plugin      Matches
----------   ----   -------   ---------   ---------   -------------------------------------
MP              0   runtime   transport   NMP         transport=usb
MP              1   runtime   transport   NMP         transport=sata
MP              2   runtime   transport   NMP         transport=ide
MP              3   runtime   transport   NMP         transport=block
MP              4   runtime   transport   NMP         transport=unknown
MP            101   runtime   vendor      MASK_PATH   vendor=DELL model=Universal Xport
MP            101   file      vendor      MASK_PATH   vendor=DELL model=Universal Xport
MP            102   file      location    NMP         adapter=vmhba2 channel=0 target=0 lun=1
MP            103   file      location    NMP         adapter=vmhba2 channel=0 target=1 lun=1
MP            104   file      location    NMP         adapter=vmhba3 channel=0 target=0 lun=1
MP            105   file      location    NMP         adapter=vmhba3 channel=0 target=1 lun=1
MP          65535   runtime   vendor      NMP         vendor=* model=*
~ #
```

Figure 5.47   Listing added claim rules

Notice that the four new rules are now listed, but the `Class` column shows them as file. This means that the configuration files were updated successfully but the rules were not loaded into memory yet.

NOTE

I truncated the PowerPath rules in Figure 5.47 for readability. Also note that using the Location type utilizes the current runtime names of the devices, and they may change in the future. If your configuration changes—for example, adding new HBAs or removing existing ones—the runtime names change, too. This results in these claim rules claiming the wrong devices. However, in a static environment, this should not be an issue.

TIP

To reduce the number of commands used and the number of rules created, you may omit the `-T` or `--target` option, which assumes a wildcard. You may also use the `-u` or `--autoassign` option to auto-assign the rule number. However, the latter assigns rule numbers starting with 5001, which may be higher than the existing claim rules for the device hosting the LUN you are planning to claim.

Figure 5.48 shows a sample command line that implements a wildcard for the target. Notice that this results in creating two rules instead of four and the "target" match is `*`.

```
wdc-tse-d98.wsl.vmware.com - PuTTY
~ # esxcli storage core claimrule add -r 104 -t location -A vmhba2 -C 0 -L 1 -P NMP
~ # esxcli storage core claimrule add -r 105 -t location -A vmhba3 -C 0 -L 1 -P NMP
~ # esxcli storage core claimrule list
Rule Class   Rule   Class     Type        Plugin       Matches
----------   -----  -------   ---------   ---------    ------------------------------------------
MP               0   runtime   transport   NMP          transport=usb
MP               1   runtime   transport   NMP          transport=sata
MP               2   runtime   transport   NMP          transport=ide
MP               3   runtime   transport   NMP          transport=block
MP               4   runtime   transport   NMP          transport=unknown
MP             101   runtime   vendor      MASK_PATH    vendor=DELL model=Universal Xport
MP             101   file      vendor      MASK_PATH    vendor=DELL model=Universal Xport
MP             104   file      location    NMP          adapter=vmhba2 channel=0 target=* lun=1
MP             105   file      location    NMP          adapter=vmhba3 channel=0 target=* lun=1
MP           65535   runtime   vendor      NMP          vendor=* model=*
~ #
```

Figure 5.48   Adding MP claim rules using a wildcard

4. Before loading the new rules, you must first unclaim the paths to the LUN specified in that rule set. You use the NAA ID as the device ID:

```
esxcli storage core claiming unclaim --type device --device naa.600601
6055711d00cff95e65664ee011
```

You may also use the shorthand version:

```
esxcli storage core claiming unclaim -t device -d naa.6006016055711d00
cff95e65664ee011
```

5. Load the new claim rules so that the paths to the LUN get claimed by NMP:

```
esxcli storage core claimrule load
```

6. Use the following command to list the claim rules to verify that they were success-fully loaded:

```
esxcli storage core claimrule list
```

Now you see that each of the new rules is listed twice—once with file class and once with runtime class—as shown in Figure 5.49.

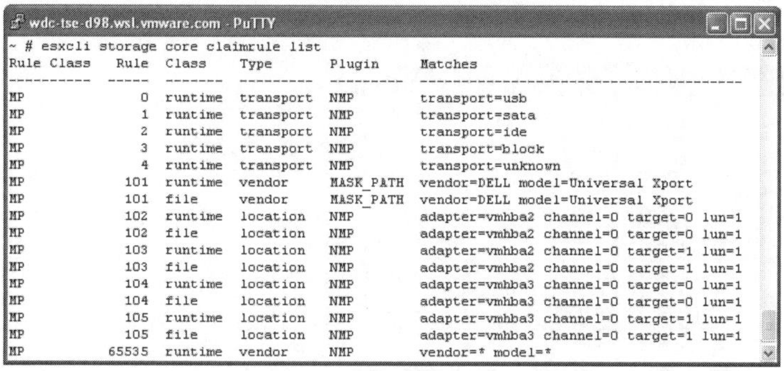

Figure 5.49   Listing MP claim rules

How to Delete a Claim Rule

Deleting a claim rule must be done with extreme caution. Make sure that you are deleting the rule you intend to delete. Prior to doing so, make sure to collect a "vm-support" dump by running `vm-support` from a command line at the host or via SSH. Alternatively, you can select the menu option Collect Diagnostics Data via the vSphere client.

To delete a claim rule, follow this procedure via the CLI (locally, via SSH, vCLI, or vMA):

1. List the current claim rules set and identify the claim rule or rules you want to delete. The command to list the claim rules is similar to what you ran in Step 6 and is shown in Figure 5.49.

2. For this procedure, I am going to use the previous example and delete the four claim rules I added earlier which are rules 102–105. The command for doing that is in Figure 5.50.

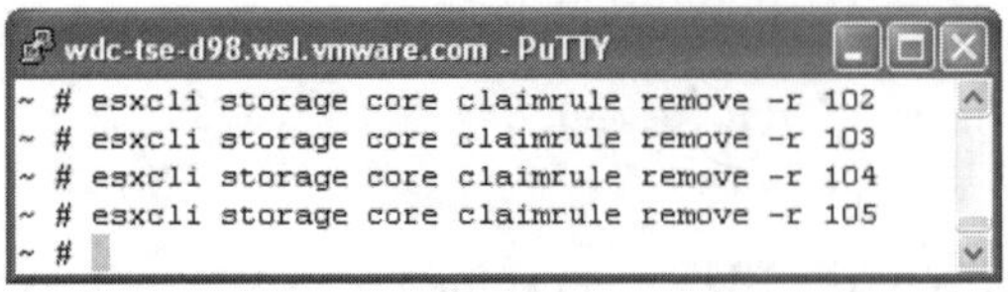

```
wdc-tse-d98.wsl.vmware.com - PuTTY
~ # esxcli storage core claimrule remove -r 102
~ # esxcli storage core claimrule remove -r 103
~ # esxcli storage core claimrule remove -r 104
~ # esxcli storage core claimrule remove -r 105
~ #
```

Figure 5.50   Removing claim rules via the CLI

You may also run the verbose command:

```
esxcli storage core claimrule remove --rule <rule-number>
```

3. Running the `claimrule` list command now results in an output similar to
   Figure 5.51. Observe that even though I just deleted the claim rules, they still show
   up on the list. The reason for that is the fact that I have not loaded the modified
   claim rules. That is why the deleted rules show runtime in their `Class` column.

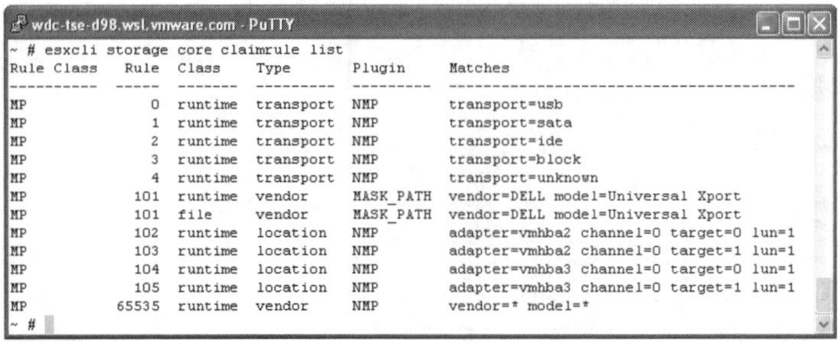

```
wdc-tse-d98.wsl.vmware.com - PuTTY
~ # esxcli storage core claimrule list
Rule Class  Rule   Class    Type       Plugin      Matches
----------  -----  -------  ---------  ---------   -----------------------------------------
MP              0  runtime  transport  NMP         transport=usb
MP              1  runtime  transport  NMP         transport=sata
MP              2  runtime  transport  NMP         transport=ide
MP              3  runtime  transport  NMP         transport=block
MP              4  runtime  transport  NMP         transport=unknown
MP            101  runtime  vendor     MASK_PATH   vendor=DELL model=Universal Xport
MP            101  file     vendor     MASK_PATH   vendor=DELL model=Universal Xport
MP            102  runtime  location   NMP         adapter=vmhba2 channel=0 target=0 lun=1
MP            103  runtime  location   NMP         adapter=vmhba2 channel=0 target=1 lun=1
MP            104  runtime  location   NMP         adapter=vmhba3 channel=0 target=0 lun=1
MP            105  runtime  location   NMP         adapter=vmhba3 channel=0 target=1 lun=1
MP          65535  runtime  vendor     NMP         vendor=* model=*
~ #
```

Figure 5.51   Listing MP claim rules

5. Because I know from the previous procedure the device ID (NAA ID) of the LUN
   whose claim rules I deleted, I ran the `unclaim` command using the `-t` device or
   `--type` option and then specified the `-d` or `--device` option with the NAA ID. I
   then loaded the claim rules using the load option. Notice that the deleted claim rules
   are no longer listed see Figure 5.52.

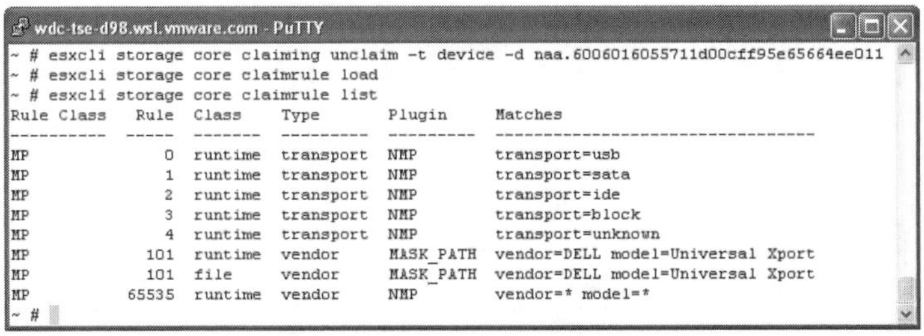

```
wdc-tse-d98.wsl.vmware.com - PuTTY
~ # esxcli storage core claiming unclaim -t device -d naa.6006016055711d00cff95e65664ee011
~ # esxcli storage core claimrule load
~ # esxcli storage core claimrule list
Rule Class   Rule   Class    Type       Plugin      Matches
----------   ----   -----    ----       ------      -------
MP              0   runtime  transport  NMP         transport=usb
MP              1   runtime  transport  NMP         transport=sata
MP              2   runtime  transport  NMP         transport=ide
MP              3   runtime  transport  NMP         transport=block
MP              4   runtime  transport  NMP         transport=unknown
MP            101   runtime  vendor     MASK_PATH   vendor=DELL model=Universal Xport
MP            101   file     vendor     MASK_PATH   vendor=DELL model=Universal Xport
MP          65535   runtime  vendor     NMP         vendor=* model=*
~ #
```

Figure 5.52   Unclaiming a device using its NAA ID and then loading the claim rules

You may also use the verbose command options:

```
esxcli storage core claiming unclaim --type device --device <Device-ID>
```

You may need to claim the device after loading the claim rule by repeating the claiming command using the "claim" instead of the "unclaim" option:

```
esxcli storage core claiming claim -t device -d <device-ID>
```

How to Mask Paths to a Certain LUN

Masking a LUN is a similar process to that of adding claim rules to claim certain paths to a LUN. The main difference is that the plug-in name is MASK_PATH instead of NMP as used in the previous example. The end result is that the masked LUNs are no longer visible to the host.

1. Assume that you want to mask LUN 1 used in the previous example and it still has the same NAA ID. I first run a command to list the LUN visible by the ESXi host as an example to show the before state (see Figure 5.53).

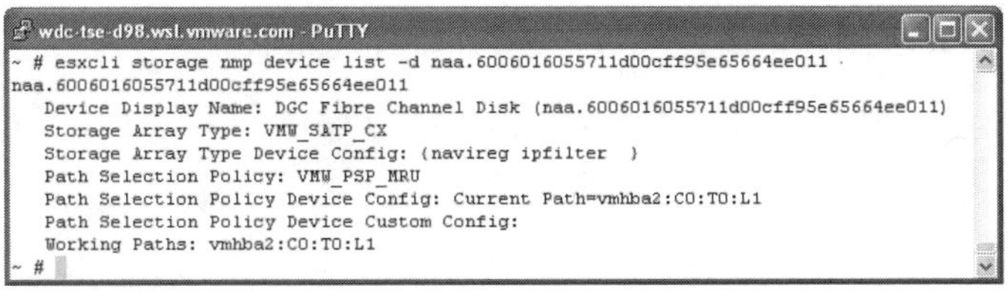

```
wdc-tse-d98.wsl.vmware.com - PuTTY
~ # esxcli storage nmp device list -d naa.6006016055711d00cff95e65664ee011
naa.6006016055711d00cff95e65664ee011
    Device Display Name: DGC Fibre Channel Disk (naa.6006016055711d00cff95e65664ee011)
    Storage Array Type: VMW_SATP_CX
    Storage Array Type Device Config: {navireg ipfilter }
    Path Selection Policy: VMW_PSP_MRU
    Path Selection Policy Device Config: Current Path=vmhba2:C0:T0:L1
    Path Selection Policy Device Custom Config:
    Working Paths: vmhba2:C0:T0:L1
~ #
```

Figure 5.53   Listing LUN properties using its NAA ID via the CLI

You may also use the verbose command option `--device` instead of `-d`.

2. Add the MASK_LUN claim rule, as shown in Figure 5.54.

```
wdc-tse-d98.wsl.vmware.com - PuTTY
~ # esxcli storage core claimrule add -r 110 -t location -A vmhba2 -C 0 -L 1 -P MASK_PATH
~ # esxcli storage core claimrule add -r 111 -t location -A vmhba3 -C 0 -L 1 -P MASK_PATH
~ # esxcli storage core claimrule list
Rule Class    Rule   Class     Type        Plugin      Matches
----------    -----  -------   ---------   ---------   ------------------------------------
MP               0   runtime   transport   NMP         transport=usb
MP               1   runtime   transport   NMP         transport=sata
MP               2   runtime   transport   NMP         transport=ide
MP               3   runtime   transport   NMP         transport=block
MP               4   runtime   transport   NMP         transport=unknown
MP             101   runtime   vendor      MASK_PATH   vendor=DELL model=Universal Xport
MP             101   file      vendor      MASK_PATH   vendor=DELL model=Universal Xport
MP             110   file      location    MASK_PATH   adapter=vmhba2 channel=0 target=* lun=1
MP             111   file      location    MASK_PATH   adapter=vmhba3 channel=0 target=* lun=1
MP           65535   runtime   vendor      NMP         vendor=* model=*
~ #
```

Figure 5.54   Adding Mask Path claim rules

As you see in Figure 5.54, I added rule numbers 110 and 111 to have MASK_
PATH plug-in claim all targets to LUN1 via vmhba2 and vmhba3. The claim
rules are not yet loaded, hence the file class listing and no runtime class listings.

3. Load and then list the claim rules (see Figure 5.55).

```
wdc-tse-d98.wsl.vmware.com - PuTTY
~ # esxcli storage core claimrule load
~ # esxcli storage core claimrule list
Rule Class    Rule   Class     Type        Plugin      Matches
----------    -----  -------   ---------   ---------   ------------------------------------
MP               0   runtime   transport   NMP         transport=usb
MP               1   runtime   transport   NMP         transport=sata
MP               2   runtime   transport   NMP         transport=ide
MP               3   runtime   transport   NMP         transport=block
MP               4   runtime   transport   NMP         transport=unknown
MP             101   runtime   vendor      MASK_PATH   vendor=DELL model=Universal Xport
MP             101   file      vendor      MASK_PATH   vendor=DELL model=Universal Xport
MP             110   runtime   location    MASK_PATH   adapter=vmhba2 channel=0 target=* lun=1
MP             110   file      location    MASK_PATH   adapter=vmhba2 channel=0 target=* lun=1
MP             111   runtime   location    MASK_PATH   adapter=vmhba3 channel=0 target=* lun=1
MP             111   file      location    MASK_PATH   adapter=vmhba3 channel=0 target=* lun=1
MP           65535   runtime   vendor      NMP         vendor=* model=*
~ #
```

Figure 5.55   Loading and listing claim rules after adding Mask Path rules

Now you see the claim rules listed with both file and runtime classes.

4. Use the reclaim option to unclaim and then claim the LUN using its NAA ID.
   Check if it is still visible (see Figure 5.56).

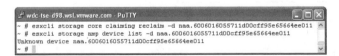

```
wdc-tse-d98.wsl.vmware.com - PuTTY
~ # esxcli storage core claiming reclaim -d naa.6006016055711d00cff95e65664ee011
~ # esxcli storage nmp device list -d naa.6006016055711d00cff95e65664ee011
Unknown device naa.6006016055711d00cff95e65664ee011
~ #
```

Figure 5.56   Reclaiming the paths after loading the Mask Path rules

You may also use the verbose command option `--device` instead of `-d`.

Notice that after reclaiming the LUN, it is now an Unknown device.

How to Unmask a LUN

To unmask this LUN, reverse the preceding steps and then reclaim the LUN as follows:

1. Remove the MASK_PATH claim rules (numbers 110 and 111) as shown in Figure 5.57.

```
wdc-tse-d9B.wsl.vmware.com - PuTTY
~ # esxcli storage core claimrule remove -r 110
~ # esxcli storage core claimrule remove -r 111
~ # esxcli storage core claimrule load
~ # esxcli storage core claimrule list
Rule Class  Rule  Class    Type       Plugin     Matches
----------  ----  -------  ---------  ---------  --------------------------------
MP             0  runtime  transport  NMP        transport=usb
MP             1  runtime  transport  NMP        transport=sata
MP             2  runtime  transport  NMP        transport=ide
MP             3  runtime  transport  NMP        transport=block
MP             4  runtime  transport  NMP        transport=unknown
MP           101  runtime  vendor     MASK_PATH  vendor=DELL model=Universal Xport
MP           101  file     vendor     MASK_PATH  vendor=DELL model=Universal Xport
MP         65535  runtime  vendor     NMP        vendor=* model=*
~ #
```

Figure 5.57   Removing the Mask Path claim rules

You may also use the verbose command options:

```
esxcli storage core claimrule remove --rule <rule-number>
```

2. Unclaim the paths to the LUN in the same fashion you used while adding the MASK_PATH claim rules—that is, using the -t location and omitting the -T option so that the target is a wildcard.

3. Rescan using both HBA names.

4. Verify that the LUN is now visible by running the list command.

Figure 5.58 shows the outputs of Steps 2–4.

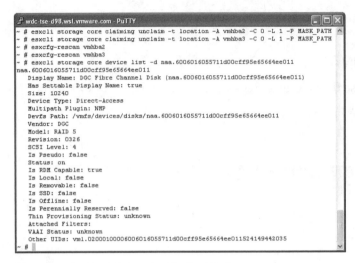

```
 wdc-tse-d98.wsl.vmware.com - PuTTY
~ # esxcli storage core claiming unclaim -t location -A vmhba2 -C 0 -L 1 -P MASK_PATH
~ # esxcli storage core claiming unclaim -t location -A vmhba3 -C 0 -L 1 -P MASK_PATH
~ # esxcfg-rescan vmhba2
~ # esxcfg-rescan vmhba3
~ # esxcli storage core device list -d naa.6006016055711d00cff95e65664ee011
naa.6006016055711d00cff95e65664ee011
   Display Name: DGC Fibre Channel Disk (naa.6006016055711d00cff95e65664ee011)
   Has Settable Display Name: true
   Size: 10240
   Device Type: Direct-Access
   Multipath Plugin: NMP
   Devfs Path: /vmfs/devices/disks/naa.6006016055711d00cff95e65664ee011
   Vendor: DGC
   Model: RAID 5
   Revision: 0326
   SCSI Level: 4
   Is Pseudo: false
   Status: on
   Is RDM Capable: true
   Is Local: false
   Is Removable: false
   Is SSD: false
   Is Offline: false
   Is Perennially Reserved: false
   Thin Provisioning Status: unknown
   Attached Filters:
   VAAI Status: unknown
   Other UIDs: vml.02000100006006016055711d00cff95e65664ee011524149442035
~ #
```

Figure 5.58   Unclaiming the Masked Paths

You may also use the verbose command options:

```
esxcli storage core claiming unclaim --type location --adapter vmhba2
--channel 0 --lun 1 --plugin MASK_PATH
```

Changing PSP Assignment via the CLI

The CLI enables you to modify the PSP assignment per device. It also enables you to change the default PSP for a specific storage array or family of arrays. I cover the former use case first because it is similar to what you did via the UI in the previous section. I follow with the latter use case.

Changing PSP Assignment for a Device

To change the PSP assignment for a given device, you may follow this procedure:

1. Log on to the ESXi 5 host locally or via SSH as root or using vMA 5.0 as vi-admin.

2. Identify the device ID for each LUN you want to reconfigure:

```
esxcfg-mpath -b |grep -B1 "fc Adapter"| grep -v -e "--" |sed 's/
Adapter.*//'
```

You may also use the verbose version of this command:

```
esxcfg-mpath --list-paths grep -B1 "fc Adapter"| grep -v -e "--" | sed
's/Adapter.*//'
```

Listing 5.5 shows the output of this command.

Listing 5.5   Listing Device ID and Its Paths

```
naa.60060e800527510000000027510000011a : HITACHI Fibre Channel Disk (naa.6006
0e800527510000000027510000011a)
    vmhba2:C0:T0:L1 LUN:1 state:active fc
    vmhba2:C0:T1:L1 LUN:1 state:active fc
    vmhba3:C0:T0:L1 LUN:1 state:active fc
    vmhba3:C0:T1:L1 LUN:1 state:active fc
```

From there, you can identify the device ID (in this case, it is the NAA ID). Note that this output was collected using a Universal Storage Platform®V (USP V), USP VM, or Virtual Storage Platform (VSP).

This output means that LUN1 has device ID `naa.60060e800527510000000027510000011a`.

3. Using the device ID you identified, run this command:

```
esxcli storage nmp device set -d <device-id> --psp=<psp-name>
```

You may also use the verbose version of this command:

```
esxcli storage nmp device set --device <device-id> --psp=<psp-name>
```

For example:

```
esxcli storage nmp device set -d naa.60060e800527510000000027510000011a
--psp=VMW_PSP_FIXED
```

This command sets the device with ID `naa.60060e800527510000000027510000011a` to be claimed by the PSP named VMW_PSP_FIXED.

Changing the Default PSP for a Storage Array

There is no simple way to change the default PSP for a specific storage array unless that array is claimed by an SATP that is specific for it. In other words, if it is claimed by an SATP that also claims other brands of storage arrays, changing the default PSP affects *all* storage arrays claimed by the SATP. However, you may add an SATP claim rule that uses a specific PSP based on your storage array's Vendor and Model strings:

1. Identify the array's Vendor and Model strings. You can identify these strings by running

```
esxcli storage core device list -d <device ID> |grep 'Vendor\|Model'
```

Listing 5.6 shows an example for a device on an HP P6400 Storage Array.

Listing 5.6   Listing Device's Vendor and Model Strings

```
esxcli storage core device list -d naa.600508b4000f02cb0001000001660000
|grep 'Model\|Vendor'
   Vendor: HP
   Model: HSV340
```

In this example, the Vendor String is HP and the Model is HSV340.

2. Use the identified values in the following command:

```
esxcli storage nmp satp rule add --satp <current-SATP-USED> --vendor
<Vendor string> --model <Model string> --psp <PSP-name> --description
<Description>
```

TIP

It is always a good practice to document changes manually made to the ESXi host configuration. That is why I used the `--description` option to add a description of the rules I add. This way other admins would know what I did if they forget to read the change control record that I added using the company's change control software.

In this example, the command would be like this:

```
esxcli storage nmp satp rule add --satp VMW_SATP_EVA --vendor HP
--model HSV340 --psp VMW_PSP_FIXED --description "Manually added to
use FIXED"
```

It runs silently and returns an error if it fails.

Example of an error:

```
"Error adding SATP user rule: Duplicate user rule found for SATP VMW_
SATP_EVA matching vendor HP model HSV340 claim Options PSP VMW_PSP_
FIXED and PSP Options"
```

This error means that a rule already exists with these options. I simulated this rule by first adding it and then rerunning the same command. To view the existing SATP claim rules list for all HP storage arrays, you may run the following command:

```
esxcli storage nmp satp rule list |less -S |grep 'Name\|---\|HP'|less
-S
```

Figure 5.59 shows the output of this command (I cropped some blank columns, including Device, for readability):

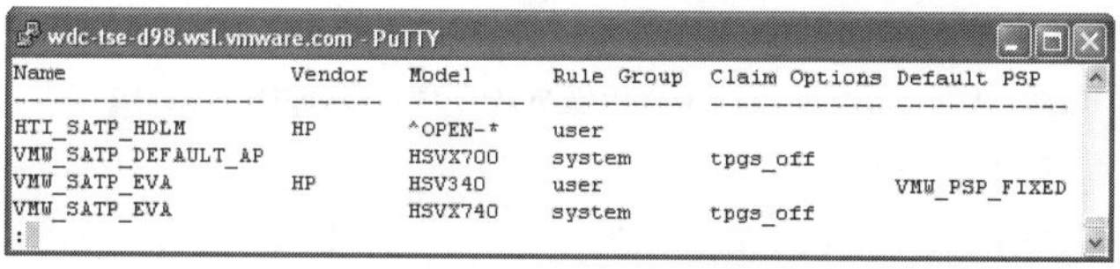

Figure 5.59   Listing SATP rule list for HP devices

You can easily identify non-system rules where the `Rule Group` column value is `user`. Such rules were added by a third-party MPIO installer or manually added by an ESXi 5 administrator. The rule in this example shows that I had already added VMW_PSP_FIXED as the default PSP for VMW_SATP_EVA when the matching vendor is HP and Model is HSV340.

I don't mean to state by this example that HP EVA arrays with HSV340 firmware should be claimed by this specific PSP. I am only using it for demonstration purposes. You *must* verify which PSP is supported by and certified for your specific storage array from the array vendor.

As a matter of fact, this HP EVA model happens to be an ALUA array and the SATP must be VMW_SATP_ALUA see Chapter 6. How did I know that? Let me explain!

- Look at the output in Figures 5.29–5.32. There you should notice that there are no listings of HP EVA arrays with Claim Options value of `tpgs_on`. This means that they were not claimed by any specific SATP explicitly.

- To filter out some clutter from the output, run the following command to list all claim rules with a match on Claim Options value of `tpgs_on`.

```
esxcli storage nmp satp rule list |grep 'Name\|---\|tpgs_on' |less -S
```

Listing 5.7 shows the output of that command:

Listing 5.7   Listing SATP Claim Rules List

Name	Device	Vendor	Model	Rule Group	Claim Options
VMW_SATP_ALUA		NETAPP		system	tpgs_on
VMW_SATP_ALUA		IBM	2810XIV	system	tpgs_on
VMW_SATP_ALUA				system	tpgs_on
VMW_SATP_ALUA_CX		DGC		system	tpgs_on

I cropped some blank columns for readability.

Here you see that there is a claim rule with a blank vendor and the Claim Options is `tpgs_on`. This claim rule claims *any* device with *any* vendor string as long as its Claim Options is `tpgs_on`.

Based on this rule, VMW_SATP_ALUA claims *all* ALUA-capable arrays including HP storage arrays based on a match on the Claim Options value of `tpgs_on`.

What does this mean anyway?

It means that the claim rule that I added for the HSV340 is wrong because it will force it to be claimed by an SATP that does not handle ALUA. I must remove the rule that I added then create another rule that does not violate the default SATP assignment:

1. To remove the SATP claim rule, use the same command used to add, substituting the add option with remove:

   ```
   esxcli storage nmp satp rule remove --satp VMW_SATP_EVA --vendor HP
   --model HSV340 --psp VMW_PSP_FIXED
   ```

2. Add a new claim rule to have VMW_SATP_ALUA claim the HP EVA HSV340 when it reports Claim Options value as `tpgs_on`:

   ```
   esxcli storage nmp satp rule add --satp VMW_SATP_ALUA --vendor
   HP --model HSV340 --psp VMW_PSP_FIXED --claim-option tpgs_on
   --description "Re-added manually for HP HSV340"
   ```

3. Verify that the rule was created correctly. Run the same command used in Step 2 in the last procedure:

   ```
   esxcli storage nmp satp rule list |grep 'Name\|---\|tpgs_on' |less -S
   ```

   Figure 5.60 shows the output.

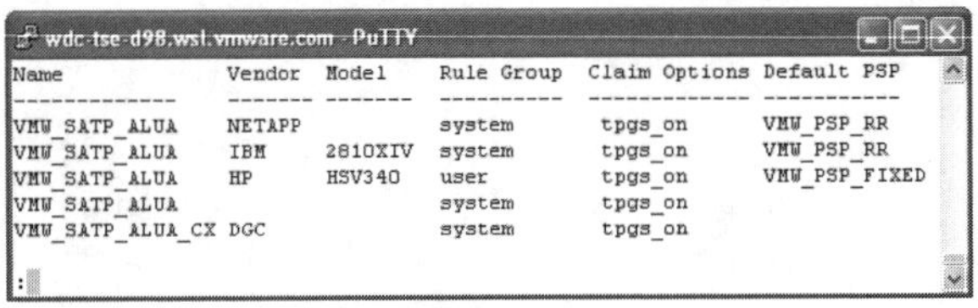

Figure 5.60   SATP rule list after adding rule

Notice that the claim rule has been added in a position prior to the catch-all rule described earlier. This means that this HP EVA HSV340 model will be claimed by VMW_SATP_ALUA when the Claim Options value is `tpgs_on`.

NOTE

If you had manually set certain LUNs to a specific PSP previously, the preceding command will not affect that setting.

To reset such a LUN to use the current default PSP, use the following command:

```
esxcli storage nmp device set --device <device-ID> --default
```

For example:

```
esxcli storage nmp device set --device naa.6006016055711d00cef95e65
664ee011 --default
```

NOTE

All EVAs today have the `tpgs_on` option enabled by default, and it CANNOT be changed by the user. So adding an EVA claim rule would only be useful in the context of trying to use a different PSP by default for all EVA LUNs or assigning PSP defaults to EVA different from other ALUA-capable arrays using the default SATP_ALUA.

Summary

This chapter covered PSA (VMware Pluggable Storage Architecture) components. I showed you how to list PSA plug-ins and how they interact with vSphere ESXi 5. I also showed you how to list, modify, and customize PSA claim rules and how to work around some common issues.

It also covered how ALUA-capable devices interact with SATP claim rules for the purpose of using a specific PSP.

## Chapter 6

ALUA

Storage arrays provide various configurations and features depending on their class and design. Depending on how the arrays handle I/O to devices presented to hosts, they can be classified as

- **Active/Active** — I/O (input/output) can be sent to Logical Unit Numbers (LUNs) via any Storage Processor (SP) and port. Most of these arrays have large cache in place, and the I/O is done on the LUN representation in cache and then the writes are flushed to the physical disks asynchronously from the I/O.

- **Active/Passive** —I/O can be sent only to any port on the Storage Processor that "owns" the LUN (also known as the Active SP). If the I/O is attempted on the LUN via ports on the "non-owner" processor (also known as Passive SP), an error is returned to the initiator that means, in simple words, "No Entry" or "No, you can't do that." I provide the actual sense codes in Chapter 7, "Multipathing and Failover."

- **Pseudo-Active/Active** (also known as "Asymmetric Active-Active")—I/O can be sent to ports on either storage processers. However, I/O sent to the "owner" processor is faster than that sent to the "non-owner" processor. The reason behind that is the path the I/O takes to get to the devices from each SP. Going through the "non-owner" SP would send the I/O via some back-end channels compared to a direct path via the "owner" SP.

The latter two types of arrays have recently started implementing a SCSI-3 specification referred to as ALUA, which stands for Asymmetric Logical Unit Access. It allows access to the array devices via both SPs but clearly identifies to the initiators which targets are on the owner SP and which are on the non-owner SP, to put it simply. ALUA support was first introduced in vSphere 4.0.

ALUA Definition

ALUA is described in the T10 SCSI-3 specification SPC-3 section 5.8 (see
http://www.t10.org/cgi-bin/ac.pl?t=f&f=spc3r23.pdf). The official description from
the above standard is

> "Asymmetric logical unit access occurs when the access characteristics of one port may differ
> from those of another port."

In simpler terms, ALUA is a type of storage device that is capable of servicing I/O to a
given LUN on two different Storage Processors but in an uneven manner.

As I mentioned briefly earlier, using ALUA, I/O to a given LUN can be sent to available
ports on any of the SPs in the storage array. This is closer to the behavior of the
Asymmetric Active/Active arrays than the Active/Passive arrays. The I/O is allowed to the
LUN but the performance of the owner SP is better than the non-owner SP. To allow the
initiators to identify which targets would provide the best I/O, the ports on each SP are
grouped together (Target Port Groups). Each Target Port Group is given a distinctive
"state" (Asymmetric Access State or AAS). The latter denotes the "optimization" of ports
on one SP compared to ports on the other SP that may be less optimized (for example,
Active-Optimized versus Active-non-optimized).

ALUA Target Port Group

According to SPC-3, a Target Port Group (TPG) is described as

> "A target port group is defined as a set of target ports that are in the same target port
> asymmetric access state at all times. A target port group asymmetric access state is defined
> as the target port asymmetric access state common to the set of target ports in a target port
> group. The grouping of target ports is vendor specific."

This simply means that a given storage array that has, say, two SPs—SPA and SPB—ports
on SPA are grouped together and ports on SPB are grouped in a separate group. Assume
that this storage array presents two LUNs—LUN1 and LUN2—to initiators in vSphere
hosts and that LUN1 is owned by SPA whereas LUN2 is owned by SPB. For the hosts
to access LUN1, it is better to access it via SPA and to access LUN2 via SPB. Relative to
LUN1, ports on SPA are in the Active-Optimized TPGs (also referred to by the abbrevia-
tions AO) and ports on SPB are in the Active-Non-Optimized TPGs (ANO).

The reverse is true for LUN2 in this example where TPGs on SPA are ANO whereas
TPGs on SPB are AO.

Figure 6.1 shows the example on an Asymmetric Active/Active array. TPG with ID=1
(represented by left-hand rectangle on SPA) is Active Optimized (AO) (represented by the

solid line connecting it to LUN1). This same TPG is Active-Non-Optimized (ANO) for LUN2 (represented by the interrupted line connecting TPG1 to LUN2).

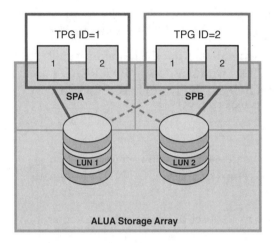

Figure 6.1   Illustration of TPGs

The reverse is true for TPG with ID=2. That is, it is AO for LUN 2 and ANO for LUN1.

On some Active/Passive ALUA-capable arrays, you may see Port Groups with "Standby" AAS instead of "ANO" on the non-owner SP.

Asymmetric Access State

Ports in an ALUA TPG can be in the same AAS at all times with respect to a given LUN. The TPGs AAS are reported to the initiators in response to the Report TPGs command. The TPG descriptor is reported in byte 1 of that response.

The possible states are

1. Active/Optimized (AO)

   Ports are on the owner SP and provided the best I/O to the LUN.

2. Active/Non-Optimized (ANO)

   Ports are on the non-owner SP. I/O to the LUN is less optimal compared to AO AAS.

3. Transitioning

The TPG AAS is in the process of switching from one state to another. For example, if the SP of an AO TPG is being rebooted or is taken offline, or the SAN (storage area network) admin manually transfers LUN ownership (on EMC CLARiiON, this is known as *trespass*), the AAS of the TPG on the alternate SP changes to AO. While this process is ongoing, the TPG AAS is *transitioning*.

While the TPG is in this state, receiving requests from the initiators would return BUSY or a CHECK CONDITION with sense Key NOT READY and ASC (Additional Sense Code) LOGICAL UNIT NOT ACCESSIBLE or ASYMMETRIC ACCESS STATE TRANSITION.

4. Standby

This state is similar to a passive SP in the non-ALUA configuration and on certain ALUA-capable arrays. It would return a CHECK CONDITION with Sense Key NOT READY.

When the TPG is in this AAS, it supports a subset of commands it accepts when it is in AO AAS. This subset of commands is

```
INQUIRY
LOG SELECT
LOG SENSE
MODE SELECT
MODE SENSE
REPORT LUNS (for LUN 0)
RECEIVE DIAGNOSTIC RESULTS
SEND DIAGNOSTIC
REPORT TARGET PORT GROUPS
SET TARGET PORT GROUPS
REQUEST SENSE
PERSISTENT RESERVE IN
PERSISTENT RESERVE OUT
Echo buffer modes of READ BUFFER
Echo buffer modes of WRITE BUFFER
```

5. Unavailable

This AAS is usually seen when the TPG access to the LUN is restricted as a result of hardware errors or other SCSI device limitations. The TPG in this state is unable to transition to AO or ANO until the error subsides.

Some ALUA storage arrays certified with vSphere 5.0 might not support some of the latter three states.

ESXi 5.0 sends the I/O to TPGs that are in AO AAS, but if they are not available, I/O is sent to TPGs that are in ANO AAS. If the storage array receives sustained I/O on TPGs that are in ANO AAS, the array transitions the TPGs state to AO AAS. Who makes that change depends on the ALUA Management Mode of the storage array. (See the next section.)

ALUA Management Modes

The dynamic nature of multipathing and failover requires the flexibility of managing and controlling the ALUA TPG's AAS. This is done via a set of commands and responses to and from the storage arrays. These commands are the following:

1. **INQUIRY** —According to SPC-3 spec section 6.4.2, in response to this command, the array returns certain pages of the VPD (Vital Product Data) or EVPD (Extended Vital Product Data). The inquiry data returned in response to this command includes the TPGs field. If the returned value in that field is non-zero, that device (LUN) supports ALUA. See Table 6.3 for the correlation between the value of TPGs field and AAS Management Modes.

2. **REPORT TARGET PORT GROUPS (REPORT TPGs)** —This command requests that the storage array sends the target port group information to the initiator.

3. **SET TARGET PORT GROUPS (SET TPGs)** —This command requests from the Storage Array to set the AAS of all ports in specified TPGs. For example, TPGs AAS can transition from ANO to AO using the SET TPGs command.

The control or management of the ALUA AAS can operate in one of four modes. Table 6.1 shows a matrix of these modes.

Table 6.1 ALUA AAS Management Modes

Mode	Managed By	REPORTPGs	SET TPGs
Not Supported	N/A	Invalid	Invalid
Implicit	Array	Yes	No
Explicit	Host	Yes	Yes
Both	Array/Host	Yes	Yes

- **Not Supported**—Response to the `REPORT TPGs` and `SET TPGs` commands is invalid. This means that the Storage Array does not support ALUA or the initiator records (CLARiiON) are not configured in a mode that supports ALUA.

- **Implicit**—The array responds to `REPORT TPGs` but not `SET TPGs` commands. In this case, setting the TPGS AAS is done only by the Storage Array.

- **Explicit**—The array responds to both `REPORT TPGs` and `SET TPGs`. In this case, setting the TPGs AAS can be done only by the initiator.

- **Both**—Same as explicit but both the array and initiator can set the TPGs AAS.

ALUA Common Implementations

The combination of ALUA AAS and Management Modes varies by vendor. Table 6.2 shows a matrix of common combinations.

Table 6.2   ALUA Common Implementations

Mode	AO	ANO	Standby	Example Array Vendor
Implicit	Yes	Yes	No	NetApp
Explicit & Implicit	Yes	Yes	No	HP EVA
				EMC CLARiiON
Explicit	Yes	No	Yes	IBM DS4000

ALUA Followover

To better explain what ALUA Followover does, let me first describe what happens without it. Storage Design that uses Active/Passive arrays must consider configurations that prevent a condition referred to as *path thrashing*. It is the case when, due to poor design or physical failure, some hosts would only have access to one SP whereas other hosts have access to the other SP and/or the incorrect Path Selection Plugin (PSP) is selected for the array. I have seen this to happen in two scenarios, which are shown in Figures 6.2 and 6.3.

Scenario 1

Figure 6.2 shows a Fibre Channel SAN design for a non-ALUA Active/Passive Array. Here host A has access to SPA only while host B has access to SPB only. LUN 1 is owned by SPA. However, because host B cannot access that SP, it requests from the array to transfer the LUN ownership to SPB. When the array complies, the result is that host A loses access to the LUN because it is no longer owned by SPA. Host A attempts to recover from this state by requesting from the array to transfer the LUN ownership back to SPA. When the array complies, host B starts this cycle again. This tug of war continues on and on while neither host can issue any I/O on the LUN.

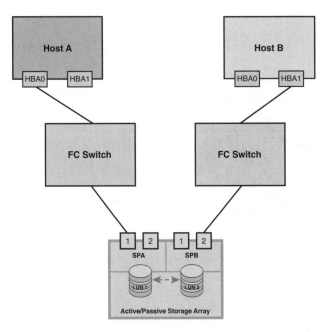

Figure 6.2   Scenario 1: Path thrashing due to wrong cabling design choice

The only solution for this problem is to correct the design where each host has access to both SPs and utilize the VMW_PSP_MRU Pluggable Storage Architecture (PSA) plug-in. Note that enabling ALUA without correcting the design may not prevent this problem.

Scenario 2

Figure 6.3 shows a variation on scenario 1. In this scenario, the Fibre Channel fabric was designed according to VMware best practices. However, both hosts were configured with VMW_PSP_FIXED instead of VMW_PSP_MRU. This by itself wouldn't result in path thrashing. However, to make matters worse, the designer decided to customize each host so that they have different preferred paths to LUN 1. These preferred path settings are represented by the interrupted lines (a path from host A and another path from host B). The expected behavior in this configuration is that as long as the defined preferred path to LUN 1 is available, the host insists on sending I/O via that path. As a result, host A attempts to send its I/O to LUN 1 via SPA and host B sends it I/O via SPB. However, LUN1 is owned by SPA and attempts to send I/O via SPB result in a check condition with a sense key ILLEGAL_REQUEST (more on this in Chapter 7). Host B insists on sending the I/O via its preferred path. So, it sends a START_UNIT or a TRESPASS command to the array. As a result, the array transfers LUN 1 ownership to SPB. Now host A gets really upset and tells the array to transfer the LUN back to SPA using the START_UNIT or TRESPASS commands. The array complies and the "tug of war" begins!

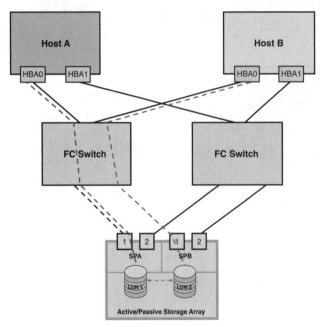

Figure 6.3   Scenario 2: Path thrashing due to wrong PSP design choice

These two examples are the reason why VMware created the VMW_PSP_MRU for use with Active/Passive arrays. In older releases prior to ESX 4.0, this used to be a policy setting per LUN. In 4.0, 4.1, and now in 5.0, MRU is a PSA plug-in. I cover the PSP design choices later in Chapter 7. What MRU does is that the host sends the I/O to the most recently used path. If the LUN moves to another SP, the I/O is sent on the new path to that SP instead of insisting on sending it to the previous owner SP. Note that MRU ignores the preferred path setting.

ALUA-capable arrays that provide AO AAS for TPGs on the owner SP and ANO AAS for TPGs on the non-owner SP allow I/O to the given LUN with high priority via the AO TPGs and, conversely, lower priority via the ANO TPGs. This means that the latter does not return a check condition with sense key ILLEGAL_REQUEST if I/O to the LUN is sent through it. This means that using VMW_PSP_FIXED with these arrays can result in a lighter version of path thrashing. In this case, I/O does not fail to be sent to the ANO TPGs if that is the preferred path. However, the I/O performance is much lower compared to using the AO TPGs. If more hosts are using the AO TPGs as the preferred path, the LUN ownership stays on the original SP that owns it. As a result, the ANO TPGs are not transitioned to AO for the offending host.

To accommodate this situation, VMware introduced a new feature for use with ALUA devices, however; it is not defined in the ALUA spec. This feature is referred to as ALUA_FOLLOWOVER.

ALUA Followover simply means that when the host detects TPG AAS change that it did not cause by itself, it does not try to revert the change even if it only has access to TPGs that are ANO. Effectively, this prevents the hosts from fighting for TPGs AAS and, instead, they follow the TPGs AAS of the array. Figures 6.4 and 6.5 illustrate ALUA_FOLLOWOVER interaction with TPGs AAS.

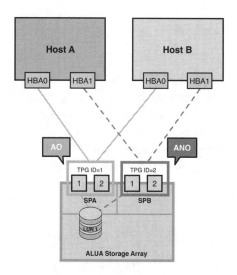

Figure 6.4   ALUA followover before failure

Figure 6.4 shows a logical storage diagram where the switch fabrics removed for diagram simplification. Here, TPG ID 1 is the AO on SPA, and both hosts send the I/O to that TPG. TPG ID 2 is ANO, and I/O is not sent to it. These TPGs are configured with Explicit ALUA Mode.

Figure 6.5 shows what happens after a path to the AO TPG fails.

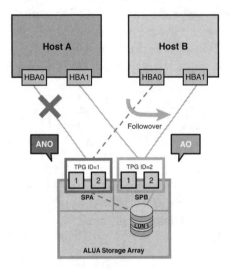

Figure 6.5   ALUA followover after failure

Figure 6.5 shows Host A lost its path to the AO TPG (based on Figure 6.4). As a result, this host takes advantage of the ALUA Explicit mode on the array and sends a SET_TPGS command to the array so that TPG ID 2 would change to AO and TPG ID 1 is changed to ANO. Host B recognizes that this change was not done by it. Because ALUA Followover option is enabled, Host B just accepts this change and does not attempt to reverse it. Consequently, the I/O is sent to TPG ID 2 because it is now the AO TPG. Notice that the array moved the LUN ownership to SPB because this is where the AO TPG is located.

> **NOTE**
> ALUA Followover is a device setting configured on the storage array. The default setting varies between vendors and models.

Some storage arrays implement the PREF (Preference) bit which enables the array to specify which SP is the preferred owner of a given LUN. This allows the storage administrator to spread the LUNs over both SPs (e.g. even LUNs on one SP and odd LUNs on the other SP). Whenever the need arises to shut down one of the SPs, the LUNs owned by that SP (say SPA) get transferred to the surviving non-preferred SP (SPB). As a result, the AAS of the port group on SPB is changed to AO. ALUA Followover honors this change and sends the next I/O intended for the transferred LUNs to port group on SPB. When SPA is brought back online, the LUNs it used to own get transferred back to it. This reverses the changes done earlier and the AAS of the port group on SPA is set to AO for the transferred LUNs. Conversely, the AAS of the port group on SPB, that no longer owns the LUNs, is changed to ANO. Again, ALUA Followover honors this change and switches the I/O back to the port group on SPA. This is the default behavior of ALUA capable HP EVA storage arrays.

Identifying Device ALUA Configuration

ESXi 5.0 host configuration that enables use of ALUA devices is a PSA component in the form of a SATP (see Chapter 5, "VMware Pluggable Storage Architecture (PSA)"). PSA claim rules decide which SATP to use based on array information returned in response to an INQUIRY command. As mentioned earlier, part of the inquiry string is the TPGs field. The claim rules are configured such that if that field's value is non-zero, the device is claimed by the defined ALUA SATP. In this section, I show how to list these claim rules and how to identify ALUA configurations from the device properties.

Identifying ALUA Claim Rule

In Chapter 5, I showed you how to list all the SATP rules. I had to split the screenshots to four quadrants so that I could show all content of the output. Here, I've tried to trim it down to list only the lines I need to show. To do so, use the following command:

```
esxcli storage nmp satp rule list |grep -i 'model\|satp_alua\|---' |less -S
```

What this command does is list all SATP rules then grep for the strings model, satp_ alua, and ---. This way, I get the column headers and the separator lines, which are the first two lines in the output. The rest of the output only shows the lines with satp_alua in them. Notice that I used the -i argument so that grep would ignore the case.

The output would look like Figure 6.6.

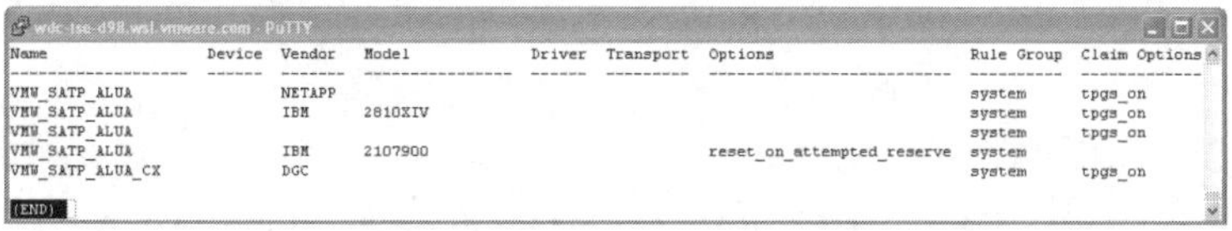

Name	Device	Vendor	Model	Driver	Transport	Options	Rule Group	Claim Options
VMW_SATP_ALUA		NETAPP					system	tpgs_on
VMW_SATP_ALUA		IBM	2810XIV				system	tpgs_on
VMW_SATP_ALUA							system	tpgs_on
VMW_SATP_ALUA		IBM	2107900			reset_on_attempted_reserve	system	
VMW_SATP_ALUA_CX		DGC					system	tpgs_on

Figure 6.6   ALUA claim rules

The following is the text of the output after removing blank colums for readability:

```
Name                Vendor  Model   Options                     Rule Group  Claim Options
----------------    ------- ------- -------------------------   ----------  ------------
VMW_SATP_ALUA       NETAPP                                      system      tpgs_on
VMW_SATP_ALUA       IBM     2810XIV                             system      tpgs_on
VMW_SATP_ALUA                                                   system      tpgs_on
VMW_SATP_ALUA       IBM     2107900 reset_on_attempted_reserve  system
VMW_SATP_ALUA_CX    DGC                                         system      tpgs_on
```

In this output, notice that the EMC CLARiiON CX family is claimed by VMW_SATP_ALUA_CX plug-in based on matches on the Model string being DGC and the Claim Options being tpgs_on.

On the other hand, both NETAPP and IBM XIV are claimed by VMW_SATP_ALUA plug-in based on matches on the Vendor String and the value of tpgs_on in the Claim Options column.

IBM DS8000, which is model 2107-900 (listed in the output without the dash), is claimed by VMW_SATP_ALUA based on the model string only, even though the claim option is not tpgs_on.

The remaining rule allows VMW_SATP_ALUA to claim devices with any vendor or model string value as long as the claim option value is tpgs_on. This means that any array not listed in the above sets of rules, which returns a non-zero value for the TPGs field in the inquiry string, gets claimed by VMW_SATP_ALUA. You may think of this as the catch-all ALUA claim rule that claims devices on all ALUA arrays that are not explicitly listed by vendor or model in the SATP claim rules.

Identifying Devices' ALUA Configurations

ALUA configurations are associated with LUNs in combination with TPGs. To list these configurations, you may run the following:

```
esxcli storage nmp device list
```

The output of this command is listed in the following figures showing examples from various storage arrays.

Example from EMC CLARiiON CX Array

Figure 6.7 shows an example of an EMC CLARiiON CX LUN configured for ALUA.

```
wdc-tse-d98.wsl.vmware.com - PuTTY
naa.60060160a2b0290001e57a70fa40e011:
   Device Display Name: DGC Fibre Channel Over Ethernet Disk (naa.60060160a2b0290001e57a70fa40e011)
   Storage Array Type: VMW_SATP_ALUA_CX
   Storage Array Type Device Config: (navireg=on, ipfilter=on){implicit_support=on;explicit_support
=on; explicit_allow=on;alua_followover=on;(TPG_id=2,TPG_state=ANO)(TPG_id=1,TPG_state=AO)}
   Path Selection Policy: VMW_PSP_FIXED
   Path Selection Policy Device Config: {preferred=vmhba34:C0:T0:L9;current=vmhba34:C0:T0:L9}
   Path Selection Policy Device Custom Config:
   Working Paths: vmhba34:C0:T0:L9
```

Figure 6.7   ALUA configuration of a CLARiiON CX FCoE device

This output shows the following configurations:

1. Storage Array Type:

   VMW_SATP_ALUA_CX—This is the same as VMW_SATP_ALUA with additional code to handle certain commands specific to CLARiiON CX ALUA arrays.

2. Storage Array Type Device Config—This line was wrapped for readability.

   The first set of curly brackets { } includes initiator registration–specific configuration. This is specific to EMC CLARiiON family of arrays. Within this set, two options are listed—navireg and ipfilter:

   ■ navireg=on—This means that NaviAgent Registration option is enabled on this host. It registers the initiator with the CX array if not already registered. Note that you need to check the initiator record on the array to make sure that the **Failover Mode** is set to **4**, which enables ALUA for this initiator. More details on this in Chapter 7.

   ■ ipfilter=on—This option filters the host's IP address so that it is not visible to the Storage Array. More on this in Chapter 7.

   The ALUA AAS Management mode options are enclosed within a second set of curly brackets { } within which is another nested pair of curly brackets for the TPGs AAS configuration.

   ALUA AAS management mode:

   ■ Implicit_support=on—This means that the array supports implicit mode of AAS management. (See Table 6.1 earlier.)

   ■ Explicit_support=on—This means that the array supports explicit mode of AAS management. (See above.)

- Explicit_allow=on—This means that the host is configured to allow the SATP to exercise its explicit ALUA capability if the need arises (for example, failed controller).

- ALUA_followover=on—This enables the alua_followover option on the host. (See the "ALUA Followover" section earlier in this chapter.)

The next set of options are within the nested pair of curly brackets {} for the TPG IDs and AAS:

- TPG_id—This field shows the Target Port Group ID. If the LUN is accessible via more than one target port group (typically two groups), both IDs are listed here. This example has TPG_id 1 and 2. Each TPG is listed within its own pair of curly brackets.

- TPG_state—This field shows the AAS of the TPG. Notice that TPG_id 1 is in AO AAS, whereas TPG_id 2 is in ANO AAS. Based on this configuration, I/O is sent to TPG_id 1.

I cover the path related options in Chapter 7.

An Example from EMC VNX

The example in Figure 6.8 shows a similar output but from an EMC VNX array.

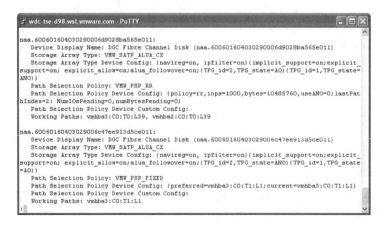

Figure 6.8   ALUA configuration of an EMC VNX FC device

In this case, the figure shows two devices on the same array. Both devices show identical information to that reported by the CX array with the following differences:

1. These devices are FC LUNs, whereas the CX example was from an FCoE device.

2. The first device in this example shows TPG_id 2 being in AO AAS, whereas on the second device TPG_id 1 is also in the same state (AO AAS). This means that the devices are spread evenly over the array's SPs. For example, TPG 1 on SPA services I/O to LUN 1 whereas TPG 2 on SPB services I/O to LUN 39. You should also notice from the Working Paths field that for LUN 39 the target portion of the path name is T0, whereas it is T1 for LUN 1. I explain in Chapter 7 how to identify which target belongs to which SP.

3. The first device is claimed by VMW_PSP_RR (Round Robin), whereas the second one is claimed by VMW_PSP_FIXED. I explain this in Chapter 7, later in this book.

Example from IBM DS8000 Array

Figure 6.9 shows a similar output from an IBM DS8000 array-based device.

Figure 6.9   ALUA configuration of an IBM DS8000 device

The output is similar in many aspects with the following differences:

1. The device is claimed by VMW_SATP_ALUA instead of VMW_SATP_ALUA_CX.

2. explicit_support=off means that the array does not support explicit mode of AAS management.

3. There is only one TPG_id, which is 0 and is in an AO AAS.

> **NOTE**
>
> Even though explicit_allow is set to on, this does not take effect because the array does not support explicit mode.

Example from IBM XIV Array

Figure 6.10 shows an output from an IBM XIV array-based device.

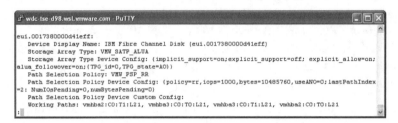

Figure 6.10   ALUA configuration of an IBM XIV device

The output is similar to that from IBM DS8000 array (refer to Figure 6.9) with the following differences:

1. The device ID uses `eui` format instead of `naa`. This is usually the result of the array supporting an ANSI revision lower than 3. (See Chapter 1, "Storage Types," for details.)

2. The PSP in use is `VMW_PSP_RR` (Round Robin) compared to FIXED. I discuss PSP choices and configuration in Chapter 7.

Example from a NetApp Array

Figure 6.11 shows an example from a NetApp array.

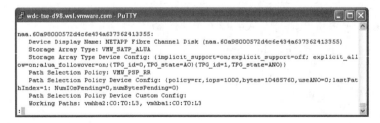

Figure 6.11   ALUA configuration of a NetApp FC device

This example is similar to the two TPGs EMC CX example in Figure 6.7 with the following differences:

1. The device is claimed by VMW_SATP_ALUA instead of VMW_SATP_ALUA_CX.

2. explicit_support=off means that the array does not support explicit mode of AAS management.

3. Device is claimed by VMW_PSP_RR instead of VMW_PSP_FIXED.

Example from an HP MSA Array

Figure 6.12 shows an example from an HP MSA array.

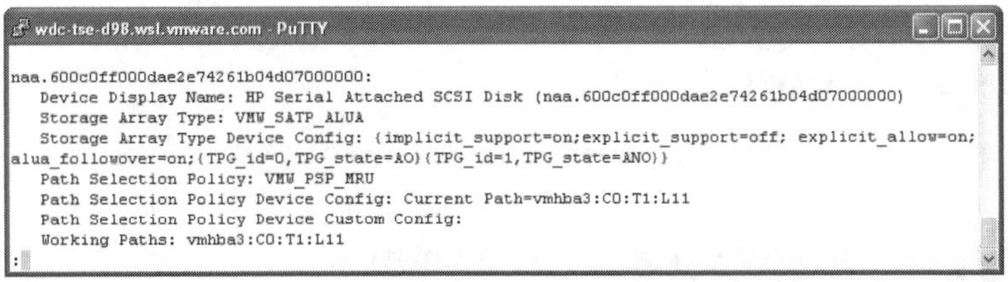

Figure 6.12 ALUA configuration of an HP MSA FC device

This example is similar to the NetApp array output (see Figure 6.11) with the difference that the PSP is VMW_PSP_MRU.

Troubleshooting ALUA

In this section I try to give some troubleshooting foundation that will hopefully help you learn how to fish (also known as TIY or Troubleshoot It Yourself)!

First, let me familiarize you with the normal log entries. When a device is discovered by vmkernel (logged to /var/log/vmkernel.log file), as I mentioned earlier, the tpgs field is included with the inquiry string. The value of that field helps vmkernel identify the AAS management mode (that is, explicit, implicit, or both).

Following are examples from the storage arrays I used in the previous section. Figure 6.13 shows vmkernel.log entries from a vSphere 5 host connected to an EMC VNX storage array.

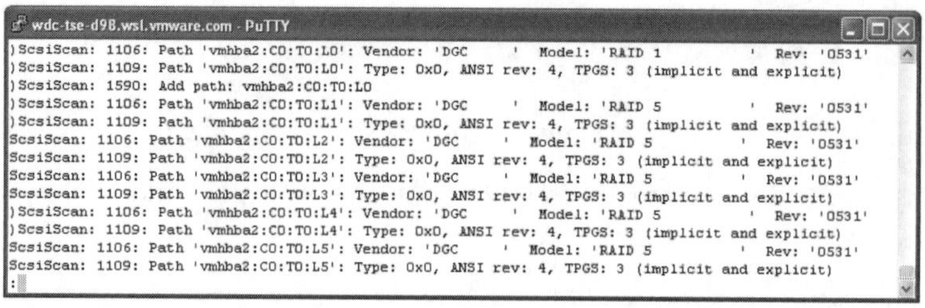

wdc-tse-d98.wsl.vmware.com - PuTTY

```
)ScsiScan: 1106: Path 'vmhba2:C0:T0:L0': Vendor: 'DGC     '  Model: 'RAID 1          '  Rev: '0531'
)ScsiScan: 1109: Path 'vmhba2:C0:T0:L0': Type: 0x0, ANSI rev: 4, TPGS: 3 (implicit and explicit)
)ScsiScan: 1590: Add path: vmhba2:C0:T0:L0
)ScsiScan: 1106: Path 'vmhba2:C0:T0:L1': Vendor: 'DGC     '  Model: 'RAID 5          '  Rev: '0531'
)ScsiScan: 1109: Path 'vmhba2:C0:T0:L1': Type: 0x0, ANSI rev: 4, TPGS: 3 (implicit and explicit)
ScsiScan: 1106: Path 'vmhba2:C0:T0:L2': Vendor: 'DGC     '  Model: 'RAID 5          '  Rev: '0531'
ScsiScan: 1109: Path 'vmhba2:C0:T0:L2': Type: 0x0, ANSI rev: 4, TPGS: 3 (implicit and explicit)
ScsiScan: 1106: Path 'vmhba2:C0:T0:L3': Vendor: 'DGC     '  Model: 'RAID 5          '  Rev: '0531'
ScsiScan: 1109: Path 'vmhba2:C0:T0:L3': Type: 0x0, ANSI rev: 4, TPGS: 3 (implicit and explicit)
)ScsiScan: 1106: Path 'vmhba2:C0:T0:L4': Vendor: 'DGC     '  Model: 'RAID 5          '  Rev: '0531'
)ScsiScan: 1109: Path 'vmhba2:C0:T0:L4': Type: 0x0, ANSI rev: 4, TPGS: 3 (implicit and explicit)
ScsiScan: 1106: Path 'vmhba2:C0:T0:L5': Vendor: 'DGC     '  Model: 'RAID 5          '  Rev: '0531'
ScsiScan: 1109: Path 'vmhba2:C0:T0:L5': Type: 0x0, ANSI rev: 4, TPGS: 3 (implicit and explicit)
:
```

Figure 6.13 VMkernel.log entries of an EMC CLARiiON ALUA device

In this example I truncated the first part of each line, which shows the data, time stamp, and host name. Notice that the `ScsiScan` lines show the `TPGS` field with a value of `3`. This means that the array supports both `implicit and explicit` ALUA modes. This is printed in English as well at the end of each line.

Figure 6.14 shows log entries from a vSphere 5 host connected to a NetApp storage array.

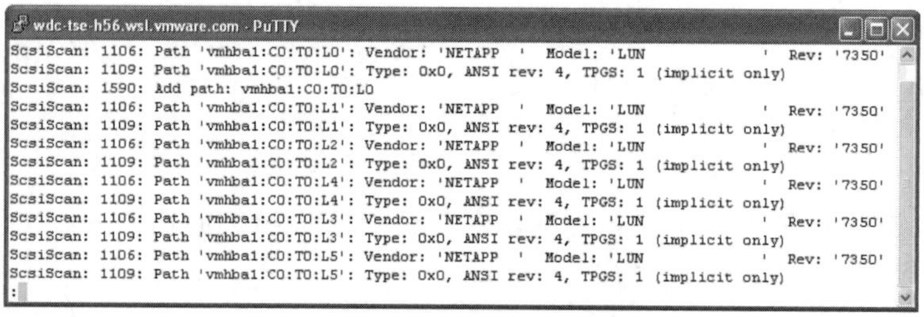

wdc-tse-h56.wsl.vmware.com - PuTTY

```
ScsiScan: 1106: Path 'vmhba1:C0:T0:L0': Vendor: 'NETAPP  '  Model: 'LUN             '  Rev: '7350'
ScsiScan: 1109: Path 'vmhba1:C0:T0:L0': Type: 0x0, ANSI rev: 4, TPGS: 1 (implicit only)
ScsiScan: 1590: Add path: vmhba1:C0:T0:L0
ScsiScan: 1106: Path 'vmhba1:C0:T0:L1': Vendor: 'NETAPP  '  Model: 'LUN             '  Rev: '7350'
ScsiScan: 1109: Path 'vmhba1:C0:T0:L1': Type: 0x0, ANSI rev: 4, TPGS: 1 (implicit only)
ScsiScan: 1106: Path 'vmhba1:C0:T0:L2': Vendor: 'NETAPP  '  Model: 'LUN             '  Rev: '7350'
ScsiScan: 1109: Path 'vmhba1:C0:T0:L2': Type: 0x0, ANSI rev: 4, TPGS: 1 (implicit only)
ScsiScan: 1106: Path 'vmhba1:C0:T0:L4': Vendor: 'NETAPP  '  Model: 'LUN             '  Rev: '7350'
ScsiScan: 1109: Path 'vmhba1:C0:T0:L4': Type: 0x0, ANSI rev: 4, TPGS: 1 (implicit only)
ScsiScan: 1106: Path 'vmhba1:C0:T0:L3': Vendor: 'NETAPP  '  Model: 'LUN             '  Rev: '7350'
ScsiScan: 1109: Path 'vmhba1:C0:T0:L3': Type: 0x0, ANSI rev: 4, TPGS: 1 (implicit only)
ScsiScan: 1106: Path 'vmhba1:C0:T0:L5': Vendor: 'NETAPP  '  Model: 'LUN             '  Rev: '7350'
ScsiScan: 1109: Path 'vmhba1:C0:T0:L5': Type: 0x0, ANSI rev: 4, TPGS: 1 (implicit only)
:
```

Figure 6.14 VMkernel.log entries of a NetApp ALUA device

Notice that the `ScsiScan` lines shows the `TPGS` field with a value of `1`. This means that the array supports `implicit` ALUA mode only. This is printed in English as well at the end of each line.

Figure 6.15 shows log entries from a vSphere 5 host connected to an IBM DS8000 storage array.

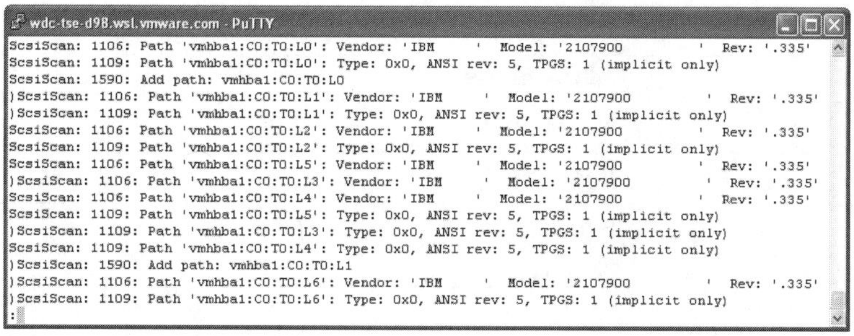

Figure 6.15   VMkernel.log entries of an IBM DS8000 ALUA device

This log shows the array as `Model: '2107900`. Notice that the `ScsiScan` lines show the `TPGS` field with a value of `1`. This means that the array supports `implicit` ALUA mode only. This is printed in English as well at the end of each line.

Figure 6.16 shows log entries from a vSphere 5 host connected to an IBM XIV storage array.

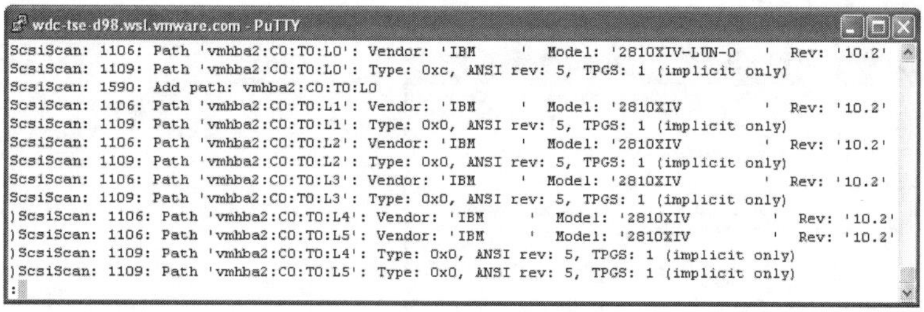

Figure 6.16   VMkernel.log entries of an IBM XIV ALUA device

This log shows the array as `Model: '2810XIV'`). Notice that the `ScsiScan` lines show the `TPGS` field with a value of `1`. This means that the array supports `implicit` ALUA mode only. This is printed in English as well at the end of each line.

At this time, I don't have access to an array that supports an explicit ALUA-only mode. However, the log from such an array would have shown the value of TPGS to be `2`. Table 6.3 summarizes the different values of TPGS field and their meaning.

Table 6.3 Meaning TPGS Field Value

TPGS Value	ALUA Mode
0	Not supported
1	Implicit only
2	Explicit only
3	Both Implicit and Explicit

Identifying ALUA Devices Path State

The next step of troubleshooting is to identify the state of the path or paths to the ALUA device. I cover the details of multipathing in Chapter 7. For now, I'm showing you how to identify the path states. The Figure 6.17 shows an output of the following command:

```
esxcli storage nmp path list
```

Figure 6.17 shows the list of four paths to LUN 20, which is on an EMC VNX array configured for ALUA.

Figure 6.17   Listing of paths to an EMC VNX ALUA device

The relevant fields for the topic of troubleshooting are

- `Group State` —Shows the Target Port Group AAS; `Active` means `AO` whereas `Active unoptimized` means ANO.

- `Storage Array Type Path Config` —This field includes `TPG_id`, `TPG_State`, `RTP_id`, and `RTP_health`.

- `TPG_id` —Similar to the output of the device list. This is the Target Port Group ID.

- `TPG_state` —Similar to the output of the device list. This matches the value equivalent to the previous field `Group State` (for example, AO or ANO).

- `RTP_id` —This is the Relative Target Port ID. It is the port ID from which the inquiry response was sent to the initiator. The Vital Product Data (VPD) included in this string includes that Relative Target Port ID. So, with two paths per HBA in this example, two inquiry strings were received by each HBA. The first of each came from RTP ID 13 and the second from RTP ID 1.

NOTE

Because both HBAs see the same RTP IDs, this means that both HBAs are connected to the same fabric. This is a possible single point of failure as I indicated in the examples in Chapter 3, "FCoE Storage Connectivity," (refer to Figure 3.24).

`RTP_Health:` This is the health status of the RTP. It can be either `UP` or `DOWN`. In this output, it is `UP`. If it were `DOWN`, the `Group State` field would have been `Dead` instead of `Active` or `Active Unoptimized`.

I cover further details in Chapter 7.

Summary

In this chapter I covered ALUA standard—how it is implemented in vSphere 5—and showed you how to identify various ALUA configurations and how they affect the hosts. Detailed interactions between ALUA and multipathing and failover are covered in Chapter 7.

Multipathing and Failover

One of the most critical elements of storage availability in the enterprise is multipathing and failover. vSphere 5, and as early as ESX 1.5, includes native multipathing (NMP) right out of the box. Although it does not provide the complex level of input/output (I/O) load balance that storage vendor's proprietary Multipathing Input/Output (MPIO) software provides, it does an excellent job with maintaining access to the shared storage that the infrastructure uses.

In ESX versions prior to 4.0, the portion of the vmkernel responsible for multipathing and failover was referred to as *legacy multipathing*. It was a monolithic code built into the vmkernel. Any changes or updates to this code required installing a new version of the vmkernel, which made it less practical for availability as it required rebooting the host after updates were installed. As the expression goes, "Necessity is the mother of invention." So, the need for better availability and more flexibility in the virtual environment lead to the birth of Pluggable Storage Architecture (PSA) which is covered in Chapter 5, "VMware Pluggable Storage Architecture (PSA)." In that chapter I provide the detailed under-the-hood architecture and configurations. In this chapter, I get into more details about how multipathing and failover work and how to identify various conditions leading to and resulting from failover events.

What Is a Path?

The I/O sent from vSphere 5 hosts to their assigned logical unit numbers (LUNs) travels through a specific route that starts with an HBA and ends at a LUN. This route is referred to as a *path*. Each host, in a properly designed infrastructure, should have more than one path to each LUN.

Figure 7.1 depicts a highly available design with no single points of failure, which I discuss in Chapter 5.

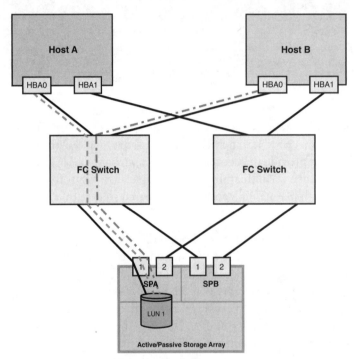

Figure 7.1   Illustration of a path to a LUN

In this example, a path to LUN1 from host A is represented by an interrupted line and Host B by an interrupted line with dots and dashes. This path goes through HBA0 to port 1 on SPA.

Such a path is represented, in the UI and CLI outputs, by the Runtime Name naming convention. Runtime Name is formerly known as Canonical Name. It is in the format of HBAx:Cn:Ty:Lz e.g. vmhba0:C0:T0:L1, which reads as follows:

vmhba0, Channel 0, Target 0, LUN1

It represents the path to LUN0 broken down as the following:

- **HBA0**—First HBA in this host. The vmhba number may vary based on the number of storage adapters installed in the host. For example, if the host already has two RAID controllers installed which assume vmhba0 and vmhba1 names, the first Fibre Channel (FC) HBA added to this host would be named vmhba2.

- **Channel 0**—Channel number is mostly zero for FC- and Internet Small Computer System Interface (iSCSI)–attached devices. If the HBA were a SCSI adapter with two channels (for example, internal connections and an external port for direct attached devices), the channel numbers would be 0 and 1.

- **Target 0**—The target definition was covered in Chapters 2, "Fibre Channel Storage Connectivity," and 4 "iSCSI Storage Connectivity." The target number is based on the order the SP ports are discovered by PSA. In this case, SPA-Port1 was discovered before SPA-Port2 and the other ports on SPB. So, that port was given target 0 as part of the runtime name.

> **NOTE**
>
> Runtime Naming, as the name indicates, does not persist between host reboots nor is it identical across hosts sharing the same LUN. This is due to the possibility that any of the components that make up that name may change due to hardware or connectivity changes. For example, a host may have an additional HBA added or another HBA removed, which would change the number assumed by the HBA.

Let's expand on this example and enumerate the remaining paths to LUN1 from Host A, which also applies to Host B.

Host A has two HBAs: vmhba0 and vmhba1, which are represented in Figure 7.1 by HBA0 and HBA1, respectively. HBA0 is connected to a fabric switch that in turn is connected to port 1 on SPA and Port 1 on SPB. HBA1 is connected to a separate fabric switch (on a separate fabric) that in turn is connected to port 2 on SPA and port 2 on SPB.

This provides two paths to the LUN from each HBA with the total of four paths. To list these four paths via the CLI, run the following command:

```
esxcli storage nmp path list --device <LUN's NAA ID>
```

You can also use the shorthand option -d instead of --device:

```
esxcli storage nmp path list -d <LUN's NAA ID>
```

The output in Figure 7.2 was collected from a host equipped with two FC HBAs named vmhba2 and vmhba3.

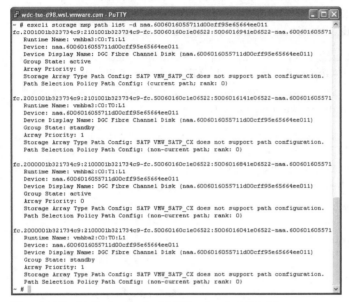

Figure 7.2   Listing paths to a LUN using its NAA ID

vmhba3 has two paths to LUN1, which are

```
vmhba3:C0:T1:L1
vmhba3:C0:T0:L1
```

vmhba2 has two paths to LUN1, which are

```
vmhba2:C0:T1:L1
vmhba2:C0:T0:L1
```

Paths would read as vmhba2, Channel 0, Target 1, LUN1, and so on.

Even though each HBA uses the same target numbers, these targets are actually different. The reason behind that is the presence of two separate fabrics to which each HBA is connected. As I illustrated in Figure 7.1, each fabric connects to different ports on SPA and SPB.

How can I tell that these targets are actually different?

Recall the details I provide in Chapters 2, 4, and 5 in which I explain the target IDs using WWPN (World Wide Port Name) for FC and iqn (iSCSI Qulaified Name) for iSCSI? This example is from an FC configuration, so let's walk through the output to identify these targets.

Table 7.1 shows the correlation between runtime names (see Chapter 2) and targets' WWPNs.

Table 7.1   Identifying Targets

Runtime Name	Target WWPN	Which SP/Port
vmhba3:C0:T1:L1	5006016941e06522	SPB/Port 1
vmhba3:C0:T0:L1	5006016141e06522	SPA/Port 1
vmhba2:C0:T1:L1	5006016841e06522	SPB/Port 0
vmhba2:C0:T0:L1	5006016041e06522	SPA/Port 0

The highlighted bytes are the unique portion of the WWPNs that help identify the EMC CLARiiON and VNX SP ports. (See Chapter 2's "FC Targets" section for details and identifiers of other known arrays ports.)

Figure 7.3 shows a similar example from an iSCSI configuration with two paths instead of four.

Figure 7.3   Listing paths to an iSCSI LUN using its NAA ID

Figure 7.3 shows two paths to a LUN with NAA ID `naa.6006016047301a00eaed23 f5884ee011`. This configuration has a single software iSCSI initiator vmhba35 that is connected to two iSCSI targets—namely `iqn.1992-04.com.emc:cx.apm00071501971. b0,t,2` and `iqn.1992-04.com.emc:cx.apm00071501971.a0,t,1`.

Based on the device display name and the Storage Array Type Plugin (SATP) that claimed this LUN (VMW_SATP_CX), the LUN is on an EMC CLARiiON CX family array. Based on the iSCSI aliases of these two targets, the LUN is accessible via SPA0 and SPB0, which were assigned target numbers 2 and 1, respectively.

Figure 7.4 shows a SAS (Serial Attached SCSI)–attached LUN that is accessible on two targets via vmhba3 and has an NAA ID `naa.600c0ff000dae2e73763b04d02000000`. Based on the device display name, the LUN is on an HP storage array.

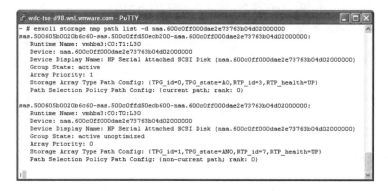

Figure 7.4   Listing paths to a SAS LUN using its NAA ID

To identify which array model it is, use this command:

```
esxcli storage core device list --device naa.600c0ff000dae2e73763b0
4d02000000
```

You may also use the shorthand option `-d` instead of `--device`:

```
esxcli storage core device list -d naa.600c0ff000dae2e73763b04d02000000
```

The output of this command is shown in Figure 7.5.

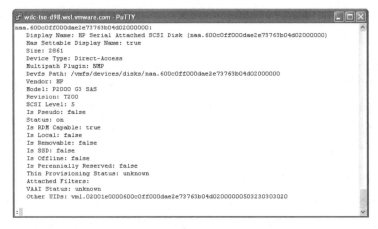

```
wdc-tse-d98.wsl.vmware.com - PuTTY
naa.600c0ff000dae2e73763b04d02000000:
   Display Name: HP Serial Attached SCSI Disk (naa.600c0ff000dae2e73763b04d02000000)
   Has Settable Display Name: true
   Size: 2861
   Device Type: Direct-Access
   Multipath Plugin: NMP
   Devfs Path: /vmfs/devices/disks/naa.600c0ff000dae2e73763b04d02000000
   Vendor: HP
   Model: P2000 G3 SAS
   Revision: T200
   SCSI Level: 5
   Is Pseudo: false
   Status: on
   Is RDM Capable: true
   Is Local: false
   Is Removable: false
   Is SSD: false
   Is Offline: false
   Is Perennially Reserved: false
   Thin Provisioning Status: unknown
   Attached Filters:
   VAAI Status: unknown
   Other UIDs: vml.02001e0000600c0ff000dae2e73763b04d02000000503230303020
```

Figure 7.5   Listing a SAS LUN's properties

This output shows the Vendor string is HP and the Model string is P2000 G3 SAS. This means that the LUN is on an HP MSA P2000 G3 SAS array.

Where Is the Active Path?

In ESX releases earlier than ESX/ESXi 4.0, there used to be an active path listed in the command-line interface (CLI) outputs as well as in the user interface (UI). This was the path through which the ESX host sends the I/O to the LUN. Starting with ESX/ESXi 4.0, the reference to active has shifted to refer to the path to the SP that owns the LUN in the Active/Passive array configuration. It also refers to all paths to a LUN on an Active/Active array. This path is identified in commands outputs as *working path* as I show you later in this section. This change continues to be true in ESXi 5.

In this section, I show you how to identify the path formerly known as the active path using the CLI as well as the UI. In short, this path is listed in the CLI as current path. In the UI, the path would be indicated by IO.

Identifying the Current Path Using the CLI

Check the examples I used in Figures 7.2, 7.3 and 7.4, for FC-, iSCSI-, and SAS-based LUNs, respectively. The Path Selection Policy Path Config field shows one of the paths as current path whereas the remaining paths show as non-current path. The former is the path through which the host sends the I/O to the LUN, while the latter are not used until the current path becomes unavailable or, when using Round Robin PSP, the I/O rotates on each of these active paths.

Identifying the IO (Current) Path Using the UI

To identify the current path through which the I/O is sent, follow this procedure:

1. Log on to the vSphere 5.0 host directly or to the vCenter server that manages the host using the VMware vSphere 5.0 Client as a user with Administrator privileges.

2. While in the Inventory—Hosts and Clusters view, locate the vSphere 5.0 host in the inventory tree and select it.

3. Navigate to the **Configuration** tab.

4. Under the **Hardware** section, select the **Storage** option.

5. Under the **View** field, click the **Devices** button.

6. Under the **Devices** pane, select one of the SAN LUNs (see Figure 7.6). In this example, its name starts with DGC Fibre Channel Disk.

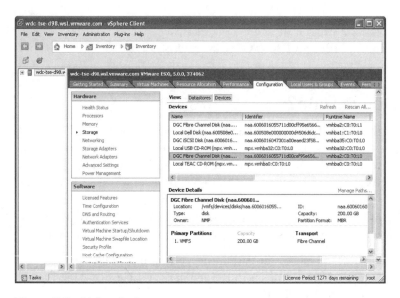

Figure 7.6   Listing devices

7. Select **Manage Paths** in the Device Details pane.

8. Figure 7.7 shows the LUN details. In this example, I sorted on the **Runtime Name** field in ascending order. The Paths section shows all available paths to the LUN in the following format:

- **Runtime Name**—vmhbaX:C0:Ty:Lz where X is the HBA number, y is the target number, and z is the LUN number.

- **Status**—Shows the path status, which is in this example is either Active or Standby. The path where the I/O is sent is marked with (I/O).

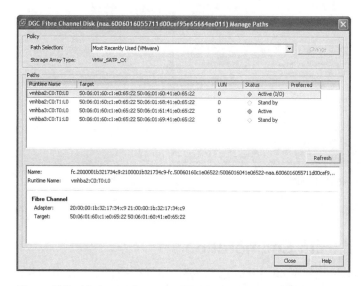

Figure 7.7 Listing paths to the FC LUN via UI

NOTE

The Preferred field is blank because the Path Selection field (which is the PSP) shows that Most Recently Used (or MRU) is in use, which ignores the preferred path option. This option is only valid with "FIXED" PSP.

Listing the paths to an iSCSI LUN is similar to the procedure I just discussed. Instead, the UI would look like Figure 7.8.

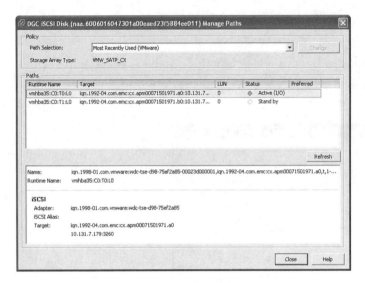

Figure 7.8   Listing paths of an iSCSI LUN via UI

LUN Discovery and Path Enumeration

Understanding how LUNs are discovered helps in identifying problems if and when they arise. In this section, I go over some SCSI commands and log entries that explain this process and how paths to LUNs are enumerated.

The process of LUN discovery and path enumeration is done via a sequence of SCSI commands and interpreting responses to such commands (SCSI Sense Codes). Table 7.2 shows a list of common SCSI commands that you may encounter on ESXi 5 hosts. (Most of these commands apply to earlier releases as well.)

Table 7.2   Common SCSI Commands

Command Name	Operation Code	Service Action
ACCESS CONTROL IN	0x86	
ACCESS CONTROL OUT	0x87	
CHANGE ALIASES	0xA4	0x0B
EXTENDED COPY	0x83	
INQUIRY	0x12	
LOG SELECT	0x4C	

Command Name	Operation Code	Service Action
LOG SENSE	0x4D	
MODE SELECT(6)	0x15	
MODE SELECT(10)	0x55	
MODE SENSE(6)	0x1A	
MODE SENSE(10)	0x5A	
PERSISTENT RESERVE IN 5	0xE	
PERSISTENT RESERVE OUT	0x5F	
PREVENT ALLOW MEDIUM REMOVAL	0x1E	
READ ATTRIBUTE	0x8C	
READ BUFFER	0x3C	
READ MEDIA SERIAL NUMBER	0xAB	0x01
RECEIVE COPY RESULTS	0x84	
RECEIVE DIAGNOSTIC RESULTS	0x1C	
REPORT ALIASES	0xA3	0x0B
REPORT DEVICE IDENTIFIER	0xA3	0x05
REPORT LUNS	0xA0	
REPORT PRIORITY	0xA3	0x0E
REPORT SUPPORTED OPERATION CODES	0xA3	0x0C
REPORT SUPPORTED TASK MANAGEMENT FUNCTIONS	0xA3	0x0D
REPORT TARGET PORT GROUPS	0xA3	0x0A
REPORT TIMESTAMP	0xA3	0x0F
REQUEST SENSE	0x03	
SEND DIAGNOSTIC	0x1D	
SET DEVICE IDENTIFIER	0xA4	0x06
SET PRIORITY	0xA4	0x0E
SET TARGET PORT GROUPS	0xA4	0x0A
SET TIMESTAMP	0xA4	0x0F

In Table 7.2, some commands require a combination of operation code and service action. Such commands show values in both the Operation Code and Service Action columns.

SCSI Sense codes are returned in response to the SCSI commands listed in Table 7.2. For a reference to commonly seen sense codes, see Tables 7.4, 7.5, 7.6, and 7.7 later in this chapter in the "Failover Triggers" section.

LUN discovery is done in the following order:

1. The host sends the REPORT LUNS command (0xA0) to the storage array.

2. The array responds with the LUN numbers that are masked (presented) to the initiators on this host.

3. The host sends the INQUIRY command (0x12) on page 0 to each of the reported LUNs. This should return the list of supported VPD (Vital Product Data) pages. VPD provides specific information about the device depending on which VPD page the device supports.

4. If the device supports VPD page 83, an inquiry command is issued on that page. This returns the device unique ID (NAA ID).

5. If the device does not support page 83, the host sends an inquiry command for VPD page 80. This provides the device Serial Number instead because NAA ID is not supported.

The VPD page provides one or more of the following identification descriptors:

- Logical unit names
- SCSI target port identifiers
- SCSI target port names
- SCSI target device names
- Relative target port identifiers
- SCSI target port group number
- Logical unit group number

Sample LUN Discovery and Path Enumeration Log Entries

The main log in ESXi 5 is /var/log/vmkernel.log file. However, there are some events that occur during system boot and are logged to /var/log/boot.gz. This file is a compressed boot log that you can read using the `zcat boot.gz |less -S` command. This is because the file is compressed to save on visorfs space (visor FS is a memory-based file system in which the ESXi compressed boot image is loaded). If you want to expand it using the `gunzip` command, don't do that in /var/log directory. Rather, copy the file to a VMFS volume or transfer it to your management workstation using scp or similar tools and expand it there.

Figure 7.9 shows a snippet from /var/log/boot.gz (after expansion). I cropped the output for readability.

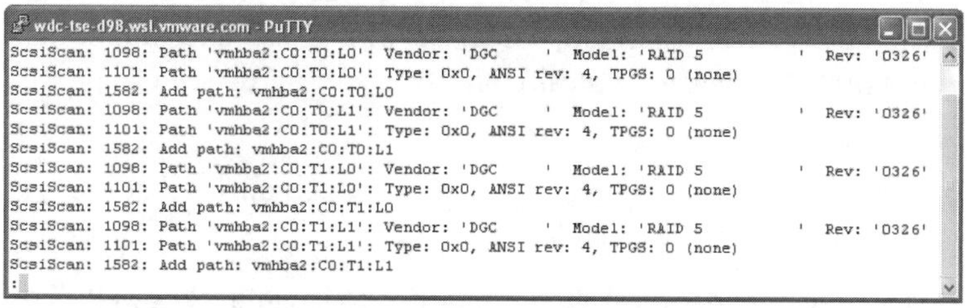

```
wdc-tse-d98.wsl.vmware.com - PuTTY
ScsiScan: 1098: Path 'vmhba2:C0:T0:L0': Vendor: 'DGC     ' Model: 'RAID 5        ' Rev: '0326'
ScsiScan: 1101: Path 'vmhba2:C0:T0:L0': Type: 0x0, ANSI rev: 4, TPGS: 0 (none)
ScsiScan: 1582: Add path: vmhba2:C0:T0:L0
ScsiScan: 1098: Path 'vmhba2:C0:T0:L1': Vendor: 'DGC     ' Model: 'RAID 5        ' Rev: '0326'
ScsiScan: 1101: Path 'vmhba2:C0:T0:L1': Type: 0x0, ANSI rev: 4, TPGS: 0 (none)
ScsiScan: 1582: Add path: vmhba2:C0:T0:L1
ScsiScan: 1098: Path 'vmhba2:C0:T1:L0': Vendor: 'DGC     ' Model: 'RAID 5        ' Rev: '0326'
ScsiScan: 1101: Path 'vmhba2:C0:T1:L0': Type: 0x0, ANSI rev: 4, TPGS: 0 (none)
ScsiScan: 1582: Add path: vmhba2:C0:T1:L0
ScsiScan: 1098: Path 'vmhba2:C0:T1:L1': Vendor: 'DGC     ' Model: 'RAID 5        ' Rev: '0326'
ScsiScan: 1101: Path 'vmhba2:C0:T1:L1': Type: 0x0, ANSI rev: 4, TPGS: 0 (none)
ScsiScan: 1582: Add path: vmhba2:C0:T1:L1
:
```

Figure 7.9 Log entries showing new paths added

Here you see LUN0 discovery via the ScsiScan function of vmkernel. The LUN properties show the Vendor, Model, and Rev fields (the first line in the output). In this example, the Vendor is DGC (Data General Corportation), which represents the EMC CLARiiON CX family of arrays. The Model in this case is the RAID type backing the LUN. Finally, the Rev field shows the storage array's firmware revisions. In this case, it is 0326 which, for the CX family, means FLARE code 26.

Then, in the second line of the log output, the device type is identified as Type: 0x0, which means Direct Access Block Device. Table 7.3 shows the list of common device types you might encounter in the vSphere 5 environment.

Table 7.3 Common Device Types

Device Type	Description
0x0	Direct access block device
0x1	Sequential access device (for example, tape drive)
0x3	Processor device
0x4	Write-once device
0x5	CD/DVD device
0x8	Tape library

The next field listed is ANSI rev, which is the SCSI standard supported by the device. In this case the value is 4, which means a later revision of SCSI-3 (for example, SAM-2—see Chapter 2 for more details). The last field is TPGS, which is 0 in this example and means that the device does not support Asymmetric Logical Unit Access (ALUA—see Chapter 6, "ALUA").

The third line in the log shows `Add path: vmhba2:C0:T0:L0`, which means that the path to LUN0 on target 0 via vmhba2 has been added.

These three lines repeat for the second path to LUN0 on target 1 via vmhba2 as well as for LUN1 via the same HBA and two targets.

The log entry for paths to the same two LUNs via the second HBA in this host (shown in Figure 7.10) are similar to Figure 7.9 with the difference being that the HBA is vmhba3.

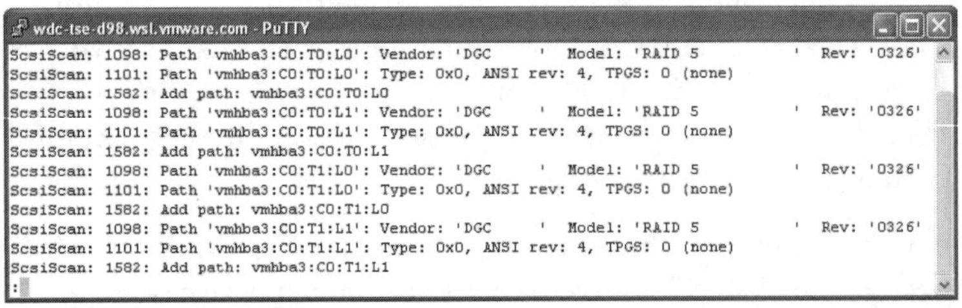

Figure 7.10 Log entries showing continuation of new paths and additional events

Finally, all discovered paths are claimed by NMP as shown in Figure 7.11.

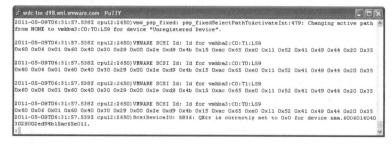

```
wdc-tse-d98.wsl.vmware.com - PuTTY
2011-07-10T16:05:18.830Z cpu3:2617)ScsiPath: 4541: Plugin 'NMP' claimed path 'vmhba3:C0:T1:L0'
2011-07-10T16:05:18.830Z cpu3:2617)ScsiPath: 4541: Plugin 'NMP' claimed path 'vmhba3:C0:T1:L1'
2011-07-10T16:05:18.830Z cpu3:2617)ScsiPath: 4541: Plugin 'NMP' claimed path 'vmhba0:C0:T0:L0'
2011-07-10T16:05:18.830Z cpu3:2617)ScsiPath: 4541: Plugin 'NMP' claimed path 'vmhba3:C0:T0:L0'
2011-07-10T16:05:18.830Z cpu3:2617)ScsiPath: 4541: Plugin 'NMP' claimed path 'vmhba3:C0:T0:L1'
2011-07-10T16:05:18.830Z cpu3:2617)ScsiPath: 4541: Plugin 'NMP' claimed path 'vmhba2:C0:T1:L0'
2011-07-10T16:05:18.830Z cpu3:2617)ScsiPath: 4541: Plugin 'NMP' claimed path 'vmhba2:C0:T1:L1'
2011-07-10T16:05:18.830Z cpu3:2617)ScsiPath: 4541: Plugin 'NMP' claimed path 'vmhba2:C0:T0:L0'
2011-07-10T16:05:18.831Z cpu3:2617)ScsiPath: 4541: Plugin 'NMP' claimed path 'vmhba2:C0:T0:L1'
2011-07-10T16:05:18.831Z cpu3:2617)ScsiPath: 4541: Plugin 'NMP' claimed path 'vmhba1:C1:T0:L0'
```

Figure 7.11   NMP claiming discovered paths

NOTE

The log entries in Figure 7.11 also include paths to locally attached LUNs that were claimed by VMW_SATP_Local, which are

vmhba0:C0:T0:L0—CD-ROM drive

vmhba1:C1:T0:L0—Local disk

After all paths to a given device have been enumerated, PSA collapses all paths to that device so that the host identifies it as a single device with multiple paths. For this to be done successfully, that device must meet the following criteria:

- The device ID (for example, NAA ID, EUI, and so on) must be identical on all paths.
- The LUN number must be identical on all paths.

There are several factors that contribute to the required uniqueness of the device ID and the LUN number, such as Symmetrix FA Director Bits configuration and choice of host type in several storage arrays on VMware's HCL.

A sample log entry for enumerating a device ID is shown in Figure 7.12.

```
wdc-tse-d98.wsl.vmware.com - PuTTY
2011-05-09T06:31:57.538Z cpu12:2650)vmw_psp_fixed: psp_fixedSelectPathToActivateInt:479: Changing active path
from NONE to vmhba3:C0:T0:L59 for device "Unregistered Device".

2011-05-09T06:31:57.538Z cpu12:2650)VMWARE SCSI Id: Id for vmhba2:C0:T1:L59
0x60 0x06 0x01 0x60 0x40 0x30 0x29 0x00 0x2e 0xd9 0x4b 0x15 0xac 0x65 0xe0 0x11 0x52 0x41 0x49 0x44 0x20 0x35

2011-05-09T06:31:57.538Z cpu12:2650)VMWARE SCSI Id: Id for vmhba2:C0:T0:L59
0x60 0x06 0x01 0x60 0x40 0x30 0x29 0x00 0x2e 0xd9 0x4b 0x15 0xac 0x65 0xe0 0x11 0x52 0x41 0x49 0x44 0x20 0x35

2011-05-09T06:31:57.538Z cpu12:2650)VMWARE SCSI Id: Id for vmhba3:C0:T1:L59
0x60 0x06 0x01 0x60 0x40 0x30 0x29 0x00 0x2e 0xd9 0x4b 0x15 0xac 0x65 0xe0 0x11 0x52 0x41 0x49 0x44 0x20 0x35

2011-05-09T06:31:57.538Z cpu12:2650)VMWARE SCSI Id: Id for vmhba3:C0:T0:L59
0x60 0x06 0x01 0x60 0x40 0x30 0x29 0x00 0x2e 0xd9 0x4b 0x15 0xac 0x65 0xe0 0x11 0x52 0x41 0x49 0x44 0x20 0x35
2011-05-09T06:31:57.539Z cpu12:2650)ScsiDeviceIO: 5836: QErr is correctly set to 0x0 for device naa.6006016040
3029002ed94b15ac65e011.
```

Figure 7.12   Enumerating device ID log entries

In this example, the PSP that claimed the device (here it is VMW_PSP_FIXED) activates the first path to the device (changing active path from NONE to vmhba3:C0:T0:L59).

The four lines that follow the path activation entry are for all four paths to the device listing the device ID `Id for vmhba...`). The bytes of the ID are listed in hexadecimal values. In this example, the ID is the first 16 bytes (the first 16 hex values in Listing 7.1 that are highlighted).

This translates to NAA ID `naa.60060160403029002ed94b15ac65e011`. The remaining 6 bytes map into ACSII characters RAID 5. The last line in Figure 7.12 shows the device ID as `naa.60060160403029002ed94b15ac65e011`, which matches the 16 bytes that I highlighted in Listing 7.1.

Listing 7.1 Locating NAA ID in Inquiry Response

```
0x60 0x06 0x01 0x60 0x40 0x30 0x29 0x00 0x2e 0xd9 0x4b 0x15 0xac 0x65 0xe0
0x11 0x52 0x41 0x49 0x44 0x20 0x35
```

To list all paths to a given device, you may run

```
esxcfg-mpath --list-paths
```

You can also use the shorthand option -b instead of --list-paths:

```
esxcfg-mpath -b
```

An example of the output is shown in Figure 7.13.

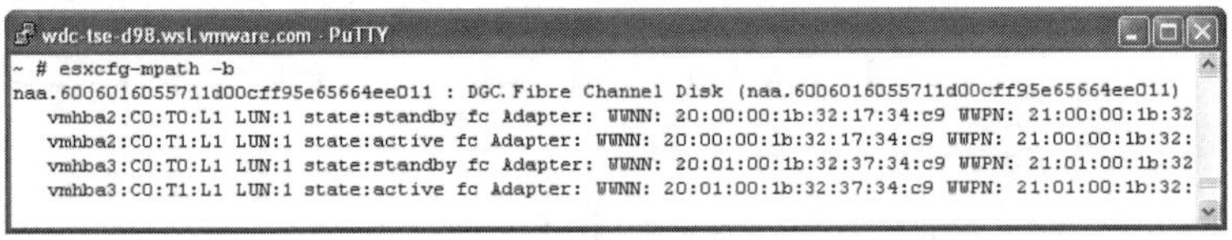

Figure 7.13 Listing paths to a LUN

The output in Figure 7.13 shows all four paths to LUN1 that I used in Figure 7.10. Here you see the discovered paths grouped under the LUN's device ID, which is the NAA ID in this case. Because that LUN has the same number (LUN1) and the same NAA ID on all four paths, they are collapsed to a single LUN with four paths. If there were a misconfiguration on the array where the device has a different LUN number, even though the device may have the same device ID, the paths would not have been collapsed in this fashion. The same is true if the device is assigned a different device ID on different targets, which would result in identifying it as a different device based on the device ID. In other words, assume the NAA ID on target 0 on vmhba2 and vmhba3 is different from that assigned on target 1 on vmhba2 and vmhba3; the result identifies the LUN as two different LUNs with two paths each.

Factors Affecting Multipathing

Several factors play important roles in the functionality of multipathing. Among these factors are the following VMkernel Advanced Settings:

- **Disk.MaxLUN**—The default value is 256 and cannot be larger than that value. When a rescan is issued, this is the maximum LUN number that is scanned on each target. So, counting from LUN0, the maximum LUN number is LUN255. As a result, LUNs presented with numbers higher than 255 are not discovered by vSphere 5.0 hosts.

> **NOTE**
>
> The maximum number of paths usable by any vSphere 5.0 host is 1024 (this applies to earlier releases as well). So, if the host is equipped with two HBAs and each of them is zoned to two targets on a storage array, the total number of paths per LUN presented from that array is four. If the array presents 256 LUNs to this host, the total number of paths is 1024 (4 paths x 256 LUNs).
>
> Depending on your design requirements, you must consider this fact when deciding on the number of LUNs presented to vSphere 5.0 hosts. In other words, if you plan to use more initiators or more targets per host, the maximum number of LUNs decreases. Also consider the paths to local devices on the host. Even though multipathing is not supported with these devices, paths to them reduce the number of paths available for SAN-attached devices.

- **Disk.SupportSparseLUN**—This is a legacy setting carried over from releases as old as ESX 1.5. The parameter listed next, when enabled, negates the need for using this one regardless of its value. Sparse LUN is the case where there is a gap in the LUN number in the sequence of discovered LUNs. For example, you have an array that presents to your host LUN numbers 0–10 and then skips the next nine LUNs so that the next group of LUN numbers is LUN 20–255. When this option is set to 0, the host stops scanning for LUNs beyond LUN10 because LUN11 is missing. It does not continue to scan for higher LUN numbers. When this option is enabled (set to 1), which is the default setting, the host continues to scan for the next LUN number until it is done with all 256 LUN numbers. Imagine what this would do to the host's boot time if it has to wait until each LUN number is scanned compounded by the number of HBAs. That is the reason why VMware introduced the next parameter (Disk.UseReportLUN).

- **Disk.UseReportLUN**—This parameter is enabled by default (set to 1). It enables the use of the command `ReportLUN`, which is sent to all targets, and the storage array should respond with the list of LUN numbers presented to the initiators in this host. This means that the host no longer needs to scan for each LUN number individually. This improves both the boot time as well as scan time. This is the only command filtered when the guest SCSI commands are passed through to the mapped LUN, which will be discussed in more detail in Chapter 13, "Virtual Disks and RDMs."

How to Access Advanced Options

To access VMKernel advanced options, follow this procedure:

1. To view or modify the advanced options that were covered in this section, among others that I discuss throughout this book, use the vSphere 5.0 Client. Log on to the vSphere host directly or via vCenter Server, and then navigate to the Configuration tab as shown in Figure 7.14.

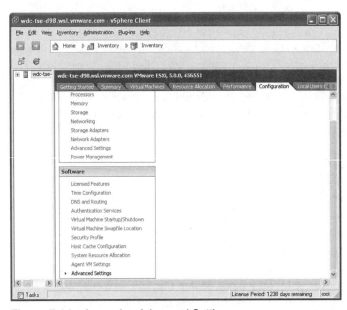

Figure 7.14   Accessing Advanced Settings

2. At the bottom of the Software section, click the **Advanced Settings** link. The screen shown in Figure 7.15 displays.

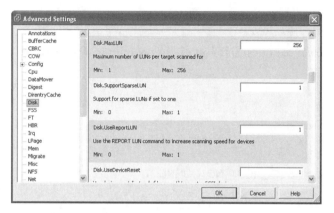

Figure 7.15   Advanced Settings

3. In the left-hand side pane, select **Disk**.

4. In the right-hand side pane, scroll down until you see the field **Disk.MaxLUN**. The three settings I discussed earlier are listed here. When done viewing the settings, click **Cancel** to close the dialog.

NOTE

Changing these options does not require rebooting for the changes to take effect.

Failover Triggers

Under normal conditions, I/O is sent on the current path until certain SCSI events occur that trigger path failover. These triggers differ depending on whether the storage array is Active/Active or Active/Passive.

SCSI Sense Codes

Before I go into the actual list of triggers, let me give you a quick primer on SCSI sense codes. Devices communicate with nodes on the SAN by sending specific hexadecimal strings that are either in response to a command or a hardware event.

The structure of the sense codes is as follow (as seen in vmkernel logs entries):

```
H:<value> D:<value> P:<value> Valid sense data <a set of 3 hexadecimal
  values>
```

- **H**—Comes from the host (initiator) and provides the host status (see Table 7.4).

  Table 7.4 provides common sense codes that you might encounter while sifting through the vSphere host logs.

Table 7.4 Host Status Codes

Code	Meaning
0x0	SCSI_HOST_OK
0x1	SCSI_HOST_NO_CONNECT
0x2	SCSI_HOST_BUS_BUSY
0x3	SCSI_HOST_TIMEOUT
0x4	SCSI_HOST_BAD_TARGET
0x5	SCSI_HOST_ABORT
0x6	SCSI_HOST_PARITY
0x7	SCSI_HOST_ERROR
0x8	SCSI_HOST_RESET
0x9	SCSI_HOST_BAD_INTR
0xA	SCSI_HOST_PASSTHROUGH
0xB	SCSI_HOST_SOFT_ERROR

- **D**—Comes from the device and provides the device status (see Table 7.5).

Table 7.5 Device Status Codes

Code	Meaning
0x0	No errors
0x2	Check condition
0x8	Device busy
0x18	Device reserved by another host

- **P**—Comes from the PSA plug-in and provides the plug-in status.

- **The set of three hexadecimal values are broken into the following:**

  - SCSI sense key (see Table 7.6).

Table 7.6 SCSI Sense Key

Code	Meaning
0x0	There is no sense information.
0x1	Last command completed successfully but used error correction in the process.
0x2	The addressed LUN is not ready to be accessed.
0x3	The target detected a data error on the medium.
0x4	The target detected a hardware error during a command or self-tests.
0x5	ILLEGAL_REQUEST. Either the command or the parameter list contains an error.
0x6	The LUN has been reset (bus reset of medium change).
0x7	Access to the data is blocked.
0x8	Reached an unexpected written or unwritten region of the medium.
0xA	COPY, COMPARE, or COPY AND VERIFY was aborted.
0xB	The target aborted the command.
0xC	Comparison for SEARCH DATA was unsuccessful.
0xD	The medium is full.
0xE	Source and data on the medium do not agree.

- Additional Sense Code (ASC) and Additional Sense Code Qualifier (ASCQ) are always reported in pairs. Sometimes these codes and the sense key are preceded by "Possible sense data" instead of "Valid sense data." (See Table 7.7.)

Table 7.7   Additional Sense Code (ASC)/Additional Sense Code Qualifier (ASCQ) Combinations

ASC	ASCQ	Meaning
0x4	0x2	LOGICAL Unit NOT READY—INITIALIZING COMMAND REQUIRED
0x5	0x3	LOGICAL Unit NOT READY—MANUAL INTERVENTION REQUIRED
0x29	0x0	POWER ON, RESET, OR BUS DEVICE RESET OCCURRED
0x29	0x2	BUS RESET OCCURRED
0x29	0x3	DEVICE RESET OCCURRED
Vendor-Specific Codes (IBM FAStT/DS4000 example)		
0x8B	0x2	QUIESCENCE HAS BEEN ACHIEVED
0x94	0x1	INVALID REQ DUE TO CURRENT LU OWNERSHIP

The combination of sense key, ASC, and ASCQ along with the host, device, and/or plug-in status would be translated to a specific SCSI event code. These codes are mostly standard across vendors with some vendor-specific codes that you might see along the way.

An example of a sense code is

```
H:0x0 D:0x2 P:0x0 Valid sense data: 0x5 0x20 0x0
```

These codes are listed on T10.org in a document named "SCSI Primary Commands - 3 (SPC-3)." Vendor-specific codes are available from the corresponding vendor.

> **NOTE**
>
> ASC and ASCQ values 0x80–0xFF are vendor specific.

Now, let's see the actual failover triggers!

Multipathing Failover Triggers

Table 7.8 lists the SCSI sense codes of events that trigger I/O path to failover to an alternate path. The columns A/P and A/A denote whether the code is relevant to Active/Active arrays or Active/Passive arrays.

Table 7.8 Path Failover Triggers

Host	Device	Key	ASC	ASCQ	A/P	A/A	Meaning
0x1	0x0	0x0	0x0	0x0	YES	YES	DID_NO_CONNECT
0x0	0x2	0x2	0x4	0x3	YES	NO	LOGICAL UNIT NOT READY - MEDIUM ERROR
0x0	0x2	0x2	0x4	0xA	YES	NO	LOGICAL UNIT NOT READY—AAS TRANSITION
0x0	0x2	0x5	0x4	0x3	YES	NO	ILLEGAL REQUEST - LOGICAL UNIT NOT READY
0x0	0x2	0x5	0x94	0x1	YES	NO	ILLEGAL REQUEST— DUE TO CURRENT LU OWNERSHIP
0x7	0x0	0x0	0x0	0x0	YES	NO	DID_ERROR (CLARiiON SP Hung)

Table 7.8 shows all the SCSI events that would trigger a path failover. I explain each of them separately. I did not list the plug-in status because it is 0x0 in all combinations listed.

- **DID_NO_CONNECT**—When the initiator loses connectivity to the SAN (for example, cable disconnected, Switch port disabled, bad cable, bad GBIC, and so on), the HBA driver reports this error. It looks like the following in the /var/log/vmkernel.log file:

  ```
  vmhba2:C0:T1:L0" H:0x1 D:0x0 P:0x0 Possible sense data 0x0 0x0 0x0
  ```

  This means that the Host status is 0x1, which matches the first row in Table 7.8.

- **LOGICAL UNIT NOT READY**—SATP claiming the device monitors the hardware state of the physical paths to the device. Part of that process, for Active/Passive arrays, is that it sends SCSI command Check_Unit_Ready to the device on all paths. Under normal conditions, the array would respond with READY for the device on all targets on the Active SP. The passive SP would respond with LOGICAL_UNIT_NOTREADY. The SATP interprets these responses to mean that the LUN is accessible from the targets that responded with READY. If, for whatever reason, the LUN used to be READY on a certain target but now it returns NOTREADY, the I/O cannot be sent there and a path failover must be done to a target that returns UNIT_READY in response to the Check_Unit_Ready command (CUR for short).

There are two possible sense codes that fall under this category: MEDIUM_ERROR or AAS TRANSITION

The MEDIUM_ERROR sense code looks like this:

```
vmhba2:C0:T1:L0" H:0x0 D:0x2 P:0x0 Valid Sense Data 0x2 0x4 0x3
```

This matches the second row in Table 7.8. This means that the LUN needs manual intervention.

AAS TRANSITION (Asymmetric Access State Transition)—which I discuss in Chapter 6—is when a target port group is transitioning from Active Optimized (AO) to Active Non Optimized (ANO) or vice versa. The sense code would look like this:

```
vmhba2:C0:T1:L0" H:0x0 D:0x2 P:0x0 Valid sense data 0x2 0x4 0xA
```

This is interpreted by the SATP to mean that I/O cannot be sent there and that a path failover must be done.

This matches the third row in Table 7.8.

- **ILLEGAL REQUEST - LOGICAL UNIT NOT READY**—The sense code for this looks like this:

```
vmhba2:C0:T1:L0" H:0x0 D:0x2 P:0x0 Valid Sense Data 0x5 0x4 0x3
```

This looks like the MEDIUM_ERROR listed earlier with the difference that the sense key is 0x5 instead of 0x2. It means that the LUN is not ready and that a manual intervention is required. Until this is done, the path should be failed over to another target that returns UNIT_READY in response to the CUR command.

This matches the fourth row in Table 7.8.

- **ILLEGAL REQUEST—DUE TO CURRENT LU OWNERSHIP**—This is different from the illegal request in the previous sense code. This one means that a command or an I/O was sent to a LUN via a target that does not own the LUN (that is, via the passive SP). The sense code looks like this:

```
vmhba2:C0:T1:L0" H:0x0 D:0x2 P:0x0 Valid Sense Data 0x5 0x94 0x1
```

This is specific to arrays made by LSI (acquired recently by NetApp) that are OEMed by IBM as FAStT and DS4000 series as well as by SUN as StorageTek series. These arrays have a feature referred to as Auto Volume Transfer (AVT). This feature, when enabled, enables LUNs owned by one of the storage processors to be automatically transferred to the passive SP to allow I/O processed through it. This simulates Active/Active configuration. However, this is not the recommended configuration for use with vSphere as it may result in a path thrashing condition (see Chapter 6, "ALUA," section "Scenario 2 in ALUA Followover"). So, with AVT disabled as recommended, I/O can only be processed via the active SP. When I/O is sent to the passive SP, this sense code is returned to the initiator.

TIP

An easy way to identify which arrays belong to this group (OEMed from LSI) is to check the SATP claim rules for devices claimed by VMW_SATP_LSI. You can check for these claim rules using the following command:

```
esxcli storage nmp satp rule list --satp VMW_SATP_LSI
```

You may also use the shorthand option -s instead of --satp:

```
esxcli storage nmp satp rule list -s VMW_SATP_LSI
```

- **DID_ERROR**—The last sense code on the list is DID_ERROR, which looks like this in the logs:

  ```
  vmhba2:C0:T1:L0" H:0x7 D:0x0 P:0x0 Possible Sense Data 0x0 0x0 0x0
  ```

  This sense code was added to handle a special case where an EMC CLARiiON array exhibits a storage processor hang. When this sense code is reported, the SATP issues additional commands to the peer SP to check with it about the status of the problematic SP. If the peer SP fails in getting a response from the problematic one, the SATP marks the latter as hung/dead and proceeds with the path failover process.

NOTE

It is possible to see this sense code in configurations with storage arrays other than the CLARiiON series. However, do not interpret it to be the same as I listed earlier. You should investigate it further.

Path States

Paths to storage devices are constantly monitored by the SATP plug-ins that claimed them. SATP plug-ins report to NMP these changes and the latter acts accordingly.

A path can be in one of the following states:

- **Active (also known as "On")**—The path is connected to the storage network and is functional. This is the normal state for all paths to targets on an Active SP. For Active/Active array configuration, all paths to the array should be in this state. Compared to Active/Passive array configuration where half the paths would be in this state if configured according to VMware's best practices.

- **Standby (formerly known as "On" in releases prior to 3.5)**—The path is connected to the storage network and is functional. This is the normal state for all paths to targets on a Passive SP. These would be the remaining half of the paths to an Active/Passive array that I mentioned in the previous bullet.

- **Dead**—The HBA lost connectivity to the Storage Network, or the target to which it is zoned is unreachable. This can be due to several factors including

  - **Cable unplugged from the HBA port**—This would show in the logs as a "loop down" error and sense code DID_NO_CONNECT.

  - **Cable unplugged from the SP port**—In this case you would not see the "loop down" error because the HBA still has a valid connection to the storage network.

  - **Bad connection** (defective GBIC, fibre cable, or Ethernet cable)—When the connection is lost, this is similar to "Cable unplugged from the HBA port."

  - **Defective switch port**—When the connection is lost, this is similar to "Cable unplugged from the HBA port."

Factors Affecting Paths States

There are several factors affecting paths states, which are covered in this section.

Disk.PathEvalTime

The Fibre Channel path state is evaluated at a fixed interval or when there is an I/O error. The path evaluation interval is defined via the advanced configuration option Disk. PathEvalTime in seconds. The default value is 300 seconds. This means that the path state is evaluated every 5 minutes unless an error is reported sooner on that path, in which case the path state might change depending on the interpretation of the reported error.

Figure 7.16 shows the Advanced Settings dialog where you select **Disk** in the sections listed in the left-hand side pane and the option is listed on the top right-hand side pane.

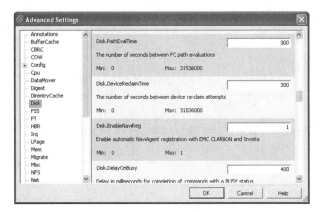

Figure 7.16 Disk.PathEvalTime Advanced settings

Reducing this value might result in faster path state detection. However, this is not advisable on a storage area network (SAN) that is changing frequently. You need to give the fabric enough time to converge to avoid unnecessary path failover due to transient events.

QLogic HBA Driver Options

QLogic FC HBA driver provides two options that control how soon the driver reports a DID_NO_CONNECT to VMkernel.

These options are visible in the QLogic proc node, which is usually at /proc/scsi/<qlogic-driver>/<n>, where <n> is the device number listed in the proc node.

To list these options and their current values, run the following command:

```
fgrep down /proc/scsi/qla2xxx/*
/proc/scsi/qla2xxx/7:Link down Timeout = 030
/proc/scsi/qla2xxx/7:Port down retry = 005
/proc/scsi/qla2xxx/8:Link down Timeout = 030
/proc/scsi/qla2xxx/8:Port down retry = 005
```

This example is for a QLogic HBA that uses driver named qla2xxx. The output shows two HBAs—number 7 and 8—and the options are

- **Link down timeout**—Default value is 30 seconds. This setting specifies the number of seconds vmkernel waits for a link down to come up. This does not affect the failover time in vSphere 5.

- **Port down retry**—Default value is 5 seconds. This setting specifies the number of seconds vmkernel waits to retry a command to a port returning port-down status.

The time it takes for VMkernel to failover to an alternate path after receiving a DID_NO_CONNECT is calculated by the following formula:

```
"Port down retry" value + 5
```

Based on the default values, the failover time is 10 seconds. In older releases of vSphere, the formula was different and the default value was 30 with failover time of 60 seconds.

> **NOTE**
>
> The equivalent option for Emulex drivers is devloss_tmo with the default value of 10 seconds. Total failover time is 10 seconds as well.
>
> There is no need to modify this setting or the QLogic driver's setting as 10 seconds failover time is sufficient in most cases.

Path Selection Plug-ins

Path Selection Plug-ins (PSPs) play a major role in failover as their main job is to select which path is used for sending I/O to the device. Depending on the PSP, failover activities vary.

VMW_PSP_FIXED

This PSP honors the preferred path setting. I/O is sent to paths marked as preferred until they become unavailable. At that time, PSP selects another path. When the preferred path becomes available, I/O fails back to it. vSphere 4.1 provided an additional plug-in—VMW_PSP_FIXED_AP—that allowed Active/Passive arrays to be configured with the preferred path option without the risk of path thrashing when used with ALUA storage arrays. The functionality of that plug-in was merged into the VMW_PSP_FIXED plug-in on vSphere 5. This would explain why several ALUA arrays now default to VMW_PSP_FIXED on vSphere 5.

VMW_PSP_MRU

This PSP ignores the preferred path setting. I/O is sent to the most recently used path that is known to work. If that path becomes unavailable, PSP selects another path to the active SP. The I/O continues to the newly selected path until it becomes unavailable.

VMW_PSP_RR

This Round Robin PSP rotates I/O to all paths to the Active SP or SP port groups that are in AO (Active Optimized) state. The rotation depends on two configurations that control the number and the size of I/O sent to the device before switching to another path.

When and How to Change the Default PSP

I discuss default PSP in Chapter 5. There I show you how to list the default PSP for each SATP. (See Figure 5.28 in the "SATP Claim Rules" section in Chapter 5.)

To recap, each SATP is configured with a default PSP as identified by the output of

```
esxcli storage nmp satp list
```

In most cases, the default configuration is sufficient. However, some storage vendors develop their own SATPs and PSPs, which require modifying the default rules for the ESXi host to take advantage of what these plug-ins have to offer. The corresponding partner provides its own documentation on how to configure the environment for its plug-ins.

In this section I show you how to make such changes and when to do it.

When Should You Change the Default PSP?

The most common use case for changing the default PSP is when you want to utilize Round Robin failover policy (VMW_PSP_RR). Although VMware supports this policy with all arrays listed on its HCL, you must check with the storage vendor before making such a change. These vendors also have documentation about specific configurations that I highlight next.

NOTE

Round Robin PSP is not supported by VMware with virtual machines (VMs) configured with MSCS (Microsoft Clustering Services, also known as Microsoft Windows Failover Clustering).

For more information, see Chapter 5.

How to Change the Default PSP

In Chapter 5, I show you how to change the PSP for a given LUN via the UI. Here, I show you how to change the default PSP for a family of arrays. As I explain in Chapter 5, the default PSPs are associated with specific SATPs. The SATP claim rules decide which array is claimed by which SATP and, in turn, which default PSP is used. So the premise of changing the default PSP is to create a PSA claim rule that associates a specific PSP with a SATP.

The example in the following listing changes the default PSP to VMW_PSP_RR for storage arrays claimed by SATP VMW_SATP_CX:

```
esxcli storage nmp satp set --default-psp VMW_PSP_RR --satp VMW_SATP_CX

Default PSP for VMW_SATP_CX is now VMW_SATP_RR
```

Run the following command to list the default PSPs and verify that the previous command has done its job:

```
esxcli storage nmp satp list
```

The output of this command is shown in Figure 7.17.

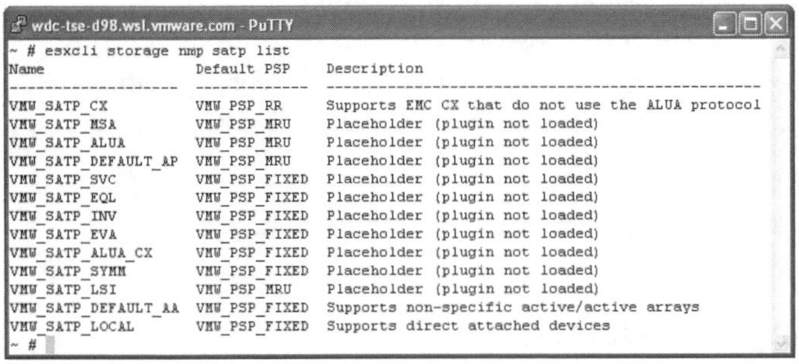

Figure 7.17   Listing default PSPs

Changing the default PSP does not apply to LUNs already discovered and claimed by other PSPs. You need to reboot the host for this to take effect.

To verify that the change took effect for a certain device, run this command:

```
esxcli storage nmp device list --device <device-ID>
```

You may also use the shorthand option -d instead of --device:

```
esxcli storage nmp device list -d <device-ID>
```

An example of the command and its output is shown in Figure 7.18.

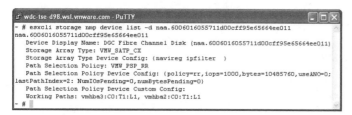

Figure 7.18   RR PSP changes took effect after reboot

Part of the output in Figure 7.18 shows the Path Selection Policy Device Config options. Table 7.9 lists these options and their corresponding values:

Table 7.9   PSP Device Config Options

Option	Value	Comments
Policy	rr	Current policy is RR because VMW_PSP_RR is in use.
Iops	1000	This is the default setting. I/O stays on one of the working paths (see the "Where Is the Active Path?" section earlier in this chapter) until 1,000 IOPS are sent, and then it switches the I/O to the next working path.
Bytes	10485760	This is the default setting. I/O stays on one of the working paths until 10485760 bytes are sent and switch the I/O to the next working path.
useANO	0	This is the default. With ALUA configuration, I/O is *not* sent to target port group in an Active-Non-Optimized state.
lastPathIndex	varies	The value listed here is the path number through which the I/O was last sent. So, if there are two active paths (1 and 2) and are based on the output in Figure 7.20, the current path in use is path 2; the next path to be used is path 1.
NumIOsPending	varies	This value list the number of I/Os pending at the time the output was collected.
numBytesPending	varies	This value lists the number of bytes pending at the time the output was collected.

LUN1 that I used in this example actually has four paths. However, because two of these paths are active and the other two are standby, only the two active paths are used by the Round Robin policy (see Figure 7.19).

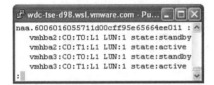

```
wdc-tse-d98.wsl.vmware.com - Pu...
naa.6006016055711d00cff95e65664ee011 :
    vmhba2:C0:T0:L1 LUN:1 state:standby
    vmhba2:C0:T1:L1 LUN:1 state:active
    vmhba3:C0:T0:L1 LUN:1 state:standby
    vmhba3:C0:T1:L1 LUN:1 state:active
:
```

Figure 7.19 Listing paths to LUN1

If this LUN were configured on an ALUA array, the two active paths would have been to a target port group in AO state and the two standby paths would have been to a target port group in ANO state. The end result would have been the same because the option useANO is set to 0.

PDL and APD

Careful designs that provide storage availability components (see Chapters 2 and 4) should prevent complete loss of connectivity to the shared storage. However, there are some uncommon situations where this might occur (for example, accidental zoning changes that result in loss of access to the originally available storage targets or storage array processors being rebooted simultaneously). Upon rescanning, these situations result in a state referred to as All Paths Down (APD). As a result, access to the affected LUNs is lost and, as a side effect, other LUNs might become unresponsive for a limited period of time or permanently. vSphere 5 and earlier releases do not support this state. However, beginning with vSphere 4.0 Update 3 and 4.1 Update 1, VMware introduced some changes that aimed to help handle such a state gracefully. vSphere 5 improved on these changes and future releases are planned to improve on it even further.

In most cases, the events leading to the APD state are transient. However, if they are not, they result in a state referred to as Permanent Device Loss (PDL). The most common examples of such events are LUN removal by either deleting the LUN on the storage array or unmapping it (unmasking). When this happens, the storage array would return to the ESXi host a specific PDL error for each path to the removed LUN. Such an error is reported as a SCSI sense code (see the "SCSI Sense Codes" section earlier in the chapter in the "Failover Triggers" section).

An example of a PDL sense code is 0x5 0x25 0x00 Logical Unit Not Supported.

In an ideal situation, vSphere administrators would get an advance warning from the storage administrators that a device (LUN) is being removed permanently from the set of LUNs presented to a given ESXi 5 host. If this is the case, you should follow these steps to prepare for this PDL:

1. Unmount the VMFS volume.

2. Detach the device (LUN).

Unmounting a VMFS Volume

Assuming that you have already used Storage VMotion or have manually moved the files on the VMFS datastore to be unmounted to their new VMFS datastore(s), you are ready to unmount the datastore on the device that is planned to be decommissioned.

You can complete the unmount operation via the UI or the CLI.

Unmounting a VMFS Datastore via the UI

You need to first verify that the datastore you plan to unmount is on the LUN that is planned to be removed.

1. Log on to the vSphere 5.0 host directly as a root user or to the vCenter server that manages the host using the VMware vSphere 5.0 Client as a user with Administrator privileges.

2. While in the Inventory—Hosts and Clusters view, locate the vSphere 5.0 host in the inventory tree and select it.

3. Navigate to the **Configuration** tab.

4. Under the **Hardware** section, select the **Storage** option

5. Under the **View** field, click the **Datastores** button.

6. Locate the VMFS datastore under the Datastores pane. To verify that it is on the LUN to be decommissioned, click the **Properties** link on the top-right corner of the Datastore Details pane as shown in Figure 7.20.

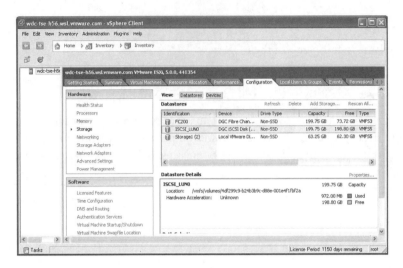

Figure 7.20　Listing the datastore to be unmounted

7. Click the **Manage Paths** button. (See Figure 7.21.)

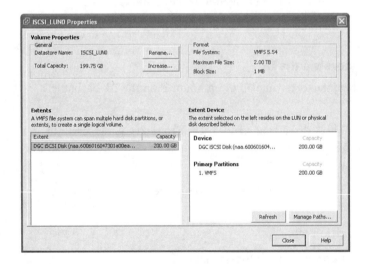

Figure 7.21　Listing properties of a datastore to be unmounted

8. The LUN number is listed under the Runtime Name (shown in Figure 7.22) vmhba34:C0:T0:L0 with an L prefix. In this example, it is L0, which means LUN0.

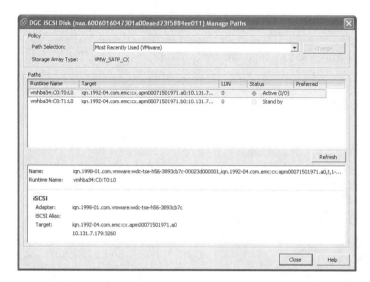

Figure 7.22   Listing paths to an iSCSI LUN

Now that you have verified that you are dealing with the correct datastore, proceed with unmounting it.

Click **Close** on each of the previous two dialogs. Right-click the datastore and select the **Unmount** option. This can be done on VMFS3 and VMFS5 volumes (see Figure 7.23).

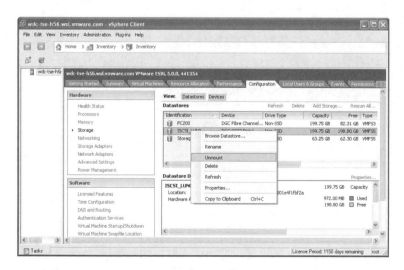

Figure 7.23   Unmounting a datastore via UI

9. If you get the dialog shown in Figure 7.24, it means that VM files are still on the datastore. Move the files to another datastore or unregister the related VM and retry the unmount operation. Acknowledge the confirmation by clicking **Next** and then **OK**.

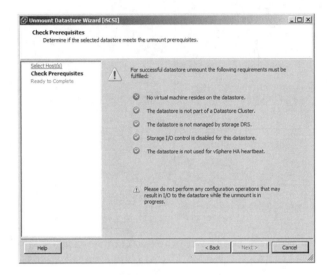

Figure 7.24   Datastore still has VMs files on it so you cannot proceed

A successful unmount operation results in the datastore being listed with grayed-out italic (see Figure 7.25).

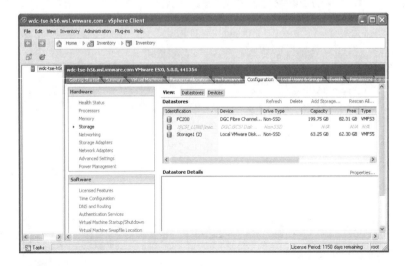

Figure 7.25   Datastore unmounted

This concludes the unmount operation. The next step is to detach the device (LUN).

TIP

To re-mount the datastore, right-click the grayed-out datastore and then select the **mount** option.

Unmounting a VMFS Datastore via the CLI

To unmount a VMFS datastore with the CLI, follow this procedure:

1. Connect to the ESXi 5 host via SSH as a root user or vMA 5.0 as vi-admin. (See Chapter 2 for details.)

2. Run the following command to verify the LUN number of the datastore you plan to unmount:

```
~ # vmkfstools --queryfs /vmfs/volumes/ISCSI_LUN0 |grep naa |sed 's/:.*$//'
```

You may also use the shorthand version of the command:

```
~ # vmkfstools -P /vmfs/volumes/ISCSI_LUN0 |grep naa |sed 's/:.*$//'
```

This returns the datastore's NAA ID and truncates the partition number from the output.

Use that ID to find the LUN number using the following:

```
~ # esxcli storage nmp device list --device naa.6006016047301a00eaed23f5884ee011 |grep Working
```

You may also use the shorthand version of the command:

```
~ # esxcli storage nmp device list -d naa.6006016047301a00eaed23f5884ee011 |grep Working
```

The output of these two commands is shown in Figure 7.26.

```
wdc-tse-h56.wsl.vmware.com - PuTTY
~ # vmkfstools -P /vmfs/volumes/ISCSI_LUN0 |grep naa |sed 's/:.*$//'
      naa.6006016047301a00eaed23f5884ee011
~ # esxcli storage nmp device list -d naa.6006016047301a00eaed23f5884ee011 |grep Working
  Working Paths: vmhba34:C0:T0:L0
~ #
```

Figure 7.26   Listing datastore's LUN

3. In this example, the LUN number is 0.

4. Proceed with unmounting the datastore using

```
esxcli storage filesystem unmount --volume-lable <datastore-name>
```

You may also use the shorthand option `-1` instead of `--volume-lable`:

```
esxcli storage filesystem unmount -1 <datastore-name>
```

The output is shown in Figure 7.27. Notice that if the command is successful, there is no status or feedback returned.

5. To verify that the datastore has been unmounted, run:

```
esxcli storage filesystem list
```

The output of this as well as the previous command is shown in Figure 7.27.

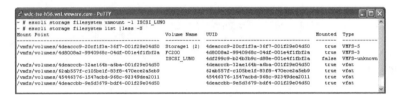

Figure 7.27 Unmounting datastore via CLI

The output shows that the Mounted status is false and that the mount point is blank. Notice that the Type shows VMFS-unknown because the volume is not mounted.

This concludes the unmount operation using the CLI.

TIP

To re-mount the datastore, repeat the command in Step 4 using `mount` instead of `unmount`.

Detaching the Device Whose Datastore Was Unmounted

In the previous procedure, you unmounted the datastore via the UI or the CLI. You are now ready to detach the device in preparation for removing it from the storage array by the storage administrator. You may accomplish this task via the vSphere 5 Client or the CLI.

Detaching a Device Using the vSphere 5 Client

Continuing with the example used for unmounting the datastore, now detach the LUN0 on vmhba34 as follows:

1. Using the vSphere 5 client navigate to the **Configuration** tab; then select the **Storage** link under the Hardware section and click the **Devices** button in the View section. (See Figure 7.28.)

Figure 7.28 Locating LUN to detach via UI

2. Right-click the device (vmhba34:C0:T0:L0) and then select the **Detach** option, as shown in Figure 7.29.

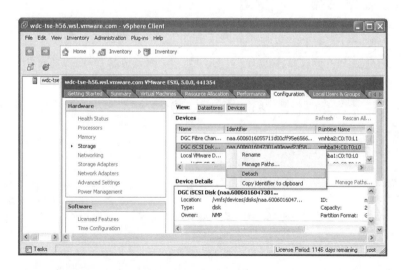

Figure 7.29 Detaching LUN via UI

3. You get the dialog shown in Figure 7.30. Select **OK** to continue.

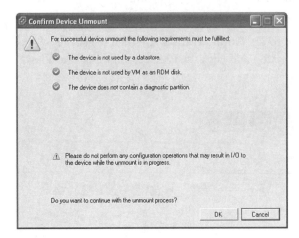

Figure 7.30   Confirming detach device

4. If you had not unmounted the datastore, you would have gotten the dialog shown in Figure 7.31 instead, and you cannot proceed until you unmount the datastore.

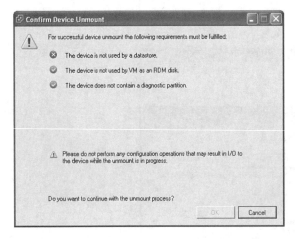

Figure 7.31   Device still has datastore mounted. Cannot proceed with detach

The host continues to "have knowledge" about the detached device until it is actually removed from the SAN and a rescan is done. In technical terms, the PSA does not "unclaim" the device, but the device state is off. The device continues to be listed in the UI as a grayed-out, italicized item in the devices list as shown in Figure 7.32.

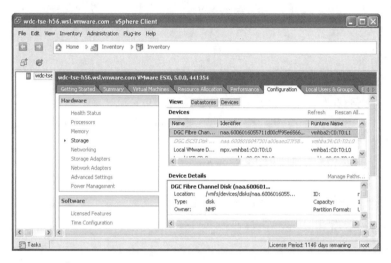

Figure 7.32   Device detached

If you need to reattach the device, simply right-click the device in the list and select the **Attach** option, as shown in Figure 7.33.

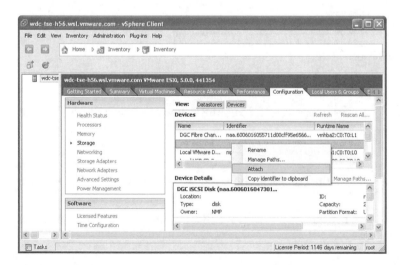

Figure 7.33   Reattaching a device

> **NOTE**
>
> Re-attaching a device does not automatically mount the datastore on that device. You must mount it manually as described in the tip at the end of the "Unmounting a VMFS Datastore via the UI" section.

Detaching a Device Using the CLI

To detach a device using the CLI, you need to know the device ID (NAA ID). Continuing with the example in the previous section, the device ID was located in Step 2 of the "Unmounting a Datastore Using the UI" section.

1. Run the following command to detach the device:

   ```
   ~ # esxcli storage core device set --state=off --device naa.6006016047
   301a00eaed23f5884ee011
   ```

   The shorthand version of this command is

   ```
   ~ # esxcli storage core device set --state=off -d naa.6006016047301a00
   eaed23f5884ee011
   ```

   The output for this command is shown in Figure 7.34.

Figure 7.34   Detaching device via CLI

2. To verify that the operation was successful, run the following command (also shown in Figure 7.34):

   ```
   ~ # esxcli storage core device detached list
   ```

   To reattach the device via the command line, repeat Step 1 using `--state=on` as follows:

   ```
   ~ # esxcli storage core device set --state=on --device naa.60060160473
   01a00eaed23f5884ee011
   ```

   The shorthand version of this command is

   ```
   ~ # esxcli storage core device set --state=on -d naa.6006016047301a00e
   aed23f5884ee011
   ```

NOTE

If the datastore was not unmounted prior to running the commands in Steps 1 and 2, you get no warning or errors via the command line and the datastore is unmounted automatically. If you reattach the device after doing so, the datastore is mounted automatically.

However, if the datastore was unmounted prior to detaching the device, reattaching it does not mount the datastore automatically.

Path Ranking

vSphere 4.1 and 5.0 provide a feature that enables you to rank the order the I/O is sent to the device over available paths when path failover is required. This feature is referred to as Path ranking. It is implemented differently in 5.0 compared to 4.1. It also works with ALUA arrays in a different fashion compared to non-ALUA arrays.

Path Ranking for ALUA and Non-ALUA Storage

In storage configurations using ALUA storage arrays (see Chapter 6), path selection is based on the Target Port Group AAS (Asymmetric Access State) which can be in one of the following states:

1. AO

2. ANO

3. Transitioning

4. Standby

To recap what I covered in Chapter 6, I/O can be sent to ports in AO state, and if none is available, I/O would be sent to ports in ANO state. If neither port group AAS are available, the last resort is to send the I/O to the ports in Standby AAS. So, as long as there are ports in AO AAS, I/O is sent only to these ports. However, when there is more than one port in the AO port group, there is no preference of to which port the I/O will be sent. If VMW_PSP_FIXED policy is used and a preferred path is set, the I/O will be sent to the preferred path. If the PREF bit is supported by and enabled on the ALUA array *and* a preferred LUN owner is set in the array configuration, the I/O will be sent to a target on the SP set as the preferred owner.

On the other hand, with non-ALUA Active/Passive storage arrays, when used by hosts configured with the VMW_PSP_MRU policy, the ports are in one of two modes: Active or Standby. With this policy, you cannot configure a "preferred path" and it is not recommended to use the VMW_PSP_FIXED policy because the arrays do not support ALUA. As an alternative and to facilitate ranking of these paths, VMware introduced a new PSP in vSphere 4.1, VMW_PSP_MRU_RANKED, which later got merged into VMW_PSP_MRU in vSphere 5.

How Does Path Ranking Work for ALUA Arrays?

Path Ranking allows vSphere Administrators to assign ranks to individual paths. The VMW_PSP_MRU plug-in goes through the Active path group state in the order I mentioned in the previous section (AO to ANO) and then to Standby and picks a path that has the highest rank for I/O.

It is important to note that as long as there are paths to ports in AO state, I/O is sent through them even when paths to ports in ANO or Standby AAS states are ranked higher.

In other words, the path selection is in this order:

1. Paths to ports in AO AAS based on the rank of each path.

2. If there are no ports in AO state, the paths to ports in ANO AAS state would be used based on the rank of each path.

3. Finally, if neither are available, the paths to ports in Standby AAS state are used based on the rank of each path.

In the output shown in Figure 7.35, notice the field named Group State in the properties of each path. Because the attached array is configured to support ALUA, one of the path Group States is active whereas the other is active unoptimized.

This is in contrast with the AAS, which is listed in the field named Storage Array Type Path Config, which are `TPG_state=AO` and `TPG_state=ANO` respectively, which also match their corresponding group state.

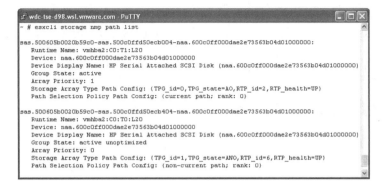

Figure 7.35   Listing paths to an ALUA LUN

Path Failover to a Ranked Path in ALUA Configuration

When an AO path with the highest rank becomes unavailable, the I/O fails over to the next highest ranked path to ports in AO state. If none is available, it fails over to the next highest ranked path to a port in ANO state and so on for Standby ports.

If all paths are ranked the same, VMW_PSP_MRU behaves as if ranking is not configured where it fails over to the next available path to a port in AO state, and if none is available, it fails over to a path to a port in ANO state and then a Standby state as detailed earlier in this chapter and in Chapters 5 and 6.

Path Failback to a Ranked Path in ALUA Configuration

VMW_PSP_MRU fails back to a better ranked path or path with a better state when such a path becomes available.

> **NOTE**
>
> This does not result in path thrashing because VMW_PSP_MRU never fails back to a path that requires activation (for example, AO to STANDBY or AO to ANO).

How Does Path Ranking Work for Non-ALUA Arrays?

VMW_PSP_MRU plug-in goes through the path Group States that are Active, and then if none are available, it goes through the path group states that are Standby. By default all paths are ranked 0, which results in I/O going through the normal MRU algorithm of path selection. When path rank values are set higher, only paths in an Active group state are used based on the rank order. The only time path ranks are used on Standby path group state is when paths on the Active group state are not available. See Figure 7.36 for an example of various paths' group states.

Figure 7.36   Listing paths to a non-ALUA LUN

In Figure 7.36, notice the field named Group State in the properties of each path. Because the attached array is Active/Passive and not configured to support ALUA, all path group states are either Active or Standby.

Notice that there are no values in the field Storage Array Type Path Config because the SATP is not an ALUA type, which is why the message SATP VMW_SATP_CX does not support path configuration is displayed.

Path Failover to a Ranked Path in Non-ALUA Configuration

When a path in an Active path group state with the highest rank becomes unavailable, the I/O fails over to the next highest ranked path in an Active path group state. If none is available, it fails over to the next highest ranked path in a Standby path group state. This triggers a trespass (on CLARiiON) or START_UNIT (on other Active/Passive arrays), which effectively transfers the LUN ownership to the formerly Passive SP, which would change the path Group State to Active.

Path Failback to a Ranked Path in Non-ALUA Configuration

VMW_PSP_MRU fails back to a better ranked path or path with a better state when such a path becomes available. This means that if the failover was to a path on an Active path group state, the failback is to the highest ranked path in an Active path group state.

Configuring Ranked Paths

Path ranking can be set via the CLI only. There is no UI available in vSphere 5 for this configuration.

Getting Path Rank

To get the path rank, run the following command:

```
esxcli storage nmp psp generic pathconfig get --path <pathname>
```

You may also use the shorthand version of the command using -p in place of --path:

```
esxcli storage nmp psp generic pathconfig get -p <pathname>
```

Example:

```
esxcli storage nmp psp generic pathconfig get -p fc.2000001b321734c9:210000
1b321734c9-fc.50060160c1e06522:5006016041e06522-naa.6006016055711d00cff95e6
5664ee011
```

Or using the runtime path name:

```
esxcli storage nmp psp generic pathconfig get -p vmhba2:C0:T0:L1
```

You get an output similar to Figure 7.37.

Figure 7.37   Listing path rank

Setting Path Rank

To set the rank of a given path, use the following command:

```
esxcli storage nmp psp generic pathconfig set --config "rank=<value>"
--path <pathname>
```

You may also use the shorthand version of the command using -c and -p in place of --config and --path, respectively:

```
esxcli storage nmp psp generic pathconfig set -c "rank=<value>" -p <path-
name>
```

Example using the physical path name:

```
esxcli storage nmp psp generic pathconfig set -c "rank=1" -p fc.2000001b321
734c9:2100001b321734c9-fc.50060160c1e06522:5006016041e06522-naa.60060160557
11d00cff95e65664ee011
```

Example using the runtime path name:

```
esxcli storage nmp psp generic pathconfig set -c "rank=1" -p
vmhba2:C0:T0:L1
```

This sets the rank to 1 for the path listed. The higher the value, the higher the rank is. After setting the rank, run the get command, listed earlier in this chapter in the "Getting Path Rank" section, to verify that it has been successfully set (see Figure 7.38).

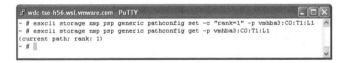

Figure 7.38   Setting path rank value

TIP

Using VMW_PSP_MRU with ALUA arrays or non-ALUA Active/Passive arrays with ranked paths enables you to set something similar to a preferred path without having to use the VMW_PSP_FIXED plug-in. You may think of this as having multiple preferred paths but with different weights.

Summary

This chapter covered multipathing and failover algorithms and provided details about failover triggers as well as factors affecting multipathing and failover. I also covered improvements introduced in vSphere 5 to better handle the APD state. Finally, it covered the little-known path ranking feature, including how it works and how to configure it.

## Chapter 8

Third-Party Multipathing I/O Plug-ins

VMware Pluggable Storage Architecture (PSA) is designed to be modular and be a foundation for VMware Storage partners to port their MPIO (Multipathing and I/O) software to run on ESXi. In this chapter I cover in some detail the MPIO plug-ins certified with vSphere 5 as of the time of this writing. In this chapter, I will provide you with an overview of each package supported by vSphere 5 and some insights into what goes on behind the scenes on ESXi after they are installed and configured. This is in no way intended to replace or substitute each package's documentation available from their corresponding vendor.

MPIO Implementations on vSphere 5

VMware Storage partners have the choice of delivering their MPIO software in one of the following formats:

- **MPP (Multipathing Plugin)** — These plug-ins run on top of PSA framework side-by-side with NMP (VMware's Native Multipathing Plugin). They may include other components that vary from partner to partner. An example of an MPP is EMC PowerPath/VE.

- **PSP (Path Selection Plugin)** —These plug-ins run on top of NMP side-by-side with other PSP already included with vSphere 5. This type of plug-in, too, may include other components that vary from partner to partner. An example of a PSP MPIO is Dell Equallogic DELL_EQL_PSP_ROUTED plug-in.

- **A combination of both PSP and SATP (Storage Array Type Plugin)** — An example is the combination of Hitachi HTI_PSP_HDLM_EXLBK, HTI_PSP_HDLM_EXLIO, HTI_PSP_HDLM_EXRR and HTI_SATP_HDLM plug-ins.

EMC PowerPath/VE 5.7

PowerPath/VE has been updated to run on ESXi 5. The certified version as of this writing is 5.7.0.00.00-b173.

As I mentioned previously, it is implemented on ESXi as an MPP (also referred to as MEM or Management Extension Module). For details on PSA, NMP, and MPP and how the pieces fit together, refer to Chapter 5, "VMware Pluggable Storage Architecture (PSA)."

Downloading PowerPath/VE

PowerPath/VE is available for download from PowerLink (http://powerlink.emc.com). You can follow these directions to locate the files:

1. Log on to PowerLink as shown in Figure 8.1.

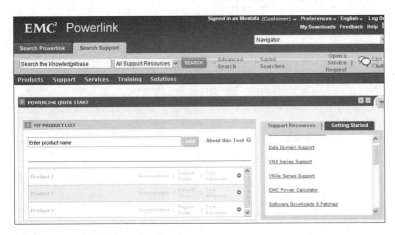

Figure 8.1   EMC Powerlink home page

2. Under the *POWERLINK QUICK START* section, if you are logged in as *Customer*, locate the Support Resources tab. Click the **Software Downloads & Patches** link.

3. On the left-hand side-bar, click the Downloads P-R link to expand it; then click the PowerPath for VMware link

4. If you logged in as *partner* (this also works as customer), select Support, Software Downloads and Licensing, Downloads P-R, PowerPath for VMware (see Figure 8.2).

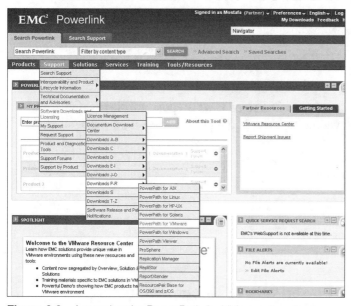

Figure 8.2 Accessing the PowerPath for VMware download page

5. I strongly recommend that you download and read "PowerPath/VE Software Download FAQ" first. It has answers to all the questions that I had, and I am sure it has answers to yours as well.

6. All you need to install PowerPath/VE is available on PowerLink. What I used was PowerPath/VE 5.7.0 for VMware vSphere – Install SW Bundle under the section conveniently labeled PowerPath/VE for VMware vSphere. The filename is PowerPath_VE_5_7_for_VMWARE_vSphere_Install_SW_Bundle.zip. The content of this zip file is subject to change in the future. At the time of this writing, the file includes the following:

   a. Three PowerPath/VE vSphere Installation Bundles (VIBs), which are LIB (Library), CIM (Common Information Model), and PLUGIN bundles for short. I list the long names later in this chapter in the "Installation Overview" section.

b. The PowerPath/VE offline bundle. It is what you use to install PowerPath/VE via VUM (and my not-top-secret-favorite method via SSH or vMA 5).

c. Both Windows and RedHat Enterprise Linux versions of RTOOLS. It is rpowermt or the Remote PowerPath Management Tool, which I discuss later in this chapter.

d. Both Windows and RedHat Enterprise Linux versions of the license server. This may or may not be included in future revisions of downloaded zip file.

7. While you are at this download page, it is advisable to also download the PowerPath Configuration Checker (PPCC), which helps you identify any changes you need to make to your ESXi hosts before installing PowerPath/VE. I do not cover this tool in this book, though.

PPCC requires output from EMCGrab or EMCReport utilities, which are available for download via the Related Items section. (See Figure 8.3.)

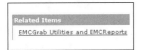

Figure 8.3   Accessing EMCGrab Utilities page

Downloading Relevant PowerPath/VE Documentations

PowerPath/VE documentation is available in the Powerlink Support section (see Figure 8.4).

Please refer to the installation and Administration instructions available for download by selecting the following menu options:

1. Support

2. Technical Documentation and Advisories

3. Software ~ P-R ~ Documentation

4. PowerPath Family

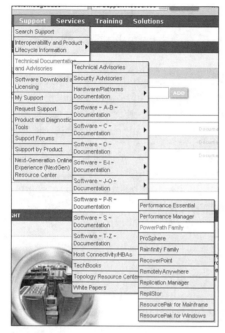

Figure 8.4 Accessing the Documentation page

5. Expand the PowerPath/VE link on the left-hand sidebar and click each document's link to download it (see Figure 8.5).

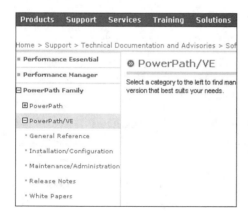

Figure 8.5 Downloading PowerPath/VE documentations

NOTE

PowerPath/VE requires that each host is licensed using one of two available licensing modes: unserved and served.

You need one unserved license for each ESXi 5 host which is locked to the System UUID of each host. This is a manual process, and it's difficult to keep track of how many licenses are used. Also, when a host is out of order or decommissioned, you might be able to request rehosting the license to a new host, but this can be done for a limited number of rehosting requests.

On the other hand, the served license mode uses a centralized Electronic License Management (ELM) Server that makes it easier to count the licensed hosts and also reassign the licenses to other hosts as needed (that is why it is referred to as Floating or Counted mode). This is flexible and more practical.

PowerPath/VE Installation Overview

1. Obtain license file(s) from EMC. If you are using unserved licenses, you need to get the system UUID from each ESXi host that you are licensing. To do so, run:

   ```
   esxcli system uuid get
   ```

2. Install RTOOLS package. Note that the Linux version cannot be installed on vMA 5 because the latter is SuSE Linux based whereas RTOOLS was built for RedHat Linux. If you plan to install the Linux version of RTOOLS, you need to install it on a separate RedHat Linux system or VM.

3. If you are using served licenses, install the License Server.

4. Install PowerPath/VE 5.7. It can be installed via one of three facilities:

   a. **VUM (vSphere Update Manager)** — This is the preferred method if you have VUM in your environment. I do not cover this facility because it is identical to installing any other offline bundle.

   b. **Auto-Deploy** — This is the facility that allows for booting ESXi from a shared image via PXE (Pre-boot eXecution Environment). It is available with vSphere 5.

   c. **vCLI (VMware vSphere CLI)** — This includes vMA 5. This can also be done via the Local CLI or via SSH if you have them enabled.

Note that ESXCLI works the same whether remotely via vCLI, via vMA 5.0, or on the local CLI. I explain this further over the next few pages.

I personally prefer using vMA 5 because I can install any VIB (vSphere Installation Bundle) or set of VIBs on multiple hosts using a few key strokes or scripts. This is manageable if you have a few hosts (five or fewer). If you have more than that and you have VUM installed in your environment, using VUM would be the recommended method of installing PowerPath/VE. Using VUM to install PowerPath/VE is similar to installing any other VIBs. Because the command line is less obvious, I share with you the procedures for vMA and Local CLI only.

5. Finally, use rpowermt commands, installed by RTOOLS, to check the license registration and device status.

What Gets Installed?

Regardless of the PowerPath/VE installation facility, what get installed are the following VIBs in this order:

1. EMC_bootbank_powerpath.lib.esx_5.7.0.00.00-b173.vib

2. EMC_bootbank_powerpath.cim.esx_5.7.0.00.00-b173.vib

   This is the PowerPath CIM Provider which is used to manage PowerPath/VE remotely via the rpowermt that I mentioned earlier.

3. EMC_bootbank_powerpath.plugin.esx_5.7.0.00.00-b173.vib

   This is the MPP plug-in itself that gets plugged into the PSA framework.

Before installing the VIBs, the ESXi host must be placed in Maintenance Mode, and it requires a reboot at the end of the installation. If you have a downtime window to reboot all hosts, you need to power off or suspend all running VMs. Otherwise, you can use a rolling outage and install on one host at a time. This is when your brilliant design comes in handy if you planned your HA/DRS cluster as N+1 or N+2 capacity. This means that you have a cluster configured for one or two host failures. It also means that the surviving hosts have enough reserve capacity to run all virtual machines (VMs) that were running on the one or two hosts you place in maintenance mode.

NOTE

Although VMware and EMC support a rolling upgrade approach where you install PowerPath/VE on one host at a time while the remaining hosts in the cluster still run NMP, this mixed-mode configuration should be on a temporary basis ONLY. You should plan on installing PowerPath/VE on ALL hosts in the cluster as soon as it is reasonably possible.

If your storage is a Symmetrix family of arrays, make sure that SPC-2 FA Director Bit is enabled. If it was not enabled and you apply this required change, be aware of a very important fact: ALL your VMFS volumes might have to be resignatured as a result of this change because the Device IDs change from "mpx.<ID>" to "NAA.<ID>," where the <ID> value is longer and partially different. This is discussed further in Chapter 15, "Snapshot Handling."

Installation Using the Local CLI

1. Copy the offline installation bundle (the filename is EMCPower. VMWARE.5.7.b173.zip as of this writing) to the shared VMFS volume. You may use the vSphere Client Browse Datastore feature or a tool such as WinSCP on Windows or SCP on Linux to securely transfer the file to an ESXi host that has access to that VMFS volume.

2. Log on to the ESXi host locally or via an SSH client (for example, Putty on Windows or ssh on Linux) as root or as a user with root privileges.

3. Place the host in maintenance mode if you have not already done so. You may do that via the vSphere Client.

4. Verify the software acceptance level setting on the host:

```
esxcli software acceptance get
PartnerSupported
```

This output means that the software acceptance level is set to PartnerSupported.

If the returned value is VMwareCertified or VMwareAccepted, you must change it to PartnerSupported. You may do so using:

```
esxcli software acceptance set --level=PartnerSupported
Host acceptance level changed to 'PartnerSupported'.
```

This is required because the PowerPath/VE VIBs were digitally signed by EMC as PartnerCertified Acceptance Level. The way acceptance level enforcement works is that you cannot install any VIBs that are lower than the current acceptance level of the host. The order of these levels is

VMwareCertified — Highest level

VMwareAccepted — Next highest

PartnerSupported — Next one down

CommunitySupported —The lowest level

So, if a host is set at a given level, you can install bundles of that level or higher, which means that with a host set to PartnerSupported acceptance level, you can install VIBs that are signed as PartnerSupported, VMwareAccepted, or VMwareCertified.

5. Perform a dry run of the installation just to make sure that you don't get any errors. To do so, run the following:

```
esxcli software vib install -d /<Path-to-offline-bundle>/EMCPower.
VMWARE.5.7.b173.zip --dry-run
```

An example is shown in Listing 8.1.

Listing 8.1 Dry Run of Installing PowerPath/VE Offline Bundle

```
esxcli software vib install --depot=/vmfs/volumes/FC200/PP57/EMCPower.
VMWARE.5.7.b173.zip --dry-run


Installation Result
   Message: Dryrun only, host not changed. The following installers will be
applied: [BootBankInstaller]
   Reboot Required: true
   VIBs Installed: EMC_bootbank_powerpath.cim.esx_5.7.0.00.00-b173, EMC_
bootbank_powerpath.lib.esx_5.7.0.00.00-b173, EMC_bootbank_powerpath.plugin.
esx_5.7.0.00.00-b173
   VIBs Removed:
   VIBs Skipped:
```

In Listing 8.1 notice that no errors result from the installation, that three VIBs are installed, and that a reboot is required.

6. Repeat the command shown in Listing 8.1 without the `--dry-run` option. Listing 8.2 shows the output.

Listing 8.2 Installing PowerPath/VE Offline Bundle

```
esxcli software vib install -d /vmfs/volumes/FC200/PP57/EMCPower.
VMWARE.5.7.b173.zip

Installation Result
   Message: The update completed successfully, but the system needs to be
rebooted for the changes to be effective.
   Reboot Required: true
   VIBs Installed: EMC_bootbank_powerpath.cim.esx_5.7.0.00.00-b173, EMC_
bootbank_powerpath.lib.esx_5.7.0.00.00-b173, EMC_bootbank_powerpath.plugin.
esx_5.7.0.00.00-b173
   VIBs Removed:
   VIBs Skipped:
```

7. Reboot the host. Don't take the host out of maintenance mode yet. You do that
   after verifying the installation. See the "Verifying Installation" section later in this
   chapter.

Installation Using vMA 5.0

Using vMA 5, the installation steps are identical to those using the local CLI listed earlier.

The only difference is that before you run the first command affecting the ESXi host, you
must change the managed target host to be that ESXi host (see Figure 8.6).

Figure 8.6 Setting the vMA managed host

For details about changing the managed host as well as the process of logging into the
vMA appliance and adding the managed target hosts, refer to Chapter 2, "Fibre Channel
Storage Connectivity," in the section "Procedure Using vMA (vSphere Management
Assistant) 5.0."

One of the many benefits of using vMA is that you can place the host in and out of maintenance mode using the CLI, as shown in Figures 8.7 and 8.8, using the esxcfg-hostops tool.

The syntax for this command would be

`esxcfg-hostops -o enter` or `esxcfg-hostops -o exit` (see Figures 8.7 and 8.8).

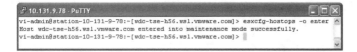

Figure 8.7 Using vMA to enter the ESXi host into maintenance mode

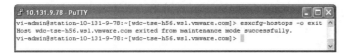

Figure 8.8 Using vMA to exit the ESXi host from maintenance mode

You can also reboot the host remotely using the same command with option `reboot` instead of `enter` or `exit`.

When you are done with the installation on one host, simply change the managed target host to another ESXi host and use the up arrow key to recall the previous commands starting with entering maintenance mode through exiting it. You can get creative and write your own script using variables to pass the offline bundle filename (and path if needed) as well as the host names.

TIP

Did you know that VMware provides sample scripts within the vMA appliance?

These sample scripts are in the /opt/vmware/vma/samples/perl and /opt/vmware/vma/samples/java directories. You can use them as a starting point and build your own scripts to your heart's content.

Verifying Installation

The installation does the following changes:

1. Installs the three VIBs listed earlier.

   To list the installed VIBs you may run

   ```
   esxcli software vib list |grep EMC
   ```

   The output is shown in Figure 8.9.

```
wdc-tse-h56.wsl.vmware.com - PuTTY                                        _ □ X
~ # esxcli software vib list |grep EMC
powerpath.cim.esx      5.7.0.00.00-b173          EMC     PartnerSupported  2011-11-16
powerpath.lib.esx      5.7.0.00.00-b173          EMC     PartnerSupported  2011-11-16
powerpath.plugin.esx   5.7.0.00.00-b173          EMC     PartnerSupported  2011-11-16
~ #
```

Figure 8.9   Listing installed PowerPath VIBs

You can also check the software profile for the three VIBs (see Figure 8.10) using

```
esxcli software profile get
```

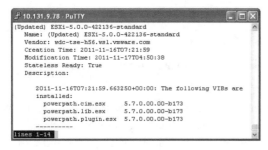

```
10.131.9.78 - PuTTY                                  _ □ X
(Updated) ESXi-5.0.0-422136-standard
   Name: (Updated) ESXi-5.0.0-422136-standard
   Vendor: wdc-tse-h56.wsl.vmware.com
   Creation Time: 2011-11-16T07:21:59
   Modification Time: 2011-11-17T04:50:38
   Stateless Ready: True
   Description:

      2011-11-16T07:21:59.663250+00:00: The following VIBs are
      installed:
         powerpath.cim.esx      5.7.0.00.00-b173
         powerpath.lib.esx      5.7.0.00.00-b173
         powerpath.plugin.esx   5.7.0.00.00-b173
         -----------
         -----------
lines 1-14
```

Figure 8.10   Listing PowerPath software profile

Note that the installed VIBs names do not include the EMC_Bootbank_ prefix or the version and build number suffix. The latter are listed as part of the properties of each VIB.

2. Registers PowerPath Plugin with PSA. This is done by jumpstart script register-emc-powerpath.json. See item 4 for details.

To list the registered plug-in (see Figure 8.11), you may run

```
esxcli storage core plugin registration list |grep "PowerPath \|Module
\|---"
```

```
wdc-tse-h56.wsl.vmware.com - PuTTY                                   _ □ X
~ # esxcli storage core plugin registration list |grep "PowerPath \|Module \|---"
Module Name          Plugin Name          Plugin Class   Dependencies
-------------------  -------------------  ------------   ------------------------
emcp                 PowerPath            MP
~ #
```

Figure 8.11   Listing PowerPath PSA module registration

In Figure 8.11, I cropped the blank column named Full Path for readability.

You may verify that the PowerPath vmkernel module (emcp) was successfully loaded (see Figure 8.12) by running

```
esxcli system module list |grep -I 'emcp\|enabled\|---'
```

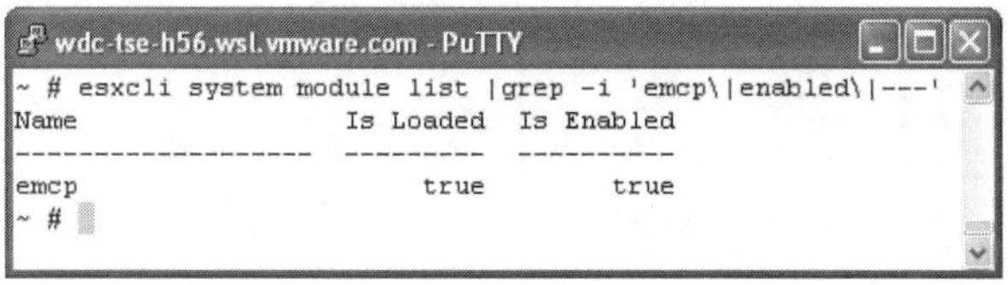

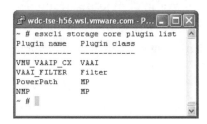

Figure 8.12   Listing PowerPath vmKernel module

The output in Figure 8.12 shows that the emcp kernel module was loaded and enabled.

You may also check that the PowerPath MPP (Multipathing Plugin) was successfully added (see Figure 8.13) by running

```
esxcli storage core plugin list
```

Figure 8.13   Listing PowerPath MP Plugin

Here you see that there is an MP class plug-in named PowerPath alongside with NMP.

3. Adds PowerPath PSA claim rules. This is done by jumpstart script psa-powerpath-pre-claim-config.json. See item 4 for details.

To list the added claim rules (see Figure 8.14), you may run

```
esxcli storage core claimrule list
```

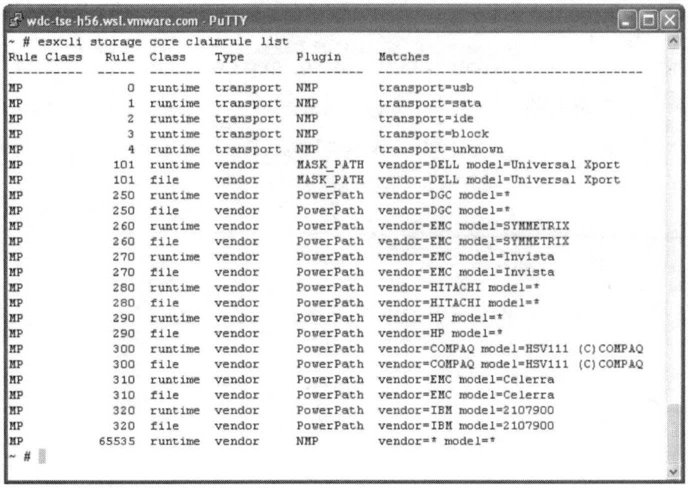

```
~ # esxcli storage core claimrule list
Rule Class   Rule  Class    Type       Plugin     Matches
----------  -----  -------  ---------  ---------  ------------------------------------
MP              0  runtime  transport  NMP        transport=usb
MP              1  runtime  transport  NMP        transport=sata
MP              2  runtime  transport  NMP        transport=ide
MP              3  runtime  transport  NMP        transport=block
MP              4  runtime  transport  NMP        transport=unknown
MP            101  runtime  vendor     MASK_PATH  vendor=DELL model=Universal Xport
MP            101  file     vendor     MASK_PATH  vendor=DELL model=Universal Xport
MP            250  runtime  vendor     PowerPath  vendor=DGC model=*
MP            250  file     vendor     PowerPath  vendor=DGC model=*
MP            260  runtime  vendor     PowerPath  vendor=EMC model=SYMMETRIX
MP            260  file     vendor     PowerPath  vendor=EMC model=SYMMETRIX
MP            270  runtime  vendor     PowerPath  vendor=EMC model=Invista
MP            270  file     vendor     PowerPath  vendor=EMC model=Invista
MP            280  runtime  vendor     PowerPath  vendor=HITACHI model=*
MP            280  file     vendor     PowerPath  vendor=HITACHI model=*
MP            290  runtime  vendor     PowerPath  vendor=HP model=*
MP            290  file     vendor     PowerPath  vendor=HP model=*
MP            300  runtime  vendor     PowerPath  vendor=COMPAQ model=HSV111 (C)COMPAQ
MP            300  file     vendor     PowerPath  vendor=COMPAQ model=HSV111 (C)COMPAQ
MP            310  runtime  vendor     PowerPath  vendor=EMC model=Celerra
MP            310  file     vendor     PowerPath  vendor=EMC model=Celerra
MP            320  runtime  vendor     PowerPath  vendor=IBM model=2107900
MP            320  file     vendor     PowerPath  vendor=IBM model=2107900
MP          65535  runtime  vendor     NMP        vendor=* model=*
~ #
```

Figure 8.14 Listing PowerPath PSA Claim Rules

The output in Figure 8.14 shows that rules 250 through 320 have been added. See item 4 to compare this list to the list of commands that added these rules. Each rule is listed with runtime and file classes. This means that the rules that were written to the configuration files (file class) have also been loaded (runtime class).

4. Adds the following JumpStart scripts to the /usr/libexec/jumpstart/plugins directory:

   a. register-emc-powerpath.json

   b. psa-powerpath-claim-load-order.json

   c. psa-powerpath-pre-claim-config.json

The first script (a) runs a command equivalent to

```
esxcli storage core plugin registration add -m emcp -N MP -P PowerPath
```

The verbose version of this command is

```
esxcli storage core plugin registration add --module-name=emcp
--plugin-class=MP --plugin-name=PowerPath
```

This command registers with PSA a vmkernel module named emcp as an MP class plug-in named PowerPath.

- The second script (b) is carried over from older PowerPath/VE versions. It is practically empty.

- The third script (c) loads the emcp vmkernel module and then adds the PSA claim rules for storage array families supported by PowerPath/VE. It runs commands equivalent to that shown in Listing 8.3.

Listing 8.3 Commands Run by "psa-powerpath-pre-claim-config.json" Script

```
esxcli system module load --module emcp

esxcli storage core claimrule add --claimrule-class MP --rule 250 --plugin
PowerPath --type vendor --vendor DGC --model *

esxcli storage core claimrule add --claimrule-class MP --rule 260 --plugin
PowerPath --type vendor --vendor EMC --model SYMMETRIX

esxcli storage core claimrule add --claimrule-class MP --rule 270 --plugin
PowerPath --type vendor --vendor EMC --model Invista

esxcli storage core claimrule add --claimrule-class MP --rule 280 --plugin
PowerPath --type vendor --vendor HITACHI --model *

esxcli storage core claimrule add --claimrule-class MP --rule 290 --plugin
PowerPath --type vendor --vendor HP --model *

esxcli storage core claimrule add --claimrule-class MP --rule 300 --plugin
PowerPath --type vendor --vendor COMPAQ --model \"HSV111 (C)COMPAQ\"

esxcli storage core claimrule add --claimrule-class MP --rule 310 --plugin
PowerPath --type vendor --vendor EMC --model Celerra

esxcli storage core claimrule add --claimrule-class MP --rule 320 --plugin
PowerPath --type vendor --vendor IBM --model 2107900
```

Listing Devices Claimed by PowerPath/VE

To verify that supported devices have been claimed by PowerPath MPP (see Figure 8.15) you may run

```
esxcli storage core device list |less -S
```

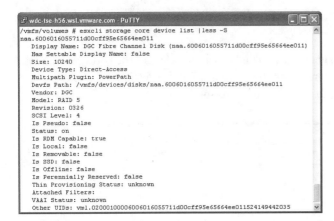

Figure 8.15   Listing PowerPath managed FC device properties

The output shown in Figure 8.15 is an example from a Fibre Channel LUN on a CLARiiON Storage Array. Notice that the Multipath Plugin is PowerPath.

Figure 8.16 shows another example of a device claimed by PowerPath, which is an iSCSI device on a CLARiiON Storage Array.

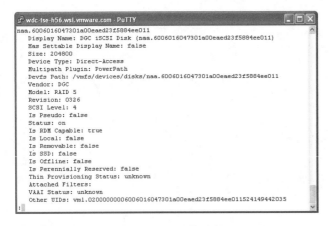

Figure 8.16   Listing PowerPath managed iSCSI device properties

Managing PowerPath/VE

You can manage PowerPath/VE remotely using rpowermt on Windows or Red Hat Linux where you installed the RTOOLS package. For details on using rpowermt, refer to the Maintenance/Configuration document available on PowerLink as I outlined in the "Downloading Relevant PowerPath/VE Documentations" section.

There is also the local powermt utility that gets installed on each ESXi server when you install PowerPath/VE. This tool is located in

```
/opt/emc/powerpath/bin
```

It enables you to run a subset of commands that are available with rpowermt.

How to Uninstall PowerPath/VE

If you are going to experiment with PowerPath/VE, you might need to uninstall it when you are done playing. You may do so following the same steps for the installation, substituting the installation step with this command:

```
esxcli software vib remove -n <bundle1>  -n <bundle2> -n <bundle3>
```

The verbose version of this command is

```
esxcli software vib remove --vibname=<bundle1>  --vibname=<bundle2>
--vibname=<bundle3>
```

Listings 8.4, 8.5, 8.6, and 8.7 show the set of commands from beginning to rebooting the host. This is all done within vMA 5.0.

Listing 8.4   Entering Maintenance Mode

```
vi-admin@station-1:~[wdc-tse-h56] > esxcfg-hostops --operation enter

Host wdc-tse-h56.wsl.vmware.com entered into maintenance mode successfully.
```

Listing 8.5   Listing PowerPath VIB Profile

```
vi-admin@station-1:~[wdc-tse-h56] > esxcli software vib list |grep powerpath

powerpath.cim.esx    5.7.0.00.00-b173   EMC PartnerSupported  2011-11-16

powerpath.lib.esx    5.7.0.00.00-b173   EMC PartnerSupported  2011-11-16

powerpath.plugin.esx 5.7.0.00.00-b173   EMC PartnerSupported  2011-11-16
```

Listing 8.6   Uninstalling PowerPath

```
vi-admin@station-1:~[wdc-tse-h56]> esxcli software vib remove --vibname
powerpath.cim.esx --vibname powerpath.lib.esx --vibname powerpath.plugin.
esx

Removal Result
   Message: The update completed successfully, but the system needs to be
rebooted for the changes to be effective.
   Reboot Required: true
   VIBs Installed:
   VIBs Removed: EMC_bootbank_powerpath.cim.esx_5.7.0.00.00-b173, EMC_
bootbank_powerpath.lib.esx_5.7.0.00.00-b173, EMC_bootbank_powerpath.plugin.
esx_5.7.0.00.00-b173
   VIBs Skipped:
```

Listing 8.7   Rebooting Host

```
vi-admin@station-1:~[wdc-tse-h56]> esxcfg-hostops --operation reboot

Host wdc-tse-h56.wsl.vmware.com rebooted successfully.
```

After the host is rebooted, while still in vMA 5.0, run the following command to verify that the VIBs were removed successfully. (The beauty of vMA is that you don't have to log on to the host after it boots back up. Because it was the last managed target, vMA uses the cached credentials in the FastPass configuration files to reconnect at the first command you run after the host is booted.)

```
esxcli software vib list |grep powerpath
```

You should not get any VIBs returned, which confirms that they are no longer installed.

Follow with a command to list the claim rules and verify that all claim rules that were added by the installer have been removed. These are claim rules numbers 250 through 320, as shown previously in Figure 8.14.

```
esxcli storage core claimrule list
```

Outputs of the two commands are listed in Figure 8.17.

```
10.131.9.78 - PuTTY
vi-admin@station-10-131-9-78:~[wdc-tse-h56.wsl.vmware.com]> esxcli software vib list |grep powerpath
vi-admin@station-10-131-9-78:~[wdc-tse-h56.wsl.vmware.com]> esxcli storage core claimrule list
Rule Class   Rule  Class    Type       Plugin     Matches
----------   ----  -------  ---------  ---------  ----------------------------------
MP              0  runtime  transport  NMP        transport=usb
MP              1  runtime  transport  NMP        transport=sata
MP              2  runtime  transport  NMP        transport=ide
MP              3  runtime  transport  NMP        transport=block
MP              4  runtime  transport  NMP        transport=unknown
MP            101  runtime  vendor     MASK_PATH  vendor=DELL model=Universal Xport
MP            101  file     vendor     MASK_PATH  vendor=DELL model=Universal Xport
MP          65535  runtime  vendor     NMP        vendor=* model=*
vi-admin@station-10-131-9-78:~[wdc-tse-h56.wsl.vmware.com]>
```

Figure 8.17　Uninstalling PowerPath

Now that you confirmed PowerPath/VE has been uninstalled, you may take the host out of maintenance mode using the following:

```
vi-admin@station-1:~[wdc-tse-h56]> esxcfg-hostops --operation exit
Host wdc-tse-h56.wsl.vmware.com exited from maintenance mode successfully.
```

Hitachi Dynamic Link Manager (HDLM)

Hitachi Dynamic Link Manager (HDLM) MPIO solution is available on several operating systems. It has been recently ported to vSphere 5 in the form of one SATP, three PSPs, and one ESXCLI extension module as follows:

- hti_satp_hdlm
- hti_psp_hdlm_exlio (Extended Least I/Os)
- hti_psp_hdlm_ex rr (Extended Round Robin)
- hti_psp_hdlm_exlbk (Extended Least Blocks)
- hex-hdlm-dlnkmgr

> **NOTE**
>
> The product information in this section is based on the latest information as of the time of this writing.

Obtaining Installation Files

To obtain HDLM for VMware installation files, contact Hitachi Data Systems or Hitachi. You will receive a set of CDs/DVDs with the software and related files and documentation. The installation files are on the DVD labeled Hitachi Dynamic Link Manager Software v7.2 Advanced (with Hitachi Global Link Manager Software).

Follow these steps on a system or a VM (running Windows version supported by HDLM) that will assist you in extracting the required installation files:

1. Install vCLI. You may download the installation file from http://communities. vmware.com/community/vmtn/server/vsphere/automationtools/vsphere_cli and then click the **Download** button under VMware vSphere CLI. Run the downloaded file and follow the prompts to install it.

2. Insert the HDLM Installation DVD into your DVD drive. (If you are installing to a VM, connect the DVD drive to the VM.)

3. If autorun is disabled on your system/VM, browse the DVD drive for the **index.html** file and run it.

4. Your browser should show a screen similar to Figure 8.18. Click the **Install** button for VMware under the Hitachi Dynamic Link Manager Software section.

Figure 8.18   Accessing HDLM installation files

5. Follow the installation prompts. See Hitachi Command Suite Dynamic Link Manager User Guide (for VMware(R)) on the documentation list in the index.html file of the Hitachi Command Suite v7.2 Software Documentation Library DVD that you received from Hitachi.

6. This process installs the HDLM Remote Management Client and places the HDLM for VMware **Offline Bundle** file in

```
<HDLM-Installation-Folder>\plugin
```

For example:

```
c:\Program files(x86)\HITACHI\DynamicLinkManagerForVMware\plugin
```

The filename as of the time of this writing is hdlm-0720000002.zip.

Installing HDLM

Installation is done via the single Offline Bundle file identified in the "Obtaining Installation Files" section: hdlm-0720000002.zip. That file includes the five plug-ins listed earlier; four PSA plug-ins and an ESXCLI extension for HDLM.

The installation process is outlined here:

1. Transfer the offline bundle zip file to a VMFS volume shared by all hosts on which you plan to install HDLM.

   You may transfer the files using one of the following tools:

   a. vSphere Client:

   Locate the datastore to which you want to transfer the files; right-click it; select **Browse Datastore;** and then click the **Upload Files to This Datastore** icon, which looks like a cylinder with a green up arrow (see Figure 8.19).

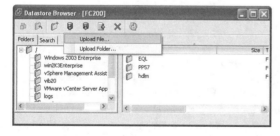

Figure 8.19   Uploading files to datastore via vSphere client

   Finally, click the **Upload File** menu and follow the prompts.

   b. A file transfer tool like WinSCP.

2. Log on to the host locally via SSH as root or use vMA 5.0. You may also use vCLI on the system on which you installed HDLM Remote Management Client because you already installed vCLI on it earlier. Using the latter, the commands are identical to what is listed, but you need to add vCLI connection options such as `--server`, `--username`, and `--password` with each command you run.

3. You can first go through an installation dry run to verify if there are any problems that would result in failure to install the output, which is shown in Figure 8.20.

```
esxcli  software  vib  install  -d  /vmfs/volumes/FC200/mpio/hdlm/
hdlm-0720000002.zip --dry-run
```

The verbose version of this command is

```
esxcli software vib install --depot /vmfs/volumes/FC200/mpio/hdlm/
hdlm-0720000002.zip --dry-run
```

Figure 8.20   HDLM installation dry run on ESXi 5

Notice that the Installation Result shows that Live Image Installer and Boot Bank Installer will be applied.

> **NOTE**
>
> Even though the Dry Run output shows `Reboot Required: false`, which means that rebooting the ESXi host after the installation is not required, you might actually need to reboot the host for certain services to be restarted. Otherwise, you can run `/sbin/services.sh restart`, which restarts these services. This can only run from the ESXi Shell via SSH or locally on the ESXi host.

4. Install the offline bundle using esxcli as follows:

```
esxcli  software  vib  install  -d  /vmfs/volumes/FC200/mpio/hdlm/
hdlm-0720000002.zip
```

The verbose version of this command is

```
esxcli software vib install --depot /vmfs/volumes/FC200/mpio/hdlm/
hdlm-0720000002.zip
```

The installation command and its output are shown in Figure 8.21.

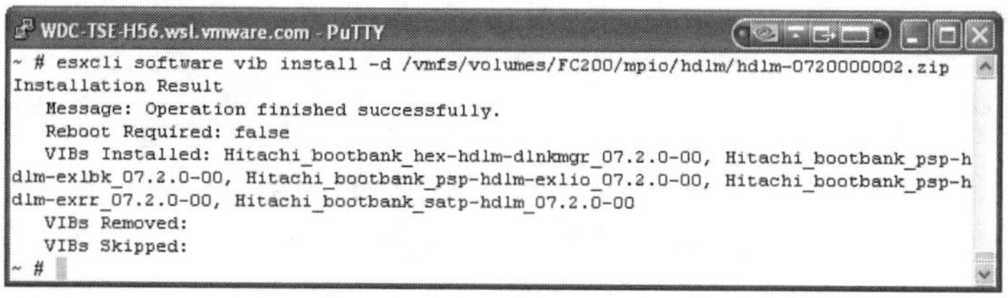

Figure 8.21   HDLM installation on ESXi 5

5. Reboot the host.

The installation configures the default PSP for HTI_SATP_HDLM as HTI_PSP_HDLM_EXLIO. However, the other two PSPs are available by changing the default PSP or changing it per device.

Changes Done to the ESXi Host Configuration by the HDLM Installation

The installation does the following changes:

1. Adds the following JumpStart scripts to /usr/libexec/jumpstart/plugins directory:

   a. nmp-hti_psp_hdlm_exlbk-rules.json

   b. nmp-hti_psp_hdlm_exlbk.json

   c. nmp-hti_psp_hdlm_exlio-rules.json

   d. nmp-hti_psp_hdlm_exlio.json

   e. nmp-hti_psp_hdlm_exrr-rules.json

   f. nmp-hti_psp_hdlm_exrr.json

   g. nmp-hti_satp_hdlm-rules.json

   h. nmp-hti_satp_hdlm.json

These jumpstart plug-ins do the following:

- Scripts with the -rules suffix load the kernel module of the PSP/SATP at boot time.
- Scripts without the -rules suffix register the plug-in with the PSA framework.

2. Registers the following modules as plug-ins as listed in Table 8.1.

Table 8.1   HDLM Plug-ins List

Module	Plug-in	Plug-in Class
hti_satp_hdlm	HTI_SATP_HDLM	SATP
hti_psp_hdlm_exlbk	HTI_PSP_HDLM_EXLBK	PSP
hti_psp_hdlm_exlio	HTI_PSP_HDLM_EXLIO	PSP
hti_psp_hdlm_exrr	HTI_PSP_HDLM_EXRR	PSP

Figure 8.22 shows the command to list the registered plug-ins.

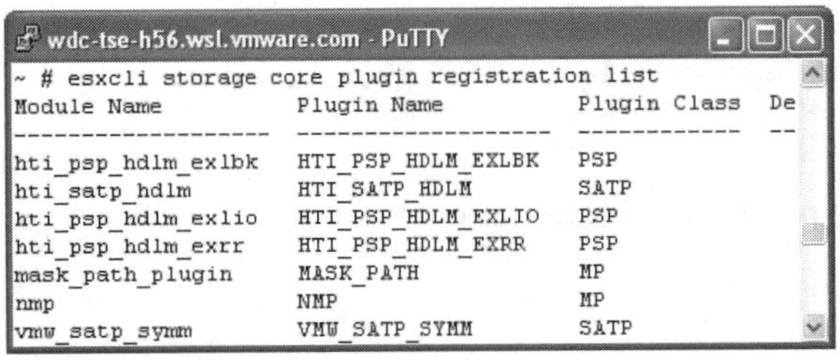

Figure 8.22   Listing HDLM PSA plug-ins registration

These are also done upon reboot by jumpstart scripts without the -rules suffix, which runs the equivalent to the commands shown in Listing 8.8.

Listing 8.8   Commands Run by PowerPath Jumpstart Scripts

```
esxcli storage core plugin registration add --module-name=hti_satp_hdlm
--plugin-class=SATP - --plugin-name=HTI_SATP_HDLM


esxcli storage core plugin registration add --module-name=hti_psp_hdlm_
exlbk --plugin-class=PSP --plugin-name=HTI_PSP_HDLM_EXLBK
```

```
esxcli storage core plugin registration add --module-name=hti_psp_hdlm_
exlio --plugin-class=PSP --plugin-name=HTI_PSP_HDLM_EXLIO
```

```
esxcli storage core plugin registration add --module-name=hti_psp_hdlm_exrr
--plugin-class=PSP --plugin-name=HTI_PSP_HDLM_EXRR
```

3. Configures HTI_PSP_HDLM_EXLIO as the default PSP for SATP HTI_SATP_HDLM.

   Figure 8.23 shows how to verify the default PSP.

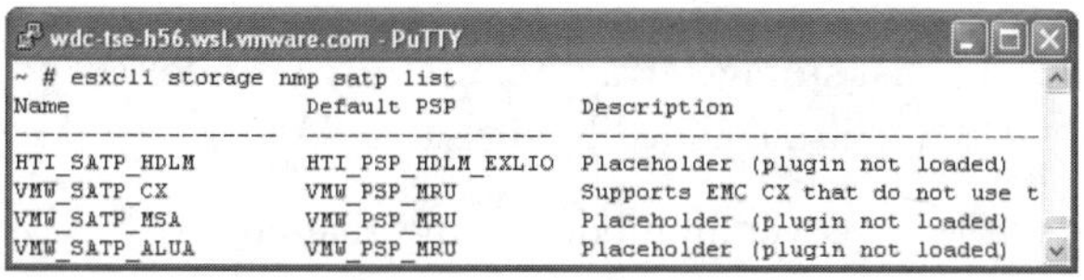

Figure 8.23   HDLM SATP default configuration

This is also done upon reboot by jumpstart script nmp-hti_satp_hdlm-rules.json, which runs the equivalent to the following command:

```
esxcli storage nmp satp set --satp HTI_SATP_HDLM --default-psp
HTI_PSP_HDLM_EXLIO
```

4. Adds three SATP rules, which associates the HTI_SATP_HDLM with the vendors and model strings listed in Table 8.2 and verified in Figure 8.24.

Table 8.2   Vendor and Model Strings Used by HDLM Claim Rules

Vendor String	Model String
HITACHI	DF600F
HITACHI	^OPEN-*
HP	^OPEN-*

The model strings in the table represent Hitachi AMS, VSP, and HP P9000 families, respectively. For the list of the supported array makes and models, check VMware HCL.

Figure 8.24 shows list of SATP Claim Rules for HTI_SATP_HDLM.

```
wdc-tse-h56.wsl.vmware.com - PuTTY
~ # esxcli storage nmp satp rule list |grep -B4 HDLM |less -S
Name                Device  Vendor  Model              Driver  Transport  Options                      Rule Group
-------------------  ------  ------  ------------------  ------  ---------  ---------------------------  ----------
HTI_SATP_HDLM               HITACHI  DF600F                                                             user
HTI_SATP_HDLM               HITACHI  ^OPEN-*                                                            user
HTI_SATP_HDLM               HP       ^OPEN-*                                                            user
```

Figure 8.24   HDLM SATP rules

This means that Storage arrays that return a vendor string of HITACHI and model strings of DF600F or ^OPEN-* are claimed by HTI_SATP_HDLM Storage Array Type Plugin (SATP).

The third row in the table and output means that storage arrays that return a vendor string of HP and return a model string of ^OPEN-* are also claimed by the same SATP.

The wildcards used in the model string ^OPEN-* cover all model strings that end with OPEN and a hyphen followed by any value (for example, OPEN-V).

This is also done upon reboot by jumpstart script nmp-hti_satp_hdlm-rules.json, which runs the equivalent to the commands in Listing 8.9.

Listing 8.9   Commands Run by "nmp_hti_satp_hdlm-rules.json" Jumpstart Script

```
esxcli storage nmp satp rule add --satp HTI_SATP_HDLM --vendor HITACHI
--model DF600F

esxcli storage nmp satp rule add --satp HTI_SATP_HDLM --vendor HITACHI
--model ^OPEN-*

esxcli storage nmp satp rule add --satp HTI_SATP_HDLM --vendor HP --model
^OPEN-*
```

Modifying HDLM PSP Assignments

Because you can have only one default PSP per SATP, you can assign a different PSP on a per-device basis. For example, you have three different LUNs on a Hitachi Adaptable Modular Storage (AMS) array that are presented to a set of ESXi 5 hosts. These hosts have been configured with the HDLM plug-ins. Each of the three LUNs has different I/O requirements that match one of the three installed HDLM PSPs. You can configure each LUN to be claimed by the PSP that matches the desired I/O criteria. This can be done via the vSphere Client, the CLI, or HDLM Remote Management Client (see section "Obtaining Installation Files" earlier in this chapter). HDLM Remote Management Client has its own CLI and is used to manage HDLM for VMware remotely. Think of it like using vMA or vCLI to manage ESXi 5 remotely.

Changing PSP Assignment Via the UI

To change the PSP Assignment via the UI, you may follow this procedure:

1. Follow Steps 1 through 7 of the "Listing Paths to a LUN Using the UI" procedure under the "Listing Multipath Details" section in Chapter 5.

2. From the **Path Selection** pull-down menu, select the desired PSP from the list (see Figure 8.25).

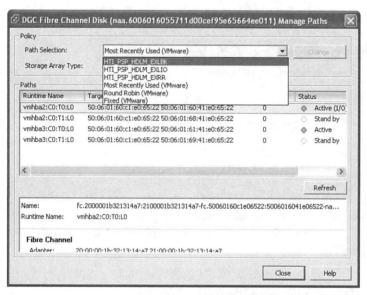

Figure 8.25 Using vSphere Client to modify HDLM PSP assignment

3. Click the Change button and then click the Close button.

4. At the device properties dialog, click the Close button to return to the vSphere Client Storage Management UI.

5. Repeat this process for each LUN using the PSP matching its I/O characteristics.

6. Repeat this process for the same set of LUNs on all ESXi 5 hosts sharing them. Make sure to use the same PSP for a given LUN on all hosts.

Changing PSP Assignment Via the CLI

To change the PSP Assignment via the CLI, you may follow this procedure:

1. Log on to the ESXi 5 host locally or via SSH as root or using vMA 5.0 as vi-admin.

2. Identify the device ID for each LUN you want to reconfigure:

```
esxcfg-mpath -b |grep -B1 "fc Adapter"| grep -v -e "--" |sed 's/
Adapter.*//'
```

You may also use the verbose version of the command:

```
esxcfg-mpath --list-paths |grep -B1 "fc Adapter"| grep -v -e "--" |sed
's/Adapter.*//'
```

The output of this command is listed in Figure 8.26.

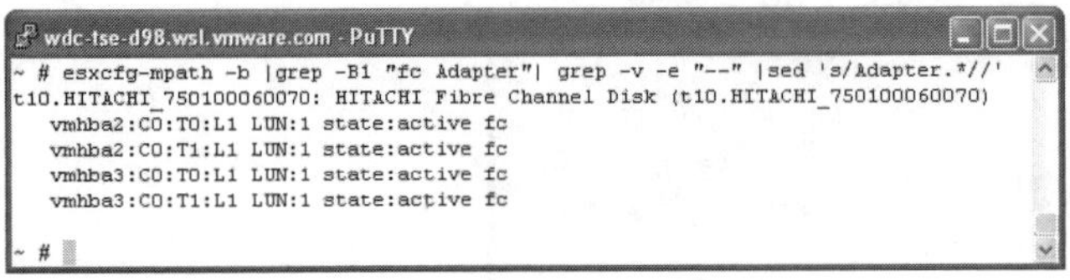

Figure 8.26 Listing a device ID on an AMS array

From there, you can identify the device ID (in this case, it is the t10 ID). Note that this output was collected using an AMS array. Universal Storage Platform® V (USP V), USP VM, or Virtual Storage Platform (VSP) would show NAA ID instead. (See Figure 8.27.)

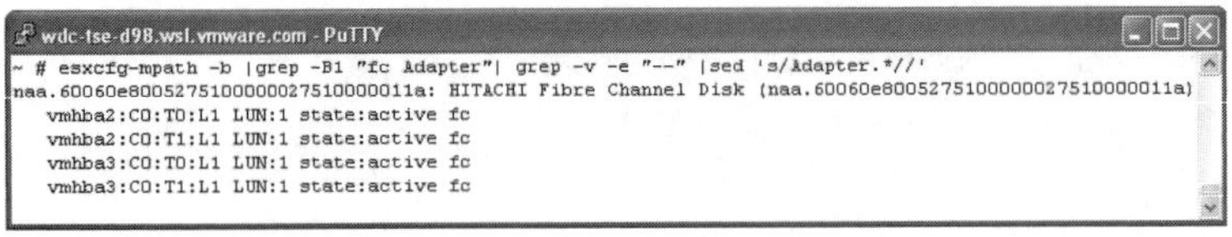

Figure 8.27 Listing a device ID on a USP array

3. Using the device ID you identified in Step 2, run this command:

```
esxcli storage nmp device set --device=<device-id> --psp=<psp-name>
```

Example for AMS LUN:

```
esxcli storage nmp device set --device=t10.HITACHI_750100060070 --psp=HTI_PSP_HDLM_EXLIO
```

Example for VSP LUN:

```
esxcli storage nmp device set --device=naa.60060e8005275100000027510000 0011a --psp=HTI_PSP_HDLM_EXLIO
```

4. Repeat Steps 2 and 3 for each device.

NOTE

HTI_SATP_HDLM was also tested, certified, and is supported for use with VMW_PSP_MRU.

See the next section, "Locating Certified Storage on VMware HCL."

Changing the Default PSP

If most of your HDLM-managed LUNs' I/O is characterized such that they benefit from using one of the HDLM PSPs other than the default one, it would be advisable to change the default PSP and then modify the exception LUNs to use a suitable one.

For example, if you have 100 LUNs whose I/O would benefit from using HTI_PSP_HDLM_EXLBK and five LUNs that would be more suited to use HTI_PSP_HDLM_EXLIO (which is the current default), you might opt to change the default PSP to the former and then change the five LUNs to use the latter.

To change the default PSP, you may use the following command:

```
esxcli storage nmp satp set --satp HTI_SATP_HDLM --default-psp HTI_PSP_HDLM_EXLBK
```

If you want to set the default PSP to be HTI_PSP_HDLM_EXRR instead, simply replace the last parameter in the command with that PSP name.

> **NOTE**
>
> If you had manually set certain LUNs to a specific PSP previously, the command does not affect that setting.
>
> To reset such a LUN to use the current default PSP, use the following command
>
> ```
> esxcli storage nmp device set --device=<device-ID> --default
> ```
>
> For example:
>
> ```
> esxcli storage nmp device set --device=naa.6006016055711d00cef95e65664
> ee011 --default
> ```

Locating Certified Storage on VMware HCL

To locate arrays certified with HDLM on VMware HCL, follow this procedure:

1. Go to http://www.vmware.com/go/hcl.

2. In the What Are You Looking For field, select **Storage/SAN** from the pull-down menu.

3. In the Product Release Version field, select **ESXi 5.0**.

4. In the Partner Name field, select the Storage Vendor's name, for example Hitachi, Hitachi Data Systems (HDS), and so on.

5. In the SATP Plugin field, select **HTI_SATP_HDLM v07.2.0-00**.

   Steps 1 through 5 are shown in Figure 8.28.

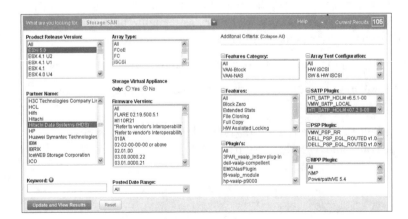

Figure 8.28   HCL search criteria for HDLM

6. Click the **Update and View Results** button.

7. Scroll down to see the list of certified arrays as shown in Figure 8.29.

Partner Name	Model	Array Type	Supported Releases					
Hitachi Data Systems (HDS)	AMS 2100	FC	ESXi	5.0				
			ESX	4.1 U2	4.1 U1	4.1	4.0 U4	...
Hitachi Data Systems (HDS)	AMS 2300	FC	ESXi	5.0				
			ESX	4.1 U2	4.1 U1	4.1	4.0 U4	...
Hitachi Data Systems (HDS)	AMS 2500	FC	ESXi	5.0				
			ESX	4.1 U2	4.1 U1	4.1	4.0 U4	...
Hitachi Data Systems (HDS)	Hitachi Virtual Storage Platform	FC	ESXi	5.0				
			ESX	4.1 U2	4.1 U1	4.1	4.0 U4	...
Hitachi Data Systems (HDS)	SMS100	FC	ESXi	5.0				
			ESX	4.1 U2	4.1 U1	4.1	4.0 U4	...

Figure 8.29 HCL search results for HDLM

8. Click the hyperlink of the Storage Array Model listed under the Model column to see the details, for example Hitachi Virtual Storage Platform.

9. Locate the row with the SATP Plugin column listing HTI_SATP_HDLM v07.2.0-00.

10. See the PSP Plugin column for the certified PSP Plugins. In this example (see Figure 8.30), all three HDLM PSP plug-ins are listed along with VMW_PSP_MRU. This means that you are free to use any combination of HTI_SATP_HDLM and any of the listed PSPs.

HTI_SATP_HDLM v07.2.0-00	HTI_PSP_HDLM_EXLBK v07.2.0-00, HTI_PSP_HDLM_EXLIO v07.2.0-00, HTI_PSP_HDLM_EXRR v07.2.0-00, VMW_PSP_MRU

Figure 8.30 HCL product details of HDLM listing

Dell EqualLogic PSP Routed

Dell's EqualLogic MPIO is implemented as a PSP. It also includes an additional component that runs in the user world, which is EqualLogic Host Connection Manager (EHCM). It is actually designed as a CIM Provider. Its main function is to manage iSCSI (Internet Small Computer System Interface) sessions to the EqualLogic array.

Downloading Documentation

You can download a reference document "Configuring and Installing the EqualLogic Multipathing Extension Module for VMware vSphere 5 and PS Series SANs" from http://www.equallogic.com/WorkArea/DownloadAsset.aspx?id=10798.

On that page, click the Download button to obtain the file named TR1074-Configuring-MEM-1.1-with-vSphere-5.pdf.

Most of the content I am sharing with you here is based on the linked Dell document and my own hands-on experience.

Downloading the Installation File and the Setup Script

To download the installation file and the setup script in one zip file, you need to have a valid login account at EQL support site. The download area is at https://support.equallogic.com/support/download.aspx?id=1484.

How Does It Work?

The PSP has knowledge of how the PS series volumes are distributed over the PS Group Members. It has a map of the physical location of data on the volumes and utilizes that to provide I/O load balancing.

The EHCM creates sessions to the EqualLogic volumes based on the SAN topology and the PSP settings (done on each ESXi host). It creates two sessions per volume slice (the portion of the volume residing on a single member of the PS series group). The maximum number of sessions per volume (the combination of sessions for all volume slices) is six. This is configurable via the Equallogic Host Connection Manager (EHCM) configuration file.

Figure 8.31 shows the Dell EqualLogic PSP Architecture.

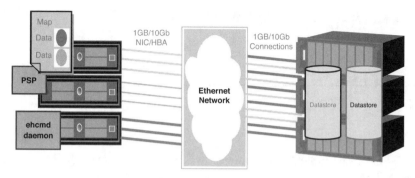

Figure 8.31   Dell EqualLogic PSP architecture

Installing EQL MEM on vSphere 5

The zip file you downloaded from EqualLogic support's download site includes the following:

- **setup.pl** — A PERL script that you use to configure the iSCSI network on the ESXi 5 host including configuring Jumbo Frame

- **dell-eql-mem-version-offline_bundle-<build_number>.zip** — Use for installing via local CLI or vMA 5.0

- **dell-eql-mem-<version>.zip** —Use for installing via VUM

I cover the installation process via Local CLI, which is identical to using vMA 5.0 after switching the managed target host to the ESXi 5 host on which you will install the VIB:

1. Copy the downloaded zip file to a VMFS volume shared by all hosts on which you plan to install this VIB. You may use a tool like WinSCP to transfer the file.

2. Log on to the ESXi 5 host directly or via SSH as root.

3. Expand the zip file to obtain the setup.pl script as well as the offline bundle

   ```
   cd /vmfs/volume/<datastore-name>
   unzip <downloaded-file>.zip
   ```

4. Run the installation command (see Figure 8.32):

   ```
   ~ # esxcli software vib install --depot=/vmfs/volumes/FC200/EQL/
   DELL-eql-mem-1.0.9.201133-offline_bundle-515614.zip
   ```

```
wdc-tse-h56.wsl.vmware.com - PuTTY
~ # esxcli software vib install -d /vmfs/volumes/FC200/EQL/DELL-eql-mem-1.0.9.201133-offline_bundle-515614.zip
Installation Result
   Message: Operation finished successfully.
   Reboot Required: false
   VIBs Installed: Dell_bootbank_dell-eql-routed-psp_1.0.9-201133
   VIBs Removed:
   VIBs Skipped:
~ #
```

Figure 8.32   Installing Dell EQL PSP

The sample file I used in this example is based on what was used for certifying the PS series with this MEM. The filename available for download from EQL might be different (version and build number).

Notice that the output states that `Reboot Required` is `false`.

Changes Done to the ESXi Host Configuration by the MEM Installation

The installation does the following changes:

- Adds JumpStart scripts psp-eql-load.json and psp-eql.json to the /usr/libexec/jumpstart/plugins directory. (See Figure 8.33.)

```
wdc-tse-h56.wsl.vmware.com - PuTTY
~ # ls /usr/libexec/jumpstart/plugins/psp-eql*
/usr/libexec/jumpstart/plugins/psp-eql-load.json
/usr/libexec/jumpstart/plugins/psp-eql.json
~ #
```

Figure 8.33   Jumpstart scripts added by Dell EQL PSP installation

- Registers module dell-psp-eql-routed as plug-in DELL_PSP_EQL_ROUTED as a PSP plug-in class. (See Figure 8.34.)

```
wdc-tse-h56.wsl.vmware.com - PuTTY
~ # esxcli storage core plugin registration list |grep -B2 ROUTED
Module Name          Plugin Name          Plugin Class  Dependencies                    Full Path
-------------------  -------------------  ------------  ------------------------------  ---------
dell-psp-eql-routed  DELL_PSP_EQL_ROUTED  PSP
~ #
```

Figure 8.34   Dell EQL PSP registration

This is also done upon host reboot by jumpstart script psp-eql.json, which runs the equivalent to this command:

```
esxcli storage core plugin registration add --module-name= dell-psp-
eql-routed --plugin-class=PSP --plugin-name=DELL_PSP_EQL_ROUTED
```

- Configures DELL_PSP_EQL_ROUTED as the default PSP for SATP VMW_SATP_EQL. (See Figure 8.35.)

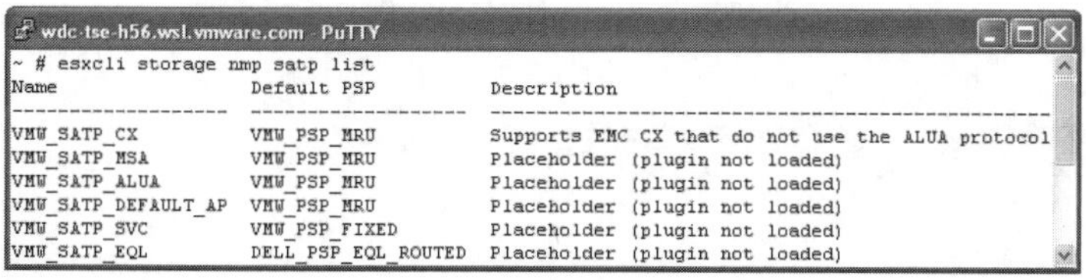
wdc-tse-h56.wsl.vmware.com - PuTTY
~ # esxcli storage nmp satp list
Name Default PSP Description
VMW_SATP_CX VMW_PSP_MRU Supports EMC CX that do not use the ALUA protocol
VMW_SATP_MSA VMW_PSP_MRU Placeholder (plugin not loaded)
VMW_SATP_ALUA VMW_PSP_MRU Placeholder (plugin not loaded)
VMW_SATP_DEFAULT_AP VMW_PSP_MRU Placeholder (plugin not loaded)
VMW_SATP_SVC VMW_PSP_FIXED Placeholder (plugin not loaded)
VMW_SATP_EQL DELL_PSP_EQL_ROUTED Placeholder (plugin not loaded)

Figure 8.35 Default Dell EQL PSP for EQL SATP

The is also done upon reboot by jumpstart script psp-eql-load.json, which runs the equivalent to this command:

```
esxcli storage nmp satp set --satp=VMW_SATP_EQL --default-psp=DELL_
PSP_EQL_ROUTED
```

Uninstalling Dell PSP EQL ROUTED MEM

To uninstall the VIB, follow these steps:

1. First get the VIB name from the installed VIBs list (see Figure 8.36):

```
esxcli software vib list |grep eql
```

Figure 8.36   Listing installed Dell EQL PSP VIB

2. Remove the VIB (see Figure 8.37) using

```
esxcli software vib remove --vibname=dell-eql-routed-psp
```

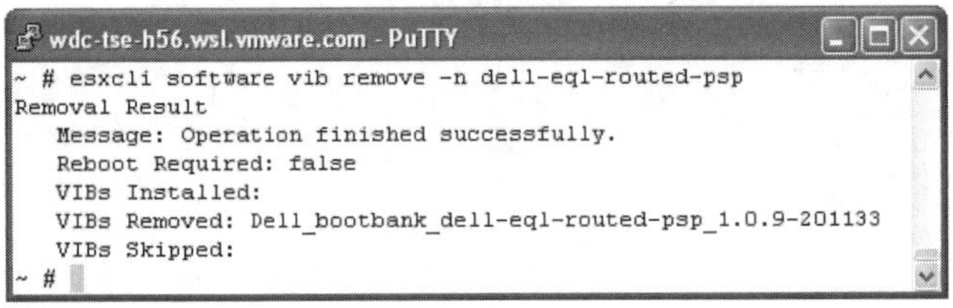

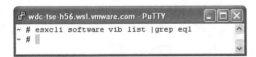

Figure 8.37   Removing Dell EQL PSP VIB

3. Verify that it was removed (see Figure 8.38) using

```
esxcli software vib list |grep eql
```

Figure 8.38   Verifying removal of Dell EQL PSP VIB

Summary

VMware Partners developed MPIO software for use on ESXi 5. There are three products available as of the time of this writing from EMC, Hitachi Data Systems, and Dell. In this chapter I provided details about installing these MPIO software packages and what changes they make to the ESXi host.

## Chapter 9

Using Heterogeneous Storage Configurations

One of the most asked questions I have had is, "Can I mix different storage arrays in my vSphere environment?"

The short answer is "yes!" This chapter explains why and how.

vSphere 5 as well as earlier releases support a maximum of 1024 paths to storage (see the "Factors Affecting Multipathing" section in Chapter 7, "Multipathing and Failover"). This number of paths is the combined paths to all devices presented to the ESXi 5 host from all storage arrays, including local storage and direct attached storage.

What Is a "Heterogeneous" Storage Environment?

As the word indicates, it is the use of *different* arrays in the environment. The word *different* applies to vendors, models, and protocols. You can use a mix of storage array models from the same vendor as well as from multiple vendors. You can also mix Internet Small Computer System Interface (iSCSI) and Fibre Channel (FC) but not for the same device from the same array via the same host. In other words, you cannot access a given device (logical unit number or LUN) via different protocols on the same array from the same host.

> **NOTE**
>
> Network Attach Storage (NAS) is also one of the classes of storage you may use in a heterogeneous storage environment. However, its effect on resources needed by existing block devices is minimal. This chapter deals with block devices only.

Scenarios of Heterogeneous Storage

The most common scenario of using heterogeneous storage is simply *storage sprawl*. You start with a storage array from a given vendor and later outgrow it. You then add more storage from whatever is available at the time. You might get a deal you cannot refuse from another storage vendor that would provide you faster, larger, and more modern storage. You have four choices:

- Install the new storage array and migrate your data from the old array. This is a waste of resources if your old array still has enough juice in it and you still have a valid maintenance agreement with the old array's vendor.

- Keep your old data in place and just add the new array. This sounds like getting the best of both worlds! Well, maybe. That depends on the class of storage of your old array, its age, and the type and speed of storage connectivity compared to the new array. Does your old array still perform and meet your current applications' SLAs (Service Level Agreements)?

- If the array provides a *storage virtualization* feature, present your old array's LUNs to the ESXi hosts as virtual LUNs on the new array and add new physical LUNs on the new array for the additional storage your host's need. I cover this topic in Chapter 11, "Storage Virtualization Devices (SVDs)." Just to summarize, this feature allows the new array to act as an initiator to the old arrays to which you present the LUNs from the old arrays. The SVD then presents the physical LUNs from the old array as virtual LUNs to your ESXi hosts. This configuration takes advantage of all other features available from the new array as if the virtual LUNs were actually located physically on the SVD.

- Some storage vendors might not provide the ability to directly import the data from the virtualized LUNs — for example, SVDs presenting back-end block devices as network file systems (NFSs). This requires creating NFSs on the virtualized LUNs. The hosts do not see these LUN and only see the NFS datastores created on them by the SVD.

Another scenario is designing a storage environment to serve as *tiered* storage, especially now that vSphere 5 introduces Storage DRS which automates migration of the virtual machine files from one datastore to another within a group of datastores that share similar capabilities.

In this scenario, you either integrate a mix of storage arrays of varying storage classes or storage arrays of the same model with varying storage classes. vSphere 5 introduced a new storage API referred to as *VASA*, which stands for vSphere APIs for Storage Awareness.

This API enables storage array vendors to report certain physical device capabilities—including RAID type and types of disks backing LUNs presented to vSphere hosts—to vCenter. The scenario may include storage arrays from the same vendor or multiple vendors of varying classes and storage capabilities. For example, you mix EMC VMAX/Symmetrix arrays with EMC CLARiiON/VNX arrays and IBM DS4000 arrays. These arrays may utilize physical disks of the following types:

- SSD
- FC SCSI
- FC SAS
- Copper SCSI
- Copper SAS
- Copper SATA

Each type is categorized in a storage tier, and you present LUNs backed by each tier to ESXi hosts within their relevant applications SLAs.

ESXi 5 View of Heterogeneous Storage

In Chapter 7 I explained multipathing, and in earlier chapters (2–4) I explained initiators and targets. Let's apply these concepts to help identify how ESXi 5 hosts *see* the various storage arrays in a heterogeneous environment.

Basic Rules of Using Heterogeneous Storage

There is a set of basic rules to observe when designing a heterogeneous storage environment. These rules can be organized in three groups: common rules, FC/FCoE rules, and iSCSI rules.

The common rules are

- Each storage array may have more than one storage processor.
- Each storage processor may have more than one port.
- Each LUN has a unique device ID.
- The total number of paths is limited to 1024 per host, which includes paths to locally attached devices.

The FC/FCoE basic rules are

- Each initiator (HBA port on the ESXi host) is zoned to certain SP ports on *all* relevant storage arrays in the environment.

- VMkernel assigns a target number to each SP port *seen* by each initiator as a unique target number.

The iSCSI basic rules are

- Some iSCSI storage arrays present each LUN on a unique target, which means that the number of targets on the array is equal to the number of LUNs presented from that array. An example of that is the Dell EqualLogic PS series.

- iSCSI software initiators can be bound to physical uplink ports (vmnics) on vSphere 5 virtual switches. This was possible on vSphere 4.x but was done manually. Now there is a UI to configure port binding on vSphere 5. A given ESXi 5 host may have multiple Hardware iSCSI initiators or a single Software iSCSI initiator. The latter can be bound to certain uplink ports.

Naming Convention

As I mentioned in Chapter 7, each path to a given LUN is identified by its *Runtime Name* or by its full *pathname*. The Runtime Name is the combination of *vmhba* number, channel number, target number, and the LUN number—for example, vmhba0:C0:T1:L5. The full pathname is the combination of the same elements using their physical IDs (it does not include the channel number) fc.20000000c971bc62:10000000c971bc62-fc.50060160c6e00 304:5006016046e00304-naa.60060160403029005a59381bc161e011 translates to

- fc.20000000c971bc62:10000000c971bc62 → HBA's WWNN:WWPN

  This is represented in the Runtime Name by vmhba0.

- fc.50060160c6e00304:5006016046e00304 → Target WWNN:WWPN

  This is the SP port that was represented in the Runtime Name by target number T1.

- naa.60060160403029005a59381bc161e011 → LUN's device ID

  This is represented in the Runtime Name by LUN5.

iSCSI devices are addressed in a similar manner but using the iSCSI Qualified Names (iqns) instead of FC WWNNs (World Wide Node Names) and WWPNs (World Wide Port Names). LUN (Device) IDs of iSCSI LUNs are similar to FC LUNs.

So, How Does This All Fit Together?

All physical identifiers in the same storage area network (SAN) are unique. When two different storage arrays present one LUN to an ESXi host using the same LUN number, each LUN has a unique device ID. As a result, ESXi 5 does not confuse both LUNs as being the same LUN. The same is true for target port IDs.

So, let's make the trip from a given initiator to LUN5 on each array using the Runtime Name elements first and then the physical pathname elements.

An example of FC LUN is

```
Runtime Name: vmhba2:C0:T1:L5
```

In this example the first hop is the HBA on the host, which is named vmhba2.

The next hop is the switch and finally the target (the channel can be ignored for now because it is always zero for HBAs other than internal RAID controllers). In this case, the target is assigned number 1. This value does not persist between reboots because it is assigned based on the order the targets are enumerated by the host. That order is based on the order of discovering these targets at boot time and during rescanning. The switch port ID to which the target is connected into the FC fabric affects that order of discovery.

To better illustrate that concept, let me take you through a set of FC cabling diagrams starting with a simple one (see Figure 9.1) and then gradually building up to a more complex environment.

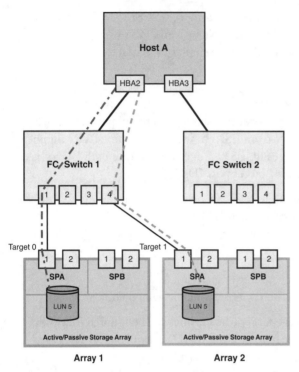

Figure 9.1   Target numbers in a simple configuration

Figure 9.1 shows the connections between hba2 on host A to LUN5 on Array 1 and
LUN5 on Array 2 via FC Switch 1. Array 1 connects to port 1 on Switch 1, and Array 2
connects to Switch 1 on port 4. As a result, because these are the only targets discovered
by Host A, the port on Array 1 was assigned target 0 whereas the port on array 2 was
assigned target 1.

NOTE

Figure 9.1 is oversimplified to illustrate the point. In this case, Switch 2 is not connected to
either storage array.

When you realize that the SAN connectivity is vulnerable to storage processors port
failure, you request from the SAN administrator to add redundant connections to the
second SP on each storage array. The end result is shown in Figure 9.2.

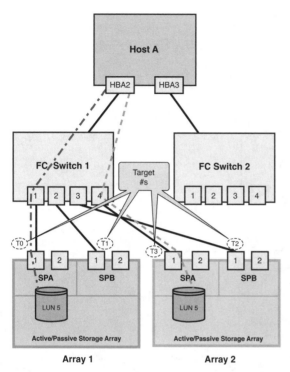

Figure 9.2   Target numbers with added paths from one switch

What the SAN administrator actually did was connect ports 2 and 3 on Switch 1 to Array 1 SPB port 1 and Array 2 SPB port 1.

Now the order of target discovery upon booting Host A makes what was previously known as Target 1 to be Target 3 because the targets connected to switch 1, ports 2 and 3, are assigned target numbers 1 and 2, respectively. (Target numbers are listed in dotted black rectangles in Figure 9.2.)

While checking Host A configurations, you notice that HBA3 is connected to the fabric but does not see any targets. You check with the SAN administrator who tells you that this switch was added recently and connected to the hosts, but no connections to the storage array have been done yet. You request that FC Switch 2 be connected to both storage arrays with redundant connections to both SP on each array. The end result is shown in Figure 9.3.

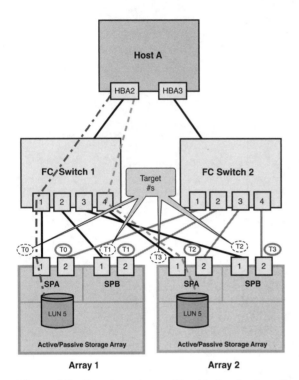

Figure 9.3 Target numbers with added paths from the second switch

How would the host see the newly added targets?

From the perspective of HBA3, they are actually numbered in a similar order starting with target 0 through target 3 (To differentiate from HBA2's targets, the target numbers are shown in solid ovals in Figure 9.3.)

Table 9.1 summarizes the target enumeration order.

Table 9.1 Order of Target Enumeration

HBA Number	Switch Number	Switch Port	Storage Array	Target Port	Active SP?	Target Number
2	1	1	1	SPA-1	Yes	0
		2	1	SPB-1	No	1
		3	2	SPB-1	No	2
		4	2	SPA-1	Yes	3

HBA Number	Switch Number	Switch Port	Storage Array	Target Port	Active SP?	Target Number
3	2	1	1	SPA-2	Yes	0
		2	1	SPB-2	No	1
		3	2	SPA-2	Yes	2
		4	2	SPB-2	No	3

I color-coded the connections to each SP to give you a visual representation of the targets' order. The best practice is symbolized as A-B/A-B. This means that the order of connection is to a port on SPA and then a port on SPB on each storage array.

With that in mind, it should be obvious from the table that connections from FC Switch 1 ports 3 and 4 to Storage Array 2 are reversed compared to the rest of the connections.

How would the target order affect the runtime names of LUN5 on each storage array? Note that I did not include the LUN numbers in the table because this applies to all LUNs presented from each array. You just add the LUN number at the end of the paths, as I show you next.

Let's use Table 9.1 to walk the first path discovered to LUN5 on Array 1 Active SP:

HBA2 → Target 0 → LUN5

Doing the same for LUN 5 on array 2 Active SP would be

HBA2 → Target 3 → LUN5

Based on this, the runtime names for LUN5 on each array (after rebooting Host A) would be

```
vmhba2:C0:T0:L5  ← LUN 5 on array 1
vmhba2:C0:T3:L5  ← LUN 5 on array 2
```

NOTE

The Runtime Name is based on the first target on which the LUN returns a READY state, which is the first path available from the initiators to the Active SP.

Why doesn't the runtime name use paths on HBA3 in this example?

The reason is that at boot time, the LUNs are discovered on HBA2 first because it was the first HBA to be initialized by the HBA's driver.

The full list paths to LUN5 on Array 1would be

```
vmhba2:C0:T0:L5 Active ← Current path
vmhba2:C0:T1:L5 Standby
vmhba3:C0:T0:L5 Active
vmhba3:C0:T1:L5 Standby
```

The paths to LUN5 on Array 2 would be

```
vmhba2:C0:T2:L5 Standby
vmhba2:C0:T3:L5 Active ← Current path
vmhba3:C0:T2:L5 Active
vmhba3:C0:T3:L5 Standby
```

Observe that the path to the Active SP for the current path is the second path in the ordered list for LUN5 on Array 2. This matches our observations from Table 9.1.

Based on your observations, you request from the SAN administrator to swap ports 3 and 4 on FC switch 1 to meet the best practices. The next time you reboot this host, the targets are renumbered as shown in Figure 9.4.

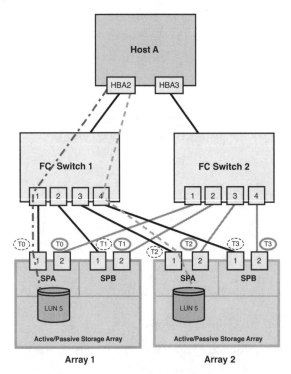

Figure 9.4   Best practices connectivity

Why Do We Care? Should We Care at All?

In releases earlier than vSphere 4.x target numbers were critical to certain functions because the only canonical (currently known as runtime) naming of LUNs and paths to them were done via the combination of HBA, Target, and LUN numbers. vSphere 4.x introduced a new naming convention that utilizes physical IDs of the same three components (HBA, Target, and LUN). This continues to be the case in vSphere 5.

So, to illustrate the new naming, let's take a look at LUN5 from Array 1 (on an EMC CLARiiON):

```
fc.20000000c971bc62:10000000c971bc62-
fc.50060160c6e00304:5006016046e00304-
naa.6006016040302900595938 1bc161e011
```

The preceding example was wrapped at the hyphens.

The substitution of the elements names is listed in Table 9.2.

Table 9.2 Naming Convention Comparison

Element	Old Name	New Name
HBA number	vmhba2	fc.20000000c971bc62:10000000c971bc62
Target number	T0	fc.50060160c6e00304:5006016046e00304
LUN number	L5	naa.6006016040302900595938 1bc161e011

See the "Naming Convention" section earlier in this chapter for explanations.

Now that you understand the new naming convention, it should be clear that the order of target discovery does not affect the target numbers and in turn the pathnames. This is not true for the display names.

Summary

The heterogeneous storage environment is supported by VMware and aids in expanding your storage environment while preserving your existing investment. You can also use it for establishing tiered storage for various applications SLAs.

Using runtime names, targets are numbered in the order they are discovered. Adding targets live results in them being enumerated in the order the new targets are added as well as by their connections to the switches. At boot time they are re-enumerated in the order they are connected to the switches.

LUNs with the same LUN number on different storage arrays are identified by their device IDs and association with the target port IDs.

## Chapter 10

Using VMDirectPath I/O

One of the least-known features introduced in vSphere 4.x that continues to be in vSphere 5 is VMDirectPath I/O. In this chapter, I explain what it is, how it works, and some practical design implementations.

What Is VMDirectPath?

Have you ever wanted to access a certain storage device directly from within a Virtual Machine (VM) but the devices is not Raw Device Mapping (RDM) capable?

Do you have a fibre-attached tape library that you want to use within a VM and provide multipathing to it?

Do you have an application that requires a specific Peripheral Component Interconnect (PCI) device accessed directly from within the VM?

The answer to these questions is a definite yes! (With caveats.)

VMDirectPath on vSphere 4.x and 5.0 uses a hardware implementation of IOMMU (I/O Memory Management Unit). This implementation is referred to as VT-d (Virtual Technology for Directed I/O) on Intel Platform and AMD IOMMU on AMD platform. The latter was experimental on vSphere 4.x, and it continues to be experimental on vSphere 5. This technology allows for passing through input/output (I/O) directly to a VM to which you dedicate a supported PCI I/O device — for example, 10Gb/s Ethernet NIC or an 8Gb FC HBA.

Which I/O Devices Are Supported?

Currently the list of supported devices is limited and there is no official HCL (Hardware Compatibility List) listing them. The current support model for these devices is the PVSP (Partner Verified and Supported Products) program. This support model means that VMware partners test and verify the implementation and interoperability of a specific I/O device within a specific configuration. Such configuration is documented in a VMware Knowledgebase (KB) article. The partner qualifying the configuration is the first line of support of such a configuration. By the time this book is in print, this might have been changed to be covered under the RPQ (Request for Product Qualification) Program. Check the VMware support website for the current support status.

TIP

The I/O device assigned to a VM is dedicated to that VM and cannot be shared with the ESXi host. Certain devices with multiple PCI physical functions may be shared with other VMs on the same host (one function per VM).

To identify which devices are known to be shareable or not, check the /etc/vmware/ passthru.map file. See Table 10.1 for a tabulation of the current version content on vSphere 5.

Table 10.1   Passthru.map File Listing

Vendor ID	Device ID	Reset Method	fptShareable
Intel 82598 (Oplin) 10Gig cards can be reset with d3d0			
8086	10b6	D3d0	Default
8086	10c6	D3d0	Default
8086	10c7	D3d0	default
8086	10c8	D3d0	default
8086	10dd	D3d0	default
Broadcom 57710/57711/57712 10Gig cards are not shareable			
14e4	164e	default	false
14e4	164f	default	false
14e4	1650	default	false
14e4	1662	link	False
Qlogic 8Gb FC card cannot be shared			
1077	2532	default	false

Vendor ID	Device ID	Reset Method	fptShareable
LSILogic 1068–based SAS controllers			
1000	0056	D3d0	default
1000	0058	D3d0	default

The basic rule is that if the device can be reset via the d3d0 reset method, it can be shareable between VMs on the same ESXi host. The possible values for the Reset Method column are flr, d3d0, link, bridge, and default.

The default method is Function Level Reset (FLR) if the device supports it. Otherwise, ESXi defaults next to link reset and then bus reset. The latter two methods can prevent the device from being shareable. These are summarized in Table 10.2.

Table 10.2 Reset Methods Comparison

Reset Method	Explanation	Device Shareable?
Function Level Reset	When the VM using the pass-through device requests a PCI reset, only the PCI function on the device is reset. For example, if there are two Ethernet ports on the NIC, only the port used by the VM is reset.	Yes
Link Reset	When a reset is required, the Physical Function (PF) link is reset instead of resetting the PCI function itself.	No
Bus Reset	When a reset is required, the PCI bus is reset instead of the PCI function itself. This affects all functions on the PCI device.	No

The last column in Table 10.1, fptShareable, means Full Pass Through Shareable. The possible values are Default, True, and False. The default value is True.

Locating Hosts Supporting VMDirectPath IO on the HCL

The list of devices verified with vSphere 4.x should still be usable on vSphere 5.

Although there is no dedicated HCL for the I/O devices, systems supporting IOMMU and certified with vSphere 5 are listed on the VMware HCL. You can search for certified systems following this procedure:

1. Go to http://www.vmware.com/go/hcl.

2. Select **Systems / Servers** from the **What Are You Looking For** pick list (see Figure 10.1).

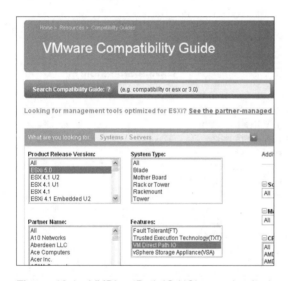

Figure 10.1   VMDirectPath IO HCL search criteria

3. Select **ESXi 5.0** as the **Product Release Version**.

4. Select **VM Direct Path IO** in the **Features** field.

5. Click the **Update and View Results** button (see Figure 10.2).

Figure 10.2   Preparing to view HCL search results

6. Scroll down to view the search results (see Figure 10.3).

Click here to **Read** Important Support Information.

Server Device and Model Information

The detailed lists show actual vendor devices that are either physically tested or are similar to the devices tested by VMware or VMw
only for the devices that are listed in this document
Click on the 'Model' for details.
Click on the 'CPU Series' for details including EVC and Fault Tolerant modes.

Search Results: Your search for " Systems / Servers" returned **8 results**.

Partner Name	Model	CPU Series	Supported Releases	
DELL	PowerEdge 1955	Intel Xeon 50xx Series	ESXi	5.0
DELL	PowerEdge R910	Intel Xeon E7-2800 Series	ESXi	5.0
DELL	PowerEdge R910	Intel Xeon E7-4800 Series	ESXi	5.0
DELL	PowerEdge R910	Intel Xeon E7-8800 Series	ESXi	5.0
DELL	PowerEdge T710	Intel Xeon 55xx Series	ESXi	5.0
Unisys Corporation	ES3000 Model 3590R G2	Intel Xeon E7-2800 Series	ESXi	5.0
Unisys Corporation	ES3000 Model 3590R G2	Intel Xeon E7-4800 Series	ESXi	5.0
Unisys Corporation	ES3000 Model 3590R G2	Intel Xeon E7-8800 Series	ESXi	5.0

Figure 10.3   Viewing HCL search results

Although the current list shows a few systems from Dell and Unisys, other systems not on
the list may work, but if issues with VMDirectPath are reported on such systems, you will
most probably not get support from VMware or the I/O device partner.

VMDirectPath I/O Configuration

After you have verified that your system is on the HCL supporting the VM Direct Path
IO feature or if you are adventurous and use a system based on Intel XEON 55xx family of
central processing units (CPUs) in a non-production environment, you are now ready to
configure VMDirectPath I/O.

1. Log on to vCenter that manages the ESXi host or directly to the host using vSphere 5 Client as an Administrator/Root user.

2. Locate the host in the inventory tree and select it.

3. Select the **Configuration** tab (see Figure 10.4).

4. Select the **Advanced Settings** link under the **Hardware** section (see Figure 10.4).

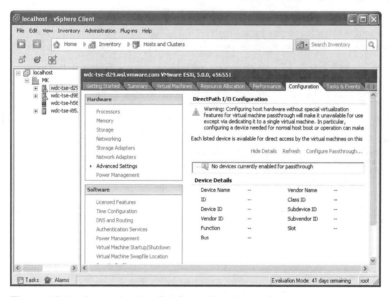

Figure 10.4   Accessing the Configure Passthrough menu

If the system is not capable of this feature, you see a `Host does not support passthrough configuration` message instead, as shown in Figure 10.5. Notice that the **Configure Passthrough** link is not enabled because the feature is not supported.

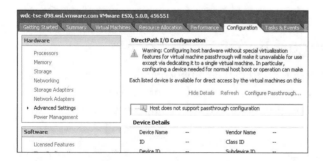

Figure 10.5   Host does not support Passthrough configuration

If your system is capable of Passthrough configuration, you see a message No devices currently enabled for Passthrough similar to what is shown in Figure 10.4.

To start the configuration process, you may follow this procedure starting from the view in Figure 10.4:

1. Click the **Configure Passthrough** link.

   You see the dialog shown in Figure 10.6. Highlighting a device displays its PCI info in the lower part of the dialog.

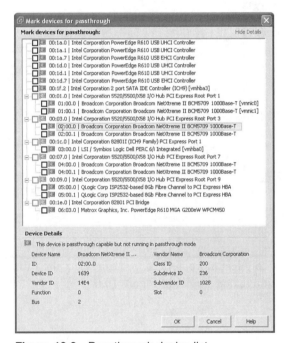

Figure 10.6   Passthrough device list

2. To enable a device, select the checkbox next to it.

3. If the device you selected has a dependent device, you see the message shown in Figure 10.7. An example of that is a dual-port network interface card (NIC) where each port shows as a separate PCI function of the device. This is due to the lack of PCI-to-PCI Bridge on the dual port card. In this example, you see the PCI ID 2.00.0 and 2.00.1. If NIC had a PCI-to-PCI bridge, it would have had a separate device or slot number for each port — for example, 2.00.0 and 2.01.0. Selecting **OK** enables

both ports. See also the tip in the "Which I/O Devices Are Supported" section earlier in this chapter.

Figure 10.7 Dependent device message

4. To complete the configuration, click the **OK** button as shown in Figure 10.8.

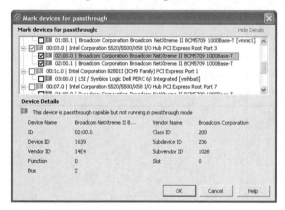

Figure 10.8 Dependent devices selection

5. You must click the **Refresh** link for the selected devices to show up in the list (see Figure 10.9). In the future, if you need to select more devices, you can select the **Edit** link, which takes you to a device selection dialog similar to Figure 10.6.

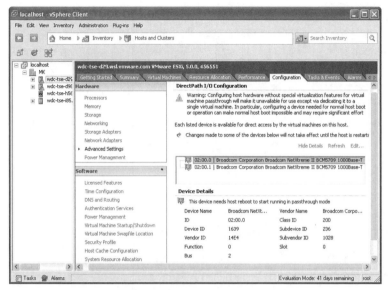

Figure 10.9   Configured devices require reboot

6. Notice that selecting one of the configured devices in Figure 10.9 shows a `This device needs host reboot to start running in passthrough mode` message in the **Device Details** section. This is due to the fact that the device was controlled by vmkernel and now you need to reboot so that it can be passed through directly to the virtual machine that you configure in the next steps.

7. After the host is rebooted, the devices should show up on the list with a green icon (see Figure 10.10).

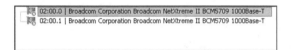

Figure 10.10   Passthrough devices ready

8. Locate the VM to which you plan to add the Passthrough PCI device, right-click it, and then select the **Edit Settings** option (see Figure 10.11).

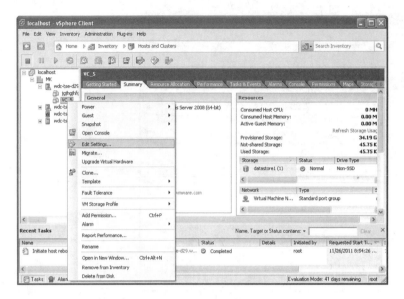

Figure 10.11 Editing a VM

9. Under the **Hardware** tab, click the **Add** button (see Figure 10.12).

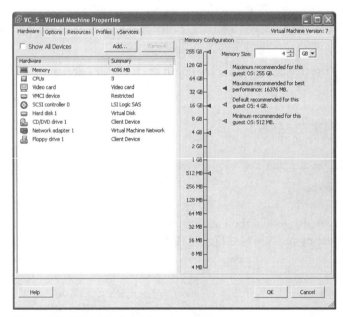

Figure 10.12 Virtual machine properties

10. Select the **PCI Devices** type and then click **Next** (see Figure 10.13).

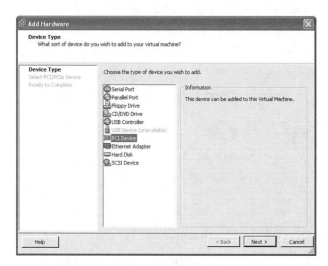

Figure 10.13   The Add Hardware dialog

11. Select the device from the pull-down list under the **Connection** section and then click **Next** as shown in Figure 10.14.

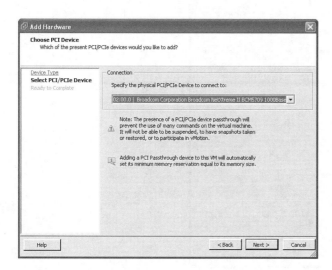

Figure 10.14   Adding a PCI device

NOTE

As the dialog in Figure 10.14 indicates, there are limitations imposed on the Virtual Machine design:

- VM cannot be suspended.
- VM cannot have a snapshot taken or restored.
- VM cannot be vMotioned, which means limited availability when it is part of a DRS cluster.
- VM cannot be protected by HA (High Availability).
- VM cannot be protected by FT (Fault Tolerance).
- The VM's minimum memory reservation is automatically set to its memory size.

12. In the **Ready to Complete** dialog, click the **Finish** button.

13. In the **Virtual Machine Properties** dialog, click **OK** to save the changes (see Figure 10.15).

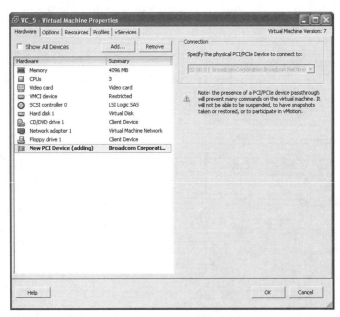

Figure 10.15   Saving VM configuration changes

14. Power on the VM. The guest OS detects the newly added device and prompts you to install its driver (see Figure 10.16). Select the relevant option to proceed with the driver installation.

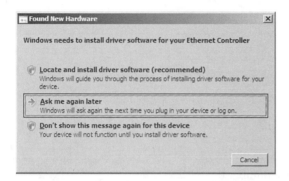

Figure 10.16   Guest detects new device

15. Figure 10.17 shows the device manager in the guest OS after installing the NIC driver. Notice that it is listed under Network Adapters as well as System Devices. If the device is a SCSI, SAS, or FC HBA, it displays under the Storage Controllers node.

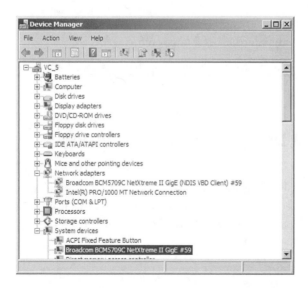

Figure 10.17   Guest OS showing configured device

What Gets Added to the VM's Configuration File?

The procedure in the previous section results in a Virtual Machine Configuration File (vmx) with the entries shown in Listing 10.1.

Listing 10.1   PCI Passthru Entries in vmx File

```
pciPassthru0.present = "TRUE"
pciPassthru0.deviceId = "1639"
pciPassthru0.vendorId = "14e4"
pciPassthru0.systemId = "4ea55642-5e38-0525-7664-00219b99ddd8"
pciPassthru0.id = "02:00.0"
sched.mem.min = "1072"
```

The first entry enables PCI Passthru device number 0.

The second entry sets the passthrough device ID based on the physical device PCI properties. If you look at Figure 10.8, you see that value listed as 1639.

The third entry sets the vendor ID from the same information in Figure 10.8.

The fourth entry sets the system ID, which is the ESXi host's UUID. You can obtain this ID using the following command:

```
esxcli system uuid get
4ea55642-5e38-0525-7664-00219b99ddd8
```

The fifth entry sets the PCI ID (which is the Slot:Device.Function format).

The last entry sets the VM's minimum memory to match the limit that was specified when this VM was created.

Practical Examples of VM Design Scenarios Utilizing VMDirectPath I/O

Some configurations were qualified by VMware partners under vSphere 4.1. As of the date of this writing, they have not been updated for vSphere 5. However, because this feature was not changed between 4.1 and 5.0, I can safely assume that what was qualified on vSphere 4.1 ends up being qualified on vSphere 5.0.

HP Command View EVA Scenario

HP qualified the following configuration:

Qualified HBAs

- Emulex LPe 1205-HP 8Gb FC HBA (456972-B21)
- Emulex LPe12000 8Gb FC HBA (AJ762A/81E)
- Emulex LPe12002 8Gb FC HBA (AJ763A/82E)
- QLogic QMH2562 8Gb FC HBA (451871-B21)
- QLogic QLE2562 8Gb FC HBA
- QLogic QLE2560 8Gb FC HBA

Qualified Software

- Minimum supported version Command View EVA (Enterprise Virtual Array) version 9.3:
  - SSSU v9.3
  - EVAPerf v9.3
- SMI-S v 9.3
  - Layered applications support
  - All layered applications currently supported with supported CVEVA (Command View EVA) version and VMDirectPath

Qualified HP Storage Arrays

- EVA 4100/6100 (HSV200-A)
- EVA 8100 (HSV210-A)
- EVA 4400 (HSV300)
- EVA 4400 (HSV300-S)
- EVA 6400 (HSV400)
- EVA 8400 (HSV450)

Qualified Guest OS

- Microsoft Windows 2008 R2 Standard
- Microsoft Windows 2008 R2 Enterprise Edition
- Microsoft Windows 2008 R2 Datacenter Edition
- Microsoft Windows 2008 R2 Webserver Edition

How Is It Used?

This configuration passes through one of the qualified Fibre Channel (FC) HBAs (Host Bus Adapters) to the VM where Command View EVA is installed to manage one of the qualified EVA Storage arrays from within the VM. This effectively replaces the physical appliance that does the same function.

Passing Through Physical Tape Devices

Configuring a VM with a passthrough HBA enables the guest OS to drive tape devices attached to the HBA. So, if the HBA is an FC initiator, the VM can gain direct access to FC-attached tape libraries and drives that are zoned to the HBA. This is different from NPIV (N_Port ID Virtualization) where the latter creates virtual N-Ports assigned to the VM and the devices are accessed as RDMs.

This also works with SAS and SCSI HBAs for direct-attached tape drives and media libraries even if they did not work on the ESXi host directly or with "generic passthrough" configuration.

If you configure more than one FC HBA, you can utilize multipathing using guest OS–based multipathing software.

Using VMDirectPath I/O does not require N-Port virtualization nor does it need RDMs configured. The host has no access to the attached devices because it does not have access to the HBA assigned to the VM.

IMPORTANT NOTE

This configuration is not supported by VMware. If your storage partner is willing to support it, make sure that they qualify it and submit the results to VMware under the PVSP program or RPQ (Request for Product Qulalification).

There have been a few issues reported to VMware regarding some I/O devices failing to work or the VMs failing to use the assigned device. I would strongly recommend that you check VMware Knowledgebase for reported issues. I would love to hear from you about your experience via my blog at http://vSphereStorage.com or twitter @mostafavmw.

What About vmDirectPath Gen. 2?

In browsing through the vSphere Client's user interface (UI), you might have stumbled upon a field called DirectPath I/O Gen. 2. What is it and how is it used?

You can actually find it in the host's Summary tab (see Figure 10.18). If the field's value is Supported, it means that the host platform supports both IOMMU and SR-IOV (Single Root I/O Virtualization). It also means that if you install PCIe network cards that support SR-IOV in this host, the cards can be used for passing through Network I/O to VMs (I explain SR-IOV in the next section). The main difference between this and the first-generation VMDirectPath I/O is that Gen. 2 is network device I/O centric, a distributed virtual switch must be configured, and the VM's virtual NIC uses VMXNET3 emulation instead of exposing the physical NIC's properties to the guest OS. Another major difference is that the I/O card is not dedicated to a single VM.

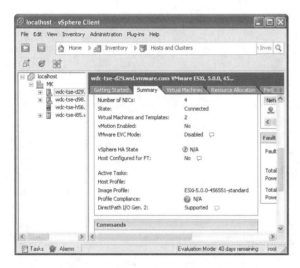

Figure 10.18   System supports DirectPath I/O Gen. 2

How Does SR-IOV Work?

PCIe devices that support SR-IOV have multiple Virtual Functions (VFs) associated with one Physical Function (PF) with a single PCI root, which is something similar to what I mention in Step 10 in the "VMDirectPath I/O Configuration" section but on a larger scale. Instead of two physical functions sharing the PCI root, multiple VFs are associated with a PF on a single PCI root.

To illustrate the difference between VMDirectPath I/O and its second generation, Figure 10.19 shows the VMDirectPath where each I/O device is assigned to a VM.

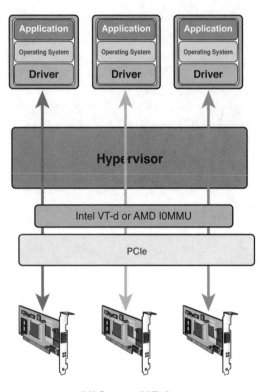

NICs or HBAs

Figure 10.19   VMDirectPath I/O direct assignment

Figure 10.20 shows the second generation's VFs, their association with PFs, and assignment to VMs.

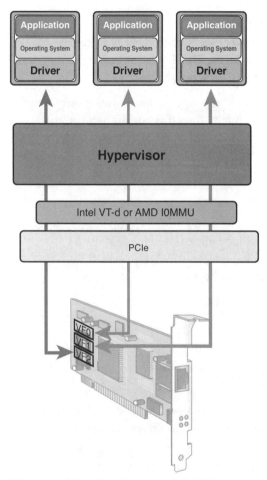

Figure 10.20   VF assignment (SR-IOV)

Figure 10.20 shows a single PCIe I/O card, which can be a NIC or an HBA that provides VFs. Each VF is assigned to a separate VM. The latter uses a VF driver for the pass-through I/O device. For example, passthrough NICs would use the VMXNET3 driver.

The virtual functions can be migrated from one device to another, thus removing the restrictions with vMotion that were imposed by the earlier generation of VMDirectPath IO.

Supported VMDirectPath I/O Devices

There is no HCL for VMDirectPath I/O devices per se. Rather, devices as well as qualified configurations, are planned to be listed on the PVSP page at http://www.vmware.com/resources/compatibility/vcl/partnersupport.php.

This page will list both generations of devices. As of the date of this writing, there were no qualified devices or configurations listed yet. By the time this book is in print, this policy might have been changed to requiring RPQ instead of PVSP. Please check the VMware support website for the current support status.

Example of DirectPath IO Gen. 2

Considering a VM running on an ESXi 5 host on a Cisco Unified Computing System (UCS) that is equipped with Cisco Virtual Machine Fabric Extender (VM-FEX) distributed switches, the following features are available with VMDirectPath IO Gen. 2 configuration (VM-FEX must be in High-Performance Mode):

- VM can be suspended and resumed.
- VM can have a snapshot taken or restored.
- VM can be vMotioned, which means it can be part of a DRS cluster.
- VM can be protected by HA (High Availability).

The trick for supporting vMotion is that the vmkernel quiesces and checkpoints the Cisco Dynamic Ethernet interface presented by the Cisco Virtual Interface Card (VIC).

The state, created by the checkpoint process, is transferred to the destination host in a similar fashion to how the memory checkpoint used to be done for vMotion.

Troubleshooting VMDirectPath I/O

Possible issues you may encounter fall into three groups: interrupt handling, device sharing, and IRQ (interrupt request) sharing.

The latter can be Virtual IRQ or Physical IRQ.

Interrupt Handling and IRQ Sharing

The default interrupt handling for PCI Passthrough on vSphere 5 is MSI/MSI-x (Message Signaled Interrupts). This works with most devices by default. If you come across a device that fails to be configured with VMDirectPath, you may need to disable MSI for the VM that uses that device. Effectively, this allows the VM to use IO-APIC (Advanced Programmable Interrupt Controller) instead of MSI. Common examples of such a device are Broadcom 57710 and 57711 when assigned to a Windows 2003 or 2008 VM.

To disable MSI for the given device in the VM, edit the VM's vmx file and add the following line:

```
pciPassthru0.msiEnabled = "FALSE"
```

If the virtual device number is higher than 0 (that is, you have more than one passthrough device), substitute the 0 with the relevant value.

There are some devices that are known to work with the MSI-enabled option set to TRUE:

- Qlogic 2500 FC HBA

- LSI SAS 1068E HBA

- Intel 82598 10Gbps NIC

Device Sharing

When an I/O device has more than one PCI function (for example, dual or quad port NIC) and there is no PCI-to-PCI Bridge on the card, most probably it is not fptShareable (full passthrough shareable). See Table 10.1 earlier for details. If you are using a device that is not listed in that table and you know it is capable of resetting itself properly using D3 to D0 power transition (D3D0 value in Table 10.1), you might need to add an entry to the /etc/vmware/pcipassthru.map file. The following is a sample of the format:

```
<Vendor ID>  <Device ID>  d3d0  default
```

To identify the device's PCI ID info, you may run the following command on the ESXi Shell locally, via SSH or via vMA 5:

```
esxcli hardware pci list
```

Listing 10.2 shows sample output listing one device:

Listing 10.2 Sample Listing of PCI Device ID Info

```
000:001:00.1
   Address: 000:001:00.1
   Segment: 0x0000
   Bus: 0x01
   Slot: 0x00
```

```
Function: 0x01
VMkernel Name: vmnic1
Vendor Name: Broadcom Corporation
Device Name: Broadcom NetXtreme II BCM5709 1000Base-T
Configured Owner: Unknown
Current Owner: VMkernel
Vendor ID: 0x14e4
Device ID: 0x1639
SubVendor ID: 0x1028
SubDevice ID: 0x0236
Device Class: 0x0200
Device Class Name: Host bridge
Programming Interface: 0x00
Revision ID: 0x20
Interrupt Line: 0x0e
IRQ: 14
Interrupt Vector: 0x88
PCI Pin: 0x66
Spawned Bus: 0x00
Flags: 0x0201
Module ID: 27
Module Name: bnx2
Chassis: 0
Physical Slot: 0
Slot Description: Embedded NIC 2
Passthru Capable: true
Parent Device: PCI 0:0:1:0
Dependent Device: PCI 0:0:1:0
Reset Method: Link reset
FPT Sharable: true
```

The values you need are highlighted for easier identification.

So, the sample line looks like this for the device in this example:

```
14e4    1639    d3d0    default
```

NOTE

Based on the sample device in Listing10.2, the `Reset Method` is `Link reset`. It also shows that the values of `Passthru Capable` as well as `FPT Shareable` are set to `true`.

These mean that without adding the entry in the pcipassthru.map file, the default values are what are reported by the PCI info shown in Listing 10.2 and that the device is Shareable and supports Full Passthru Sharing. Adding the entries in the file overrides Reset Method only because you are leaving the fptShareable set to default.

Summary

VMDirectPath I/O has been available since vSphere 4.x and continues to exist in vSphere 5. You can use it to pass through physical storage or network devices, which expose the physical I/O card to the guest OS. The latter installed the physical card's driver. Design scenarios include FC-attached and direct-attached tape drives and media libraries and other devices that otherwise are not available via vmkernel.

A second generation of VMDirectPath IO is introduced in vSphere 5 that utilizes SR-IOV. This has not been fully implemented yet, and I have seen it with Network I/O Passthrough. As of the date of this writing, I have not seen an HBA implementation yet.

SR-IOV spec is available from PCI-SIG at http://www.pcisig.com/specifications/iov/single_root/.

An introduction paper is available from Intel at http://www.intel.com/content/dam/doc/application-note/pci-sig-sr-iov-primer-sr-iov-technology-paper.pdf.

## Chapter 11

Storage Virtualization Devices (SVDs)

Storage vendors competing in the enterprise had to come up with ways to first coexist with and then migrate from their competitors' storage. This need begat a storage feature that is the topic of this chapter: Storage Virtualization Devices (SVDs). As simple as it may sound, it is a complex concept and varies from one vendor to another. This chapter deals with this topic from a vSphere 5 perspective. It is not intended to be an in-depth discussion of the SVD configuration details.

SVD Concept

The concept can be simplified as follows:

Take existing third-party block storage and present it to initiators as if it is the SVD's own storage. The SVD then presents virtualized storage as block devices or network file systems.

How Does It Work?

Virtualizing storage can be done via any—or a mix—of the following approaches:

- **Address Space Remapping**—The SVD abstracts the physical location of the data and provides a logical representation of that data to the initiators. For example, more than one LUN (logical unit number) on the back-end array (the one being virtualized) can be pooled together as one large LUN. The front-end array (the SVD itself) keeps a mapping table of which blocks of the virtual LUN (the one it presents to the initiators) are mapped to which blocks on the back-end LUNs.

- **Metadata**—This is "data about data" that presents the big picture to the initiators. In simple words, the metadata holds the "structure" of the data presented to the initiators and might include the mapping table mentioned in the previous point. The device details—LUN size, boundaries, RAID type, and so on—are presented by the metadata of the SVD. This is somewhat like VMFS presenting a physical device to a VM as a RAW Device Mapping (RDM). The properties of the device are stored in the virtual machine file system (VMFS) metadata, but the physical block locations are obtained from the storage array hosting the physical LUN.

- **I/O Redirection**—When I/O is sent from the initiator to a specific block on the virtualized device, it gets redirected to the mapped physical block on the back-end device. It is somewhat like how VMkernel redirects the I/O sent from a VM to an RDM. This function is based on one or more of these three mechanisms (see Figure 11.1).

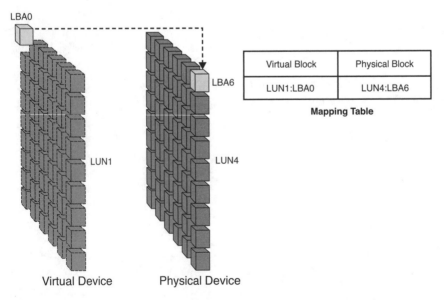

Figure 11.1   I/O redirection and address space mapping

For example, when I/O is sent to a block on the virtual device (Logical Block Address 0 (LBA0) on LUN1), it gets redirected to the Logical Block Address of the block on the physical device (for example, LBA6 on LUN4) based on the mapping table defined by the Address Space Remapping. The metadata would have pointers to the data on the virtual LUN so that the initiator would know where the data is located.

SVD Architecture

SVDs are available mostly in hardware configuration with specialized firmware. There are some varieties that are available in software form. However, the latter are certified with vSphere in association with certain hardware configurations or software-only configuration. For example, IBM SVC, HDS USPv, and NetApp V-series were certified as hardware solutions, whereas others such as Falcon Store NSS Gateway were certified as a Storage Virtual Appliance.

Figure 11.2 shows a diagram depicting the SVD architecture.

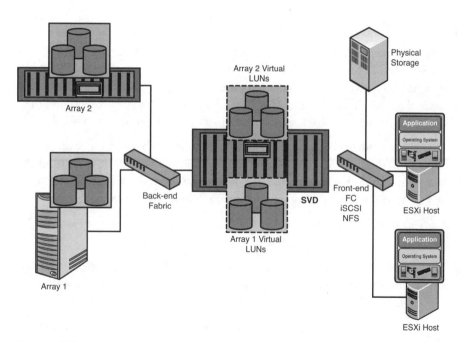

Figure 11.2 SVD architecture

SVD storage connects to two different sets of fabrics: front-end and back-end fabrics. The front-end fabric connects the hosts to the SVD, and the back-end fabric connects the SVD to the back-end storage arrays. The front-end fabric may be substituted with iSCSI or NFS protocols in the few configurations certified with iSCSI or NFS front-end. Regardless of the front-end protocol, the back-end is only supported with Fibre Channel (FC) connectivity between the SVD and the back-end storage.

In this configuration the SVD acts as an initiator to the back-end storage arrays while it acts as a target for the ESXi hosts.

NOTE

In the case of FC front- and back-ends, the fabric separation can be physical or logical. The FC back-end can be done via zoning where the hosts and the front-end array's ports are in one set of zones, whereas the front-end array and back-end array's ports are in a separate set of zones.

Constraints

The SVD configuration certified for vSphere 5 restricts the back-end storage arrays' connectivity to FC only. Other protocols are not supported for back-end storage. The ESXi hosts must never be given access to the back-end arrays while zoned to the SVD. This is to prevent data corruption because the hosts may treat the physical LUNs and the virtual LUNs as different devices. Back-end LUNs must never be presented to hosts.

If the physical LUNs on the back-end storage have VMFS3 or VMFS5 volumes on them, the virtual LUNs representing them are seen by the ESXi hosts as snapshot LUNs and the VMFS volumes are not mounted automatically. I discuss the behavior of snapshot technologies with VMFS datastores (or volumes) in Chapter 15, "Snapshot Handling."

The ESXi hosts can access the VMFS volumes via the virtual LUNs by one of two methods:

- **Resignature the VMFS volumes**—This is the process of regenerating a new VMFS volume signature and writing it to the metadata. This result is a renamed volume with a prefix *snap*.

- **Force mount the VMFS volumes**—This is a new feature in vSphere 5 that allows the vSphere Administrator to mount a VMFS volume that resides on a snapshot LUN without having to resignature the VMFS volume.

I discuss these methods in Chapter 15 as well.

Migrating Back-End Storage to the SVD

If your final goal of utilizing the SVD is to migrate your data to the new storage array and then decommission the old storage, you can proceed further beyond the configuration discussed in this chapter by using features provided by the SVD to migrate the data from the physical LUNs to physical storage on the SVD to back the virtual LUNs. This process is transparent to the front-end initiators (ESXi hosts) and does not usually impose a negative effect on I/O performance. When the data is completely migrated, the virtual LUN is switched to being a physical LUN internally by the SVD. At this point, the SVD acts as a physical storage array like any others, connected to the initiators via the front-end fabric.

SVD Design Decisions

There are several choices to consider in your SVD design. Here, I group them into two major groups: front-end and back-end choices.

Front-End Design Choices

There are several design choices for the front-end, which I cover in this section.

Which SVD?

The choice of SVD is yours based on the features available, supported storage tiers, supported protocols, capacity, and so on.

The front-end array must be on VMware HCL (Hardware Compatibility List) as an SVD certified with ESXi 5. The back-end array must also be certified with ESXi 5 (with FC connectivity). To verify that, you may follow these steps:

1. Go to http://www.vmware.com/go/hcl.
2. Select **Storage/SAN** from the pull-down menu as shown in Figure 11.3.

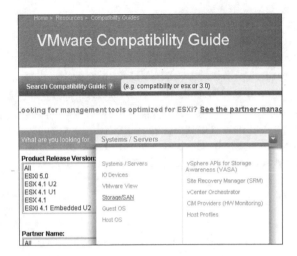

Figure 11.3   Accessing storage/SAN HCL page

3. Select **ESXi 5.0** in the **Product Release Version:** box. (See Figure 11.4.)

4. Select **SVD** in the **Array Type**: box.

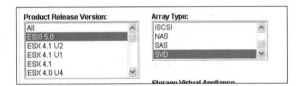

Figure 11.4   Selecting release and array type

5. Click the storage vendor's name under the **Partner Name** box. You may select more than one by pressing **Ctrl** and clicking on each partner's name.

6. Click the **Update and View Results** button.

7. Scroll down to see the results.

Which Protocol?

The next design choice for the front-end is the supported protocols. As I mentioned earlier, SVDs are supported with the FC protocol as well as Fibre Channel over Ethernet (FCoE), Internet Small Computer System Interface (iSCSI), and network file system

(NFS). If you plan to use the SVD as a migration tool to the SVD's physical storage, you might want to consider the additional storage capacity that you plan to use after the migration is completed. For example, you might want to add more disks on the array to accommodate the data to be migrated from the back-end storage.

Which Bandwidth?

As for the connection speed, your choice is limited by what is listed on the HCL for the SVD. To identify which speeds are supported, follow these steps as a continuation of the HCL search mentioned earlier:

1. In the search results, locate the storage array you plan to use and select the hyperlink under the **Model** column for the array as shown in Figure 11.5.

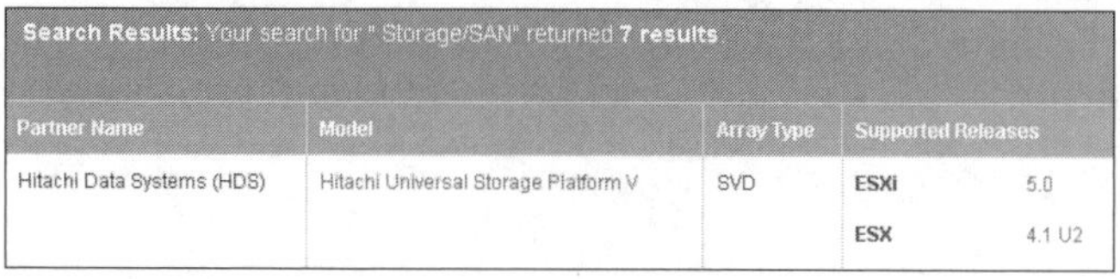

Search Results: Your search for " Storage/SAN" returned **7 results**

Partner Name	Model	Array Type	Supported Releases	
Hitachi Data Systems (HDS)	Hitachi Universal Storage Platform V	SVD	ESXi	5.0
			ESX	4.1 U2

Figure 11.5   Search results

2. The array details are displayed (see Figure 11.6).

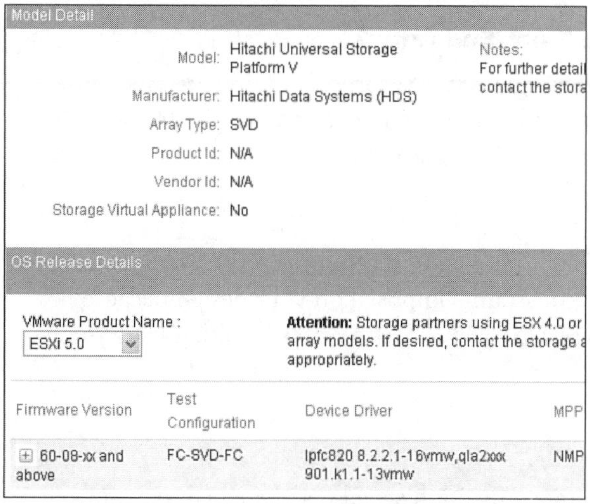

Model Detail

Model:	Hitachi Universal Storage Platform V	Notes: For further detail contact the stora
Manufacturer:	Hitachi Data Systems (HDS)	
Array Type:	SVD	
Product Id:	N/A	
Vendor Id:	N/A	
Storage Virtual Appliance:	No	

OS Release Details

VMware Product Name : ESXi 5.0	**Attention:** Storage partners using ESX 4.0 or array models. If desired, contact the storage appropriately.		
Firmware Version	Test Configuration	Device Driver	MPP
⊞ 60-08-xx and above	FC-SVD-FC	lpfc820 8.2.2.1-16vmw,qla2xxx 901.k1.1-13vmw	NMP

Figure 11.6   Array details

The connection speed would be based on the **Test Configuration** column's value as shown in Table 11.1.

Table 11.1 Test Configuration and Connection Speeds

Test Configuration	Front-end Connection Speed	Back-end Connection Speed
FC-SVD-FC	FC 4Gb or 2Gb	FC 4Gb or 2Gb
8G FC-SVD-FC	FC 8Gb	FC 4Gb or 2Gb
ISCSI-SVD-FC	iSCSI 1 Gb or 10Gb	FC 4Gb or 2Gb
NAS-SVD-FC	Ethernet 1Gb or 10Gb	FC 4Gb or 2Gb

To narrow your search result to one of these test configurations, simply add a step right before Step 6 by selecting the desired test configuration from the **Array Test Configuration** field (see Figure 11.7).

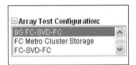

Figure 11.7 Selecting the test configuration

How About Initiator Records on the Front-End Array?

The front-end array must be configured with initiator records, FA Director Bits, Host Records, and so on based on the storage vendor's recommendations similar to those they provided as if you are configuring the array with physical LUNs.

Back-End Design Choices

The back-end array choices are actually constraints imposed on your design because they are existing configurations, and you have to consider the risks resulting from these constraints and mitigate these risks.

Which Bandwidth?

The common scenario is that the back-end connection speed may be equal to or slower than the front-end connection speed because the former are older generations with slower ports. Your configuration's effective speed is the least common denominator of both the front-end and the back-end connection speeds. In most cases, using the SVD for the purpose of migrating storage from the back-end to the SVD, the existing hosts may be equipped with FC HBAs with speeds matching the back-end connection speed. This is another constraint imposed on your design. You can mitigate this by later adding faster FC HBAs to the ESXi hosts after the storage migration is complete and the back-end is disconnected.

Which Protocol?

If the front-end array supports additional protocols—for example, FCoE or iSCSI—you may plan on adding matching initiators in the ESXi hosts. For example, your choice of storage arrays provides 10Gbps iSCSI SP ports and your network design provides this bandwidth. You can migrate one host at a time (using vMotion to vacate the host) and then replace the FC HBAs with 10Gbps iSCSI initiators. You then present the same LUNs on the SVD to the host via iSCSI protocol. Make sure that the LUN number and UUID are not changed. After booting, the upgraded ESXi host should start enjoying the added bandwidth.

Initiator Records

Because the front-end arrays pose as initiators to the back-end arrays, you need to check with the corresponding front-end array's configuration requirements.

LUN Presentation Considerations

I briefly touched on this topic earlier in the "Constraints" subsection of the "SVD Architecture" section.

Depending on the storage array vendor and model, the back-end LUNs' properties might not be preserved when presenting their equivalent SVD virtual LUNs. These properties are

- LUN number
- Device ID (for example, NAA ID)

I discuss this in further detail later in Chapter 15, but here is the gist of it:

VMFS datastore's signature is partly based on the LUN number as well as the device ID. If either of these values change (especially the device ID), the ESXi hosts treat this datastore as if it is on a snapshot LUN. This is a major constraint that can be addressed in this environment by VMFS datastore resignature. I discuss other alternatives in Chapter 15.

RDM (RAW Device Mapping) Considerations

If your ESXi hosts use LUNs on back-end array as RDMs, you need to re-create the RDM entries on the "resignatured" VMFS volumes because the original entries were created using the original LUN properties (LUN number and Device ID). I provide further details and procedure in Chapter 13, "Virtual Disks and RDMs."

TIP

If the main business requirement for the design is to migrate the data from the old arrays to the new ones, I strongly recommend using a phased approach in which you begin with a heterogeneous storage configuration by adding the new array to the SAN as an additional physical storage and then utilize Storage vMotion to move the VMs from the old datastores to the new ones. This has an effect on your design because you need to consider the target LUN sizing, I/O SLAs, and availability.

Storage vMotion moves the RDM entries to the target datastore. However, you need to plan a downtime to migrate the mapped physical LUNs to the new storage array and re-create the RDM entries.

After the data migration is complete, you may move on to the next phase in which you disconnect and decommission the old storage arrays.

Pros and Cons of Using SVDs

SVDs offer many advantages that you can leverage compared to the older storage arrays that hide behind them:

- Migrate your old data with less downtime. (I can't say "no downtime" because you need to resignature the VMFS datastores.)

    Hmm! Storage vMotion does that, too (Data Migration, that is), and with no downtime (unless you have RDMs see Chapter 13).

- Migrate your current data from over-utilized storage arrays.

    I've heard of that before! Oh yeah! vSphere 5 does this using Storage DRS (Dynamic Resource Scheduler) automatically.

- Data replication, mirroring, snapshots, and so on if your old array does not provide it and the SVD does.

- SVD might have larger cache, faster processors, faster ports, and larger command queue. One needs to consider the costs associated with adding an SVD as compared to upgrading the storage array.

On the other hand, there are a few disadvantages to using SVDs:

- VMFS datastores most likely require being resignatured. This also requires reregistering all VMs residing on these datastores. Using Storage vMotion avoids this because you would be moving the VMs to a new datastore instead of using a virtualized LUN on an SVD.

- Migrating RDMs requires re-creating their VMFS entries.

- You cannot take rotating outages of the ESXi hosts to migrate the data because you should never present the back-end LUNs to some hosts while other hosts access them via the SVD's virtual LUNs. This means that all hosts in the cluster must be down while the switchover is done. Alternatively, you can follow the approach outlined in the following "Migration Process" section.

Migration Process

Let me take you through the journey from the old array to the new one with a stop in the twilight zone! Oh, I meant the SVD.

1. Connect the SVD to the fabric that will serve as the front-end fabric.

2. Connect the SVD to the fabric that will serve as the back-end fabric.

3. Zone the SVD SP ports, designated to the connectivity with the back-end storage, to the SP ports on the back-end storage.

4. Shut down all VMs running on the back-end storage.

5. For all ESXi hosts, follow the procedure "Unmounting a VMFS Volume" in Chapter 7, "Multipathing and Failover," to unmount the back-end–based VMFS volumes.

6. For all ESXi hosts, follow the procedure "Detaching the Device Whose Datastore Was Unmounted" in Chapter 7 to detach the LUNs associated with the VMFS volumes you unmounted in Step 5.

7. Remove all hosts from the zones with the old storage array on the back-end fabric.

8. Add all hosts to the zones with the SVD on the front-end fabric.

9. Create the virtual LUNs on the SVD mapping to the physical LUNs on the old storage array.

10. Present the virtual LUNs to one ESXi host using the same LUN numbers as the old one (this is for ease of management rather than functionality).

11. Using the ESXi host mentioned in Step 10 (via vCenter Server), mount the VMFS datastores presented by the virtual LUNs. This gives you the choice to resignature the datastores. See the detailed procedure "Resignaturing Datastores" and other alternatives in Chapter 15.

12. Present the virtual LUNs to the remaining ESXi hosts and rescan to discover the virtual LUNs and mount the VMFS datastores.

13. Using vCenter, remove the orphaned virtual machines from the inventory and browse the datastores to register the VMs on their corresponding ESXi hosts.

14. Make sure to place the VMs in the resource pools to which they belonged prior to this procedure.

15. Power on the VMs and all should be back to normal (a better normal I hope).

If your goal is to decommission the old storage array, start the data migration process to the SVD. It is better to plan this for off-peak hours. After this process is completed, switch the virtual LUNs to physical mode depending on the SVD's specific procedures (see the SVD's documentation for additional details). Finally, disconnect the SVD from the back-end fabric when all back-end data has been migrated to the SVD.

Summary

SVDs present older back-end arrays' LUNs to initiators as if they are physically located within the SVDs themselves. Back-end connectivity is limited to the FC protocol, whereas the front-end varies by SVD and spans FC, iSCSI, and NFS. Data migration is one of the main features of most SVDs. After the data is migrated, you can decommission the back-end arrays as needed. VMFS volumes on the back-end arrays are detected as being on snapshot LUNs when presented to the host via the SVD. RDM entries need to be re-created regardless of keeping the RAW LUNs on the back-end arrays or migrating them to the SVDs.

## Chapter 12

VMFS Architecture

vSphere 5 and its near predecessors are inherently highly scalable clustered environments. From the very beginning of the life of ESX, VMware Virtual Machine File System (VMFS) has been the core element that holds the environment together.

VMFS is the core component of vSphere's storage virtualization as it abstracts the underlying storage and presents it to Virtual Machines (VMs) in various formats: virtual disks, PassthruRDMs, nonPassthruRDMs, snapshots, and so on. More on that later!

History of VMFS

VMFS evolved from a flat file system to a highly specialized clustered file system over four generations.

VMFS1

The first version of VMFS, which shipped with ESX 1.x, was a flat file system (did not provide directories) and provided three modes: Private, Public, and Shared.

Private mode VMFS was used for storing virtual disks of VMs that are not shared between hosts. This resided mostly on local storage internal to the host or directly attached to it.

Public mode VMFS was used on shared storage for storing virtual disks of VMs that can run on more than one ESX host and used file locking mechanism to prevent the same virtual disks from being opened by multiple hosts concurrently.

Shared mode VMFS was used exclusively for MSCS-clustered VMs. This mode did not enforce file-level locking and left that function to the clustering software within the guest OS. Shared mode VMFS was created on local or shared storage to support cluster-in-a-box (CIB) and cluster-across-boxes (CAB).

Due to the fact that the file system was flat, VM configuration files had to be stored in a hierarchy of directories on a local EXT2 filesystem (in the early days, the VM configuration file extension was cfg, which was changed to vmx in later releases). The directory structure used to be located within the user's home directory, which provided some level of ACL (Access Control List) based on local users' Linux-style accounts.

I had an ESX 1.5.2 host running in my home office closet for more than five years, and its uptime was most of these five years (apart from a couple of prolonged power outages that depleted my UPS battery). I had so many panics on my physical Linux hosts and BSODs (Blue Screen of Death) on my physical Windows desktop, I almost forgot that I was still running the ESX 1.5.2 host.

VMFS2

With the release of ESX 2, VMware upgraded the file system to version 2, which was also a flat file system. However, the Private mode was deprecated.

TIP

You may see a private mode file system on ESXi 5 but not on VMFS file system. Rather, it is a property of the ESXi 5 bootbanks, which are VFAT file systems.

VMFS2 added multi-extent capability to extend the datastore onto additional logical unit numbers (LUNs) up to 32 extents.

ESX 2.5 introduced vMotion, which requires the use of Public mode VMFS2 datastores shared between hosts in datacenter.

VMFS3

Virtual Infrastructure 3 (VI3) introduced the first hierarchical version of VMFS and added file system journaling for enhanced resiliency and recoverability. Also, with this release, the Shared mode was deprecated leaving Public as the sole mode available from VMFS. Now you know the origin of that mode you may have observed in the properties of VMFS3 and 5 file systems (see Figure 12.1).

Figure 12.1 VMFS3 properties

VI3 also introduced Logical Volume Manager (LVM) for VMFS3, which enhanced the ability to span a VMFS datastore onto multiple LUNs to form a larger datastore beyond 2TB in size. This simply concatenates multiple smaller LUNs into a larger VMFS3 volume up to 32 extents. The main difference between VMFS3 and VMFS2 is that loss of any of the extents (other than the head extent) will not invalidate the rest of the VMFS3 datastore (more on that later in this chapter in the "Span or Grow?" section).

LVM also handles resignature of VMFS3 or VMFS5 datastores that are detected to be on snapshot LUNs. (For more details, see Chapter 15, "Snapshot Handling").

VI3 supported VMFS2 but in Read-Only mode for the sole purpose of live migration of VMs from the old VMFS2 datastores to VMFS3 datastores. This was done using the early version of Storage vMotion, which was command-line based in the first release of VI3 via Remote command-line interface (RCLI) or VIMA (Virtual Infrastructure Management Assistant).

The Storage vMotion process organized the VMs in directories on the target VMFS3 datastore.

VMFS5

vSphere 5 continues support for VMFS3 in addition to introducing VMFS5. The latter provides improved scalability and architectural changes to enable scalability which include the following:

- GUID Partition Table (GPT) to support larger datastore extent size greater than 2TB

- Single block size (1MB) that supports all file sizes. VMFS3 maximum file size was tied to various block sizes ranging from 1 to 8MB.

- Smaller sub-block size (8KB) compared to 64KB in VMFS3.

- Datastores can be tagged as ATS-only volumes after the Storage Arrays, hosting the LUNs backing them, are detected as supporting the ATS VAAI primitive (Atomic Test and Set). I cover this in Chapter 16, "VAAI."

VMFS 3 on Disk Layout

I cannot share with you the exact VMFS layout because it is proprietary VMware IP. However, I am allowed to share with you some publicly available diagrams that I used in some of VMworld and Partner Exchange presentations.

Figure12.2 depicts VMFS3 layout.

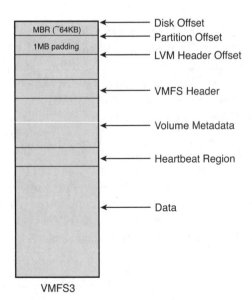

Figure 12.2   VMFS3 on disk layout

The regions illustrated in Figure 12.2 are

- VMFS3 partition offset — It is at a certain location relative to the disk offset. I show you how to identify this location later in this chapter under the "Re-creating a Lost Partition Table for VMFS3 Datastores" section.

- LVM — The next area in the file system is the Logical Volume Manager (LVM) Header. It starts 1MB from the partition offset. (Remember this fact later when I show you how to restore the partition table.) It exists on all devices on which the volume is spanned and holds the following:

    - Number of extents that are logical building blocks of the file system.

    - Number of devices on which the volume is spanned. These are commonly referred to as *extents* or *physical extents* and should not be confused for the previous item.

    - Volume size.

    - Is this a snapshot? This is an attribute that is turned on by VMFS when it identifies that the LUN housing the datastore has a different device ID from that stored in the metadata. I explain the snapshot volumes later in Chapter 15.

- Metadata — The following area is the Volume Metadata. It exists on all devices on which the volume is spanned. The following regions make up the metadata and are represented by five systems files (see Figure 12.3). These files are hidden (with a leading period and .sf suffix). They are the Volume Header and four resource system files.

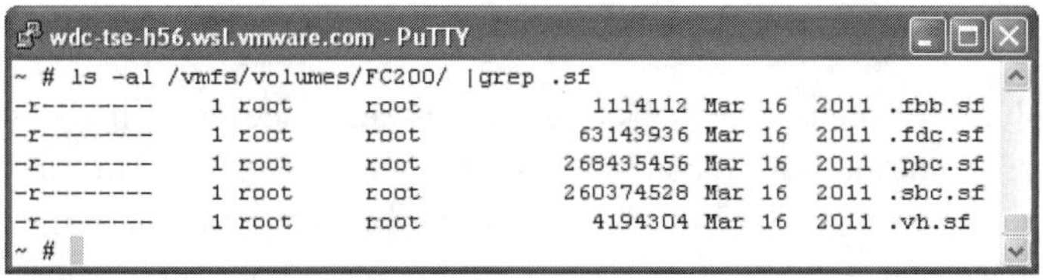

```
~ # ls -al /vmfs/volumes/FC200/ |grep .sf
-r--------    1 root     root       1114112 Mar 16  2011 .fbb.sf
-r--------    1 root     root      63143936 Mar 16  2011 .fdc.sf
-r--------    1 root     root     268435456 Mar 16  2011 .pbc.sf
-r--------    1 root     root     260374528 Mar 16  2011 .sbc.sf
-r--------    1 root     root       4194304 Mar 16  2011 .vh.sf
~ #
```

Figure 12.3 VMFS3 System Files

- Volume Header (vh) defines the volume structure including

    - The volume name — There is a misconception that the "volume name" is located in the LVM header, but it is actually in the Volume Header within the datastore's metadata.

- VMFS3 UUID — This is the volume's unique identifier, which is partially composed of MAC address of the uplink used by the management port on the ESXi host that was used to first create or resignature the volume. This is also referred to as the volume "signature." I discuss this in Chapter 15.

- Accessing the datastore via the ESXi Shell or via SSH is via a directory structure:

  `/vmfs/volumes/<volume-UUID>`

  or

  `/vmfs/volumes/<volume-label>`

- The volume label is actually a symbolic link to the volume UUID. Such links are automatically created by vmkernel at the time it mounts the datastore based on the volume name. To see the link, use the `ls -al` command as shown in Figure 12.4.

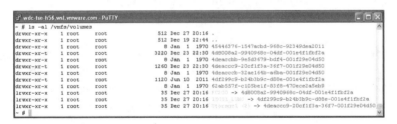

Figure 12.4 VMFS labels are symbolic links

- The first column of the output shows the file system modes, which are Unix/Linux style modes modifiable using chmod. The first mode in this example is either d or l. The former means that this is a directory and the latter means that this is a link. The remaining modes are the permissions for the Group, User, and Others in the form of rwx which means Read, Write, and Execute. The last mode for the Others is sometimes t which means Sticky. The sticky bit means that the directory or link can only be modified by root or the owner:

- The second column shows the number of inodes — also known as file descriptors — used by this directory entry.

- The third and fourth columns show the group and usernames of the file owner, which is the account used to create the entry.

- The fifth column shows the size in bytes. This is the size of the file or the directory (not the directory's content size).

- The sixth column is the date and time stamp of the last time the file or the directory was modified.

- The last column shows the file or directory name and if the entry is a symbolic link, it would show to which entry it is linked.

NOTE

The output shown in Figure 12.4 shows some UUIDs that have no symbolic links. These are related to visorFS.

- **The Extent ID** — This is the ID that the LVM header uses to identify which physical extent of the datastore this device holds.

- **Disk Block Size** — Do not confuse this with the File Block Size.

The following file system resources are organized in clusters. Each resource in the cluster has associated metadata and locks (see Figure 12.5).

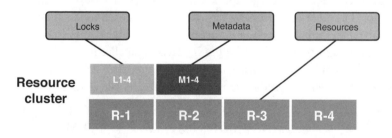

Figure 12.5   VMFS3 resource cluster

The clusters are grouped into Cluster Groups. The latter repeat to make the file system (see Figure 12.6).

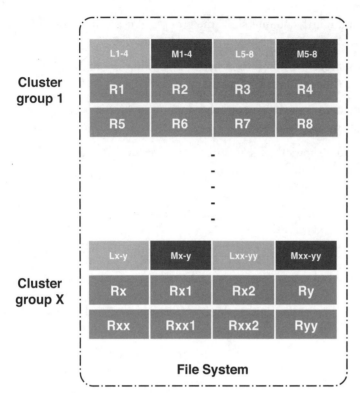

Figure 12.6   Cluster groups form file system

- **File Descriptor Cluster (fdc)** — File descriptors (inodes) keep track of the location of file data using a fixed number of addresses (256) stored within each inode. These addresses may be sub-blocks, file blocks (see Figure 12.7), or pointer blocks (see Figure 12.8). They are for sub-blocks when the file is 64KB or smaller in size. They are for file blocks when the file is more than 1MB but not larger than 256 * file block size. They are for pointer blocks when the file is larger than 256 * file block size.

- **Sub-Block Cluster (sbc)** — Files that are equal to or smaller than VMFS3 sub-block size occupy a sub-block each (64KB). If a file grows beyond a VMFS3 sub-block size, it is no longer sub-allocated. This helps reduce wasting space occupied by smaller files. VMFS5 provides smaller sub-blocks (8KB), which I cover later under the "File Allocation Improvements" section.

An example of a file block direct addressing is shown in Figure 12.7.

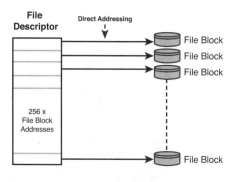

Figure 12.7   VMFS3 direct block addressing

An example of indirect block addressing using pointer blocks is shown in Figure 12.8.

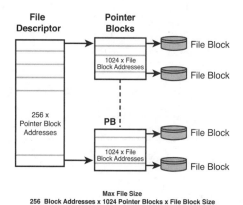

Figure 12.8   VMFS3 indirect block addressing

- **Pointer Block Cluster (pbc)** — When a file is larger than the direct Block Addressing limit (refer to Figure 12.7) where each File Descriptor holds 256 block addresses * file block size, indirect block addressing is used. In the latter, the file descriptors hold pointer block addresses instead of file block addresses. Each pointer block holds up to 1024 file block addresses. Pointer blocks are used for indirect addressing. Figure 12.8 shows an indirect addressing block diagram. Each file descriptor holds 256 pointer block addresses. Each pointer block in turn holds (or references) 1024 file block addresses. Pointer blocks are assigned to hosts in cluster groups for better efficiency.

To better understand the correlation between the file size and VMFS3 resources, see Table 12.1.

Table 12.1   File Size Correlation with VMFS3 Resources

File Size	Type of Addresses Stored in File Descriptor	Type of Resources Files that the Data Is Stored In
< 1MB	Sub-block	Sub-blocks
>= 1MB, <= 256 * X MB	File block	File blocks
> 256 * X MB	Pointer block	File blocks

- **File Block Bitmap (fbb)** — These are the bitmap of the file blocks' data on disk. File blocks themselves are fixed-size basic units of storage on the VMFS file system. VMFS3 provided four different file block sizes that support different max file sizes. These are listed in Table 12.2.

Table 12.2   VMFS3 File Block Sizes

File Block Size	Max File Size
1MB	256GB (minus 512bytes)
2MB	512GB (minus 512bytes)
4MB	1TB (minus 512bytes)
8MB	2TB (minus 512bytes)

The formula for these max file sizes is (256 pointer block addresses per file descriptor * 1024 file block addresses per pointer block * file block size)

Example of 1MB file block: 256*1024*1MB = 256GB

NOTE

Max file size is always short by 512 bytes.

TIP

You can list the pointer blocks and sub-blocks counts on VMFS3 using the following command:

```
vmkfstools -Ph -v10 /vmfs/volumes/FC200/

VMFS-3.54 file system spanning 1 partitions.
File system label (if any): FC200
Mode: public
Capacity 199.8 GB, 39.1 GB available, file block size 1 MB
Volume Creation Time: Wed Mar 16 00:47:30 2011
Files (max/free): 30720/4792
 Ptr Blocks (max/free): 64512/64285
 Sub Blocks (max/free): 3968/0
UUID: 4d8008a2-9940968c-04df-001e4f1fbf2a
Partitions spanned (on "lvm"):
        naa.6006016055711d00cef95e65664ee011:1
DISKLIB-LIB   : Getting VAAI support status for /vmfs/volumes/FC200/
Is Native Snapshot Capable: NO
```

- **The heartbeat region** — I explain in Chapter 14, "Distributed Locks," the function of this region when I explain locking mechanisms and concurrent access to the shared VMFS datastores.

VMFS5 Layout

Figure 12.9 depicts VMFS5 on disk layout.

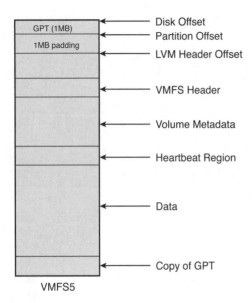

Figure 12.9   VMFS5 on disk layout

VMFS5 layout is somewhat similar to VMFS3, but it has some major differences including the following:

- The partition is GUID Partition Table (GPT) based (see the "GPT on Disk Layout" section later in this chapter). The move to adopt this format was to break loose from the limitations of MBR's (Master Boot Record) 32-bit address space.

  - GPT address space allows vSphere to utilize LUNs larger than 2TB as VMFS5 extents as well as PassthruRDMs (see the "Double Indirect Addressing" section later in the chapter). For more information about GPT, see Wikipedia http://en.wikipedia.org/wiki/GUID_Partition_Table.

  - GPT allows for a theoretical maximum disk and partition size of 8 Zettabytes (1024 Exabytes)! However, vSphere 5 limits this to 64TB which is the largest LUN size it supports.

  - GPT supports more than four primary partitions compared to MBR.

NOTE

When a VMFS3 is upgraded to VMFS5, it retains its MBR partition table.

After the datastore is grown beyond 2TB size, the MBR partition table is switched to GPT.

- At the end of the device there is a secondary GPT. However, vSphere 5 does not provide tools for utilizing this for partition table recovery (at least not yet!)

- In-between the two regions I discussed in the first two bullets lies the VMFS5 partition layout. The latter appears similar to VMFS3, but I am over simplifying this because I am not authorized disclose the actual details. However, what I can share with you are some architectural changes that aim at improving VMFS scalability and performance.

These changes are listed in the following sections.

Spanned Device Table

VMFS3 and VMFS5 are capable of spanning a volume onto multiple LUNs (see the "Span or Grow?" section later in this chapter). VMFS5 introduced a new property, Spanned Device Table, which stores the device IDs (for example, NAA IDs) for easier identification of extents. This table is stored in the Spanned Device Descriptor on the first device of the spanned VMFS datastore (also referred to as device 0 or head extent).

To list the content of this table, you may do the following:

1. Identify the device ID of the head extent using the following:

   ```
   vmkfstools -Ph /vmfs/volumes/<datastore-name>
   ```

   For example, if the volume name is Datastore1, the command would be

   ```
   vmkfstools -Ph /vmfs/volumes/Datastore1
   ```

   The output would be something like Listing 12.1.

Listing 12.1 Listing Extents' Device ID

```
VMFS-5.54 file system spanning 2 partitions.
File system label (if any): Storage1
Mode: public
Capacity 414.5 GB, 277.1 GB available, file block size 1 MB
```

```
UUID: 4bd783e0-1916b9ae-9fe6-0015176afd6e
Partitions spanned (on "lvm"):
     naa.6006016012d021002a49e23fa349e011:1
     naa.6006016012d021002b49e23fa349e011:1
```

This means that the datastore is spanned on two devices. The first one is the head extent.

2. Use the head extent device ID you located (including the partition number) to list the Spanned Device Table as shown in Figure 12.10.

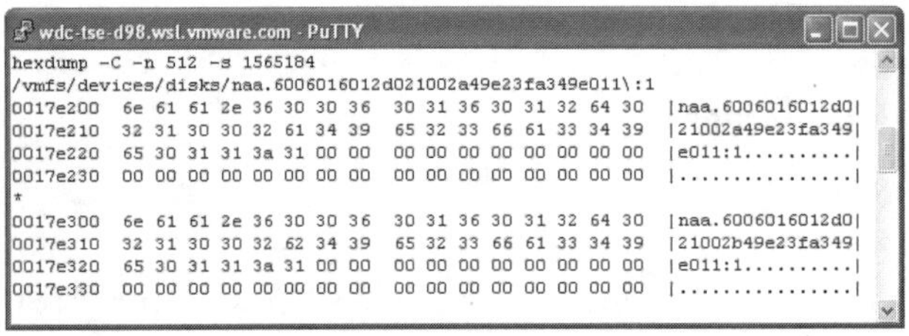

Figure 12.10   Listing spanned device table

The displayed text in the right column of the output is the list of devices matching the earlier output of vmkfstools.

NOTE

As long as the head extent remains accessible, you can get the information listed in items 1 and 2. The spanned datastore can survive any of its extents going offline other than the Head Extent. If this happens and the datastore is missing one of these extents, any input/ output (I/O) destined to blocks on the missing extent result in an I/O error while I/O to the rest of the datastore is successful.

To identify the missing device, you can run the vmkfstools command; the output shown in Listing 12.2 clearly states which device is offline.

Listing 12.2 Listing Volume Extent's Device ID

```
VMFS-5.54 file system spanning 2 partitions.
File system label (if any): Storage1
Mode: public
Capacity 414.5 GB, 277.1 GB available, file block size 1 MB
UUID: 4bd783e0-1916b9ae-9fe6-0015176afd6e
Partitions spanned (on "lvm"):
     naa.6006016012d021002a49e23fa349e011:1
     (device naa.6006016012d021002b49e23fa349e011:1 might be offline)
     (One or more partitions spanned by this volume may be offline)
```

File Allocation Improvements

To illustrate the following points, let's first get some verbose VMFS5 properties by running the command shown in Listing 12.3.

Listing 12.3 Listing VMFS5 Properties

```
vmkfstools -Ph -v10 /vmfs/volumes/Storage1/

VMFS-5.54 file system spanning 1 partitions.
File system label (if any): Storage1 (2)
Mode: public
Capacity 63.2 GB, 62.3 GB available, file block size 1 MB
Volume Creation Time: Sun Jun  5 00:24:41 2011
Files (max/free): 130000/129990
Ptr Blocks (max/free): 64512/64496
Sub Blocks (max/free): 32000/32000
Secondary Ptr Blocks (max/free): 256/256
File Blocks (overcommit/used/overcommit %): 0/971/0
Ptr Blocks  (overcommit/used/overcommit %): 0/16/0
Sub Blocks  (overcommit/used/overcommit %): 0/0/0
UUID: 4deaccc9-20cf1f3a-36f7-001f29e04d50
Partitions spanned (on "lvm"):
        mpx.vmhba1:C0:T0:L0:3
DISKLIB-LIB   : Getting VAAI support status for /vmfs/volumes/Storage1/
Is Native Snapshot Capable: NO
```

The following are VMFS5 improvements to file allocation:

1. Block size is now 1MB only, which supports all file sizes. There is no longer a need to specify larger block sizes to be able to support larger file sizes.

   Listing 12.3 shows the output taken from a freshly created VMFS5 datastore. The block size is listed as 1 MB; in contrast, VMFS3 provided block sizes 1, 2, 4, and 8 MB which supported max file sizes.

2. Maximum number of files increased to 130,000 compared to 30,720 on VMFS3.

3. Maximum file size increased to 64TB. However, this is currently limited to PassthruRDMs. This means that virtual disk file size is still limited to 2TB.

4. Maximum datastore size remains at 64TB. However, extent size can be more than 2TB with the max being 64TB.

5. Sub-block allocation is now 8KB block size compared to 64KB on VMFS3 effectively increasing the number of sub-blocks.

6. Small File Packing (also known as Zero Level Address or ZLA) — When a file size is smaller than 1KB, it is stored within its own file descriptor (inode). When the file grows beyond that size, its data is copied out to a sub-block if it has not reached 8KB in size. When it grows beyond that, it is stored in file blocks.

7. Improved efficiency of handling Pointer Block Cluster (pbc) caching.

8. Added .pb2.sf system file to support pbc growth in a future release. Currently, the max limit of total number of pbc is 64512. Figure 12.11 shows VMFS5 system files. They are the same system files as in VMFS3 (refer to Figure 12.3) with the addition of .pb2.sf to VMFS5.

```
wdc-tse-h56.wsl.vmware.com - PuTTY
~ # ls -al /vmfs/volumes/Storage1\ \(2\)/
drwxr-xr-t   1 root     root             1120 Jun  5  2011 .
drwxr-xr-x   1 root     root              512 Dec 23 19:13 ..
-r--------   1 root     root           458752 Jun  5  2011 .fbb.sf
-r--------   1 root     root        267026432 Jun  5  2011 .fdc.sf
-r--------   1 root     root          1179648 Jun  5  2011 .pb2.sf
-r--------   1 root     root        268435456 Jun  5  2011 .pbc.sf
-r--------   1 root     root        262733824 Jun  5  2011 .sbc.sf
-r--------   1 root     root          4194304 Jun  5  2011 .vh.sf
~ #
```

Figure 12.11   VMFS5 System files

Double Indirect Addressing

Freshly created VMFS5 datastore provides 1MB file blocks only. To support varying file sizes beyond 256GB, it resorts to using double indirect addressing. If you look at VMFS3 implementation of indirect addressing you notice that the maximum number of file blocks is fixed and the max file size depends on the file block size. On the other hand, VMFS5 has a fixed file block size (1MB), and to be able to address file sizes beyond 256GB, each secondary pointer block points to 1024 primary pointer block. Because the latter can store up to 1024 file block addresses, it effectively increases the addressable file blocks 1024 folds (see Figure 12.12).

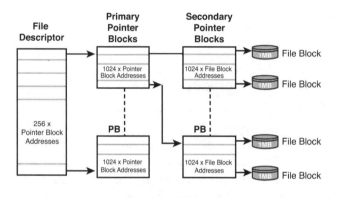

Theoretical Max File Size
256 Pointer Block x 1024 Pointer Blocks x 1024 File Blocks x 1MB File Block Size

Figure 12.12   VMFS5 double indirect block addressing

This architecture would provide a theoretical max file size of 256TB based on the following formula:

256 block addresses per file descriptor * 1024 addresses per secondary pointer block * 1024 file block addresses per primary pointer block * 1MB per file block

(256*1024*1024*1MB =256TB)

However, vSphere 5 limits the max virtual disk size to 2TB, but the max size of PassthruRDM as well as the LVM (max datastore size) are limited to 64TB.

The secondary pointer blocks resources are partially used in vSphere 5. They are limited to 256 addresses. This would explain the 64TB limit, which, based on the formula, is the resultant of 256*256*1024*1MB.

If we revisit Table 12.1, the revised version of that table for VMFS5 would be Table 12.3.

Table 12.3 File Size Correlation with VMFS5 Resources

File Size	Type of Addresses Stored in File Descriptor	Secondary Pointer Blocks Used?	Type of Resources File That the Data Is Stored In
< 1MB	Sub-block	No	Sub-blocks
>= 1MB, <= 256*1MB	File block	No	File blocks
> 256MB, <=256 *1024*1MB	Pointer block	No	File blocks
>256GB, <=256*256*1024*1MB (64TB)	Pointer block	Yes	File Blocks

Common Causes of Partition Table Problems

I have seen several cases where a VMFS3 partition table is corrupt or lost. The most common cause is presenting the VMFS3 LUN to non-ESXi hosts, especially those running Windows. You are probably familiar with the dialog you get when you first run the Disk Management tool on a Windows OS that prompts you to "initialize the disk." Even if you do not partition it or format it using this tool, initializing the disk results in overwriting the partition table. Positive proof of that was evident from the dump of the first few sectors of the LUN housing the VMFS volume where I frequently found the Windows signature.

The same can happen, although by a different mechanism, with Linux or Solaris hosts given access to the VMFS3 LUN.

The next most common cause is user error.

VMware has introduced some mechanisms to prevent such corruption, except for hardware/firmware issues, to prevent the partition table that is in use from being clobbered or deleted.

I have not seen this as much recently. However, older logs had shown the following messages:

```
in-use partition modification is not supported
Can't clobber active ptable for LUN <Device ID>
```

It is strongly recommended that you utilize a logical grouping of initiator records on storage arrays — for example, host groups — and assign the LUNs to that group only. This prevents accidental presentation of ESXi hosts' LUNs to non-ESXi hosts.

Another less common cause is storage array rebuilding the RAID set after losing one of the backing disks. Sometimes with a faulty cache or firmware some blocks fail to be written to the disk and all you see on these blocks are some fixed pattern similar to that used by the disk manufacturer to test the media. This has been fixed later by the storage vendors with which VMware has collaborated on identifying this mode of corruption. Depending on which blocks were affected, the partition table could get corrupt.

Re-creating a Lost Partition Table for VMFS3 Datastores

For the increasingly rare occasion that you would face a situation where the partition table is gone or corrupt, let me share with you a process that can help you re-create it. This process works most of the time as long as the corruption does not extend into the metadata.

Normal Partition Table

Before I begin with the process, let me first review how the normal partition table looks!

To list the partition table, you use fdisk. This tool is based on Linux which was modified to support VMFS3 file system. The command to list it on ESXi 5 is

```
fdisk -lu /vmfs/devices/disks/<device ID>
```

or

```
fdisk -lu /dev/disks/<device ID>
```

NOTE

/vmfs/devices is a symbolic link to /dev on ESXi 5

The output of a healthy partition table looks like Figure 12.13.

Figure 12.13 Listing a VMFS3 healthy partition table

In this example I used -lu option to get the units in sectors that are physical disk blocks 512bytes in size. You see why I need to use this unit when I go through the process of rebuilding the partition table.

If you use -l instead, you get something like this:

```
fdisk -l /dev/disks/naa.6006016055711d00cef95e65664ee011

Disk /dev/disks/naa.6006016055711d00cef95e65664ee011: 214.7 GB,
214748364800 bytes
255 heads, 63 sectors/track, 26108 cylinders
Units = cylinders of 16065 * 512 = 8225280 bytes

                          Device Boot  Start End    Blocks      Id
System
/dev/disks/naa.6006016055711d00cef95e65664ee011p1  1    26108  209711486 fb
VMFS
```

Notice that the outcome is using Cylinders as units whose size is 16065 * 512, which makes it difficult to count blocks in the procedure.

Now let's continue with the first output. It shows that the VMFS partition with ID fb starts at sector 2048, which means it starts 1MB from the disk offset. The partition ends at sector 419425019. Note that fb is the System ID for VMFS. This was an available ID at the time VMware first extended fdisk for use with ESX. Another ID VMware also uses is f, which is for vmkcore or vmkernel core dump partition. You would usually encounter the latter type on ESXi boot devices.

Repairing Corrupt or Lost Partition Table

Now, on to the important part of this section; the actual process of repairing the partition table.

The outline of the process is the following:

1. Identify the device name that represents the affected LUN.
2. Locate the LVM header offset.
3. Calculate the partition offset.
4. Use fdisk to re-create the partition table.
5. Mount the datastore.

Identifying Device Name

1. List the VMFS datastores and their associated device names using `esxcli`. Figure 12.14 show the output of command:

   ```
   esxcli storage vmfs extent list
   ```

   This command lists all VMFS datastores extents and their associated device names and partition numbers.

Figure 12.14   Listing VMFS extents (devices)

2. List all devices on this host using the `esxcfg-scsidevs` command. In this example, I used the `-c` option to get a compact list of devices and their associated Console Device names. (Figure 12.15 was cropped to show only the relevant columns.)

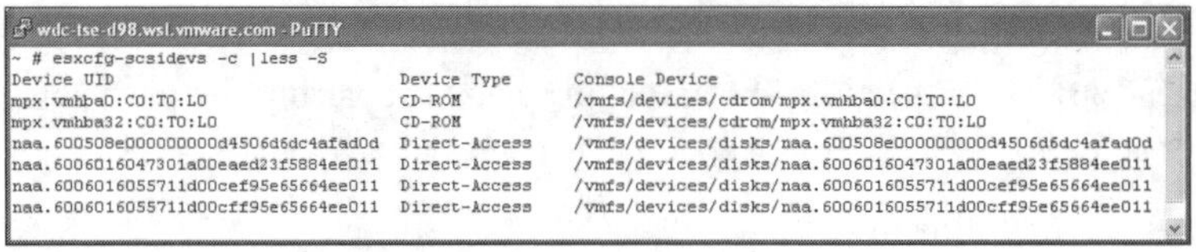

Figure 12.15   Listing all storage devices

3. Notice that I have four `Direct-Access` devices but my previous output showed three VMFS datastores. Comparing both outputs, I can identify the device ID and console device name of the potentially affected LUN, which is `naa.6006016055711 d00cff95e65664ee011`.

From Steps 1 and 2 the device name I need to use with this procedure is

`/dev/disks/naa.6006016055711d00cff95e65664ee011`

Notice that I changed /vmfs/devices to /dev because the former is linked to the latter, and it makes the command line shorter.

To verify that you located the affected device, you can run `fdisk -lu` to list its partition table.

```
fdisk -lu /dev/disks/naa.6006016055711d00cff95e65664ee011

Disk /dev/disks/naa.6006016055711d00cff95e65664ee011: 10.7 GB, 10737418240
bytes
255 heads, 63 sectors/track, 1305 cylinders, total 20971520 sectors
Units = sectors of 1 * 512 = 512 bytes

Disk /dev/disks/naa.6006016055711d00cff95e65664ee011 doesn't contain a
valid partition table
```

What If the Datastore Has Extents?

If you have a datastore with extents and one or more of these extents suffer from a damaged or lost partition table *and* the head extent is intact, the best way to identify the affected devices is by running

`vmkfstools -P /vmfs/volume/<volume-name>`

This should list the extents and their device names. Use the device name whose status is offline. The rest of the procedure stays the same.

If the head extent is also affected, attempt to rebuild the partition tables on all affected devices and, if it's successful, it all comes together and the volume is mounted.

Locating LVM Header Offset

To located the LVM header offset, you may use hexdump as shown in Listing 12.4.

Listing 12.4 Locating the LVM Header Offset Using hexdump

```
hexdump /dev/disks/naa.6006016055711d00cff95e65664ee011

00001f0 0000 0000 0000 0000 0000 0000 0000 aa55
0000200 0000 0000 0000 0000 0000 0000 0000 0000
*
0200000 d00d c001 0003 0000 0015 0000 1602 0000
0200010 0000 0000 0000 0000 0000 0000 0000 0000
```

Using the hexdump utility included with ESXi 5, you can list the hex content of the device.

The LVM header offset would show d00d c001 as the first 4 bytes. The following 2 bytes show the major VMFS version. In this example it is 0003, which means that this volume was VMFS3 version. If it were VMFS5, the value would have been 0005.

TIP

Do not use the -C option with hexdump because it lists the output in reverse byte order. For example, d00d c001 would be listed as 0d d0 01 c0 which can get you confused.

Based on the dump shown in Listing 12.4, the LVM header offset is at 0200000 address.

Calculating the Partition Offset

Now, let's use the LVM header offset to count backward 1MB, which is how far it lies from the partition offset:

1. Convert the LVM header offset value from hex to decimal:

   0200000 Hex = 2097152 Decimal

2. Convert the byte count to sectors (divide by 512, which is the sector size):

   2097152 / 512 = 4096 sectors

3. Subtract the number of sectors that add up to 1MB (2048 sectors of 512 bytes each):

4096– 2048 = 2048

This means that the partition starts at sector 2048.

Using fdisk to Re-create the Partition Table

The process of re-creating the partition table is fairly straightforward using these steps:

```
fdisk -u /dev/disks/naa.6006016055711d00cff95e65664ee011
```

This uses fdisk to specify sectors instead of cylinders.

Now use the following options and values:

- n (to create a new partition)
- p (to specify that this is a primary partition)
- 1 (to specify that this is the first partition)
- 2048 (to set the partition offset)
- [enter] (to accept the default value for the last sector)
- t (to change the system type)
- fb (to specify VMFS as the system type)
- w (to write the changes and exit fdisk)

Mounting the Recovered Datastore

To mount the VMFS datastore, rescan the device for VMFS datastore by running

```
vmkfstool -V
```

This is a hidden option that probes the filesystem and mounts the datastore found on the re-created partition table. To verify if the datastore was mounted successfully, check the content of /vmfs/volumes directory using

```
ls /vmfs/volume
```

Re-creating a Lost Partition Table for VMFS5 Datastores

VMFS5 datastores have a relatively similar partition table geometry using GPT instead of MBR.

The process of identifying the partition offset is identical to that of VMFS3, as discussed in the previous section. The only difference is that the major version of VMFS is 5 instead of 3 in the hexdump.

The process of re-creating the partition table utilizes partedUtil instead of fdisk.

GPT on Disk Layout

Before I delve into the process details, let's first review the GPT on disk layout.

Figure 12.16 shows the GUID partition table scheme.

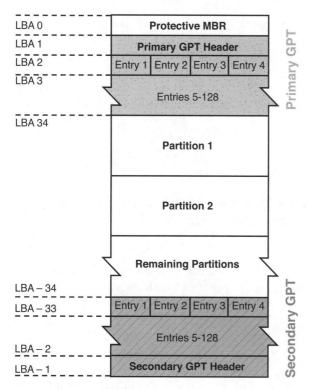

Figure 12.16   GPT layout

The layout in Figure 12.16 shows the following:

- The first LBA (Sector), which is LBA0, is occupied by a Protective MBR.

- The Primary GPT Header on LBA1 (second disk sector).

- LBA2 has the first four entries followed by entries 5 through 128 which end on LBA33. VMFS partition can be anywhere beginning from LBA34 (35th disk sector).

- The secondary GPT header is on the last LBA on the disk. So, it starts at LBA -1, which means that if the device has 1024000 sectors, the last LBA would be number 1024000 minus 1 or 1023999.

- The backup entries 5 through 128 are on the previous 31 sectors (LBA -2 through LBA -32).

- The remaining entries 1 through 4 are on the previous sector (LBA -33).

This means that the usable sectors on the device begin on LBA 34 and end on LBA -34.

To illustrate this, let's examine the following output:

```
partedUtil getptbl /dev/disks/naa.6006016055711d00cff95e65664ee011

gpt
1305 255 63 20971520
1 2048 20971486 AA31E02A400F11DB9590000C2911D1B8 vmfs 0
```

This command lists the healthy gpt partition table from the device I used as a recovery example. This output was before the partition table was removed.

The output shows the following:

- The partition type — in this example, it is gpt. Another value you might see is msdos which is what you see when you use partedUtil with a VMFS3 partition created by pre-ESXi 5 hosts.

- The second line shows the disk geometry in the format of (C, H, S, Sectors) or Cylinders, Heads, Sectors per track, and Total Sector count.

- The last line shows the VMFS partition details in the format of (Partition Number, Offset (first sector), Last Sector, GUID, Partition type, and finally the attribute).

The GUID is specific to VMFS. You can get this value from the following output:

```
partedUtil showGuids

Partition Type        GUID
  vmfs                AA31E02A400F11DB9590000C2911D1B8
```

```
vmkDiagnostic          9D27538040AD11DBBF97000C2911D1B8
VMware Reserved        9198EFFC31C011DB8F78000C2911D1B8
Basic Data             EBD0A0A2B9E5443387C068B6B72699C7
Linux Swap             0657FD6DA4AB43C484E50933C84B4F4F
Linux Lvm              E6D6D379F50744C2A23C238F2A3DF928
Linux Raid             A19D880F05FC4D3BA006743F0F84911E
Efi System             C12A7328F81F11D2BA4B00A0C93EC93B
Microsoft Reserved     E3C9E3160B5C4DB8817DF92DF00215AE
Unused Entry           00000000000000000000000000000000
```

The partition type is vmfs and the attribute is always 0 for VMFS partitions.

```
partedUtil getUsableSectors /dev/disks/naa.6006016055711d00cff95e65664ee011
```

34 20971486

This command lists the first and last usable sector on the device. Based on the gpt on disk layout details I provided in the getptbl command, the last usable sector is LBA -34. This example shows that the total number of sectors on this device is 20971520. If you subtract 34 to get the last usable sector, that would be (20971520 - 34 = 20971486), which matches the getptbl command output.

Re-creating the Partition Table

The syntax to re-create the partition table is

```
partedUtil setptbl "/dev/disks/<DeviceName>" DiskLabel "partNum startSec-
tor endSector type/guid attribute"
```

Required parameters:

- **DeviceName** — Use the NAA ID of the affected device including path—for example, /dev/disks/naa.6006016055711d00cff95e65664ee011.

- **DiskLabel** —This is the partition type which for our purpose can be either msdos or gpt. The former creates a partition fdisk style, (MBR) whereas the latter creates a partition for use with ESXi 5 datastores. To rebuild a VMFS5 partition table, this must be gpt.

- **partNum** —This is the partition number. Because any of VMFS5 datastores are stored on a single partition (other than local storage used for booting ESXi or Boot-from-SAN LUNs), the partition number is always 1.

- **startSector** —This is the partition offset that you calculated from the hexdump analysis in the "Locating LVM Header Offset" section. In our example, it is 2048.

- **endSector** —This is the last usable sector I discussed in the "GPT on Disk Layout" section. So, to get the last usable sector number, you subtract 34 from the total number of sectors of the affected device.

  To refresh your memory, you get the size of the device in sectors, by running

  ```
  partedUtil get /dev/disks/<device-ID>
  ```

  If this does not work, possibly because the primary gpt was also damaged or deleted, you may use fdisk instead using:

  ```
  fdisk -lu /dev/disks/<device-ID>
  ```

  For example:

  ```
  fdisk -lu /dev/disks/naa.6006016055711d00cff95e65664ee011

  Disk /dev/sdd: 10.7 GB, 10737418240 bytes
  255 heads, 63 sectors/track, 1305 cylinders, total 20971520 sectors
  ```

  In this example, the total number of sectors on this device is 20971520. To get the last usable sector, subtract 34 from that and you get 20971486.

6. The GUID is AA31E02A400F11DB9590000C2911D1B8, which I listed earlier in the output of

   ```
   partedUtil showGuids
   ```

7. The partition attribute, which is always 0 for VMFS partitions.

Using these guidelines, the command to re-create the partition table for this example would be

```
partedUtil setptbl "/dev/disks/naa.6006016055711d00cff95e65664ee011" gpt "1
2048 20971486 AA31E02A400F11DB9590000C2911D1B8 0"
```

After the partition table has been re-created, you can mount the datastore automatically by running:

```
vmkfstools -V
```

If the operation is successful, you should see the datastore listed in the /vmfs/volumes directory.

TIP

Check the /var/log/vmkernel.log for the following error:

LVM: 2907: [naa.6006016055711d00cff95e65664ee011:1] Device expanded (actual size 20969439 blocks, stored size 20964092 blocks)

This message means that the last sector used in re-creating the partition table did not match the original value. You can simply calculate the difference and add it to the `partedUtil` command you used to re-create the table. So, in this example, I had deliberately used a "last sector" value that was 5347 sectors short of the correct last usable sector.

You do not need to delete the table you created. Just rerunning the command with the new values overwrites the current table.

ONE MORE TIP

If you see the following message in /var/log/vmkernel.log

WARNING: Partition: 434: No Prot MBR for "naa.6006016055711d00cff95e65664ee011". GPT entries will be skipped

This means that the "protective MBR" on the first sector was deleted or corrupt. Re-creating the table as outlined this section should recover from this situation as long as the corruption was limited to the first 34 sectors of the device.

YET ANOTHER TIP

In the very rare situation where the primary GPT is corrupt while the protective MBR is still intact, you would get the following output when you run "partedUtil getptbl" command:

```
partedUtil getptbl /dev/disks/naa.6006016055711d00cff95e65664ee011

Error: The primary GPT table is corrupt, but the backup appears OK,
so that will be used.

Gpt

1305 255 63 20971520
```

If this is the case, you might be able to recover the Primary GPT using `partedtUtil fix` `<device-name>` which copies secondary GPT and places it in the primary GPT blocks.

Preparing for the Worst! Can You Recover from a File System Corruption?

The procedures previously discussed assume that the extent of the corruption was limited to certain sectors whose structure is repairable using generally available tools such as fdisk and partedUtil. However, damage beyond the VMFS partition offset that involves the metadata is much harder to repair without enlisting the services or a data recovery service such as Kroll-Ontrack or Seagate (see VMware KB 1015413 http://kb.vmware.com/kb/1015413).

To improve your chances of recovering your VMFS file system, you should have a BC/DR (Business Continuity/ Disaster Recovery) plan that provides backup of your data, storage replication/mirroring/snapshots and so on, recovery site(s), as well as infrastructure/fabric redundancy. Let me share with you a few tips that can improve your chances using simple tasks that do not take too much of your time.

Maintain a List of Your VMFS Partition Tables

The easiest way to gather the partition table it to collect vm-support dumps either locally on the host or preferably via vSphere Client 5 connected to vCenter Server.

Collecting Diagnostics Data

To collect vm-support dumps, follow this procedure:

1. Log on to vCenter Server using the vSphere 5 client.

2. Select Administration, Export System Logs. (See Figure 12.17.)

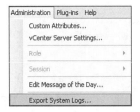

Figure 12.17   Accessing the Export System Logs menu

3. In the Source dialog (see Figure 12.18), expand the inventory tree and select the list of ESXi hosts from which you want to collect the dumps. If you want all hosts in the datacenter or the Cluster, select the checkbox next to one of the latter two. If you want to collect vCenter Server logs and vSphere Client logs, select the checkbox

at the bottom of the dialog and then click **Next**. Note that I manually uncheck the boxes next to the hosts that are not responding.

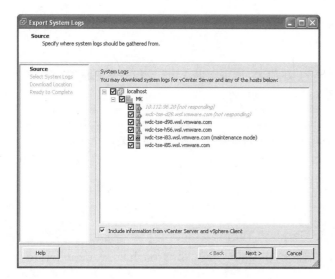

Figure 12.18 Selecting hosts for exporting system logs

4. In the Select System Logs dialog, you may accept the defaults and click **Next** to continue. If you want to reduce the dump size, you may uncheck all but the log types you want to collect. To understand what gets collected by each selection, read the corresponding manifests located in /etc/vmware/vm-support directory on one of the ESXi 5 hosts.

5. In the Download Location dialog, specify a folder accessible your vSphere 5 Client desktop and then click **Next**.

6. Review the summary, and if it matches your choices, click **Finish** to start the collection process.

7. The final dialog shows the progress of the log collection tasks. When it is completed, the logs are located in the folder you specified in Step 5 within a folder named after the following pattern:

    `VMware-vCenter-support-YYYY-MM-DD@HH-MM-SS`

    The vm-support dumps are named after the following pattern:

    `ESXiHostName-vmsupport-YYYY-MM-DD@HH-MM-SS.tgz`

8. When the need arises to use the collected data, you can do the following:

    a. Transfer the dump to an ESXi host or a Linux host.

    b. Extract the dump using

```
tar zxvf <dump-file-name>
```

    c. The extracted files are in a directory named after the following pattern:

```
esx-ESXiHostname-YYYY-MM-DD--HH.MM
```

    d. Before proceeding with utilizing the content of the extract dump, you must first reconstruct some output that was collected in chunks. You do so by running

```
cd <path-to-extracted-dump>
./reconstruct.sh
```

Which Parts of the Dump Provide Partition Table Details?

After expanding the vm-support dump as outlined in Steps 8b through 8d, you can locate the output of

```
esxcfg-info -a
```

in the /commands directory.

In this output you find all publicly available ESXi host properties and configuration as of the time the dump was collected. It is organized in a text-based tree structure. Branches are known as VSI Nodes, which include objects that hold certain properties.

Each VMFS volume's info, including its extents and partition table, is located in nodes like those listed in Figure 12.19.

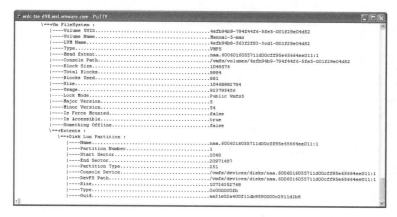

Figure 12.19 VMFS5 VSI Nodes

Here you see all properties of the VMFS volume. This helps you identify the following:

- Volume's UUID (signature).

- VMFS version (in this example, the major version is 5 and the minor one is 54).

- The device ID (NAA ID) which is the Name field listed under Extents, which also includes the partition number after a colon (:).

- The start sector (in this example it is 2048).

- The end sector (in this example it is 20971487). Notice that this value is always one sector larger compared to the partedUtil outputs. I am investigating this discrepancy as of the time of this writing.

Manually Collecting Partition Info Summary

If you have a small number of hosts, or otherwise have the time, you may collect a list of partitions from each host using

```
esxcli storage core device partition list
```

This gives you output similar to Figure 12.20.

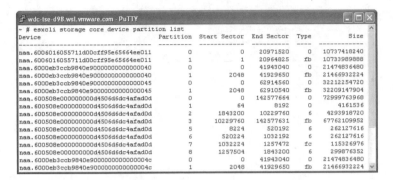

Figure 12.20   Listing partitions on all devices

The list includes the following:

1. **Device ID** — This is NAA ID of the LUN on which VMFS datastore resides.

2. **Partition number** — When the partition number listed is 0, this means that the listing represents the whole LUN, which is why the start sector is 0. Conversely, the end sector in this case refers to the last LBA (Logical Block Address) on the LUN.

   The output shown in Figure 12.20 was collected from an ESXi 5 host with typical configuration, which boots from a local disk because one of the devices has eight partitions (1 through 8).

3. **Start Sector** — This is the first LBA in the partition. If the value is 0, the partition number is also 0 because the listing is for the whole device. A value higher than 0 means the actual LBA numbers on which the partition offset is located.

4. **End Sector** — This is the last LBA in the partition. For devices with a single partition, this value should match the last usable sector obtained by the partedUtil getUsableSectors command listed earlier in this chapter in the "GPT on Disk Layout" section.

   For listings representing the whole device, this value represents the last LBA on the LUN.

NOTE

This output is derived from the VSI nodes I mentioned in relation to Figure 12.19. As such, I want to draw your attention to the fact that the end sector from this output is always one sector more than what you get from partedUtil outputs. So, keep this in mind when you will calculate the partition's last sector for the purpose of rebuilding the partition table.

For example, if you get the partition table listing of the boot device that has eight partitions (device ID naa.600508e000000000d4506d6dc4afad0d). you observe this as well. See the third column values in the following output for comparison. (I arranged the output for readability.) So, if you collect this output, it would be a more reliable calculation.

```
partedUtil getptbl /dev/disks/naa.600508e000000000d4506d6dc4afad0d
gpt
8875 255 63 142577664
1 64        8191       C12A7328F81F11D2BA4B00A0C93EC93B systemPartition 128
5 8224      520191     EBD0A0A2B9E5443387C068B6B72699C7 linuxNative     0
6 520224    1032191    EBD0A0A2B9E5443387C068B6B72699C7 linuxNative     0
7 1032224   1257471    9D27538040AD11DBBF97000C2911D1B8 vmkDiagnostic   0
8 1257504   1843199    EBD0A0A2B9E5443387C068B6B72699C7 linuxNative     0
2 1843200   10229759   EBD0A0A2B9E5443387C068B6B72699C7 linuxNative     0
3 10229760  142577630  AA31E02A400F11DB9590000C2911D1B8 vmfs            0
```

5. **Partition Type** — For VMFS partitions, the type is always fb in this output even though it is a GUID partition table, which means that the type should have been VMFS. This output uses the partition type similar to that used by fdisk regardless of the partition table format.

6. **Partition Size** — The size is in sectors. Notice that for listings whose partition number is 0, the size represents the total number of sectors in the LUN.

Maintain a Set of Metadata Binary Dumps

One more step you can take to improve your chances of data recovery is to regularly collect metadata binary dumps of the first 32MB of the devices on which VMFS3 or VMFS5 datastores reside as well as their extents, if any, using dd.

The syntax for collecting the dumps is

```
dd if=/dev/disks/<device-name> of=/<path-to-enough-space>/<Vol-x>-dump.bin
count=32 bs=1M
```

Just fill in the path to where you want to store the dumps and give each a name denoting the VMFS volume name from which it is collected.

This command collects 32MB from the device offset, which includes the Protective MBR/Primary GPT and VMFS metadata binary dump. This is sufficient for most file system and partition table recovery.

To collect backup of other resources that may also be affected by corruption, it is a good idea to increase the size of the dump to the first 1200MB of each device. This is what VMware support would ask you to collect if you report VMFS corruption.

The syntax for this is the same as the previous dd command but the count is 1200 instead of 32, as follows:

```
dd if=/dev/disks/<device-name> of=/<path-to-enough-space>/<Vol-x>-dump.bin
count=1200 bs=1M
```

Save the collected dumps in a safe place!

Span or Grow?

Careful design that accounts for expected workloads and capacity requirements usually provisions storage that satisfies these requirements. However, there is always a possibility that new business requirements will justify a design change.

A VMFS3 or VMFS5 datastore can be spanned onto additional LUNs or grown onto additional free space added to the existing device. However, before making this decision, you should also consider using storage DRS (Dynamic Resource Scheduler), which can effectively provide additional space that meets both I/O and Availability SLAs (Service Level Agreements).

For completeness sake, I discuss both extending and expanding VMFS3 and VMFS5.

Spanning VMFS Datastores

Adding physical LUNs to an existing VMFS3 or VMFS5 datastore spans the file system over these LUNs. The first LUN used to create the datastore is referred to as the head LUN because it includes part of the metadata without which the VMFS datastore cannot be mounted. The added LUNs are referred to as extents. VMFS3 and later can tolerate loss of any of the extents except for the head extent. If non-head extent is unavailable, the VMFS3 or 5 datastores remain accessible. Any I/O destined to blocks on the missing extent result in I/O errors.

How to Span a VMFS Datastore onto a New Extent

To span a VMFS datastore onto a new extent, follow this procedure:

1. Log on to vCenter Server using vSphere 5 Client as a user with Administrator/Root privileges.

2. Navigate to one of the hosts in the cluster/datacenter in the inventory tree.

3. Select the Configuration tab and then select **Storage** under the Hardware section.

4. In the Datastores pane, select the VMFS volume you want to span and click the **Properties** link in the Datastore Details pane (see Figure 12.21).

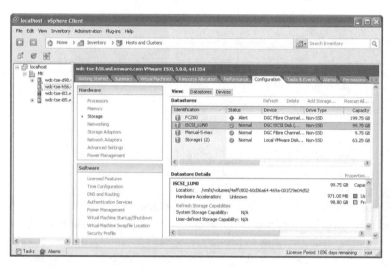

Figure 12.21 Selecting a datastore to span

5. In the Volume Properties dialog (see Figure 12.22), observe the Extent Device section where you see the total device capacity (in this example 200GB) and the primary partitions capacity, which indicate that the latter is using full device capacity. This means that you cannot grow this volume and that to increase its size, additional space is needed. You can get this space by either adding a new LUN to this host or by resizing the existing LUN on the array. Using the latter enables you to grow the volume. I cover this in the "Growing VMFS Datastores" section later in this chapter.

6. Click the **Increase** button (see Figure 12.22).

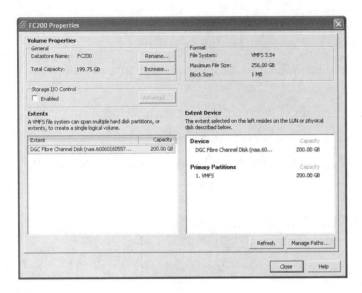

Figure 12.22 Datastore properties

7. In the Increase Datastore Capacity dialog, you see all devices that are not part of a VMFS volume or mapped via an RDM (see Figure 12.23). vCenter Server hides such devices to protect them from being used. Otherwise, it results in corrupting the file system already on these devices. Select a device to add. In this example, I am using VMFS3 datastore, but this procedure also applies to VMFS5. Notice the note at the bottom of the dialog stating "This datastore uses VMFS3. In order to use extents larger than 2TB, you must upgrade this datastore to VMFS5." As long as the capacity of each device that will be added as an extent is 2TB or less, you should be able to proceed. Larger device capacity is usable by VMFS5 only.

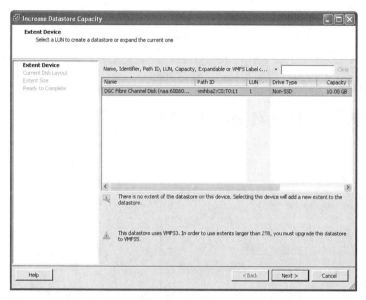

Figure 12.23   Selecting a device to add to a VMFS3

If this datastore were VMFS5, you would see the dialog in Figure 12.24 instead.
Click **Next** to proceed.

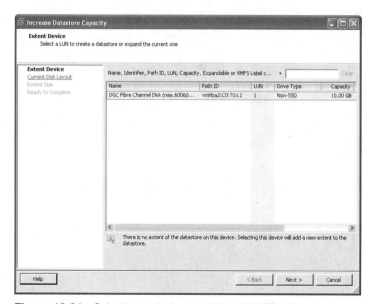

Figure 12.24   Selecting a device to add to a VMFS5 datastore

Notice that there is no warning about the device size in the dialog in Figure 12.24.

8. The Current Disk Layout dialog (see Figure 12.25) shows the head extent's disk layout and the new extent is blank. Click **Next** to continue.

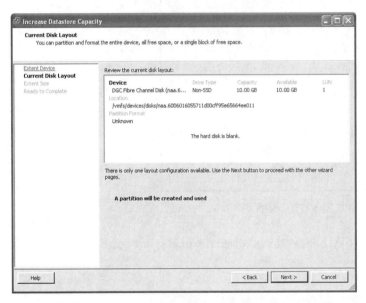

Figure 12.25   Spanning VMFS volume — Disk Layout

9. The resulting dialog (see Figure 12.26) enables you to use the maximum available space on the device or use less by selecting the **Custom Space Setting** radio button and specifying a smaller capacity. For this example, I'm using the whole device. Click **Next** to continue.

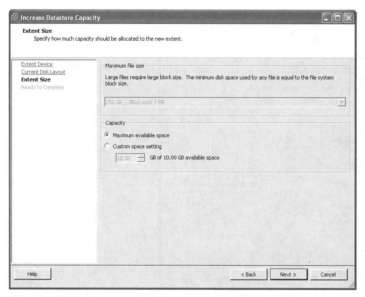

Figure 12.26 Spanning VMFS volume — Extent Size

NOTE

Notice that the block size cannot be changed as it must match the head extent's block size. Because this file system is VMFS3, you must use a block size that supports the largest file size you plan to use on this datastore.

If you plan to use a larger file size than the head extent's block size supports, the best approach is to upgrade the head extent prior to spanning it onto this new device. Doing so upgrades it to VMFS5, which, as I mentioned earlier, uses a single block size (1MB) to support all file sizes previously requiring larger block sizes.

10. The final dialog shows the new spanned volume size as well as the extent's disk layout (see Figure 12.27). Notice that the partition format is MBR because this is VMFS3. If this were a VMFS5 datastore, it would have been GPT instead. Click **Finish** when complete.

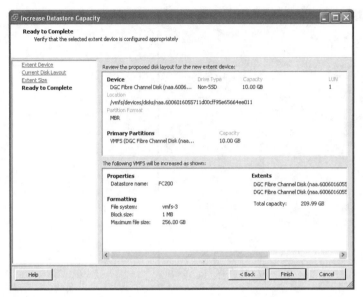

Figure 12.27   Spanning VMFS3 datastore — Ready to complete

11. vCenter Server triggers a rescan operation on all hosts sharing this volume so that they all can recognize the newly added capacity.

TIP

Although it is not enforced by vCenter Server, it is not advisable to span VMFS datastores onto extents of differing properties (RAID type, Physical Disk Types, Disk Interface type, Disk RPM rating, Storage Processor Port Speed, and Protocol).

The LUNs should practically be identical in all properties except for the capacity, which can vary according to your need and availability. Using vStorage API for Storage Awareness (VASA) can help you identify these properties from within vCenter Server.

How Does LVM Know the Members of Datastore?

VMFS3 volume header includes an extent ID as well as the volume UUID. At the load time or upon rescanning for VMFS datastores, LVM reads the metadata on each device. If it finds multiple devices share the same VMFS volume UUID, it assembles the volume using the extent ID starting with the head extent that has the first extent ID.

VMFS5 LVM header has the Spanned Device Table that lists the device IDs of all the volume's extents. This makes it easier to identify the members of the spanned volume.

How Is Data Spread over Extents?

When a datastore has extents, data is written to them in a fashion that all extents are used concurrently, not sequentially. There is a misconception that data is written sequentially on the first extent and then when it is full the next extent gets used. This is not true. VMFS Resource Manager, which is built in to the file system kernel modules, uses all extents that make up the spanned VMFS volume when hosts require allocating new space on that volume. The resource manager bases its block allocation decisions on a variety of factors that I cannot publically disclose. The net effect is that blocks from any LUN in a spanned VMFS volume may be allocated at any time. The exact sequence varies by volume, connectivity, and sequence of events among other factors. The VMFS resources are assigned to each host in resource groups across all available extents. Hosts distance the physical location of the files they create from those written by other hosts. However, they try to keep the objects they manage within close vicinity.

Spanning VMFS Pros and Cons

In medicine, each drug has several effects. For treating some diseases one or more of these effects are therapeutic and the rest are just side effects. Depending on the desired outcome from taking that drug the classification of these effects change.

The same concept lends itself to the computer industry, which usually refers to it as pros and cons. (I am tempted to use the joke about the Congress and Progress but I will restrain myself.)

Pros

Spanning a VMFS volume can provide the following benefits:

- Obviously, it adds more space to a space constrained VMFS datastore.

- Because SCSI reservations are done on the head extent only, spanning a VMFS volume reduces the SCSI reservations overall. However, this can be achieved better by using VMFS5 with a VAAI-enabled array that supports ATS primitive. VAAI would also help with VMFS3 datastores but VMFS5 has the property "ATS Only" that improves on using ATS without the need to check if the array supports it. I explain this in detail in Chapter 16.

- It can possibly reduce "hot spots" on the array because the data is spread over multiple extents on different disk groups.

- If the extents are on devices on different storage arrays or on the same or different controllers on the same array, this may help reduce the Device Queue exhaustion under high I/O utilization. This benefit is on the array's end only. The initiator is still limited to the max queue depth provided by the HBA's driver.

- Using Spanned Datastores with VMFS5 no longer imposes the limitation of the file block size. So, you can span the datastore to use fewer larger files. However, if these files belong to fewer VMs, then the benefit of using VMFS5 — which also adds the use of ATS-Only mode and effectively eliminates SCSI-2 reservations as long as the array supports that primitive — ends up diminishing the need to use such lower number of files. On the other hand, you must pay attention to your defined RTO; will you be able to restore such a large file fast enough to meet that SLA?

Cons

Spanning a VMFS has the following side-effects, drawbacks, or disadvantages:

- There is no easy way to identify which files live on which extent. So, if you happen to lose an extent, you only lose the data on that extent while the surviving ones keep chugging along. (You may say that this is a benefit by itself.) The only way you can tell what was affected is by observing which VMs get I/O errors writing to the missing blocks. How would you mitigate this risk? Backup!!!! Do that on the hardware level and the file level. Taking hardware snapshots or making a replica of the business-critical VMs/datastores/extents should help you recover more quickly compared to having one large single extent-based datastore of the same size as the spanned one. The time it takes you to restore the humongous datastore may go way beyond your RTO (Recovery Time Objective). Another way to mitigate this is to use Datastore Clusters with Storage DRS.

- Losing the head extent can result in losing the whole datastore. However, this is the same outcome if you are using a large LUN equal in size to the total size of extents making up the spanned datastore.

Growing VMFS Datastores

Many storage arrays provide the capability of growing LUNs. In the past, utilizing this space required manual changes to the partition table where you add a new partition in the added space and then create a VMFS extent on it in the same fashion you usually do with spanning VMFS volumes. Beginning with vSphere 4.0, VMware introduced a new feature of growing a VMFS datastore onto free space available on the physical LUN on which it resides. This effectively resizes the partition and modifies the metadata to add the new space as available resources.

Architecturally speaking, the end result is similar to freshly creating the VMFS volume on the device. The main difference between using this feature with VMFS3 and VMFS5 is that the latter can be grown onto LUNs larger than 2TB in size.

How to Grow a VMFS Volume

You can grow a VMFS volume using the vSphere 5 client or vmkfstools via the CLI.

Procedure Using vSphere 5 Client

To grow a VMFS datastore using the vSphere 5 Client, follow this procedure:

1. Log on to vCenter Server using vSphere 5 Client as a user with Administrator/Root privileges.

2. Navigate to one of the hosts in the cluster/datcenter in the inventory tree.

3. Select the Configuration tab; then select **Storage** under the Hardware section.

4. In the Datastores pane, select the VMFS volume you want to grow; then click **Properties...** link in the Datastore Details pane (Figure 12.28).

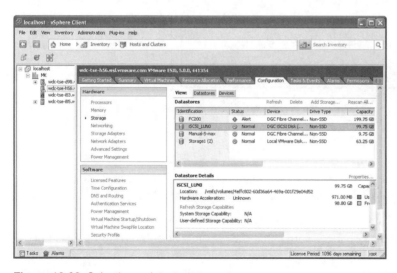

Figure 12.28 Selecting a datastore to grow

5. In the Volume Properties dialog, observe the Extent Device section where you will see the total device capacity (in this example 200GB) and the Primary Partitions capacity indicates that the latter is using half of the total device capacity (see Figure 12.29). This means that we can double the VMFS volume capacity using the remaining free capacity. Also, in this example, I am using VMFS5 datastore, but this procedure also applies to VMFS3 as long as the device capacity is 2TB or less. Larger device capacity is usable by VMFS5 only.

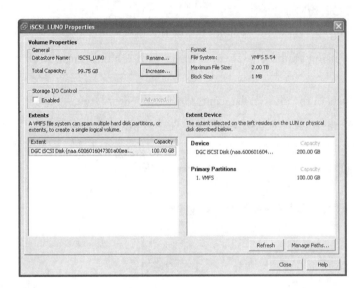

Figure 12.29 Volume properties

6. Take a note of the device ID (in this example, it is the NAA ID) under the Extents section; then click the **Increase…** button in the General section.

7. In the Increase Datastore Capacity dialog, select the device with the same device ID you noted in the last step. Notice that the Expandable column shows Yes. This means that you are OK to proceed. Notice the information listed on the bottom part of the dialog informing you that "the datastore already occupies one or more extents on this device" (see Figure 12.30). Click the **Next** button to proceed.

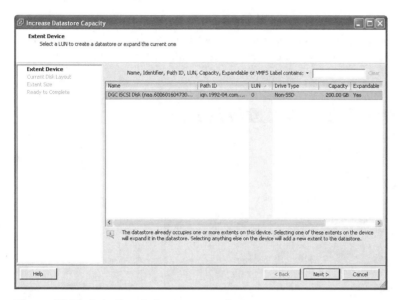

Figure 12.30 Selecting device to grow volume

8. The resulting disk layout dialog (see Figure 12.31) shows that there is one Primary Partition and that the Free space that will be used to expand the VMFS volume. Click **Next** to proceed.

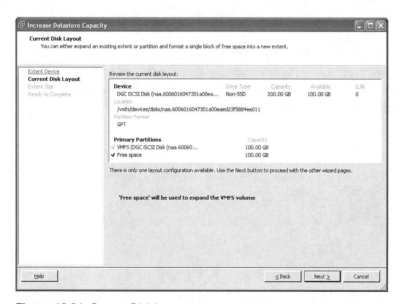

Figure 12.31 Current Disk Layout

9. You are almost there! The Extent Size dialog (see Figure 12.32) allows you to use the Maximum available space or use a Custom space setting, which allows you to use part of the available space. In this example, I will use all available space. Click **Next** to proceed.

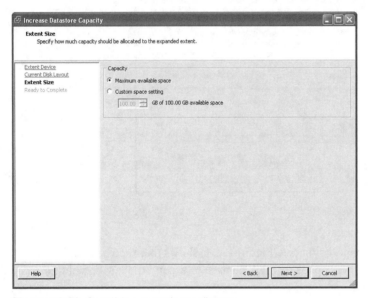

Figure 12.32 Specifying capacity to allocate

10. The Ready to Complete dialog (see Figure 12.33) shows the final settings that will be applied to the volume. Notice that the Primary Partition will be resized to utilize full device capacity instead of adding a second primary partition utilizing the free capacity you specified in the previous step. Click **Finish** to complete the operation.

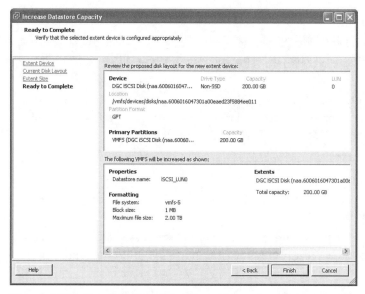

Figure 12.33 Ready to Complete "Grow Volume" process

11. Observe the Recent Tasks pane (see Figure 12.34) and you should notice that the following actions took place in that order:

   a. Compute disk partition information.

   b. Compute disk partition information for resize.

   c. Expand VMFS datastore.

   d. Finally, rescan VMFS on all ESXi hosts in the Datacenter.

Name	Target	Status	Details	Initiated by	Requested Start Ti...	Start Time
Rescan VMFS	wdc-tse-i83.ws...	Completed		System	12/31/2011 7:07:09 ...	12/31/2011
Rescan VMFS	wdc-tse-i85.ws...	Completed		System	12/31/2011 7:07:09 ...	12/31/2011
Rescan VMFS	wdc-tse-d98.w...	Completed		System	12/31/2011 7:07:09 ...	12/31/2011
Expand VMFS datastore	wdc-tse-h56.w...	Completed		root	12/31/2011 7:06:57 ...	12/31/2011
Compute disk partition information for resize	wdc-tse-h56.w...	Completed		root	12/31/2011 7:06:56 ...	12/31/2011
Compute disk partition information	wdc-tse-h56.w...	Completed		root	12/31/2011 7:06:56 ...	12/31/2011

Figure 12.34 Tasks done to grow volume

Step D ensures that all hosts in the datacenter can see the added capacity to the VMFS volume. This prevents other hosts in the cluster/datacenter from accidentally repeating this process if they had not seen the added capacity.

> **NOTE**
>
> Comparing this process to that of adding a new device as an extent on which to span the VMFS volume, the only difference is that in Step 7 you would select a different device from that used by the datastore already.
>
> In this case, instead of modifying the partition table on the head extent, the VMFS metadata is modified to reflect the added extent and its resources. See the previous section for details of spanning a VMFS volume.

This concludes the procedure.

Procedure Using vmkfstools

Growing the datastore onto the newly added device capacity is not as straightforward as using the vSphere 5 Client and is error prone since it requires the following high-level steps:

1. Use partedUtil to resize the partition.

   This process will effectively overwrite the GPT partition table and relocate the secondary GPT to the last sectors on the device. The VMFS partition is also resized. To find out the last sector that will be used by the resized partition, you would use partedUtil getUsableSectors option.

2. Use vmkfstools -G option to grow the volume.

As you see, using partedUtil can introduce errors that may result from typographical errors or miscalculations of the last sector number. It is a lot safer and faster to utilize the UI instead.

Upgrading to VMFS5

The upgrade process from VMFS3 to VMFS5 can be done live while VMs are actively running on the datastore. It is a very simple process that can be done via the UI or the CLI.

Before doing that, you must make sure that all hosts sharing the datastores you plan to upgrade have been themselves upgraded to ESXi 5. Once the datastore is upgraded, you cannot reverse the process and all hosts running versions pre-5.0 will lose access to the upgraded datastores.

Upgrade Process Using the CLI

To upgrade VMFS 3 to VMFS5 datastore using the CLI, follow this procedure:

1. Log in to ESXi host directly, via SSH or vMA 5.0.

2. Run the upgrade command using the following syntax:

   ```
   vmkfstools -T /vmfs/volumes/<volume-name>
   ```

3. You are prompted with a reminder about the older ESX versions on hosts sharing the datastore. The prompt asks you to select 0 (Yes) or 1 (No) to continue or abort the process, respectively. Select **0** then **Enter** to continue. (See Figure 12.35.)

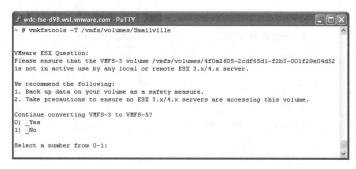

Figure 12.35   Upgrading VMFS via the CLI

The upgrade process continues showing the following text:

```
Checking if remote hosts are using this device as a valid file system. This
may take a few seconds...
Upgrading file system /vmfs/volumes/Smallville...
done.
```

4. Rescan from all ESXi 5 hosts sharing the upgraded datastore. This is the main drawback of using the CLI to upgrade the datastore. In comparison, the UI process listed next triggers rescan automatically after the upgrade is complete.

To verify the outcome, run the command in the following listing:

```
vmkfstools -Ph /vmfs/volumes/Smallville/
VMFS-5.54 file system spanning 1 partitions.
File system label (if any): Smallville
Mode: public
```

```
Capacity 9.8 GB, 9.2 GB available, file block size 2 MB
UUID: 4f0a2605-2cdf65d1-f2b3-001f29e04d52
Partitions spanned (on "lvm"):
        naa.6006016055711d00cff95e65664ee011:1
Is Native Snapshot Capable: NO
```

The new version is now listed in the output as VMFS-5.54. I highlighted the relevant text. Notice the file block size is still 2MB because the VMFS3 datastore was originally formatted with that block size.

Table 12.4 compares Upgraded VMFS5 datastores to those freshly created.

Table 12.4   Comparing Upgraded VMFS5 Datastores to Freshly Created Datastores

Features	Upgraded VMFS5	Formatted VMFS5
File-block size	1, 2, 4, and 8MB	1MB
Sub-block size	64KB	8KB
Partition type	MBR (GPT when grown)	GPT
Number of sub-blocks, file descriptors, and pointer blocks	Inherited from VMFS3	Limits proportionate to filesystem size
ATS only support (see Chapter 16)	No	Yes

Upgrade Related Log Entries

Events related to the upgrade process are posted to /var/log/vmkernel.log file. See the following listing for entries from the previous example. I cropped the date and time stamps for readability:

```
cpu0:6155853)FS3: 199: <START pb2>
cpu0:6155853)256 resources, each of size 4096
cpu0:6155853)Organized as 1 CGs, 64 C/CG and 16 R/C
cpu0:6155853)CGsize 4259840. 0th CG at 65536
cpu0:6155853)FS3: 201: <END pb2>
cpu0:6155853)Vol3: 3347: Successfully upgraded file system 4f0a28e3-
4ea353b6-08b6-001e4f1fbf2a to 5.54 from 3.54
```

Do you recall the pb2 I discussed earlier in this chapter in the "VMFS5 Layout" section?

The first five lines of this log show the creation of this new system file. It also shows the following properties:

- Resources: 256
- Resource size: 4096

- Number of Resource Clusters (R/C): 16

- Number of Clusters per Cluster Group (C/CG): 64

- Number of Cluster Groups (CGs): 1

- Cluster Group size (CGsize): 4259840

- Offset of Cluster Group number 0 (0th. CG): 65536

Upgrade Process Using the UI

To upgrade VMFS3 to VMFS5 using the UI, follow this procedure:

1. Log in to vCenter as Root, Administrator, or equivalent.

2. Locate one of the ESXi 5 hosts, sharing the volume to upgrade, in the inventory. Select its Configuration tab and then select **Storage** under the Hardware section.

3. Click the VMFS3 datastore you plan to upgrade.

4. Click the **Upgrade to VMFS-5** link (see Figure 12.36).

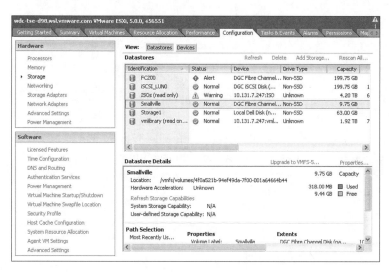

Figure 12.36 UI — Upgrade to VMFS-5 option

5. If you still have ESXi hosts older than 5.0, you see the dialog shown in Figure 12.37. To remedy this, click the **View Incompatible Hosts** link, which displays a list of hosts that you must upgrade before proceeding. Click **Cancel** to dismiss the dialog.

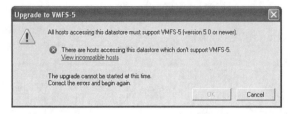

Figure 12.37   Error you get if older hosts still access the old volume

6. If, after upgrading the identified hosts, you no longer see the Upgrade to VMFS-5 link, click the **Rescan All** link at the top right-hand side of the Datastores pane.

7. Now you should be able to click the `Upgrade to VMFS5` link, which should result in the dialog shown in Figure 12.38. Click **OK** to proceed with the upgrade.

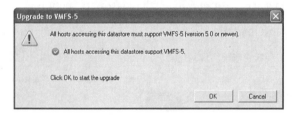

Figure 12.38   OK to proceed

8. When the upgrade process is complete, vCenter Triggers a rescan on all ESXi 5 hosts sharing the datastore.

9. To verify the outcome, check the value displayed in the File System field under the Formatting section in the Datastore Details section (see Figure 12.39). In this example, it is VMFS 5.54. Also notice that the block size remained at 2MB, which was the original volume's file block size.

Figure 12.39   Locating the upgraded volume's version in the UI

If you check /var/log/vmkernel.log file for the upgrade events, notice that they match those that I listed earlier when I ran the upgrade via the CLI. However, this time around, I had originally formatted the VMFS3 datastore using ESXi 4.1. This would explain the last line in the set of log entries shown in the next line:

```
Successfully upgraded file system 4f0a521b-94ef49da-7f00-001a64664b44 to
5.54 from 3.46
```

Notice that the previous version is 3.46 compared to 3.54 listed earlier under the CLI procedure. The reason is that the higher "minor" version of the file system was created using ESXi 5.0. The difference in minor versions has no effect on features available for VMFS3 on ESXi 5.0.

What If VMFS5 Datastore Is Presented to ESXi 4.x?

Assume that your SAN administrator accidentally presented a device on which a VMFS5 volume resides, what would happen?

The answer is "nothing will happen!" The reason is that the older version of the vmkernel has a module for VMFS3 only. The latter identifies the major version is 5, and gracefully fails to mount the VMFS5 datastore.

How about another variation on this scenario?

In the section for upgrading using the CLI, the process depends on *you* to verify that all hosts accessing this datastore have been upgraded to ESXi 5. Let's assume you overlooked one or two hosts. The process still continues, and the datastore is upgraded to version 5.54.

What actually happens with the older hosts? You should see something like the following messages in /var/log/vmkernel on the 4.x hosts:

```
WARNING: LVM: 2265: [naa.6006016047301a00eaed23f5884ee011:1] LVM major
version mismatch (device 5, current 3)

FSS: 3647: No FS driver claimed device 'naa.6006016047301a00eaed23f5884
ee011:1': Not supported

FSS: 3647: No FS driver claimed device '48866acd-d8ef78ec-5942-
001a6436c322': Not supported
```

I added blank lines between each message for readability. The first message states that the LVM version on the datastore is newer. What is on the disk is version 5; what the host has in memory is version 3. This means that the host has not rescanned the storage area network (SAN) since the datastore was upgraded.

The second and third lines are the same but one references the device ID (NAA ID) and the other references the volume signature (UUID). What they mean is that this host has a VMFS kernel module that does not support this version. As a result, none of the FS drivers (file system drivers) claimed the device(s).

Summary

VMFS5 is the latest version of VMware-clustered file system that introduced several scalability and performance enhancements. In this chapter I shared with you the file system history, architecture, and recovery tips.

Chapter 13

Virtual Disks and RDMs

VMware vSphere 5, and earlier releases, abstract the storage and presents it to virtual machines in various forms which are virtual disks, Raw Device Mappings (RDMs), and generic pass-through SCSI devices. This chapter deals with virtual disks and RDMs.

The Big Picture

To better understand how virtual disks and RDMs are abstracted, see Figure 13.1 for a high-level diagram.

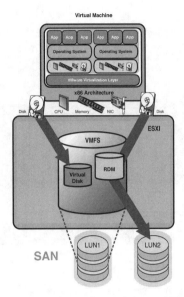

Figure 13.1   Virtual disks and RDMs

In Figure 13.1, virtual machine file system (VMFS) datastore was created on LUN1 on the storage area network (SAN). A virtual disk is a file on the VMFS datastore. When the virtual disk is attached to the virtual machine, it sees it as a VMware SCSI Disk. In contrast, an RDM is created on the VMFS datastore that is simply a file that acts as a pointer to LUN2. When the RDM is attached to the virtual machine, it sees it as one of two possible modes; a VMware SCSI Disk or a Native Physical LUN (for example, CLARiiON RAID5 LUN). I explain the differences in the "Virtual Mode RDMs" and "Physical Mode RDMs" sections later in this chapter.

Virtual Disks

Virtual disks are files created on VMFS or NFS (Network File System) datastores. These files use a .vmdk extension and are made up of more than one file depending on the type of virtual disk they represent.

The main file is referred to as the Virtual Disk Descriptor File, which is an ASCII (actually, UTF-8 encoded) text file that defines the structure of the virtual disk. Listing 13.1 is an example of such a file:

Listing 13.1   Sample Virtual Disk Descriptor File

```
# Disk DescriptorFile
version=1
encoding="UTF-8"
CID=fffffffe
parentCID=ffffffff
isNativeSnapshot="no"
createType="vmfs"

# Extent description
RW 33554432 VMFS "vSphere Management Assistant 5.0_1-flat.vmdk"

# The Disk Data Base
#DDB

ddb.virtualHWVersion = "4"
ddb.longContentID = "0481be4e314537249f0f1ca6fffffffe"
ddb.uuid = "60 00 C2 93 7f fb 16 2a-1a 66 1f 50 ed 10 51 ee"
ddb.geometry.cylinders = "2088"
ddb.geometry.heads = "255"
ddb.geometry.sectors = "63"
ddb.adapterType = "lsilogic"
```

The Virtual Disk Descriptor File has the following sections:

- `Disk DescriptorFile` — The fields in this section are listed in Table 13.1.

Table 13.1   Virtual `Disk DescriptorFile` Section Fields

Field	Possible Values	Notes
CID	fffffffe or lower hexadecimal value	Content ID is unique per disk hierarchy. Read more details in the "Linked Clones" section.
ParentCID	ffffffff for the top-level virtual disk and lower for children in a snapshot or linked clone	Snapshot files or linked clone files identify their parent virtual disk by its parent virtual disk's Content ID (CID). Read more details in the "Linked Clones" section.

Table 13.1   Continued

Field	Possible Values	Notes
isNativeSnapshot	No or Yes	For use by a future vSphere release.
createType	Vmfs	Virtual disk.
	vmfsRawDeviceMap	Virtual mode RDM.
	vmfsPassthroughRawDeviceMap	Physical mode RDM.
	twoGbMaxExtentSparse	2GB sparse disk.
	vmfsSparse	Virtual disk snapshot.

- Extent description — Lists the virtual disk extent files and is made up of four sections listed in Table 13.2. The actual field names are not stated in the vmdk file. All values are listed on one line under the Extent Description section in the vmdk file.

Table 13.2   Extent Description Fields

Field	Possible Values	Notes
Access	RW	Inherited from older releases. On ESXi 5 it is always RW (read-write).
Size	device block count	Size of the extent file in 512-byte disk blocks.
Type	VMFS	Virtual disk extent. One extent per virtual disk.
	VMFSRDM	RDM extent (both virtual and physical). One extent per RDM.
	SPARSE	Extents of Virtual Disk created via vmkfstools using 2gbsparse option. (Read more details in the "Creating Virtual Disks Using vmkfstools" section.)
	VMFSSPARSE	Extents of virtual disks of a VM snapshot.
Extent Files	*-flat.vmdk	This is where the Virtual Disk data gets written.
	*-rdm.vmdk	This is the VMFS pointer to the raw device (virtual mode).
	*-rdmp.vmdk	This is the VMFS pointer to the raw device (physical mode).
	*.s00(n).vmdk	These represent the 2GB segments of the sparse virtual disk. The size can be smaller than 2GB. The (n) represents the extent number counting from 1.

- The `Disk Database` — This section lists the virtual disk properties as seen by the VM. It includes the seven fields listed in Table 13.3 (and one additional field for thin provisioned virtual disks).

Table 13.3   Disk Database Fields

Field	Possible Values	Notes
ddb.virtualHWVersion	4 or 8	Virtual hardware version.
ddb.longContentID	Hexadecimal value	Long Content ID is used to resolve conflicts in CID. For example, if there are multiple descriptor files with the same CID, the Long CID is used as a unique ID instead.
ddb.uuid	Hexadecimal value	Random text. Unique to the virtual disk. Generated from the SHA1 hash of the host ID, time stamp, and a random number.
ddb.geometry.cylinders	Decimal value	The number of cylinders of the disk presented to the guest OS.
ddb.geometry.heads	Decimal value	The number of heads of the disk presented to the guest OS.
ddb.geometry.sectors	Decimal value	The number of sectors of the disk presented to the guest OS.
ddb.adapterType	lsilogic, buslogic or ide	Matches the virtual storage adapter used by the VM.
ddb.thinProvisioned	1	Denotes that the virtual disk was created as thin provisioned. This field will not have a value other than 1. If the virtual disk is not thin provisioned, this property would not exist in the descriptor file.

Virtual Disk Types

Virtual disks on ESXi 5–based VMFS3 or VMFS5 datastores are categorized according to their disk provisioning as the following:

- **Zeroed thick** — In the UI, this is referred to as *flat disk*. Disk blocks are pre-allocated at creation time, but the blocks are zeroed out (zeros written to the blocks) upon first write. The file is created faster because all that is done is to create the metadata file entry and specify the file blocks that it occupies but that are not zeroed out.

- **Eager zeroed thick** — Disk blocks are pre-allocated and zeroed out at creation time. This is the most secure type of virtual disks because any previous data that might have been on the allocated disk blocks is overwritten with zeros. On VMFS3 or -5 datastores that are on non-VAAI (VMware vStorage APIs for Array Integration) storage arrays (see Chapter 16, "VAAI") the creation process takes more time compared to the creation time for the zeroed thick type and is proportionate to the virtual disk size. If the storage array supports WRITE_SAME (also known as block zeroing) primitive, the block zeroing is offloaded to the storage array. This significantly reduces the file creation time.

- **Thin** — This type of virtual disk is analogous to thin provisioning physical LUNs (logical unit numbers). The virtual disk file size is predefined, but the disk blocks are not allocated at the time the file is created.

Table 13.4 compares all three types.

Table 13.4 Virtual Disk Types Comparison

Characteristics	Zeroed Thick	Eager Zeroed Thick	Thin
Disk allocation	Fully pre-allocated.	Fully pre-allocated.	On demand.
Block placement on file system	Higher chance of using contiguous file blocks.	Same as zeroed thick.	Depending on how active the datastore is at the time the file is grown, the allocated blocks might not be contiguous.
Block zeroing	On demand upon first write.	At the time of creating the file.	At the time the file is grown.
Reading previously unwritten blocks	Blocks not read from disk. Rather, memory buffers are filled with zeros. This is very fast because zeroing memory is extremely faster than zeroing disk.	Read request sent to disk. This might return stale data from disk. This is slower than zeroed thick because it reads from disk instead of memory.	Same as zeroed thick.

Characteristics	Zeroed Thick	Eager Zeroed Thick	Thin
Writing previously unwritten blocks	Blocks are zeroed before sending the write to disk. This results in higher latency of the original write (from guest OS). This is much slower than eager zeroed thick.	Write requests are sent to disk because the blocks were zeroed at the time of creating the file.	Block is allocated and zeroed on disk first. Then the write is sent to disk. This is slightly slower than zeroed thick and has a higher latency of the original write (from the guest OS). Allocating blocks results in some distributed locking traffic unless the VAAI ATS and Write_ Same primitives are supported.
Reading previously written blocks	Requests sent to disk. If this occurs while the first write to the blocks are still in progress, the reads are queued until the writes are done.	Request is forwarded to disk. No other overhead.	Same as zeroed thick.
Writing previously written blocks	Same as reading previously written blocks.	Same as reading previously written blocks.	Same as zeroed thick.
Physical disk space usage	Does not need more space while the VM is running because the file blocks were pre-allocated.	Same as zeroed thick.	Because the file blocks are allocated on demand, the guest may be paused if the VMFS volume runs out of space or, if on thin provisioned LUN, the LUN reaches its maximum capacity. See more details in the "Thin-on-Thin Configuration" section later in this chapter.
Appearance in vSphere UI	Thick provision lazy zeroed.	Thick provision eager zeroed.	Thin provision.
Datastore Compatibility	VMFS3	VMFS3	VMFS3
	VMFS5	VMFS5	VMFS5
	NFS*	NFS*	NFS (Default type)

* NFS datastore on storage arrays must support VAAI NAS (Network Attached Storage) primitives. See more details about VAAI in Chapter 16. For thin provisioned virtual disks, VAAI support is not required as this is the default format for NFS datastores.

Thin on Thin

Using thin provisioned virtual disks on thin provisioned LUNs poses the risk of LUNs running out of space before thin virtual disks reach their maximum provisioned capacity. To mitigate this risk, VMware introduced alarms and VOBs (vSphere Observations) to alert the vSphere Administrator of two possible states:

- **Out of Space Warning** — Storage array vendors can provide a Free Space Soft Threshold Limit setting on the array. When set, a warning is sent to the ESXi host that attempted to write blocks and resulted in reaching the threshold. The write operation would succeed, though. This warning can be sent in-band or out-of-band. This means that it can be sent as a SCSI error directly to the host (as a check condition with sense key 0x6 ASC 0x38 ASCQ 0x7) or as a VASA (VMware vStorage APIs for Storage Awareness) event polled by the VASA provider installed in the vSphere environment. Storage vendors opt to use one or the other but not both. The vSphere environment can be configured to move virtual disks to other datastores if using the Storage DRS feature.

- **Out of Space Error** — This is a similar setting to be configured on the Storage Array as a hard threshold that generates an Out-of-Space error (to the host directly as a check condition with sense key 0x6 ASC 0x27 ASCQ 0x7). This results in failing the I/O (input/output) that resulted in reaching the hard threshold of free space. Similar integration with Storage DRS is implemented in vSphere 5.

Virtual Disk Modes

Virtual disk modes dictate how these virtual disks are affected by VM snapshots (see the "Snapshots" section later in this chapter):

- **Dependent** — This is the default mode. It means that when a snapshot of the VM is taken the virtual disk has a snapshot created.

- **Independent** — The virtual disk is independent from VM snapshot activities. So, when a VM snapshot is taken, the virtual disk does not have a snapshot created. In this mode the virtual disk can be set as persistent or non-persistent:

  - **Persistent** — Data written to the virtual disk persists when the VM is powered off and then powered on.

  - **Non-persistent** — Data written to the virtual disk are redirected to a delta file (also know as a REDO file) that is discarded upon powering off the VM. Note that just rebooting the Guest Operating System (GOS) does not result in discarding the delta files. Only powering off the VM does.

Creating Virtual Disks Using the UI

Virtual disks are created in the process of creating a VM as well as editing existing VMs to add new virtual disks.

Creating Virtual Disks During VM Creation

Choosing the custom VM creation path enables you to specify the type, mode, and location of the virtual disks that you define as outlined in this procedure.

1. Log on to vCenter Server 5 via vSphere Client 5 as a user with Administrator privileges.

2. Navigate to and select the Datacenter or Cluster in which you want to create the new VM.

3. Use Ctrl+N keyboard hotkey or right-click the Datacenter or Cluster object in the inventory tree then select **New Virtual Machine** (see Figure 13.2).

Figure 13.2   New Virtual Machine command

4. Select the **Custom** radio button and then click **Next** (see Figure 13.3).

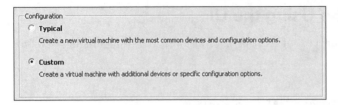

Figure 13.3   Selecting the Custom VM option

5. Type the VM name and select in which inventory location you want to store the VM. Click **Next.**

6. Select the host on which you want to run the VM and then click **Next**.

7. Select the storage on which to store the VM files.

8. In the Virtual Machine Version dialog select **7** if you want the VM shared with hosts earlier than ESXi 5 or select **8** if you plan to run it on ESXi 5 or later (see Figure 13.4).

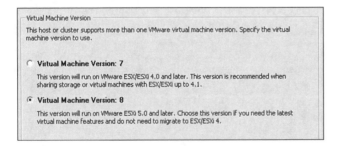

Figure 13.4   Selecting the VM version

This choice dictates the Virtual hardware version used by the VM, version 7 or 8, respectively.

9. Select the Guest OS type, the number of virtual sockets and cores per virtual socket, the VM Memory Size, and the Virtual NIC count and type in the subsequent the dialogs, respectively.

10. Select the virtual SCSI Controller (see Figure 13.5). The default selection is based on your choice of Guest OS selected in Step 9. See the section "Virtual Storage Adapters" for more details.

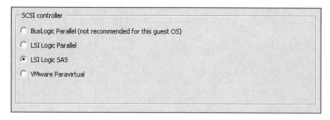

Figure 13.5   Selecting the virtual SCSI controller

11. Select the **Create a New Virtual Disk** radio button and click **Next.**

12. Specify the Capacity, Disk Provisioning, and Location of the virtual disk. (See Figure 13.6.)

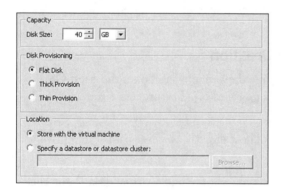

Figure 13.6   Selecting virtual disk capacity, disk provisioning, and VM location

13. Select the Virtual Device Node and the Mode of the Virtual Disk. Click **Next** (see Figure 13.7).

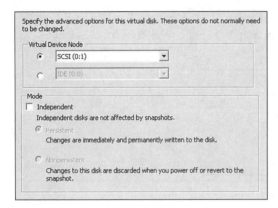

Figure 13.7   Selecting the virtual device node and mode

14. Review your selections and click **Finish** to create the VM.

The Virtual Disk created using this procedure is stored in the location you selected in Step 12 and is named after the Virtual Machine name you specified in Step 3.

Creating a Virtual Disk After VM Creation

You may add virtual disks to existing VMs while they are powered on if the guest OS supports hot-add; otherwise, the VM must be powered off. The process is the same regardless of the power state.

1. Log on to vCenter Server or to the ESXi host directly as a user with admin privileges.

2. Locate the VM in the inventory to which you want to add a virtual disk. Right-click it and then select **Edit Settings** (see Figure 13.8).

Figure 13.8 Editing VM settings

3. In the resulting dialog, click the **Add** button.

4. Select **Hard Disk** from the list of devices and then click **Next**.

5. Follow Steps 11 through 13 under the previous section "Creating Virtual Disks During VM Creation."

6. Click **Finish** to conclude the virtual disk creation.

   The new virtual disk shows in the device list as New Hard Disk (adding) (see Figure 13.9).

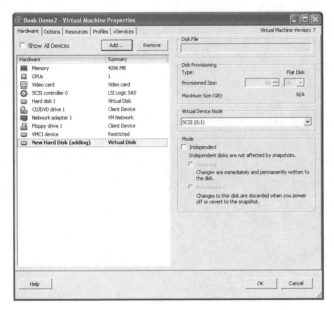

Figure 13.9   Result of adding a new virtual disk

7. To save the changes to the VM, click **OK**.

> **NOTE**
>
> In Step 6 of this procedure you can change the virtual device node as well as the virtual disk mode if you forgot to select them during the earlier steps.
>
> I discuss the design choices for the virtual device node in the "Virtual Storage Adapters" section later in this chapter.

Creating Virtual Disks Using vmkfstools

vmkfstools is the ESXi tool to use for managing VMFS datastores and Virtual Disks. It is available on the ESXi 5 host as well as vMA 5.0 and vCLI 5. If you run vmkfstools without any parameters, it displays available options shown in Listing 13.2.

Listing 13.2 vmkfstools Options

```
~# vmkfstools
vmkfstools: unrecognized option

OPTIONS FOR VIRTUAL DISKS:

vmkfstools -c --createvirtualdisk #[gGmMkK]
               -d --diskformat [zeroedthick|
                                thin|
                                eagerzeroedthick]
               -a --adaptertype [buslogic|lsilogic|ide]
           -w --writezeros
           -j --inflatedisk
           -k --eagerzero
           -K --punchzero
           -U --deletevirtualdisk
           -E --renamevirtualdisk srcDisk
           -i --clonevirtualdisk srcDisk
               -d --diskformat [zeroedthick|
                                thin|
                                eagerzeroedthick|
                                rdm:<device>|rdmp:<device>|
                                2gbsparse]
               -N --avoidnativeclone
           -X --extendvirtualdisk #[gGmMkK]
               [-d --diskformat eagerzeroedthick]
           -M --migratevirtualdisk
           -r --createrdm /vmfs/devices/disks/...
           -q --queryrdm
           -z --createrdmpassthru /vmfs/devices/disks/...
           -v --verbose #
           -g --geometry
           -I --snapshotdisk srcDisk
           -x --fix [check|repair]
           -e --chainConsistent
     vmfsPath
```

The relevant options for this chapter are those listed in the "Options for Virtual Disks" section. I removed the other options from the output.

In the output shown in Listing 13.2, the reference to vmfsPath in the context of virtual disk options represents the virtual disk filename including the path to the VMFS datastore. It is also worth noting that a subset of the virtual disk–related options apply to manipulating virtual disk files on NFS datastores as well. I point these out where appropriate.

Creating a Zeroed Thick Virtual Disk Using vmkfstools

Zeroed Thick Virtual Disks have pre-allocated blocks on the datastore (see Table 13.4 earlier in this chapter), but the blocks are not zeroed out at creation time. This is the default type for virtual disks created on VMFS3 or VMFS5 datastores. You can create this type of a virtual disk using vmkfstools using this command:

```
vmkfstools --createvirtualdisk <size> --diskformat zeroedthick --adapter-
type <type> /<vmfs-path to VM directory>/<Virtual Disk file name>
```

The shorthand version of this command is

```
vmkfstools -c <size> -d zeroedthick -a <type> /<vmfs-path to VM
directory>/<Virtual Disk file name>
```

Example:

```
vmkfstools --createvirtualdisk 40G --diskformat zeroedthick --adaptertype
lsilogic /vmfs/volumes/datastore1/Book-Demo/bookdemo-disk2.vmdk
```

This creates a 40GB zeroed thick virtual disk named bookdemo-disk2.vmdk in datastore named datastore1 in a VM directory named Book-Demo.

The size option accepts a single letter *g*, *m*, or *k* in upper- or lowercase representing GB, MB, and KB units, respectively. The number preceding the letter is the virtual disk size in the specified unit.

Creating an Eager Zeroed Thick Virtual Disk Using vmkfstools

Eager zeroed thick virtual disks have pre-allocated blocks on the datastore, and all blocks have zeros written to them. This ensures that if there were any data from files previously occupying the allocated blocks, they get overwritten with zero patterns.

To create such a file using vmkfstools, you use the same command in the previous section substituting zeroedthick with eagerzeroedtick as follows:

```
vmkfstools --createvirtualdisk <size> --diskformat eagerzeroedthick
--adaptertype <type> /<vmfs-path to VM directory>/<Virtual Disk file name>
```

The shorthand version of this command is

```
vmkfstools -c <size> -d eagerzeroedthick -a <type> /<vmfs-path to VM
directory>/<Virtual Disk file name>
```

Example:

```
vmkfstools --createvirtualdisk 40G --diskformat eagerzeroedthick --adapter-
type lsilogic /vmfs/volumes/datastore1/Book-Demo2/bookdemo-disk3.vmdk
```

Listing 13.3 shows a sample output.

Listing 13.3   Output of Creating Eager Zeroed Thick Virtual Disk

```
Creating disk '/vmfs/volumes/datastore1/Book-Demo2/bookdemo-disk3.vmdk' and
zeroing it out...
Create: 74% done.
```

As the file creation progresses, the percentage done is incremented in the Create line until it reaches 100%.

To measure how long it takes for the file creation to complete, you may run the command in Listing 13.4.

Listing 13.4   Measuring Time to Create Eager Zeroed Thick Virtual Disk

```
time vmkfstools -c 40G --diskformat eagerzeroedthick --adaptertype lsilogic
/vmfs/volumes/iSCSI_LUN0/Book-Demo2/bookdemo-disk4.vmdk
Creating disk '/vmfs/volumes/iSCSI_LUN0/Book-Demo2/bookdemo-disk4.vmdk' and
zeroing it out...
Create: 100% done.
real    3m 16.99s
user    0m 1.68s
sys     0m 0.00s
```

The command `time` tracks the time taken for the task to complete. The value you need to track is listed in the real field. In this example it took 3 minutes, 16 seconds, and 99 milliseconds to create a 40GB eager zeroed thick virtual disk on the datastore named iSCSI_LUN0.

Running the same command to create the same virtual disk on a datastore located on a VAAI-capable storage array completes almost immediately because the process of writing zeroes is offloaded to the storage array. I discuss this further in Chapter 16.

Creating a Thin Virtual Disk Using vmkfstools

Thin virtual disks blocks are allocated as needed when data is written to the virtual disk and the file grows in size. This is the default type for virtual disks created on NFS datastores.

To create a thin virtual disk using vmkfstools, use this command:

```
vmkfstools --createvirtualdisk <size> --diskformat thin --adaptertype
<type> /<vmfs-path to VM directory>/<Virtual Disk file name>
```

The shorthand version of the command is

```
vmkfstools -c <size> -d thin -a <type> /<vmfs-path to VM
directory>/<Virtual Disk file name>
```

Example:

```
vmkfstools --createvirtualdisk 40G --diskformat thin --adaptertype lsilogic
/vmfs/volumes/datastore1/Book-Demo2/bookdemo-disk5.vmdk
```

This creates a 40GB thin virtual disk file named book-demo-disk5.vmdk on a datastore named datastore1.

Listing File System Usage by Thin Virtual Disks

To VMs, thin virtual disks appear to be pre-allocated, but they actually occupy the blocks used by data written to the virtual disk only. To demonstrate that, let's run a couple of commands.

The following command lists a virtual disk file named book-demo-thin-flat.vmdk in the current directory. I named thin for demonstration purposes. Normally thin virtual disks are named whatever you name them and the provisioning type is not included in the filename. This file is the extent of the virtual disk with a descriptor file named book-demo-thin.vmdk.

```
ls -al book-demo-thin*
-rw-------    1 root     root            4294967296 Mar 25 02:39 book-demo-
thin-flat.vmdk
-rw-------    1 root     root                   499 Mar 25 02:39 book-demo-
thin.vmdk
```

The size of the extent file is 4294967296 bytes, which is 4GB (4GB × 1024MB × 1024KB × 1024bytes). This is the size the file system reports to the virtual machine that uses it as a virtual disk.

Now, let's see the actual number of disk blocks this file occupies on the file system (see Listing 13.5).

Listing 13.5   Count of Blocks Used by Thin Virtual Disk

```
stat book-demo-thin-flat.vmdk
  File: "book-demo-thin-flat.vmdk"
  Size: 4294967296      Blocks: 0          IO Block: 131072 regular file
Device: d03aaeed4049851bh/15004497442547270939d Inode: 88096004    Links: 1
Access: (0600/-rw-------)  Uid: (   0/   root)  Gid: (   0/   root)
Access: 2012-03-25 02:39:10.000000000
Modify: 2012-03-25 02:39:10.000000000
Change: 2012-03-25 02:39:10.000000000
```

The command `stat` lists the filename, its size, and how many disk blocks it occupies. In this example, the file size matches what we got from the directory listing. However, the block count is zero! Why is it zero? The answer is Small File Packing or Zero Level Addressing discussed under the "File Allocation Improvements" section in Chapter 12, "VMFS Architecture."

Where is the file actually stored if it occupies zero blocks? It is stuffed into the VMFS file descriptor block (inode). In this example the inode number is 88096004. When a VM writes data to this file and it grows beyond 1K in size, it is placed in a VMFS sub-block (64k for VMFS3 and 8K for VMFS5) until it grows beyond the sub-block size, which is when it occupies whole File System block (1MB for newly created VMFS5 or whatever block size used to format VMFS3). See the "File Allocation Improvements" section in Chapter 12.

In comparison, see what a thick disk block allocation looks like in Listing 13.6.

Listing 13.6   Count of Blocks Used by Thick Virtual Disk

```
stat book-demo-thick-flat.vmdk
  File: "book-demo-thick-flat.vmdk"
  Size: 4294967296      Blocks: 8388608    IO Block: 131072 regular file
Device: d03aaeed4049851bh/15004497442547270939d Inode: 71318788    Links: 1
Access: (0600/-rw-------)  Uid: (   0/   root)  Gid: (   0/   root)
Access: 2012-03-25 02:36:33.000000000
Modify: 2012-03-25 02:36:33.000000000
Change: 2012-03-25 02:36:33.000000000
```

In this example, I created a thick virtual disk with the exact size as the thin one and I used the word *thick* in the file name for demonstration purposes. The output of stat shows that the size is 4294967296, which is 4GB, and the number of disk blocks are 8388608. If you multiply the number of block by the disk block size which is 512bytes, you get 4294967296 which is the total file size in bytes.

Cloning Virtual Disks Using vmkfstools

The process of creating a copy of a virtual disk via vmkfstools is referred to as *cloning*. It used to be known as importing but because the output can be any supported virtual disk type which can be different from the original virtual disk, the term *cloning* is more appropriate. Do not confuse this process with that available in vCenter Server which clones the whole VM. The latter clones the VM configuration along with the virtual disks. This process is also used by View Composer, which creates full clones or linked clones. I explain that further in Chapter 15, "Snapshot Handling."

To clone a virtual disk, you need to decide on the following items:

- Source virtual disk name
- Target virtual disk name
- Target virtual disk format

The first two items are self-explanatory. The third item can be any of the following disk formats:

- zeroedthick (zeroed thick)
- thin (thin)
- eagerzeroedthick (eager zeroed thick)
- rdm (virtual mode RDM)
- rdmp (physical mode RDM)
- 2gbsparse (2GB sparse disk)

I already covered the first three types. I discuss RDMs later in this chapter in the "Raw Device Mapping" section.

2GB sparse disk format is the default VMware Workstation and VMware Fusion virtual disk format. To clone a virtual disk using this disk format you may use this command:

```
vmkfstools --clonevirtualdisk <source-virtual-disk) --diskformat 2gbsparse
<target-virtual-disk>
```

The shorthand version is

```
vmkfstools -i <source-virtual-disk) -d 2gbsparse <target-virtual-disk>
```

Example:

```
vmkfstools -i book-demo-thin.vmdk -d 2gbsparse book-demo-thin-clone.vmdk
```

This clone results in the creation of the files shown in Listing 13.7.

Listing 13.7   Sparse Files Created by Cloning Option

```
ls -al book-demo-thin-clone*
-rw-------  1 root root   327680 Mar 25 20:40 book-demo-thin-clone-s001.vmdk
-rw-------  1 root root   327680 Mar 25 20:40 book-demo-thin-clone-s002.vmdk
-rw-------  1 root root    65536 Mar 25 20:40 book-demo-thin-clone-s003.vmdk
-rw-------  1 root root      619 Mar 25 20:40 book-demo-thin-clone.vmdk
```

The smallest file is the virtual disk descriptor file: book-demo-thin-clone.vmdk.

The remaining files are the extents of the virtual disk with a suffix s00x where x is a sequential numeric value starting from 1.

Listing 13.8 shows a sample of the relevant content from the descriptor file.

Listing 13.8   Content of a Sparse Disk Descriptor File

```
# Disk DescriptorFile
version=1
encoding="UTF-8"
CID=fffffffe
parentCID=ffffffff
isNativeSnapshot="no"
createType="twoGbMaxExtentSparse"

# Extent description
RW 4192256 SPARSE "book-demo-thin-clone-s001.vmdk"
RW 4192256 SPARSE "book-demo-thin-clone-s002.vmdk"
RW 4096 SPARSE "book-demo-thin-clone-s003.vmdk"

# The Disk Data Base
#DDB

ddb.deletable = "true"
```

In this example, the `createType` property is `twoGbMaxExtentSparse`, which means that the virtual disk is divided into extents of 2GB or smaller in size. The extents are specified in the `Extent description` section of the descriptor file.

The extents in this example are

- `book-demo-thin-clone-s001.vmdk`

- `book-demo-thin-clone-s002.vmdk`

- `book-demo-thin-clone-s003.vmdk`

The first two extents are less than 2GB in size each (4192256 disk blocks of 512 bytes each). The last extent is the balance of the 4GB. All three extents are of the SPARSE type. It is evident from the directory listing shown in Listing 13.7 that the extents' size on disk is smaller than the provisioned size. Note that source virtual disk from which I cloned; this one was freshly created and had no data written to it at the time I cloned it. If there were data written to the source virtual disk, the target virtual disk extents would have been larger than this example. They would have been equivalent to the non-zero blocks cloned from the source virtual disk.

To identify the number of VMFS blocks these extents occupy on the datastore, run the `stat` command as shown in Listing 13.9.

Listing 13.9   Count of Blocks Used by a Sparse Disk

```
stat book-demo-thin-clone* |grep 'vmdk\|Blocks'
  File: "book-demo-thin-clone-s001.vmdk"
  Size: 327680         Blocks: 2048        IO Block: 131072 regular file
  File: "book-demo-thin-clone-s002.vmdk"
  Size: 327680         Blocks: 2048        IO Block: 131072 regular file
  File: "book-demo-thin-clone-s003.vmdk"
  Size: 65536          Blocks: 2048        IO Block: 131072 regular file
  File: "book-demo-thin-clone.vmdk"
  Size: 619            Blocks: 0           IO Block: 131072 regular file
```

In this output I grepped for text that includes vmdk and Blocks to filter out the rest of the output and list on the filename and related size information. Here you should notice that the number of blocks used by each extent is 2048 disk blocks, which are equal to 1MB. The reason they used only 1MB is that the file size is less than 1MB and more than 8KB in size. In other words, they are smaller than the VMFS5 file block size and larger than the VMFS5 sub-block size. If the datastore were VMFS3 volume or upgraded from VMFS3, the last two files would have occupied a 64KB sub-block each instead. This is also why the descriptor file, which is the last one on the list, occupies zero blocks because it is smaller than 1KB in size.

> **NOTE**
>
> You cannot freshly create a virtual disk using the vmkfstools `2gbsparse` option. This option is only available when you use the vmkfstools `--clonevirtualdisk` option.

Raw Device Mappings

Certain virtualized applications — for example, Microsoft Clustering Services (MSCS) or Storage Layered Applications — require direct access to raw storage devices. vSphere enables these applications via Raw Device Mappings (RDMs). These mappings are pointers to the physical LUN and stored on VMFS datastores. These RDMs can be attached to virtual machines in the same fashion you do with virtual disks. The VMFS metadata entry representing the RDM pointer on the file system occupies no data blocks. I show you how that works later in this section.

RDMs are available in two modes:

- **Virtual Mode RDMs** (also known as *non-pass-through RDMs*) — Hide the physical properties of the mapped device and VMs using them see these RDMs as VMware SCSI Disk similarly to how they see the virtual disks.

- **Physical Mode RDMs** (also known as *pass-through RDMs*) — Expose the physical properties of the mapped LUNs and the virtual machines using them to see these RDMs as a physical LUN directly presented from the storage array. All SCSI commands issued by the guest OS to the mapped LUNs are passed through to the storage array unmodified. The only SCSI command that is not passed through is `REPORT_LUN` as the VM cannot discover targets not presented to it via RDMs.

Creating Virtual Mode RDMs Using the UI

The process of creating Virtual Mode RDMs is relatively similar to that of creating virtual disks:

1. Log on to vCenter Server as a user with Administrator or Root permissions.

2. Locate the VM to which you want to add the RDM in the inventory. Right-click and select **Edit Settings.**

3. Click the **Add** button and then select **Hard Disk.** Click **Next**.

4. Select the **Raw Device Mappings** radio button and then click **Next** (see Figure 13.10).

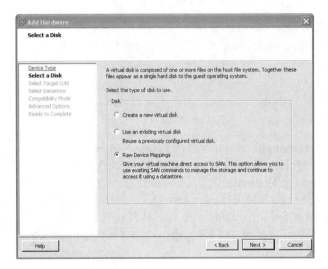

Figure 13.10 Creating an RDM

5. Select the LUN you want to map and then click **Next** (see Figure 13.11).

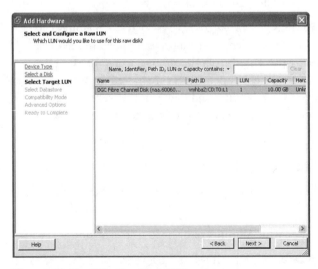

Figure 13.11 Selecting the LUN to map

6. Select where you want to store the LUN mapping. You can either store it with the VM or specify a datastore. Select the corresponding radio button. If you store the LUN mapping on a datastore, select that datastore from the list. Click **Next** after you make your selection (see Figure 13.12).

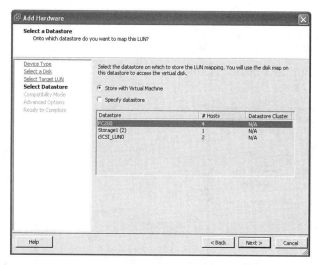

Figure 13.12   Selecting the datastore for RDM entry

7. Select the **Virtual** radio button under the Compatibility section and then click **Next** (see Figure 13.13).

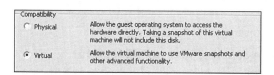

Figure 13.13   Selecting the RDM compatibility mode

8. Select the first radio button under the Virtual Device Mode section and then select one of the modes from the pull-down selection. It is a common practice to select a different virtual SCSI adapter number from that assigned to the guest OS's system disk. In this example it is **SCSI(1:0)**, which means that the RDM will be attached as the first device on the second virtual SCSI adapter which is SCSI1 (see Figure 13.14). Click **Next**.

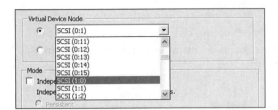

Figure 13.14   Selecting virtual device node

9. Review your selections and then click **Finish** (see Figure 13.15).

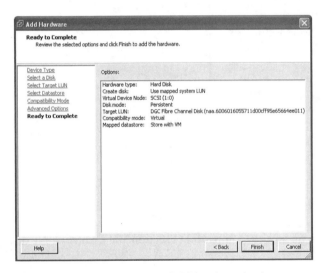

Figure 13.15   Reviewing and finishing the selection

The added RDM shows up in the listed of VM devices as New Hard Disk (adding) as shown in Figure 13.16. In this dialog, you should also see the mapped device, which is the LUN's NAA ID (A), the Virtual Device Node (B), and the RDM Compatibility Mode (C).

10. Click **OK** to save the changes to the VM configuration.

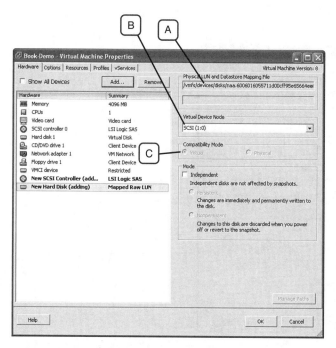

Figure 13.16   RDM ready to be added

NOTE

Because the RDM you created in this procedure is a virtual mode, the section labeled Mode shows that the option for setting the Independent mode is available. This is due to the fact that the virtual mode RDM is treated like a virtual disk from the VM's point of view. This option is not available for physical mode RDMs.

---

11. To see the actual datastore mapping file representing the RDM, edit the virtual machine settings again and see the second field under the Physical LUN and Datastore Mapping File section (see Figure 13.17, A). In this example, the mapping file is Book-Demo_1.vmdk. Note that the Physical LUN now shows as the vml file instead of the NAA ID. This is simply a symbolic link to the device as described in the "Listing RDM Properties Using vmkfstools" section later in this chapter. Click **Cancel** when done.

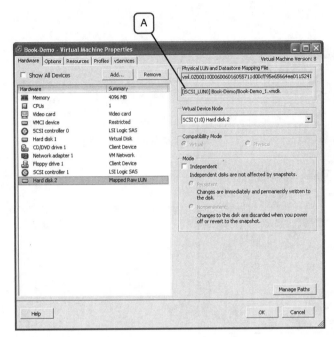

Figure 13.17   Viewing RDM properties

Creating Physical Mode RDMs Using the UI

To create a physical mode RDM, follow the procedure in the "Creating a Virtual Mode RDM" section earlier in the chapter, with the following exceptions:

- In Step 7, select the **Physical** radio button instead of **Virtual**.
- In Step 10, the Independent Mode option is not available (see Figure 13.18).

Figure 13.18   Adding a physical mode RDM

Creating RDMs Using the Command-Line Interface

You can create RDMs, both virtual and physical modes, using the vmkfstools -r and -z commands respectively. See Listings 13.10 and 13.11 for command-line examples.

Listing 13.10   vmkfstools Command to Create a Virtual Mode RDM

vmkfstools --createrdm /vmfs/devices/disks/<naa ID> /vmfs/volumes/<Datastore>/<vm-directory>/<rdm-file-name>.vmdk

The short-hand version is

```
vmkfstools -r /vmfs/devices/disks/<naa ID> /vmfs/volumes/<Datastore>/<vm-
directory>/<rdm-file-name>.vmdk
```

Example:

```
vmkfstools -r /vmfs/devices/disks/naa.6006016055711d00cff95e65664ee011 /
vmfs/volumes/iSCSI_LUN0/Book-Demo/Book-Demo_2.vmdk
```

Listing 13.11   vmkfstools Command to Create Physical Mode RDM

```
vmkfstools --createrdmpassthru /vmfs/devices/disks/<naa ID> /vmfs/
volumes/<Datastore>/<vm-directory>/<rdm-file-name>.vmdk
```

The short-hand version is

```
vmkfstools -z /vmfs/devices/disks/<naa ID> /vmfs/volumes/<Datastore>/<vm-
directory>/<rdm-file-name>.vmdk
```

Example:

```
vmkfstools -z /vmfs/devices/disks/naa.6006016055711d00cff95e65664ee011 /
vmfs/volumes/iSCSI_LUN0/Book-Demo/Book-Demo_3.vmdk
```

Listing RDM Properties

After an RDM is created, you might need to identify its properties. The user interface (UI) as shown in Figure 13.18 earlier only shows the vml name of the mapped device. The VMFS entries of a given RDM appear to be similar to virtual disks. Each RDM has two vmdk files on the datastore on which you created the RDM. These files are the virtual machine descriptor file and the RDM pointer file.

To list the files in the VM directory you may run

```
ls -al /vmfs/volumes/<datastore>/<vm-directory> |sed 's/.*root //'
```

This assumes that the file owner is root. This command truncates the output to remove the word root and all text before it leaving only the size, date, and time stamp as well as the filenames. A sample output is shown in Listing 13.12.

Listing 13.12   Listing VM Files

```
ls -al /vmfs/volumes/iSCSI/Book-Demo/ |sed 's/.*root //'
      4294967296 Feb 14 04:44 Book-Demo-flat.vmdk
             468 Feb 14 04:44 Book-Demo.vmdk
               0 Feb 14 04:44 Book-Demo.vmsd
            1844 Apr  9 19:47 Book-Demo.vmx
             264 Apr  9 19:47 Book-Demo.vmxf
     10737418240 Apr  9 17:51 Book-Demo_1-rdm.vmdk
             486 Apr  9 17:51 Book-Demo_1.vmdk
     10737418240 Apr  9 19:01 Book-Demo_2-rdm.vmdk  ← Pointer
             486 Apr  9 19:01 Book-Demo_2.vmdk  ← Descriptor
     10737418240 Apr  9 19:14 Book-Demo_3-rdmp.vmdk
             498 Apr  9 19:14 Book-Demo_3.vmdk
```

In this example there are three RDMs descriptor files (I marked one of them with ←
descriptor) named Book-Demo_1.vmdk through Book_Demo_3.vmdk. The RDM pointer
files (I marked one of them with ← pointer), which are equivalent to the virtual disk extent
files, have a suffix of rdm or rdmp. Files with rdm suffix are pointers to a virtual mode
RDM. Conversely, files with rdmp suffix are pointers to physical mode RDMs, which are
also known as pass-through RDMs.

Based on the file size of each RDM pointer file, they appear to be 10GB in size. These
match the mapped LUNs' size. However, because these are not actual file blocks on the
datastore, they should have been zero bytes in size. To find out the actual size of these
files, you may run

```
cd /vmfs/volumes/<datastore>/<vm-directory>
stat *-rdm* |awk '/File/|||/Block/{print}'
```

A sample output is shown in Listing 13.13.

Listing 13.13 Output of Commands Listing RDM Pointers Block Count

```
stat *-rdm* |awk '/File/|||/Block/{print}'
  File: "Book-Demo_1-rdm.vmdk"
  Size: 10737418240     Blocks: 0          IO Block: 131072 regular file
  File: "Book-Demo_2-rdm.vmdk"
  Size: 10737418240     Blocks: 0          IO Block: 131072 regular file
  File: "Book-Demo_3-rdmp.vmdk"
  Size: 10737418240     Blocks: 0          IO Block: 131072 regular file
```

This output clearly shows that, although the size is 10GB (listed here in bytes), the actual
number of blocks is zero for all three files. This is easily explained by the fact that the
actual file blocks are mapped to blocks on the physical LUN that each RDM represents.

Listing 13.14 shows the content of a virtual mode RDM descriptor file.

Listing 13.14 Content of a Virtual Mode RDM Descriptor File

```
# Disk DescriptorFile
version=1
encoding="UTF-8"
CID=fffffffe
parentCID=ffffffff
isNativeSnapshot="no"
createType="vmfsRawDeviceMap"
```

```
# Extent description
RW 20971520 VMFSRDM "Book-Demo_1-rdm.vmdk"

# The Disk Data Base
#DDB

ddb.virtualHWVersion = "8"
ddb.longContentID = "2d86dba01ca8954da334a0e4ffffffffe"
ddb.uuid = "60 00 C2 9c 0e da f3 3f-60 7a f7 fe bc 34 7d 0f"
ddb.geometry.cylinders = "1305"
ddb.geometry.heads = "255"
ddb.geometry.sectors = "63"
ddb.adapterType = "lsilogic"
```

The highlighted lines in the output are unique to virtual mode RDMs:

- The `createType` field value is `vmfsRawDeviceMap`, which means virtual mode RDM.

- The `Extent description` section shows the RDM sectors count, which is in 512-byte disk blocks. It also shows the extent type, which is `VMFSRDM`. This type is also used by physical mode RDMs as well, which I show you in Listing 13.15.

Listing 13.15 shows the content of a physical mode RDM descriptor file.

Listing 13.15   Content of a Physical Mode RDM Descriptor File

```
# Disk DescriptorFile
version=1
encoding="UTF-8"
CID=ffffffffe
parentCID=ffffffff
isNativeSnapshot="no"
createType="vmfsPassthroughRawDeviceMap"

# Extent description
RW 20971520 VMFSRDM "Book-Demo_3-rdmp.vmdk"

# The Disk Data Base
#DDB

ddb.virtualHWVersion = "8"
```

```
ddb.longContentID = "307b5c6b4c696020ffb7a8c7ffffffffe"
ddb.uuid = "60 00 C2 93 34 90 2c ca-c9 96 f2 a6 7f a6 65 e1"
ddb.geometry.cylinders = "1305"
ddb.geometry.heads = "255"
ddb.geometry.sectors = "63"
ddb.adapterType = "buslogic"
```

Again, I highlighted the lines in the output that are unique to physical mode RDMs:

- The `createType` field value is `vmfsPassthroughRawDeviceMap`, which means physical mode RDM (also known as pass-through RDM).

- The `Extent description` section shows the RDM sectors count, which is in 512-byte disk blocks. It also shows the extent type, which is VMFSRDM. As I mentioned in the explanation of the virtual mode RDM, this extent type is common between both types of RDMs.

Now that I showed you the file structure of RDMs, it's time to identify the RDM properties to locate which device it maps. You can do this using vmkfstools as well as the UI.

Listing RDM Properties Using vmkfstools

To list RDM properties using vmkfstools, you may follow these steps:

Use `vmkfstools --queryrdm`, or the shorthand version `vmkfstools -q`, to identify the vml ID of the mapped LUN (see Listing 13.16).

This option lists the RDM properties, which includes the RDM type — for example, pass-through RDM or non-pass-through RDM.

Listing 13.16   Using vmkfstools to List RDM Properties

```
vmkfstools -q /vmfs/volumes/FC200/win2K3Enterprise/win2K3Enterprise.vmdk

Disk /vmfs/volumes/FC200/win2K3Enterprise/win2K3Enterprise.vmdk is a
Passthrough Raw Device Mapping
Maps to: vml.02000100006006016055711d00cff95e65664ee011524149442035
```

I highlighted vml id in the output.

Use the vml ID with `esxcli storage core device` command to find the device ID of the mapped LUN (see Listing 13.17).

The syntax is

```
esxcli storage core device list --device=<vml ID>
```

Or the shorthand version is

```
esxcli storage core device list -d <vml ID>
```

Listing 13.17   Identifying Device ID Using vml ID

```
esxcli storage core device list --device=vml.02000100006006016055711d00cff9
5e65664ee011524149442035 |grep naa
naa.6006016055711d00cff95e65664ee011
    Display Name: DGC Fibre Channel Disk (naa.6006016055711d00cff95e65664
ee011)
    Devfs Path: /vmfs/devices/disks/naa.6006016055711d00cff95e65664ee011
```

I highlighted the device ID in the output. The NAA ID is usually sufficient to identify the LUN. However, if you need to identify the LUN number as well, you run this command using the NAA ID you just identified:

```
esxcli storage nmp device list --device=<NAA ID> |grep Current
```

Or the shorthand version is

```
esxcli storage nmp device list -d <NAA ID> |grep Current
```

Listing 13.18 shows the output of this command.

Listing 13.18   Identifying the LUN Number Based on Device ID

```
esxcli storage nmp device list --device=naa.6006016055711d00cff95e65664
ee011 |grep Current
    Path Selection Policy Device Config: Current Path=vmhba3:C0:T1:L1
```

The output shows that this LUN's runtime name is vmhba3:C0:T1:L1, which means that the LUN number is LUN 1 on storage array port on Target 1. See the "FC Targets" section in Chapter 2, "Fibre Channel Storage Connectivity," for details.

Listing RDM Properties Using the UI

To list RDM properties using the UI, follow these steps:

1. While logged on to the vCenter Server using vSphere 5 client as an administrator, locate the VM in the inventory tree.

2. Right-click the VM listing and then select **Edit Settings.**

   You should see a dialog similar to that shown in Figure 13.19.

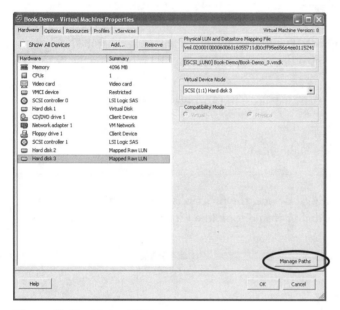

Figure 13.19   Listing RDM properties using the UI

3. Locate the device showing **Mapped Raw LUN** in the summary column and select it.

4. Click the **Manage Paths** button on the lower-right corner of the dialog.

5. The device ID is listed in the lower pane of the resulting dialog. The ID is right after the last dash in the Name field. (See Figure 13.20.)

Figure 13.20   Listing RDM's NAA ID

In this example, the device ID is

```
naa.6006016055711d00cff95e65664ee011
```

TIP

If you look closer at the vml and NAA ID in this example, you will notice that the NAA ID is actually part of the VML ID or the other way around; the vml ID is based on the NAA ID of the device.

vml.02000100006006016055711d00cff95e65664ee011524149442035

naa.6006016055711d00cff95e65664ee011

For example, the matching bytes are highlighted.

If the mapped LUN is an iSCSI device, the process is the same as with the FC example, but the last step's dialog would look like Figure 13.21.

Figure 13.21   Listing iSCSI RDM NAA ID

Virtual Storage Adapters

VMs utilize virtual disks and RDMs as SCSI disks attached to a virtual SCSI HBA. Some virtual disks may be also connected to an IDE adapter.

Virtual machine configuration files (*.vmx) show the type of virtual storage adapter.

For example, running the following command while in a virtual machine directory returns its list of virtual SCSI HBAs:

```
fgrep -i virtualdev *.vmx |grep scsi

scsi0.virtualDev = "lsisas1068"
scsi1.virtualDev = "lsilogic"
scsi3.virtualDev = "buslogic"
```

This example shows that the VM has three different virtual SCSI HBAs:

- Virtual SCSI HBA number 0 is `lsisas1068`, which is LSI Logic SAS type

- Virtual SCSI HBA number 1 is `lsilogic`, which is LSI Logic Parallel type

- Virtual SCSI HBA number 2 is `buslogic`, which is BusLogic Parallel type

Selecting the Type of Virtual Storage Adapter

To select the type of virtual storage adapter, follow this procedure using vSphere Client 5 while logged in as an administrator or root user:

1. Locate the VM in the inventory, right-click it, and select Edit Settings.

2. Click on the SCSI controller you want to modify in the list of devices and then click the **Change Type** button (see Figure 13.22).

Figure 13.22 Modifying the virtual SCSI controller type

3. Select the SCSI Controller Type by clicking the radio button next to the type you want to choose (see Figure 13.23).

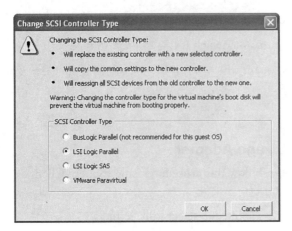

Figure 13.23   Selecting the virtual SCSI controller type

Figure 13.24 shows the device list with the original `SCSI controller 1` marked with `(replacing)` and the new one at the bottom of the list marked with `(replacement)` that shows the new type.

4. Click **OK** to apply the changes.

Figure 13.24   Virtual HBA type changes ready to apply

VMware Paravirtual SCSI Controller

Paravirtualization is a technique that allows ESXi to present to the GOS a high-performance virtual SCSI controller that is almost identical to the underlying physical SCSI controller.

This high-performance virtual SCSI controller is referred to as VMware Paravirtual SCSI Controller (PVSCSI). It utilizes specialized GOS kernels that support paravirtualization. Such a combination provides better I/O throughput and reduces CPU utilization. To find out if your GOS is supported, follow this procedure to check VMware HCL (Hardware Compatibility List):

1. In a browser, go to http://www.vmware.com/go/hcl.

2. Select the file in Figure 13.25 as follows:

    a. What you are looking for: Guest OS (A)

    b. Virtual Hardware: Paravirtualization (VMI) (B)

    c. Product Release Version: ESXi 5.0 and ESXi 5.0 U1 (C)

3. Click the **Update and View Results** button (D) and scroll down to see the results.

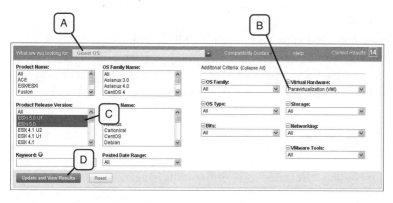

Figure 13.25   Searching VMware HCL for supported PVSCSI Guest OS

Configuring a VM to Use PVSCSI

To configure a VM to use PVSCSI, follow Steps 1 through 4 under the previous section, "Selecting the Type of Virtual Storage Adaptor." However, in Step 3 you need to select VMware `Paravirtual` as the adapter type.

> **WARNING**
>
> Do not change the type of virtual SCSI controller to which the GOS system disk is attached. Doing so may render the GOS unbootable.

PVSCSI Limitations

The following limitations are imposed on the PVSCSI controllers:

- If you hot add or hot remove a virtual disk to the VM attached to the PVSCSI controller, you must rescan the SCSI BUS from within the GOS.

- If the virtual disks attached to the PVSCSI controller have snapshots, they will not benefit from the performance improvements.

- If the ESXi host memory is overcommitted, the VM does not benefit from the PVSCSI performance improvement.

- PVSCSI controllers are not supported for GOS boot devices (see the earlier warning).

- MSCS clusters are not supported with PVSCSI.

Known Issues with PVSCSI

Although Windows Server 2008 and Windows Server 2008R2 are not listed on the HCL as supported with PVSCSI, several customers have been using it without issues. However, VMware received several reports of sever performance degradation on these operating systems when using PVSCSI under high disk I/O. The following message is logged to the guest's event logs:

```
Operating system returned error 1117 (The request could not be performed
because of an I/O device error.)
```

According to vSphere 5.0 Update 1 Release Notes, it fixed this issue.

Virtual SCSI Bus Sharing

You might have noticed in Figure 13.24 that there is a section named SCSI Bus Sharing. This feature is designed mainly to support MSCS clustered VMs.

There are two bus sharing policies: virtual and physical. Do not confuse them with RDM Compatibility Modes bearing the same names. What the SCSI Bus Sharing does is to allow multiple VMs to open the same shared virtual disks or RDMs concurrently.

You accomplish this by turning off file locking for virtual disks attached to virtual SCSI controllers with bus sharing enabled. To prevent concurrent writes to the shared virtual disks, the GOS must provide the functionality that elects which node in the cluster is allowed to write to the shared disks. This is provided by MSCS and the use of quorum disks.

Table 13.5 compares virtual and physical bus sharing policies.

Table 13.5   Virtual and Physical Bus Sharing Comparison

Feature	Virtual	Physical	None
Virtual Disks Concurrent Access	Yes	No	No
Virtual Mode RDMs Concurrent Access	Yes	Yes	No
Physical Mode RDMs Concurrent Access	No	Yes	No
Supported with VM Snapshots (see next section)	No	No	Yes
Supported with Multi-Writer Locking (see footnote)	No	No	Yes

Multi-Writer Lock is discussed in Chapter 14, "Distributed Locks."

Virtual Machine Snapshots

Have you ever been in a situation when you install an OS patch or update that renders it unbootable or keeps crashing? You probably wished you could turn back the time to right before you installed the problematic patches.

I once got a VMware T-Shirts that had an "Undo Your Whole Day" slogan on the back of the shirt. This was the slogan we used when VMware first introduced the concept that allows you to do that — go back in time that is.

This feature was referred to as REDO logs. They enabled you to discard changes made to the VM after the REDO logs were created.

Now the VM is all grown up and so are its features. The concept of REDO logs evolved into virtual machines snapshots. They enable you to take a point-in-time snapshot of the Virtual Machine state, which includes the virtual disks and optionally, if the VM was powered on at the time, take a snapshot of the VM memory.

These states are saved to a set of files stored in the VM directory. Before taking the first snapshot, let me show you the baseline set of files in the VM directory (see Listing 13.19).

Listing 13.19 Virtual Machine Files before Taking Snapshot

```
ls -Al |sed 's/.*root//'
          8589934592 Apr 13 04:13 Book-Demo3-flat.vmdk
                 497 Apr 13 04:13 Book-Demo3.vmdk
                   0 Apr 13 04:13 Book-Demo3.vmsd
                1506 Apr 13 04:13 Book-Demo3.vmx
                 265 Apr 13 04:13 Book-Demo3.vmxf
```

Table 13.6 lists the extensions of these files and their functions.

Table 13.6 VM File Extensions

File Extension	Function	Comments
vmdk	Virtual Disk	There are two files with that extension for each virtual disk. The file without -flat suffix is the descriptor file that I covered in Virtual Disks section earlier in this chapter. The other file with -flat suffix is the extent file which, I also covered in the same section as the descriptor file
vmsd	Virtual Machine Snapshot Dictionary	It defines the Snapshot Hierarchy. More about that in this section. The file is blank prior to taking any snapshots
vmx	Virtual Machine Configuration File	Defines the Virtual Machine structure and virtual hardware.
vmxf	Virtual Machine Foundry File	Holds information used by vSphere Client when it connect to the ESXi host directly. This is a subset of information stored in the vCenter Server Database.

Creating the VM's First Snapshot While VM Is Powered Off

To create a snapshot, follow this procedure using vSphere Client 5:

1. Log in to vCenter Server as an Administrator or root user.

2. Locate the VM in the Inventory tree and right-click it, select the **Snapshot** menu, and then select the **Take Snapshot** submenu (see Figure 13.26).

Figure 13.26 Creating a VM snapshot

3. When prompted, fill the Name and Description fields with the Snapshot Display Name and its description respectively and then click **OK** (see Figure 13.27). Note the two checkboxes that are grayed out. This is because the VM is not powered on at the time the snapshot is taken. I discuss these checkboxes later in this section.

Figure 13.27 Entering the snapshot name and description

You should see a task created in the Recent Tasks pane showing the Create virtual machine snapshot status is in progress. The status changes to completed when it's done.

Let's see now which files were added or modified when the snapshot was created. Listing 13.20 shows three new files created and two files modified.

Listing 13.20   VM Directory Listing After First Snapshot Created

```
ls -Al |sed 's/.*root//'
              20480 Apr 13 05:03 Book-Demo3-000001-delta.vmdk
                323 Apr 13 05:03 Book-Demo3-000001.vmdk
              18317 Apr 13 05:03 Book-Demo3-Snapshot1.vmsn
         8589934592 Apr 13 04:13 Book-Demo3-flat.vmdk
                497 Apr 13 04:13 Book-Demo3.vmdk
                464 Apr 13 05:03 Book-Demo3.vmsd
               1513 Apr 13 05:03 Book-Demo3.vmx
                265 Apr 13 04:13 Book-Demo3.vmxf
```

Table 13.7 lists the added and modified files and explanations.

Table 13.7   Files Added or Modified by Snapshot Creation

Filename	Descriptions	Comments
Book-Demo3-000001-delta.vmdk	Delta Disk Extent	New data written after snapshot is taken gets redirected to this extent file. Its type is vmfsSparse.
Book-Demo3-000001.vmdk	Delta Disk Descriptor File	Descriptor file defining the snapshot virtual disk. See Listing 13.20 for content.
Book-Demo3-Snapshot1.vmsn	VM Snapshot File	This is the actual snapshot file, which is the state of the VM configuration. It actually combines the original unmodified content of both vmx and vmxf files. If the VM were powered on at the time of taking the snapshot and I chose to take a snapshot of the VM's memory, this file would have included that as well as the CPU state.
Book-Demo3.vmsd	VM Snapshot Dictionary	This file used to be blank before the snapshot was taken. Now it includes the snapshot hierarchy. See Listing 13.21 for content.

Filename	Descriptions	Comments
Book-Demo3.vmx	VM Configuration File	The value of scsi0:0.fileName is changed to be the Delta Disk Descriptor filename.

To better understand the relationships between these files, let me walk you through the relevant content from each file. I'm doing that in the order of relevance. Note that all added files are named based on the VM Name, which is also the default system disk virtual disk name. In this example it is Book-Demo3:

1. The VM Configuration file (vmx) is modified as follows:

   Before snapshot:

   ```
   scsi0:0.fileName = "Book-Demo3.vmdk"
   ```

   After snapshot:

   ```
   scsi0:0.fileName = "Book-Demo3-000001.vmdk"
   ```

   This means that the virtual disk attached to scsi0:0 is now the delta disk file descriptor.

2. The delta disk descriptor file content is shown in Listing 13.21. It shows that the delta disk is a sparse file with vmfsSparse type.

Listing 13.21   Delta Disk Descriptor File Content

```
# Disk DescriptorFile
version=1
encoding="UTF-8"
CID=fffffffe
parentCID=fffffffe
isNativeSnapshot="no"
createType="vmfsSparse"
parentFileNameHint="Book-Demo3.vmdk"
# Extent description
RW 16777216 VMFSSPARSE "Book-Demo3-000001-delta.vmdk"

# The Disk Data Base
#DDB

ddb.longContentID = "a051b9fb9b43b7ae0b351f1dfffffffe"
```

The highlighted lines are explained in Table 13.8.

Table 13.8   Delta Disk Descriptor Properties

Property	Virtual	Comments
parentCID	fffffffe	The parent disk's Content ID.
isNativeSnapshot	no	For use in a future release that will allow the snapshot creation to be handled by the storage array directly.
createType	vmfsSparse	All delta disks are sparse files regardless of their parent disks type.
parentFileNameHint	Book-Demo3.vmdk	The name of the parent disk. This disk stays unmodified..
Extent Description	Multi-values	The relevant values are the type, again, is VMFSSPARSE and the extent filename is that with the -delta suffix.

Parent disk remains unmodified. When the VM is powered on, that file is opened with Read-Only locks. This is the same function done by the VADP API (vStorage APIs for Data Protection) when it backs up a virtual disk while the VM is running. This allows the backup software to copy the parent disk since the Read-Only lock allows Multi-Readers to access and open the parent virtual disk for reads.

> **NOTE**
>
> Many types of storage arrays implement snapshot-backup capabilities. These technologies are often implemented in one of two fashions: Copy-On-Write (EMC) or Pointer-Based (NetApp and ZFS-based arrays). These technologies provide a means for arrays to provide LUN and file system snapshots. With VMware, storage partners, like NetApp, are able to provide file-based snapshots. Because VMDKs are files that can take advantage of such technology, this capability provides a more granular level of functionality.

3. The virtual machine snapshot dictionary file (vmsd) stores the properties that define the snapshot hierarchy, which is the relationship between snapshot files and the snapshot to which they belong. Listing 13.22 shows the content of this file.

Listing 13.22 Virtual Machine Snapshot Dictionary File Content

```
.encoding = "UTF-8"
snapshot.lastUID = "1"
snapshot.current = "1"
snapshot0.uid = "1"
snapshot0.filename = "Book-Demo3-Snapshot1.vmsn"
snapshot0.displayName = "Before installing patch xyz"
snapshot0.description = "Snapshot taken before installing patch xyz"
snapshot0.createTimeHigh = "310664"
snapshot0.createTimeLow = "1673441029"
snapshot0.numDisks = "1"
snapshot0.disk0.fileName = "Book-Demo3.vmdk"
snapshot0.disk0.node = "scsi0:0"
snapshot.numSnapshots = "1"
```

Because this is the first snapshot taken for the VM, there is only one snapshot definition listed, and its ID is 1. All properties in that file have a prefix: `snapshot0`. The list of properties without the prefix are better explained in Table 13.9.

Table 13.9 Properties in the Virtual Machine Snapshot Dictionary File

Property	Value	Comments
`lastUID`	1	ID of the most recently created snapshot.
`current`	1	ID of the snapshot currently in use.
`uid`	1	Snapshot ID.
`filename`	"Book-Demo3-Snapshot1.vmsn"	Name of the Snapshot file.
`displayName`	"Before installing patch xyz"	Snapshot name entered in the dialog shown in Figure 13.29.
`description`	"Snapshot taken before installing patch xyz"	Description of snapshot entered in the dialog shown in Figure 13.29.
`numDisks`	1	Number of virtual disks that are *not* configured as independent. This is the number of virtual disks that will have delta files.
`disk0.filename`	"Book-Demo3.vmdk"	Name of the first parent virtual disk.
`disk0.node`	scsi0:0	Parent virtual disk node.
`numSnapshots`	1	Total number of snapshots take for this VM.

These properties dictate how the Snapshot Manager displays the current hierarchy of the snapshots in the UI. Figure 13.26 shows the hierarchy of the first snapshot of this VM. To display the Snapshot Manager, right-click the VM in the inventory and then select **Snapshot menu** followed by **Snapshot Manager submenu**. This opens the dialog shown in Figure 13.28.

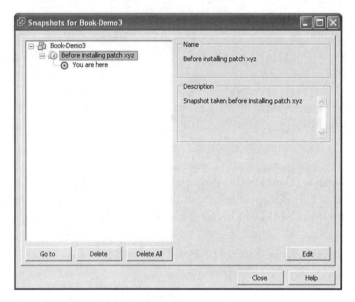

Figure 13.28   Displaying Snapshot Manager

In this figure you can easily identify the parent disk, the snapshot display name, and description. The You Are Here Marker is the current state that points to the snapshot. I explain the Go To and Delete buttons in the "Snapshot Operations" section later in this chapter.

Creating a VM Second Snapshot While Powered On

Now take a second snapshot. This time, the VM is powered on. Follow the same steps you used to create the first snapshot:

1. Log in to vCenter Server as an Administrator, root, or virtual machine power user.

2. Locate the VM in the Inventory tree, right-click it, and then select the **Snapshot** menu and then the **Take Snapshot** submenu.

3. When prompted, fill the Name and Description fields with the Snapshot Display Name and its description, respectively and then click **OK** (see Figure 13.29). Note the two checkboxes that are now available because the VM is powered on. The first one, Snapshot the Virtual Machine's Memory, is selected by default. This is self-explanatory. The second checkbox uses the same function that the VADP uses to take a snapshot before backing up the parent virtual disk. As the option indicates, VMware Tools must be installed in the VM for this to work. The reason is that part of the tools installation is a set of scripts that are run when this function is used.

Figure 13.29   Entering the snapshot name and description of a Power On VM

Let's see which files were added or modified in the VM directory. Listing 13.23 shows the VM directory after the second snapshot was created.

Listing 13.23   VM Directory Content After Creating Second Snapshot (Powered On)

```
ls -Al |sed 's/.*root//'
            20480 Apr 13 05:03 Book-Demo3-000001-delta.vmdk
              323 Apr 13 05:03 Book-Demo3-000001.vmdk
            20480 Apr 13 08:27 Book-Demo3-000002-delta.vmdk
              330 Apr 13 08:27 Book-Demo3-000002.vmdk
            18317 Apr 13 05:03 Book-Demo3-Snapshot1.vmsn
       1074980997 Apr 13 08:29 Book-Demo3-Snapshot2.vmsn
       1073741824 Apr 13 08:02 Book-Demo3-f1994119.vswp
       8589934592 Apr 13 04:13 Book-Demo3-flat.vmdk
              497 Apr 13 04:13 Book-Demo3.vmdk
              890 Apr 13 08:27 Book-Demo3.vmsd
             2585 Apr 13 08:27 Book-Demo3.vmx
              265 Apr 13 04:13 Book-Demo3.vmxf
```

The highlighted files were added or modified. Notice that the size of the Book-Demo3-Snapshot2.vmsn file is much larger than the snapshot1 one. This is because the VM is powered on, and I have chosen to snapshot the VM's memory. The CPU state and the memory state are both kept in the corresponding snapshot file.

Book-Demo3-000002.vmdk and Book-Demo3-000002-delta.vmdk are the virtual disk snapshot for this new snapshot. However, its parent disk is not the same as the first snapshot's parent. How did I know that? Listing 13.24 shows the descriptor file.

Listing 13.24   Content of Second Snapshot's Delta Disk Descriptor File

```
# Disk DescriptorFile
version=1
encoding="UTF-8"
CID=fffffffe
parentCID=fffffffe
isNativeSnapshot="no"
createType="vmfsSparse"
parentFileNameHint="Book-Demo3-000001.vmdk"
# Extent description
RW 16777216 VMFSSPARSE "Book-Demo3-000002-delta.vmdk"


# The Disk Data Base
#DDB

ddb.longContentID = "a051b9fb9b43b7ae0b351f1dfffffffe"
```

I highlighted the relevant properties in the listing. The `parentFileNameHint` clearly shows that the parent disk is Book-Demo3-000001.vmdk which is the first snapshot's delta disk. This means that all new data get redirected to Book-Demo3-000002-delta.vmdk file.

Also note that the vmx file has been changed to reflect that the new delta file is the current virtual disk attached to scsi0:0.

After the first snapshot:

```
scsi0:0.fileName = "Book-Demo3-000001.vmdk"
```

After the second snapshot:

```
scsi0:0.fileName = "Book-Demo3-000002.vmdk"
```

In addition, the vmsd file now shows an additional snapshot whose properties are prefixed with `snapshot1` (see Listing 13.25).

Listing 13.25   vmsd File Content

```
.encoding = "UTF-8"
snapshot.lastUID = "2"
snapshot.current = "2"
snapshot0.uid = "1"
snapshot0.filename = "Book-Demo3-Snapshot1.vmsn"
snapshot0.displayName = "Before installing patch xyz"
snapshot0.description = "Snapshot taken before installing patch xyz"
snapshot0.createTimeHigh = "310664"
snapshot0.createTimeLow = "1673441029"
snapshot0.numDisks = "1"
snapshot0.disk0.fileName = "Book-Demo3.vmdk"
snapshot0.disk0.node = "scsi0:0"
snapshot1.uid = "2"
snapshot1.filename = "Book-Demo3-Snapshot2.vmsn"
snapshot1.parent = "1"
snapshot1.displayName = "After Installing App X"
snapshot1.description = "Second snapshot taken after installing Application
X"
snapshot1.type = "1"
snapshot1.createTimeHigh = "310667"
snapshot1.createTimeLow = "1030355829"
snapshot1.numDisks = "1"
snapshot1.disk0.fileName = "Book-Demo3-000001.vmdk"
snapshot1.disk0.node = "scsi0:0"
snapshot.numSnapshots = "2"
```

I highlighted the lines that were added or changed.

All lines prefixed with `snapshot1` are the properties of the newly added snapshot. They look identical to those of the first snapshot file but with different values. A new property was added: `snapshot1.parent`. It simply states that this snapshot's parent is another snapshot whose ID is 1, which is the first snapshot we covered earlier. Also note that the `numSnapshots` value is now 2. This means that the total count of snapshots for the VM is currently 2.

The `snapshot1.uid` is 2. Why wasn't it given a higher number? The reason is that this number is the next number in sequence after the value of the field named `snapshot.` `lastUID` in the previous version of the vmsd file. If you look at Table 13.9, you will notice that the value was 1. If it were higher, the second snapshot's UID would have been higher than 2.

Figure 13.30 shows how these properties look in the Snapshot Manager's UI.

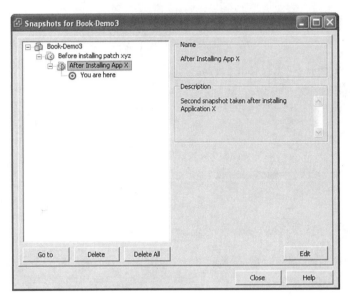

Figure 13.30   Listing second snapshot

Note that now the *You are here* marker points to the second snapshot.

Snapshot Operations

Available snapshot operations are

- Go to a snapshot.
- Delete a snapshot.
- Revert to a snapshot.
- Consolidate a snapshot (a new feature in vSphere 5). I explain each operation separately.

Go to a Snapshot Operation

Consider the following scenario: I am testing an application that is still in beta and I am not comfortable with what damage it can do to my VM. So, I take a snapshot before installing the application. In Figure 13.29, the snapshot is labeled Before Installing App X (instead of taking it after installing the app as I did in the previous section). Then what I expected happens, the VM crashed. I'm not certain I can reproduce the crash. So, I take a snapshot to save the state of the VM showing the problem. Because the application is a beta quality, there is no live support for it. I decide that I need to rule out patch xyz, which I installed before the application, as the root cause of the problem. So, the plan is to go to the VM state before I installed patch xyz and then take another snapshot. Then I can install the application.

Figure 13.31 displays the Snapshot Manager (cropped) showing the current state:

1. Click the snapshot labeled **Before Installing Patch xyz** and then click the **Go To** button.

Figure 13.31   Snapshot Manager showing a crashed VM snapshot

The dialog in Figure 13.32 opens. Note that the icon for the **Before Installing Patch xyz** does not have the power on symbol (the right-pointing triangle) like the other two below it. This means that when it was taken, the VM was powered off. So, when I click the **Go To** button, the VM is powered off because it was the state of the VM at that time.

2. Click **Yes** in the resulting dialog (see Figure 13.32).

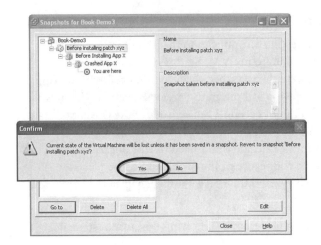

Figure 13.32   Confirming the Go To operation

3. After the process is done, the snapshot manager should look like Figure 13.33, and the VM is powered off.

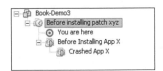

Figure 13.33   The completed Go To operation

4. Now let's take another snapshot before installing App X. If the Snapshot Manager is still open, click **Close**. Make sure the VM is still selected (A) in the inventory tree, and then click the **Take a Snapshot of This Virtual Machine** button (B) (see Figure 13.34).

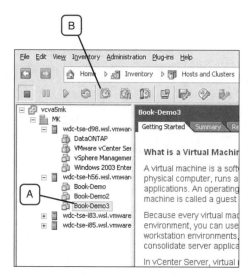

Figure 13.34   Taking a new snapshot to create a new branch

5. Enter the snapshot name and description (for example, Side Branch Before Installing App X), and then click **OK**.

6. Power the VM on and install App X. So far, so good! The application seems stable.

7. To be on the safe side, let's take a snapshot in this state. Click the **Take a Snapshot of This Virtual Machine** button, enter the snapshot name and description (for example, After Installing App X), and click **OK**.

8. Click the **Snapshot Manager Toolbar** (A) button to display the current snapshot hierarchy (B) (see Figure 13.35).

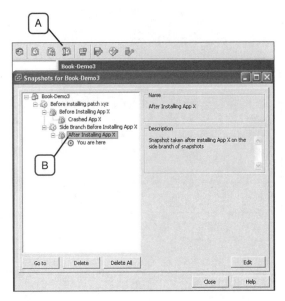

Figure 13.35   Listing second snapshot branch in Snapshot Manager

> **TIP**
>
> Keep an eye on the target! That is the **You Are Here** marker. This represents the current state of the VM since you took the last snapshot. Assume that the VM is powered off at this time. If you want to discard what you did since you took the snapshot, select the snapshot to which the target is pointing and then click the **Go To** button. You should observe that the VM is now powered on and is at the state taken by that snapshot.

Delete a Snapshot Operation

After taking a VM snapshot the original VM CPU, optionally, memory states are kept in the VM snapshot file (vmsn), and the original unmodified data is kept in the parent virtual disk file. All changes to the CPU and memory state are kept in the running VM memory and don't get written to a snapshot file until you take another snapshot. Continuing with the example from the previous section, assume that App X, installed on the OS without a patch, is proven to be stable. You can safely delete the snapshot because you no longer need to restore the VM to its App X state. I want to delete the Side Branch

Before Installing App X snapshot and keep the most recent one. The following procedure continues from the end of the procedure from the "Go to a Snapshot Operation" section. The VM is now running in the state After Installing App X:

1. Still referring to Figure 13.35 at the end of the previous section, click **Side Branch Before Installing App X** snapshot and then click the **Go To** button. Click **Yes** to continue. Snapshot Manager should look like Figure 13.36 now, and the VM is powered off.

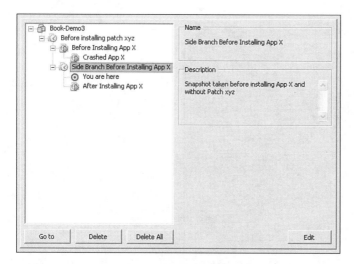

Figure 13.36   Going to parent snapshot before deleting it

2. Click the **Delete** button. You get the *Confirm Delete* dialog. Click **Yes** to proceed with deleting the snapshot.

   The Snapshot Manager should look like Figure 13.37, and the VM is still powered off.

Figure 13.37   Side branch snapshot deleted

What actually happened here is that all the changes that were written to the delta file of the Side Branch Before Installing App X snapshot got written to its parent virtual visk. This means that these changes can no longer be discarded.

3. To switch to the state with the installed App X, select the **After Installing App X** snapshot and then click the **Go To** button.

4. Click **Yes** to confirm the operation. The Snapshot Manager should look like Figure 13.38.

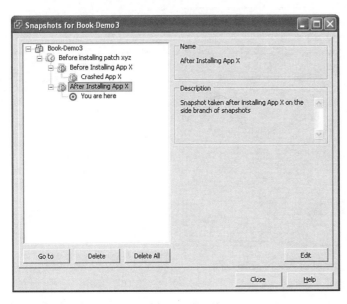

Figure 13.38   Going to child snapshot

5. Click **Close**.

Consolidate Snapshots Operation

Snapshot consolidation searches for snapshot hierarchies, or delta disks, to combine without violating data dependency. The outcome of consolidation is the removal of redundant disks. This improves virtual machine performance and saves storage space.

Identifying Consolidation Candidates

To identify which VMs require snapshot consolidation, follow this procedure:

1. Log on to vCenter Server as Administrator or root user.

2. Navigate to Home, Inventory, VMs and Templates (see Figure 13.39).

Figure 13.39   Switching to the VMs and Templates view

3. Select the **Virtual Machines** Tab (A).

4. Right-click on any of the column headers (B) and select **Needs Consolidation (C)** (see Figure 13.40).

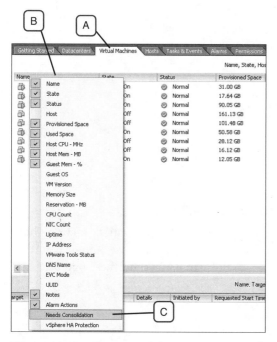

Figure 13.40   Adding a Needs Consolidation column

5. The column is added to the far right-hand side of the view. You may move it by clicking and dragging the column header to the desired location in the view. If a VM needs consolidation, the value of this column will be Yes. Otherwise, it would be No.

6. Right-click a VM that needs consolidation and then click **Snapshot** followed by **Consolidate** (see Figure 13.41).

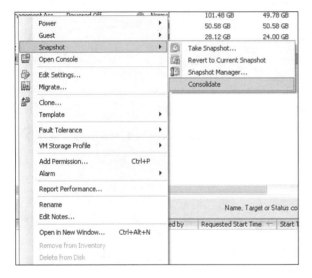

Figure 13.41   The Consolidate Snapshot command

7. Confirm the operation when prompted by clicking **Yes**.

What Actually Happens When Snapshots Are Consolidated?

Continuing with the example I used under the "Delete Snapshot Operation" section, the deletion left a delta disk behind. To find out which one, I collected some outputs before and after the consolidation process. Listings 13.26 through 13.29 show these outputs.

Listing 13.26   Virtual Disk Descriptors Before Consolidation

```
323 Apr 14 20:26 Book-Demo3-000001.vmdk
330 Apr 14 20:29 Book-Demo3-000002.vmdk
330 Apr 15 00:57 Book-Demo3-000003.vmdk
346 Apr 15 03:27 Book-Demo3-000004.vmdk
330 Apr 15 04:10 Book-Demo3-000005.vmdk
520 Apr 15 03:27 Book-Demo3.vmdk
```

Listing 13.27   Virtual Disk Descriptors After Consolidation

```
323 Apr 14 20:26 Book-Demo3-000001.vmdk
330 Apr 14 20:29 Book-Demo3-000002.vmdk
346 Apr 15 04:47 Book-Demo3-000004.vmdk
330 Apr 15 04:47 Book-Demo3-000005.vmdk
520 Apr 15 03:27 Book-Demo3.vmdk
```

Comparing the listings, it is obvious that one delta disk was removed (which I highlighted in listing 13.26). This is the virtual disk descriptor for the delta file used by the snapshot I deleted earlier. Because its blocks have been converged with its parent disk, it is no longer needed. To find out which was its parent disk, I ran the following command:

```
fgrep vmdk Book-Demo3-00000?.vmdk |grep parent
```

The outputs before and after the consolidation process are shown in Listings 13.28 and 13.29.

Listing 13.28   Snapshot Parent Disks Before Consolidation

```
fgrep vmdk Book-Demo3-00000?.vmdk |grep parent
Book-Demo3-000001.vmdk:parentFileNameHint="Book-Demo3.vmdk"
Book-Demo3-000002.vmdk:parentFileNameHint="Book-Demo3-000001.vmdk"
Book-Demo3-000003.vmdk:parentFileNameHint="Book-Demo3-000004.vmdk"
Book-Demo3-000004.vmdk:parentFileNameHint="Book-Demo3.vmdk"
Book-Demo3-000005.vmdk:parentFileNameHint="Book-Demo3-000003.vmdk"
```

Listing 13.29   Snapshot Parent Disks After Consolidation

```
fgrep vmdk Book-Demo3-00000?.vmdk |grep parent
Book-Demo3-000001.vmdk:parentFileNameHint="Book-Demo3.vmdk"
Book-Demo3-000002.vmdk:parentFileNameHint="Book-Demo3-000001.vmdk"
Book-Demo3-000004.vmdk:parentFileNameHint="Book-Demo3.vmdk"
Book-Demo3-000005.vmdk:parentFileNameHint="Book-Demo3-000004.vmdk"
```

Listing 13.28 shows, from the bottom up, that delta disk Book-Demo3-000005.vmdk had a parent disk Book-Demo3-000003.vmdk. It also shows that delta disk Book-Demo3-000003.vmdk had a parent disk Book-Demo3-000004.vmdk. So, when the snapshot that used Book-Demo3-000003.vmdk as the delta disk was deleted, the content of that disk was combined with its parent Book-Demo3-000004.vmdk. This left the snapshot using Book-Demo3-000005.vmdk delta desk still pointing to the deprecated delta disk Book-Demo3-000003.vmdk.

The consolidation process corrected this discrepancy by modifying Book-Demo3-000005.vmdk to point to its new parent Book-Demo3-000004.vmdk, which was evident by Listing 13.29.

How about the VM snapshot dictionary? It, too, should be corrected. Listings 13.30 and 13.31 show before and after consolidation for the output of

```
fgrep vmdk Book-Demo3.vmdk
```

This command lists all references to virtual disks in the dictionary file, which shows their association with their corresponding snapshot.

Listing 13.30   Virtual Disks Association with Snapshots Before Consolidation

```
fgrep vmdk Book-Demo3.vmsd
snapshot0.disk0.fileName = "Book-Demo3.vmdk"
snapshot1.disk0.fileName = "Book-Demo3-000001.vmdk"
snapshot2.disk0.fileName = "Book-Demo3-000003.vmdk"
snapshot3.disk0.fileName = "Book-Demo3-000002.vmdk"
```

Listing 13.31   Virtual Disks Association with Snapshots After Consolidation

```
fgrep vmdk Book-Demo3.vmsd
snapshot0.disk0.fileName = "Book-Demo3.vmdk"
snapshot1.disk0.fileName = "Book-Demo3-000001.vmdk"
snapshot2.disk0.fileName = "Book-Demo3-000004.vmdk"
snapshot3.disk0.fileName = "Book-Demo3-000002.vmdk"
```

The highlighted line in Listings 13.30 and 13.31 show that snapshot2 was changed from using Book-Demo3-000003.vmdk to Book-Demo3-000004.vmdk, which is consistent with the changes I demonstrated in Listing 13.28 and Listing 13.29.

The diagram shown in Figure 13.42 shows the combined relations from the previous six listings before and after consolidation.

> **NOTE**
>
> If your storage array does not support VAAI block device or NAS primitives (see Chapter 16), the process of deleting or consolidating snapshots might have a negative effect on performance.

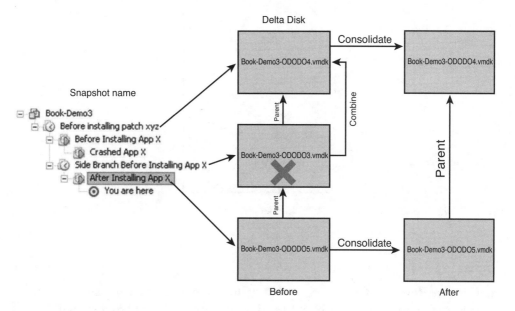

Figure 13.42 Snapshot consolidation process flow

Reverting to Snapshot

Let's continue further with the example I used in the last few sections. I now have an application that is stable but somehow the VM got infected by a virus that I am unable to clean without reinstalling the GOS. I had to power off the VM to prevent it from spreading to other VMs. Because all changes done to the VM, after taking the After Installing App X, get written to what is represented by the You Are Here state, all I need is to discard current state and return to the snapshot itself (see Figure 13.43). The process of discarding the current state is referred to as Revert to Current Snapshot.

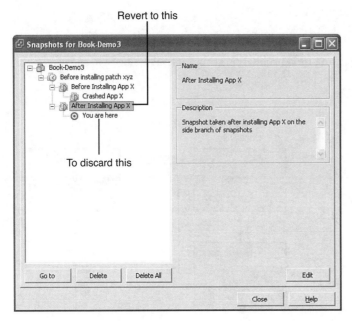

Figure 13.43   Snapshot hierarchy of current snapshot state

To revert to a snapshot, follow this procedure:

1. Click the **Revert to Current Snapshot** button (A) or right-click on the VM in the inventory tree (B) and then select **Snapshot, Revert to Current Snapshot** (C) menu (see Figure 13.44).

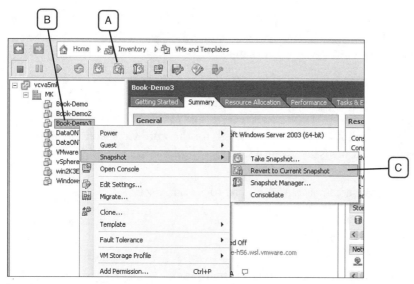

Figure 13.44   Revert to Current Snapshot command

2. Click **Yes** to confirm the operation.

Notice that the VM is now powered on even though it was off before I reverted to the current snapshot. The reason for that is how I took the snapshot originally; the VM was powered on and I chose to take a memory snapshot.

Linked Clones

Looking back at the setup of the example I used so far, I realized that because I have two branches of snapshots, why don't I use both branches concurrently?

For example, App X tech support finally got back to me on my beta support call that I submitted when the app crashed on the OS with patch xyz. However, I can't stop what I am doing with the stable branch of snapshots. I stepped back from my white board with all my scribbles that depicted my snapshot hierarchy and took a look at the bigger picture. It looked like what I saw with a VMware VDI (Virtual Desktop Infrastructure) setup I did a while back in which multiple VMs share a parent disk and get deployed in seconds with minor customization efforts. I thought to myself, "I think I can get away with this for a short period." What I had in mind was to create a temporary linked clone of my VM using the crashed state snapshot if I connected the temporary VM to an isolated network. So, I went for it, and it saved me a ton of time that I might have wasted trying to re-create the crash state.

First, I needed to identify the virtual disk used by the snapshot called Crashed App X by using the following procedure:

1. Search the VM Snapshot Dictionary file (vmsd) for the word Crashed to identify the snapshot prefix in that file (see Listing 13.32).

Listing 13.32   Locating Snapshot Prefix of the Crashed App X Snapshot

```
fgrep Crash Book-Demo3.vmsd
snapshot3.displayName = "Crashed App X"
```

I highlighted the snapshot prefix, which is snapshot3.

2. Search the vmsd for the virtual disk name associated with the snapshot prefix (see Listing 13.33).

Listing 13.33   Locating the Delta Virtual Disk Used by a Snapshot

```
fgrep snapshot3.disk Book-Demo3.vmsd
snapshot3.disk0.fileName = "Book-Demo3-000002.vmdk"
snapshot3.disk0.node = "scsi0:0"
```

I highlighted the virtual disk name. Also note the node name, which is scsi0:0.

3. Create a new VM using custom options to use an existing disk. Browse for the file name identified in Step 2 and select it. Make sure to change the virtual network to use a port group on a virtual switch connected to a different network from that of the original VM.

4. To be able to preserve the crashed state, I decided to set the virtual disk as independent, nonpersistent. What this does is create a REDO log to store all changes done while the VM is powered on. The REDO log gets discarded when the VM is powered off.

5. Go through the debugging needed for the crashed VM. If you need to start over again, just power off the VM and then power it on.

6. When done, delete the VM but make sure to not delete the virtual disk.

NOTE

Using linked clones is supported by VMware in a VDI and Lab Manager/VMware vCloud Director environments only. If you decide to play with linked clones in vSphere environment, make sure that it is not in production environment and not on a permanent basis.

Summary

In this chapter, I have introduced the basics of virtual disks and RDMs' structure, layout, and type, which are eager zeroed thick, zeroed thick, and thin. I also explained the various virtual disks types from the file systems perspective, that is, SPARSE, VMFSSPARSE, and VMFSRDM.

I discussed RDMs (both virtual and physical modes) in detail.

I explained virtual machine snapshots and how they affect their virtual disks. In addition, I covered deleting, going to, reverting to, and consolidating snapshots. I gave you a quick glance at linked clones and how they correlate to certain snapshot hierarchies.

## Chapter 14

Distributed Locks

By default a logical unit number (LUN) is not designed to be accessed simultaneously by multiple hosts. VMware developed Virtual Machine File System (VMFS), their clustered file system, to allow ESXi hosts concurrent access to shared datastores. To prevent corruption resulting from more than one host writing to the same file or metadata area, an on-disk distributed locking mechanism is used. To put it simply, VMFS "tells" each host which areas in the metadata and disk it can update. It tracks this via on-disk lock records in the metadata. At the time each ESXi host was first installed and configured, it is assigned a unique ID referred to as Host UUID (Universally Unique Identifier). You can locate this ID on each host by running:

```
esxcli system uuid get
4d7ab650-e269-3374-ef05-001e4f1fbf2c
```

When an ESXi host first mounts a VMFS3 or VMFS5 volume, it is assigned a slot within the VMFS heartbeat region where the host writes its own heartbeat record. This record is associated with the host UUID. All subsequent operations done by this host on the file system that require metadata updates are associated with this heartbeat record. However, for the host to create its heartbeat record, it must first get a lock on its slot in the heartbeat region to which it will write that record. This, like any other updates to the metadata, requires SCSI-2 reservation on the VMFS LUN or head extent (if it is a spanned volume) if the array does not support vStorage APIs for Array Integration (VAAI) primitive Atomic Test and Set (ATS). I discuss ATS in detail in Chapter 16, "VAAI."

> **NOTE**
>
> SCSI-2 reservations are nonpersistent and are acquired by one host at a time.

Basic Locking

The typical sequence of distributed locking operations on pre ESXi 3.5 is Reserve-Read-Modify-Write-Release. This translates to the following:

1. ESXi host requests a SCSI-2 reservation from the storage array on the LUN.

2. The ESXi host reads the on-disk lock records into memory.

   Figure 14.1 shows a block diagram representing the VMFS building block, which is the Resource Cluster (see Chapter 12, "VMFS Architecture," in the "VMFS 3 on Disk Layout" section).

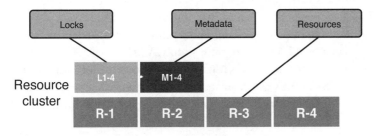

Figure 14.1   VMFS3 Resource Cluster

   On-disk locks are kept close to the metadata records they protect.

3. The ESXi host acquires a free on-disk lock, writes it to disk, and then releases the SCSI-2 reservation.

4. The ESXi host modifies, in memory, the metadata protected by the lock(s) but does not write it to disk yet.

5. If the host ID is not set in the heartbeat region, the host also updates the following in an available heartbeat slot:

   - **Host ID**—This is the system UUID, which you can list using the esxcli system uuid get command.

- **Generation Number**—This number is set when the host first created its heartbeat record. From that point on, it updates the live-ness (see the next bullet). If the host loses access to the datastore or otherwise crashes leaving a stale heartbeat record, it breaks the lock on its own heartbeat and a new generation number is set.

- **Live-ness**—This is also referred to as the time stamp. It is changed by the host on a regular interval. If it fails to update the time stamp, other hosts interpret that the host is dead or has lost access to the datastore.

- **Journal offset**—This is where the heartbeat's journal is located on disk. It is used by other hosts that need to break a dead host's lock by replaying the heartbeat's journal. (See the next section, "What Happens When a Host Crashes?")

6. If the host needs additional on-disk locks, it repeats Steps 1–4 but does not write the changes to disk yet. Each of these cycles requires a separate SCSI-2 reservation.

7. The host then writes the updated metadata to the journal.

8. The journal is then committed to the file system.

9. The host releases the on-disk locks.

If the requested lock was to modify certain VMFS resources or the metadata—creating a file or growing it, the relevant `File Descriptor Clusters` (FDCs) are assigned to this host in the form of a cluster group. If the files require `pointer blocks` (ptr) and/or `secondary pointer blocks` (secondary ptr) in addition to the range of file blocks, the host updates these resources and associates them with its own heartbeat record. ESXi 4 and later increased the size of the VMFS resource clusters, which makes them easier to cache.

> **NOTE**
>
> The VMFS resources are kept close to their metadata on disk. This provides better performance.

What Happens When a Host Crashes?

In a situation where a host suffers from a crash, it might leave behind stale locks on the VMFS datastore. If you have configured the HA (High Availability) feature, it attempts to power on the protected virtual machines (VMs) on one of the surviving hosts in the cluster. However, due to the stale locks, this might not be possible. For this operation to succeed, the host attempting to power on the VM does the following:

1. Checks the heartbeat region of the datastore for the lock owner's ID.

2. A few seconds later, it checks to see if this host's heartbeat record was updated. Because the lock owner crashed, it is not able to update its heartbeat record.

3. The recovery host ages the locks left by this host. After this is done, other hosts in the cluster do not attempt to break the same stale locks.

4. The recovery host replays the heartbeat's VMFS journal to clear and then acquire the locks.

5. When the crashed host is rebooted, it clears its own heartbeat record and acquires a new one (with a new generation number). As a result, it does not attempt to lock its original files because it is no longer the lock owner.

Optimistic Locking

Optimistic locking was introduced in ESX 3.5, which enabled the host to modify all metadata protected by free locks and then request a single SCSI-2 reservation when it is ready to write these changes to disk.

The revised process follows:

1. ESXi host reads on-disk locks into memory.

2. The host modifies all metadata that is protected by free locks in memory (in other words, they were not locked by other hosts at that time) instead of doing this one record at a time.

3. Before the host can write these metadata updates to the journal, it acquires all the necessary disk locks with one SCSI-2 reservation.

4. All metadata updates are written to the journal.

5. The journal is committed to disk.

6. The host releases all on-disk locks.

Optimistic locking requires a lot fewer SCSI-2 reservations and reduces the chances of SCSI (Small Computer System Interface) reservation conflicts.

If, at the time the host attempts to acquire the on-disk locks (Step 3), another host had stolen the locks, this ESXi host would fall back to the standard locking mechanism for the whole batch of locks it tried to acquire optimistically.

Dynamic Resource Allocation

As the contention for and/or occupancy of on-disk locks increases, the optimistic locks are decreased. So, in an extremely busy environment, this mechanism might still run into reservation conflicts. So, to reduce the number of locks required for these operations, the number of resources per cluster (for example, FDC and PBC) were increased, which may increase chances of cross-host contention. To work around that, the number of clusters per resource group was also increased, but this might increase contention and distance between the data and its metadata.

The combination of Optimistic Locking and Dynamic Resource sizing helps with operations such as:

- File creation
- File deletion
- File extension

However, they do not help with File Open operations such as

- Powering VMs on
- Resuming VMs
- Migrating VMs with vMotion

These operations require a SCSI reservation to lock the files for exclusive access by the VMs.

SAN Aware Retries

As you see from the above, SCSI reservation conflicts are prone to happen in a busy environment that is overutilized or undersized (for example, too few datastores for the number of running VMs across multiple ESXi hosts, which results in contention for SCSI reservations). To help reduce the effect on the running VMs, VMware introduced the SAN Aware Retries mechanism in vSphere 4.

To better explain what it does, let's look at the block diagram shown in Figure 14.2.

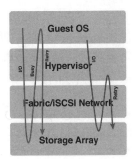

Figure 14.2   SAN Aware Retries

This block diagram shows the path of an I/O and its related error when there are SCSI Reservation conflicts. The arrow on the left side shows that the I/O traverses the hypervisor and the SAN from the VM on its way to the storage array.

Without SAN Aware Retries the following is the journey of the I/O:

1. The VM sends the I/O.

2. If the hypervisor encounters SCSI reservation conflicts, a Device Busy error is returned to the guest OS.

3. The guest OS retries the I/O until the host runs out of conflict retries, at which point the I/O fails and the failure is reported to the guest OS.

With **SAN Aware Retries** the following is the journey of the I/O represented in Figure 14.2 by the shorter arrow on the right side:

1. The VM sends the I/O.

2. If the hypervisor encounters SCSI reservation conflicts, it retries the I/O (not the reservation).

3. The guest OS does not receive a Device Busy error as frequently as without SAN Aware Retries. If the hypervisor exhausts the conflict retries, the guest receives an I/O failure error.

4. The guest OS retries the I/O.

As a result, the guest OS receives significantly fewer Device Busy errors.

Optimistic I/O

Optimistic locking and dynamic resource allocation do not address SCSI reservations resulting from a File Open operation at VM power on time. These are characterized by the following:

- Most of the File Open operations are to read and re-read VM files such as *.vmx (virtual machine configuration file) or *.vmdk (virtual disks). See Chapter 13, "Virtual Disks and RDMs," for further detail about VM files.

- Most of these files are closed almost immediately after being read.

- As application complexity increases, the number of the File Open operations increase as well.

vSphere 4.x introduced optimistic I/O to address this issue. It leverages optimistic locking for reading, re-reading, validating, and invalidating file contents without using SCSI reservations.

The way this works is by requesting the optimistic locks and proceeding with the read I/O assuming that the locks will succeed. This approach results in significant reduction in SCSI reservations during VMs boot time (also known as boot storm).

List of Operations That Require SCSI Reservations

There are two groups of operations that require SCSI-2 reservations: VMFS datastore–specific operations and on-disk locks–related operations.

VMFS Datastore–Specific Operations

Such operations result in metadata modifications such as

- Creating a datastore

- Spanning or growing a datastore

- Re-signature of datastore

On-Disk Locks–Related Operations

In the previous sections I discussed the distributed locking mechanism and how it requires on-disk lock acquisition. It should be clear from that discussion that SCSI reservations are required to complete such operations in the absence of ATS. Examples of these operations are

- Powering on a VM (optimistic I/O alleviates the need for the reservation)

- Acquiring a lock on a file

- Creating or deleting a file

- Creating a virtual machine template (the previous two bullets apply here)

- Deploying a VM from a template

- Creating a new VM

- Migrating a VM with vMotion (this involves both the source and target hosts on the shared datastore)

- Growing a file—for example, snapshot file or thin provisioned virtual disk (see Chapters 13).

MSCS-Related SCSI Reservations

One of the most common questions I receive is related to Microsoft Windows Failover Clustering Services (MSCS) (also known as MSCS or Microsoft Clustering Services), their form of host failover clustering, and how it interacts with storage shared between its cluster nodes.

I am not going to discuss MSCS itself here. Rather, only its effect on shared storage and the types of SCSI reservations used.

MSCS SCSI-2 Reservations

Windows 2003 and earlier implemented MSCS to utilize SCSI-2–style reservations on the quorum and shared data disks. The latter are mostly RDMs (Raw Device Mappings), which I cover in Chapter 13. They can also be virtual disks if both cluster nodes reside on the same ESXi host and will not be migrated onto separate hosts in the future (also known as CIB or Cluster-in-a-Box). The active node of the MSCS cluster acquires a reservation on the shared storage and does not release this reservation. That reservation is reset by one of the passive nodes if the active node fails to send its heartbeat over the network as well as onto the quorum disk. The process of releasing the reservation is done by the passive node by sending a `Device Reset` SCSI command to the shared storage. This results in the storage array releasing the reservation. The passive node then sends a SCSI reservation request that gets granted since the active node is either offline or had received a "poison pill" from the passive node if it is reachable over the network.

The activities are handled differently by the ESXi host depending on how the MSCS-clustered VMs are configured—that is CAB (Cluster across Boxes) or CIB.

NOTE

The virtual SCSI HBA (Host Bus Adapter) used by the cluster nodes for the shared storage must be LSI logic parallel, which is a parallel SCSI HBA supporting SCSI-2 standard.

Cluster-in-a-Box Shared Storage

In this configuration both nodes reside on the same ESXi host. This provides the vmkernel visibility into what each node is doing to the shared storage. As a result, there is no need to communicate via the shared storage in the form of SCSI reservation events. This means that the shared storage can be in the form of either virtual disks or virtual mode RDM (non-passthrough RDM). Concurrent access to such shared storage configurations is arbitrated via file-level locks. In other words, the active node is granted a Read-Write lock on the file until the passive node takes over the active role, at which time it sends a `Device Reset` command to the shared storage. VMkernel translates this command to releasing the lock acquired by the active node. When this is done, the lock on the file is granted to the new active node. Note that I am referring to the shared storage "file" regardless of it being a virtual disk or a virtual mode RDM because the latter is treated like a virtual disk from the lock-handling perspective. If a VM on another host attempts to access the LUN mapped by this RDM, it fails because the other host (with the CIB nodes) has a SCSI reservation on it based on the lock granted to the active MSCS node.

Cluster-Across-Boxes Shared Storage

In this configuration each node in the cluster resides on a separate host. This means that each host has no knowledge of what the VM on the alternate host is doing to the shared storage and the only way for them to have such knowledge is via SCSI reservations. For this to work correctly, the shared storage must be physical mode RDM (also known as passthrough RDM). In this RDM mode, SCSI reservation requests are passed through to the storage array. In other words, the active node of the MSCS cluster acquires SCSI-2 reservations on the shared storage (both quorum and data disks). If the passive node attempts to write to the shared storage, it receives an error because it is reserved by the active node.

When the active node fails to communicate its heartbeat, the passive node sends a `Device Reset` command to the storage array. This results in releasing the reservation, and the passive node sends a reservation request that is granted by the array.

MSCS SCSI-3 Reservations

MSCS on Windows 2008 uses PGR (Persistent Group Reservation), which is a SCSI-3. This is the main reason why Windows Server 2008 VMs must be configured with LSI

Logic SAS (Serial Attached SCSI) virtual SCSI HBA for the shared storage because that virtual adapter supports the SCSI-3 standard required for supporting PGR.

> **NOTE**
>
> Regardless of which version of Windows you use for MSCS, virtual disks and virtual mode RDMs are supported *only* with CIB configurations. Physical mode RDMs are the only supported shared store for CAB configurations.
>
> If your cluster nodes do not use shared storage—for example, Exchange CCR (Cluster Continuous Replication) or DAG (Database Availability Group)—there is no effect on SCSI reservations beyond what is used by non-clustered VMs.

Perennial Reservations

Having MSCS cluster nodes spread over several ESXi hosts necessitates the use of passthrough RDMs, which are shared among all hosts on which a relevant cluster node will run. As a result, each of these hosts have some RDMs reserved whereas the remaining RDMs are reserved by the other hosts. At boot time, LUN discovery and Device Claiming processes require a response from each LUN. Such a response takes much longer for LUNs reserved by other hosts. This results in an excessively prolonged boot time of all hosts with that configuration. The same issue might also affect the time it takes for a rescan operation to complete.

vSphere 5 introduced the concept of perennial reservations, which is a device property that makes it easier for an ESXi 5 host to recognize if a given LUN is reserved by another host perennially. At boot time or upon rescanning, the host does not wait for a response from a LUN in that state. This improves boot and rescan times on ESXi 5 hosts sharing MSCS shared LUNs.

To identify if a LUN is perennially reserved, run this command:

```
esxcli storage core device list -d <device-ID>
```

You may also use the verbose version of this command:

```
esxcli storage core device list --device <device-ID>
```

Listing 14.1 is a sample output of a LUN that is *not* marked as reserved (the property is highlighted in Listing 14.1).

Listing 14.1 Sample Output of a LUN That Is NOT Reserved

```
esxcli storage core device list -d naa.6006016055711d00cff95e65664ee011

naa.6006016055711d00cff95e65664ee011
    Display Name: DGC Fibre Channel Disk (naa.6006016055711d00cff95e65664
ee011)
    Has Settable Display Name: true
    Size: 10240
    Device Type: Direct-Access
    Multipath Plugin: NMP
    Devfs Path: /vmfs/devices/disks/naa.6006016055711d00cff95e65664ee011
    Vendor: DGC
    Model: RAID 5
    Revision: 0326
    SCSI Level: 4
    Is Pseudo: false
    Status: on
    Is RDM Capable: true
    Is Local: false
    Is Removable: false
    Is SSD: false
    Is Offline: false
    Is Perennially Reserved: false
    Thin Provisioning Status: unknown
    Attached Filters:
    VAAI Status: unknown
    Other UIDs: vml.02000100006006016055711d00cff95e65664ee011524149442035
```

You need to set this option manually for all LUNs mapped as RDMs for MSCS shared storage on all ESXi 5 hosts sharing them. This setting is stored within the host's configuration (in /etc/vmware/esx.conf file). You enable this option using the following esxcli command:

```
esxcli storage core device setconfig -d <ID> --perennially-reserved=true
```

Listing 14.2 shows an example of setting the perennially reserved option.

Listing 14.2 Setting a Perennially Reserved Option

```
esxcli storage core device setconfig -d naa.6006016055711d00cff95e65664
ee011 --perennially-reserved=true

esxcli storage core device list -d naa.6006016055711d00cff95e65664ee011
naa.6006016055711d00cff95e65664ee011
   Display Name: DGC Fibre Channel Disk (naa.6006016055711d00cff95e65664
ee011)
   Has Settable Display Name: true
   Size: 10240
   Device Type: Direct-Access
   Multipath Plugin: NMP
   Devfs Path: /vmfs/devices/disks/naa.6006016055711d00cff95e65664ee011
   Vendor: DGC
   Model: RAID 5
   Revision: 0326
   SCSI Level: 4
   Is Pseudo: false
   Status: on
   Is RDM Capable: true
   Is Local: false
   Is Removable: false
   Is SSD: false
   Is Offline: false
   Is Perennially Reserved: true
   Thin Provisioning Status: unknown
   Attached Filters:
   VAAI Status: unknown
   Other UIDs: vml.02000100006006016055711d00cff95e65664ee011524149442035
```

The first command in Listing 14.2 sets the option to true, and the second command lists the device properties of the LUN you just configured. Notice that the `Is Perennially Reserved` value is now true.

> **NOTE**
>
> This property cannot be set via a host profile in this release. As a result, this configuration cannot persist between reboots of Auto-Deployed ESXi hosts.

How to Locate the Device ID for a Mapped LUN

This topic is discussed in greater detail in Chapter 13, but I touch on it here for convenience.

Procedure Using the CLI

Using the CLI logged on to the ESXi Shell either directly, via SSH, or via vMA 5.0, use the following process:

1. Use `vmkfstools -q` to identify the vml ID of the mapped LUN.

   The output of this command is shown in Listing 14.3.

Listing 14.3 Identifying the vml ID of a Mapped LUN

```
vmkfstools -q /vmfs/volumes/FC200/win2K3Enterprise/win2K3Enterprise.vmdk

Disk /vmfs/volumes/FC200/win2K3Enterprise/win2K3Enterprise.vmdk is a
Passthrough Raw Device Mapping
Maps to: vml.02000100006006016055711d00cff95e65664ee011524149442035
```

I highlighted the vml ID in the output.

2. Use the vml ID with the `esxcfg-scsidevs` command to find the device ID of the mapped LUN.

   The output of this command is shown in Listing 14.4.

Listing 14.4 Identifying the RDM Device ID Using Its vml ID

```
esxcfg-scsidevs -l -d vml.02000100006006016055711d00cff95e65664
ee011524149442035

naa.6006016055711d00cff95e65664ee011
    Device Type: Direct-Access
    Size: 10240 MB
    Display Name: DGC Fibre Channel Disk (naa.6006016055711d00cff95e65664
ee011)
    Multipath Plugin: NMP
    Console Device: /vmfs/devices/disks/naa.6006016055711d00cff95e65664ee011
    Devfs Path: /vmfs/devices/disks/naa.6006016055711d00cff95e65664ee011
    Vendor: DGC        Model: RAID 5              Revis: 0326
    SCSI Level: 4  Is Pseudo: false Status: on
    Is RDM Capable: true  Is Removable: false
    Is Local: false Is SSD: false
```

```
Other Names:
    vml.020001000060060160557l1d00cff95e65664ee011524149442035
VAAI Status: unknown
```

I highlighted the device ID in the output.

Procedure Using the UI

To locate the device ID for a mapped LUN using the UI, follow this procedure:

1. While logged on to the vCenter Server using vSphere 5 client as an administrator, locate the MSCS cluster node VM in the inventory tree.

2. Right-click the VM listing and then select **Edit Settings**.

   You should see a dialog similar to Figure 14.3.

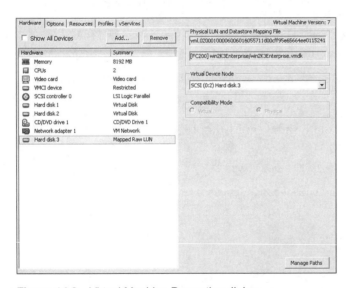

Figure 14.3   Virtual Machine Properties dialog

3. Locate the device showing **Mapped Raw LUN** in the summary column and select it.

4. Click the **Manage Paths** button on the lower-right corner of the dialog.

5. The device ID is listed in the lower pane of the resulting dialog. The ID is right after the last dash in the **Name** field (see Figure 14.4).

Figure 14.4 Listing the device ID of an FC device

In this example, the device ID is

`naa.6006016055711d00cff95e65664ee011`

TIP

If you look closer at the vml and NAA ID in this example, notice that the NAA ID is actually part of the VML ID or the other way around; the vml ID is based on the NAA ID of the device.

`vml.02000100006006016055711d00cff95e65664ee011524149442035`

`naa.6006016055711d00cff95e65664ee011`

For example, the matching bytes are highlighted.

If the mapped LUN is an iSCSI device, the process is the same as the previous example but the last step's dialog looks like Figure 14.5.

Figure 14.5 Listing a device ID of an iSCSI device

Under the Hood of Distributed Locks

Most of the issue related to distributed locks can be identified by reading the vmkernel logs. I share with you some normal and problematic logs along with explanations.

> **NOTE**
>
> Log entries were cropped or wrapped for readability.

Heartbeat Corruption

There were some reported cases where the heartbeat record of a host got corrupt. As a result, it could neither clear its heartbeat record nor acquire any locks that it requires for its normal operation.

In this case, the vmkernel logs show an error like Listing 14.5:

Listing 14.5   Sample Log Entries of Corrupt Heartbeat

```
vmkernel: 25:21:39:57.861 cpu15:1047)FS3: 130: <START [file-name].vswp>
vmkernel: 25:21:39:57.861 cpu15:1047)Lock [type 10c00001 offset 52076544 v
69, hb offset 4017152
vmkernel: gen 109, mode 1, owner 4a15b3a2-fd2f4020-3625-001a64353e5c mtime
3420]
vmkernel: 25:21:39:57.861 cpu15:1047)Addr <4, 1011, 10>, gen 36, links 1,
type reg, flags 0x0, uid 0, gid 0, mode 600
vmkernel: 25:21:39:57.861 cpu15:1047)len 3221225472, nb 3072 tbz 0, zla 3,
bs 1048576
vmkernel: 25:21:39:57.861 cpu15:1047)FS3: 132: <END [file-name].vswp>
```

Listing 14.6 shows another example of a corrupt heartbeat:

Listing 14.6   Another Sample Log of a Corrupt Heartbeat

```
vmkernel: 0:00:20:51.964 cpu3:1085)WARNING: Swap: vm 1086: 2268: Failed
to open swap file '/volumes/<vol-UUID>/<vm-directory>/<file-name.vswp>':
Invalid metadata

vmkernel: 0:00:20:51.964 cpu3:1085)WARNING: Swap: vm 1086: 3586: Failed to
initialize swap file '/volumes/4730e995-faa64138-6e6f-001a640a8998/mule/
mule-560e1410.vswp': Invalid metadata
```

You might need to contact VMware technical support for assistance. Be prepared with a binary dump of the first 30MB or 1200MB of the device on which the VMFS volume resides. Technical support will attempt to repair the heartbeat records for the affected host.

File System Corruption

During the beta of ESXi 5, a file system corruption was reported by an internal user. During the process of resignaturing a VMFS datastore, another host attempted the same process. The following are the relevant log messages from this case.

Listing 14.7 shows log entries of VMFS corruption.

Listing 14.7 Sample Log Entries of Corrupt VMFs

```
cpu7:2128)FS3: ReportCorruption:379: VMFS volume snap-6787757b-datastore-
X/4cfed840-657ae77f-9555-0026b95121da on naa.6006016019322800835528fe3c40
2e011:1 has been detected corrupted

cpu7:2128)FS3: ReportCorruption:381: While filing a PR, please report the
names of all hosts that attach to this LUN, tests that were running on
them,

cpu7:2128)FS3: ReportCorruption:383: and upload the dump by `dd if=/vmfs/
devices/disks/naa.6006016019322800835528fe3c402e011:1 of=X bs=1M count=1200
conv=notrunc`,

cpu7:2128)FS3: ReportCorruption:384: where X is the dump file name on a
different volume

cpu15:2128)FS3: DescriptorVerify:323: Volume Descriptor mismatch

cpu15:2128)FS3: DescriptorVerify:325: (Check if volume is involved in a
Format/Upgrade/dd from other hosts)

cpu15:2128)FS3: DescriptorVerify:326: In Memory Descriptor:magic
0x2fabf15e, majorVer 12, minorVer 51 uuid 4cfed840-657ae77f-
9555-0026b95121da, label <snap-6787757b-datastore-X>creationTime
1291049806config 6, diskBlockSize 512, fileBlockSize 1048576

cpu15:2128)FS3: DescriptorVerify:328: On Disk Descriptor:magic 0x2fabf15e,
majorVer 12, minorVer 51 uuid 4cfed79c-94250e53-64b8-0026b9511d8d, label
<snap-2042dfa8-datastore-X>creationTime 1291049806config 6, diskBlockSize
512, fileBlockSize 1048576
```

The last two lines in this example show the file system's UUID in memory is different from that on disk. To identify which host is the offending one, the last segment of the on-disk UUID is the MAC address of that host's management port. In this case it is 00:26:b9:51:1d:8d. I believe that this was fixed in the final release build as we have not seen this issue reported outside the beta. Notice that the file system version is identified as majorVer 12 and minorVer 51. This was a prerelease version. The released version is majorVer 14 and minorVer 54, which translates to version 5.54.

Notice the new enhancement in the log message where it identifies the corruption and provides you with the command line you need to use to collect the file system binary dumps needed for repairing the corruption.

Marking the Heartbeat and Replaying Journal

In this example, the ESXi host attempts to clear or mark the heartbeat and replays the journal.

Listing 14.8 shows an example of replaying the heartbeat journal.

Listing 14.8   Replaying the Heartbeat Journal

```
HBX: FS3_MarkOrClearHB:4752: Marking HB [HB state abcdef02 offset 3158016
gen 5 stampUS 3345493920478 uuid 4cc0d786-d2f90077-9479-0026b9516a0d jrnl
<FB 1800> drv 12.51] on vol 'snap-6787757b-datastore-X'

HBX: FS3_MarkOrClearHB:4829: Marked HB [HB state abcdef04 offset 3158016
gen 5 stampUS 4064734308197 uuid 4cc0d786-d2f90077-9479-0026b9516a0d jrnl
<FB 1800> drv 12.51] on vol 'snap-6787757b-datastore-X'

J3: ReplayJournal:2970: Replaying journal at <FB 1800>, gen 5

HBX: FS3PostReplayClearHB:3985: Cleared pulse on vol 'snap-6787757b-
datastore-X' for [HB state abcdef01 offset 3158016 gen 6 stampUS
4064734365500 uuid 00000000-00000000-0000-000000000000 jrnl <FB 0> drv
12.51]
```

The message prefix is HBX (Heartbeat). The first two messages are attempting to mark the heartbeat first with HB state abcdef02, then with HB state abcdef04. After this is done, it replays the journal, which in this case is at file block 1800. This message prefix was J3 (Journal).

The last message in the example is prefixed with HBX, and the code is FS3PostReplay-ClearHB, which is the code that clears the Heartbeat after Journal has been replayed. Notice the heartbeat UUID is all zeros.

Checking Whether a Lock Is Free

The following messages demonstrate the activities a host does to check whether a given lock is free.

Listing 14.9 shows log entries of checking if a lock is free.

Listing 14.9   Checking Whether a Lock Is Free

```
cpu2:176604)DLX: FS3RecheckLock:3349: vol 'datastore-X', lock at 4327424:
Lock changed from:

cpu2:176604)[type 10c00001 offset 4327424 v 20, hb offset 3407872gen 29,
mode 1, owner 4e693687-57255600-7546-001ec933841c mtime 2568963num 0 gblnum
0 gblgen 0 gblbrk 0]

cpu2:176604)DLX: FS3RecheckLock:3350: vol 'datastore-X', lock at 4327424:
To:

cpu2:176604)[type 10c00001 offset 4327424 v 22, hb offset 3407872gen 29,
mode 1, owner 4e693687-57255600-7546-001ec933841c mtime 2662975num 0 gblnum
0 gblgen 0 gblbrk 0]

cpu2:176604)DLX: FS3LeaseWaitAndLock:4109: vol 'datastore-X': [Retry 0]
Lock at 4327424 is not free after change

cpu2:176604)DLX: FS3LeaseWaitOnLock:3565: vol 'datastore-X', lock at
4327424: [Req mode 1] Checking liveness:

cpu2:176604)[type 10c00001 offset 4327424 v 22, hb offset 3407872gen 29,
mode 1, owner 4e693687-57255600-7546-001ec933841c mtime 2662975num 0 gblnum
0 gblgen 0 gblbrk 0]

cpu2:176604)DLX: FS3CheckForDeadOwners:3279: HB on vol 'datastore-X'
changed from [HB state abcdef02 offset 3407872 gen 29 stampUS 337574575701
uuid 4e693687-57255600-7546-001ec933841c jrnl <FB 22186800> drv 14.56]

cpu2:176604)DLX: FS3CheckForDeadOwners:3280: To [HB state abcdef02
offset 3407872 gen 29 stampUS 337580579826 uuid 4e693687-57255600-7546-
001ec933841c jrnl <FB 22186800> drv 14.56]

cpu2:176604)DLX: FS3LeaseWaitAndLock:4089: vol 'datastore-X', lock at
4327424: [Req mode: 1] Not free:
```

1. The first line in Listing 14.9 shows that the Disk-Lock code (DLX) is checking a lock for the file system on a datastore named datastore-X. The lock location is at 4327424 offset. It reports that the lock has changed.

2. The second line shows the lock info before it was changed, which is the following:

   - Lock type.

   - Lock offset.

   - Lock version.

   - Heartbeat offset.

   - Heartbeat generation.

   - Lock mode: This can be a value between 0 and 3. Table 14.1 lists the meaning of each of these lock modes.

Table 14.1   VMFS Lock Modes

Lock Mode	Meaning	Comments
0	Unlocked	Lock is free.
1	Exclusive Lock	This is the mode commonly used to lock files frequently modified by one host—for example, virtual disks, and VM Swap Files.
2	Read-Only Lock	This is used mostly at VM power on to allow the host to read the virtual machine configuration files (*.vmx) and virtual disk files (*.vmdk) in a linked clone configuration. This is the type of lock used with optimistic I/O, which uses Optimistic Locking. Using ATS facilitates acquiring these locks without reservations.
3	Multi-writer Lock	It allows multiple hosts to write to shared virtual disks concurrently. The arbitration of who should write to these files is done by the clustering software running within the guest OS.

The following are some practical examples of lock mode uses.

Multi-writer locks are the most dangerous type of locks, and unless they're used with a qualified clustering solution — for example, Oracle RAC — they can lead to corruption of files locked by this mode. This log entry shows the UUIDs of the multiple lock owners. These owners are hosts sharing this file using this mode. If you are familiar with VMware Workstation, this lock mode is similar to what you achieve by using vmx option `Disk.Locking = FALSE`:

- **Lock owner UUID**—The last segment of this ID is the MAC address of the management port on the host that owns this lock.

- **Num**—This is the number of hosts holding the lock. For Read-only and Multi-writer locks, this value can be more than 1.

3. The third and fourth lines show the lock record after it was changed. I highlighted the changed values.

4. The fifth line was generated by VMFS `wait on lock` code because it identified that the lock is not free.

5. The sixth line onward is the beginning of the process of checking for the `liveness` of the lock owner. It does this by checking the heartbeat slot of the lock owner for a change of the heartbeat region. If it is changed, it means that the lock owner is alive and was able to write to its heartbeat. This is done by the `check for dead owners` code.

Taking Over a Lock

The messages in Listing 14.10 are related to breaking a lock.

Listing 14.10 Breaking a Lock

```
cpu3:228427)DLX: FS3CheckForWrongOwners:3302: Clearing wrong owner for
lock at 184719360 with [HB state abcdef01 offset 3313664 gen 1076 stampUS
938008735 uuid 00000000-00000000-0000-000000000000 jrnl <FB 0> drv 14.58]

cpu2:228427)Resv: UndoRefCount:1386: Long reservation time on naa.60060160
55711d00cff95e65664ee011 for 1 reserve/release pairs (reservation held for
3965 msecs, total time from issue to release 4256 msecs).

cpu2:228427)Resv: UndoRefCount:1396: Performed 5 I/Os / 7 sectors in (8t 0q
01 8i) msecs while under reservation

cpu2:228427)Resv: UndoRefCount:1404: (4 RSIOs/ 7 sectors),(0 FailedIOs / 0
sectors)

cpu2:228427)FS3Misc: FS3_ReleaseDevice:1465: Long VMFS rsv time on
'datastore-X' (held for 4297 msecs). # R: 3, # W: 1 bytesXfer: 7 sectors
```

```
cpu3:228427)DLX: FS3LeaseWaitOnLock:3686: vol 'datastore-X', lock at
66318336: [Req mode 1] Checking liveness:

cpu3:228427)[type 10c00001 offset 66318336 v 2887, hb offset 3469312 gen
2763, mode 1, owner 4efb041c-235d1b95-f0cb-001e4f43718e mtime 27954 num 0
gblnum 0 gblgen 0 gblbrk 0]
```

1. The first line has the following elements:

   - **DLX**—This refers to the vmkernel code that handles disk locks.

   - **FS3CheckForWrongOwners**—This is the part of the disk lock code that checks for wrong owners of on-disk locks. It starts the process of clearing the lock by first listing the current lock information. Such information includes

     - Lock location

     - Heartbeat state

     - Heartbeat offset

     - Heartbeat generation

     - Time stamp; listed here as stampUS

     - Host UUID that owns the lock; listed here as all zeros

     - Journal location

2. The second line is a SCSI reservation and release pair showing the time it took between both events. In this case it is a long reservation time as it held the reservation for more than 3 seconds when normally it should not take more than a few milliseconds. Notice the message begins with Resv, which is the code that handles SCSI reservations. This reservation was held on the device whose ID is the NAA ID I marked in bold italic.

3. The third line shows how many I/Os are done on how many sectors while the device was under reservation.

4. The fourth line shows the count of reservation I/Os on how many sectors (four I/Os on seven sectors) and that there were no failed I/Os.

5. The fifth line shows the device release action.

6. The sixth line shows that the host has requested a lock at sector **66318336** on the volume named **datastore-X**.

7. The final line shows that an exclusive lock (mode 1) at sector 66318336 is now owned by host UUID 4efb041c-235d1b95-f0cb-001e4f43718e. This exclusive lock is on that sector only. What this log does not show is that this lock protects a certain File Descriptor Cluster that occupies a specific Resource. The log entry would have looked like <FD c1 r21>. This translates to File Descriptor Cluster 1 Resource 21.

Summary

vSphere releases prior to 5.0 introduced enhancements in distributed lock handling. In the absence of VAAI-capable storage arrays, these mechanisms are still used by vSphere 5. A new device property in vSphere 5 is perennial device reservation, which helps improve boot and rescan time for hosts with RDMs reserved by MSCS nodes on other ESXi hosts. I discuss VAAI in Chapter 16.

## Chapter 15

Snapshot Handling

Data is written to storage devices frequently in such a dynamic environment as vSphere 5. Losing a few hours' worth of data, for whatever reason, could translate to a large amount of data loss. Storage arrays provide varying forms of Business Continuity/Disaster Recovery (BC/DR) capability to help mitigate this risk. Examples of these capabilities are

- Snapshots

- Replicas

- Mirrors

In this chapter, I cover details affecting VMFS (virtual machine file system) datastores.

What Is a Snapshot?

A *storage snapshot* is a static view of data at a certain point in time. It is commonly implemented as pointers to unmodified blocks on the primary LUN as of the time of taking the snapshot. If and when any of the blocks are to be modified, the unmodified block is copied to the snapshot LUN (logical unit number), and then the modification is written to the block on the primary LUN. The end result is two LUNs: the primary LUN with the current state of data and the snapshot LUN with a combination of blocks copied before being modified and pointers to unmodified blocks on the primary LUN. The snapshot LUN coexists with the primary LUN on the same storage array. It is read-only but can be configured for read-write operations and presented as a separate LUN.

What Is a Replica?

As the name indicates, a *replica* is a block-for-block copy of a storage device (LUN). Depending on the type and frequency of replication—that is, synchronous (sync) or asynchronous (async)—the replica (copy) LUN (R2) has identical content of the primary LUN (R1) at any point in time (sync) or is missing the modified blocks of the R1 LUN since the last replication took place.

The distance and latency of the connection between storage arrays hosting a pair of replicas (R1 and R2) influences the design decision of choosing between sync and async replication. For the topic at hand, I am only highlighting the relevant details to the effects of replication on VMFS datastores. So, for now, a synchronous replica has identical content while an asynchronous one (R2) lags behind the R1 content by the replication period at the most. VMFS datastore signature is identical on R1 and R2 LUNs.

What Is a Mirror?

One of the types of RAID is RAID1, in which two devices are attached to the same storage adapter and all write I/O (input/output) is sent to both devices concurrently, which results in identical content. This is referred to as *mirroring*. RAID adapters have cache of ECC RAM type or better. The cache can be read, write, or both read and write. Depending on the presence of battery backup on the RAID adapter, the write cache can be write-back (with battery backup) or write-through (without battery backup).

A similar concept is used by most storage arrays, which use a much larger cache and the caching algorithm varies from one vendor to another. The bottom line is that storage arrays can do more types of RAID. However, in the storage array's case, RAID is done at a lower level where a set of disks are grouped together as disk pools. One or more RAID types can be created on each pool. For example, one disk pool can host RAID1 and RAID5 concurrently or just RAID1 on one pool and RAID5 on another. Anyhow, the RAID set can then be carved up into multiple LUNs protected by the underlying RAID set.

Such LUNs can be mirrored so that any write operation done on one gets done on the mirror at the same time. I name the primary LUN M1 and the mirror M2. Both M1 and M2 can be on the same storage array or on separate ones within synchronous distance or closer—for example, two buildings in the same campus or across the river between Manhattan and Brooklyn. The latter scenario is commonly referred to as a metro area network (MAN).

A mirror pair has M1 read-write and M2 read-only or write-protected. When the need arises to use M2 in the absence of M1, mirror can be broken and M2 is changed to writable. When M1 becomes available, the you can change the mirroring roles so that M2 syncs up with M1 and then write-protect M2 after M1 is back online. The VMFS Datastore is identical between M1 and M2. Furthermore, for some arrays, both LUNs may have the same device ID if the storage array firmware provides the option.

VMFS Signature

When a new VMFS3 or VMFS5 datastore is created, it is assigned a unique identifier referred to as Volume UUID (universally unique identifier). This is stored in the logical volume manager (LVM) Header along with the device ID, for example, NAA ID.

Here is a sample Volume UUID:

```
4d7bebaa-721eeef2-8c0a-001e4f1fbf2c
```

The Volume UUID is composed of four portions:

1. **System Time** — System time at volume creation
2. **TSC Time** — Internal time stamp counter kept by the CPU
3. **Random** — A random number
4. **MAC** — Management Port uplink (VMNIC) MAC address of the host used to create or resignature the datastore

If the VMFS5 datastore is spanned across multiple LUNs, the LVM header also holds the Spanned Device Table (see Chapter 12, "VMFS Architecture," in the section "Spanned Device Table"), which lists the device IDs of all volume extents.

Listing Datastores' UUIDs via the Command-Line Interface

To list a datastore's UUID via the command-line interface (CLI), you may run this command:

```
esxcli storage filesystem list
```

The output looks like that shown in Figure 15.1.

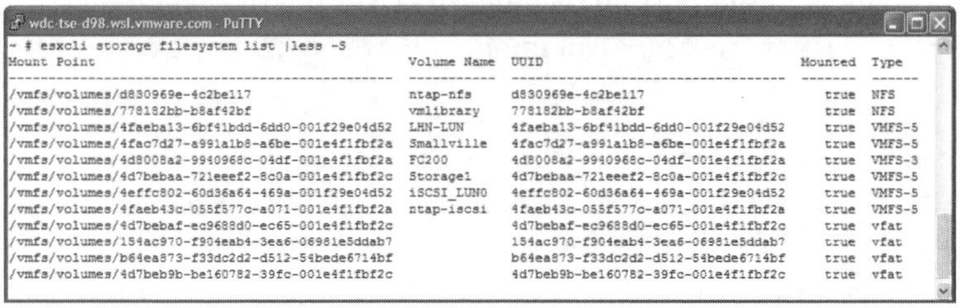


```
~ # esxcli storage filesystem list |less -S
Mount Point                                        Volume Name  UUID                                 Mounted  Type
-------------------------------------------------  -----------  -----------------------------------  -------  ------
/vmfs/volumes/d830969e-4c2be117                    ntap-nfs     d830969e-4c2be117                       true  NFS
/vmfs/volumes/778182bb-b8af42bf                    vmlibrary    778182bb-b8af42bf                       true  NFS
/vmfs/volumes/4faeba13-6bf41bdd-6dd0-001f29e04d52  LHN-LUN      4faeba13-6bf41bdd-6dd0-001f29e04d52     true  VMFS-5
/vmfs/volumes/4fac7d27-a991a1b8-a6be-001e4f1fbf2a  Smallville   4fac7d27-a991a1b8-a6be-001e4f1fbf2a     true  VMFS-5
/vmfs/volumes/4d8008a2-9940968c-04df-001e4f1fbf2a  FC200        4d8008a2-9940968c-04df-001e4f1fbf2a     true  VMFS-3
/vmfs/volumes/4d7bebaa-721eeef2-8c0a-001e4f1fbf2c  Storage1     4d7bebaa-721eeef2-8c0a-001e4f1fbf2c     true  VMFS-5
/vmfs/volumes/4effc802-60d36a64-469a-001f29e04d52  iSCSI_LUN0   4effc802-60d36a64-469a-001f29e04d52     true  VMFS-5
/vmfs/volumes/4faeb43c-055f577c-a071-001e4f1fbf2a  ntap-iscsi   4faeb43c-055f577c-a071-001e4f1fbf2a     true  VMFS-5
/vmfs/volumes/4d7bebaf-ec9688d0-ec65-001e4f1fbf2c               4d7bebaf-ec9688d0-ec65-001e4f1fbf2c     true  vfat
/vmfs/volumes/154ac970-f904eab4-3ea6-06981e5ddab7               154ac970-f904eab4-3ea6-06981e5ddab7     true  vfat
/vmfs/volumes/b64ea873-f33dc2d2-d512-54bede6714bf               b64ea873-f33dc2d2-d512-54bede6714bf     true  vfat
/vmfs/volumes/4d7beb9b-be160782-39fc-001e4f1fbf2c               4d7beb9b-be160782-39fc-001e4f1fbf2c     true  vfat
```

Figure 15.1 Listing datastores' UUID

I cropped the output to fit this page. The text I truncated was the size column and the free column. What is displayed is the list of datastores under the Volume Name column, and the rest is self explanatory.

Effects of Snapshots on VMFS Signature

If the device ID of a LUN, on which there is a VMFS3 or VMFS5 volume, is changed, the following takes place:

1. When the host rescans for new devices, it discovers the presented LUN.
2. When the host rescans for datastores, the vmkernel compares the physical device ID to that stored in the VMFS datastore LVM. It identifies a mismatch and does not automatically mount the discovered datastore.
3. If the snapshot LUN is an extent of a spanned VMFS datastore and the remaining extents were not snapshot and presented to the host, the ESXi host refuses to resignature or force-mount the volume.

   You may check for this condition using this command:

   ```
   esxcli storage vmfs snapshot list
   ```

   Listing 15.1 shows the output of this command.

Listing 15.1 Listing VMFS Snapshot of a Spanned Datastore

```
esxcli storage vmfs snapshot list
4faeba13-6bf41bdd-6dd0-001f29e04d52
   Volume Name: LHN-LUN
   VMFS UUID: 4faeba13-6bf41bdd-6dd0-001f29e04d52
   Can mount: false
   Reason for un-mountability: some extents missing
   Can resignature: false
   Reason for non-resignaturability: some extents missing
   Unresolved Extent Count: 1
```

Notice that the reasons for un-mountability and for non-resignaturability are both some extents missing.

This protects accidental resignaturing of any of the extents of a spanned VMFS volume.

How to Handle VMFS Datastore on Snapshot LUNs

For a snapshot LUN–based VMFS datastore to be mounted on an ESXi 5 host, it needs a new Volume UUID written to it (resignature) or to be force-mounted with its signature unmodified. The choice between both options depends on whether or not the primary LUN from which the snapshot LUN was taken is presented to the same host. If the primary and snapshot LUNs are not presented to the same host and will not be presented to it at any time in the future, it would be safe to force-mount the datastore. Otherwise, you must resignature the snapshot datastore before you mount it alongside its primary LUN. If you do not resignature the snapshot datastore, you are guaranteed to corrupt the datastore on both primary and snapshot LUNs accessed concurrently by the same host.

If you have multiple ESXi 5 hosts sharing a set of datastores, they all must access these datastores uniformly—that is, do not force-mount a snapshot on one host in the cluster while other hosts access the datastore on the primary LUN. vCenter Server has some validation checks in place to prevent this from happening as long as you do not manage any host in the cluster by logging in to it directly.

In ESX version 3.5 and older, there were LVM Advanced VMkernel options to resignature snapshot datastore in bulk or to allow them to be mounted unmodified. These options were LVM.EnableResignature and LVM.DisallowSnapshotLun, respectively. The first option enables automatic resignature of the snapshot datastores. The second option allows snapshot datastores to be mounted without resignature. These options are now hidden from the UI as well as ESXCLI in vSphere 5 and 4.x, and they have been replaced with per-datastore operations to provide better control and reduce accidental operations that might result in data corruption.

Resignature

The process to resignature a VMFS datastore is the same for both VMFS3 and VMFS5. It can be done via the user interface (UI) or ESXCLI.

Resignature a VMFS Datastore Using the UI

To resignature a VMFS Datastore using the UI, you may follow this procedure:

1. Log on to vCenter Server as an Administrator or root user.

2. In the inventory tree, select the ESXi host on which you will mount the datastore.

3. Click the **Configuration** tab; then select **Storage** under the Hardware section.

4. Click the **Datastores** button in the View pane and click the **Add Storage** link.

5. Select the **Disk/LUN** radio button in the Select Storage Type dialog and then click **Next.**

6. Select the LUN representing the snapshot and then click **Next.** (See Figure 15.2.)

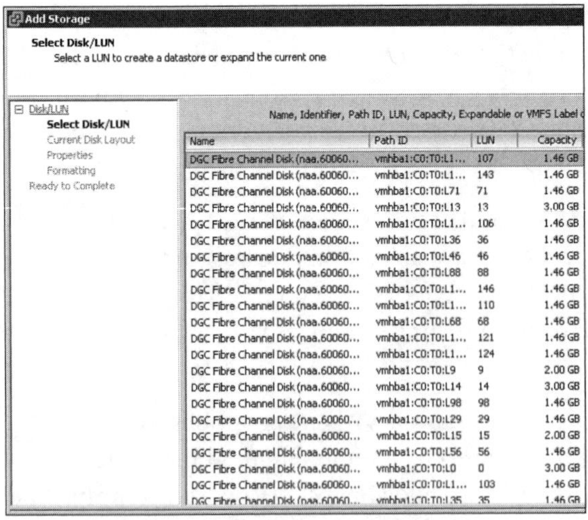

Figure 15.2   Select snapshot LUN

7. Select the **Assign a New Signature** radio button in the Add Storage dialog and then click **Next**. (See Figure 15.3.)

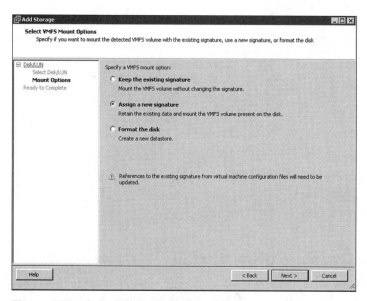

Figure 15.3   Selecting the resignature Option

8. Review the summary and click **Finish** (see Figure 15.4).

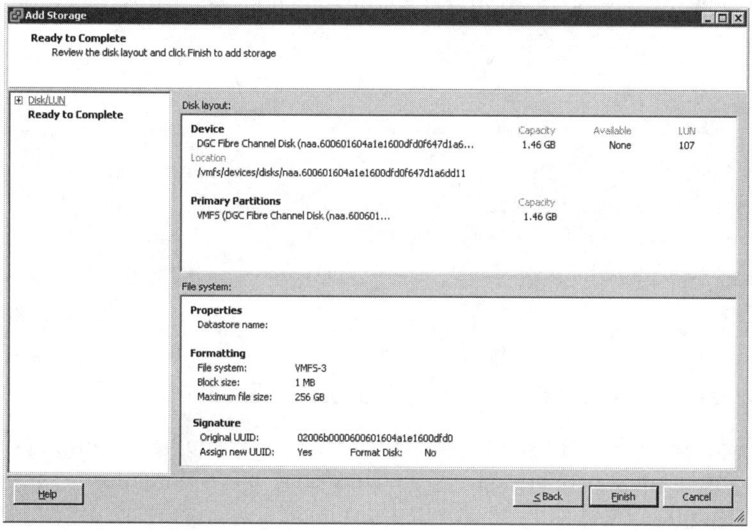

Figure 15.4   Review selections

The VMFS datastore is now mounted and renamed according to the convention `snap-<random-number>-<original-volume-name>` e.g. `snap-1ba3c456-Smallville`. (See Figure 15.5.)

Identification	Status	Device	Drive Type	Capacity
vmlibrary (read only)	Normal	10.131.7.247:vml...	Unknown	1.92 T
iSCSI_LUN0	Normal	DGC iSCSI Disk (...	Non-SSD	199.75 G
FC200	Normal	DGC Fibre Channel...	Non-SSD	199.75 G
Storage1	Alert	Local Dell Disk (n...	Non-SSD	63.00 G
snap-1ba3c456-Smallville	Normal	DGC Fibre Channel...	Non-SSD	9.75 G
esxi-nfs	Normal	10.131.9.85:/vol/...	Unknown	3.34 G

Figure 15.5   Snapshot datastore mounted

To use the VMs on this datastore, right-click the datastore, select the **Browse Datastore** menu, navigate to each VM directory, locate its vmx file, right-click it, and then select the **Add to Inventory** option.

Resignature a VMFS Datastore Using ESXCLI

Using ESXCLI to resignature VMFS datastores is a process done on all snapshot LUN–based datastores accessible by the host. It uses a hidden option which will be deprecated in future releases. This process is time consuming and takes longer, per datastore, than the time it takes to resignature and then mount the same datastore via the UI. Although this is a supported operation by VMware, it is not recommended for a large number of datastores if your Recovery Time Objective (RTO) is shorter than the time it takes for this operation to complete.

> **NOTE**
>
> VMware Site Recovery Manager does this process programmatically on the recovery site in a much shorter time compared to using ESXCLI. The reason behind the longer time experienced by ESXCLI is in how some of the APIs used by ESXCLI serialize certain operations and wait for acknowledgement of each operation. This is to guarantee data integrity and prevent race conditions.

Use the following steps to resignature and mount the datastore via ESXCLI:

1. Log on to ESXi locally via SSH or use the vMA 5.0 appliance. If you have multiple hosts on which to mount the resignatured VMFS datastores, it would be more practical to use vMA 5.0 as I will show you in this example.

2. Continuing with the example of using vMA, logged in as vi-admin user, run the vifp listservers command to verify that the ESXi host was previously added to the managed targets list (see Listing 15.2).

Listing 15.2 Listing vMA 5 Managed Targets

```
vifp listservers

wdc-tse-d98.wsl.vmware.com       ESXi
prme-iox215.eng.vmware.com       ESXi
wdc-tse-h56.wsl.vmware.com       ESXi
wdc-tse-i83.wsl.vmware.com       ESX
10.131.11.215                    vCenter
```

In this example, I have four ESXi hosts and one vCenter server registered on this vMA 5 appliance.

3. If the host you want to manage is not on the return list, you may add it using the vifp addserver option:

```
vifp addserver wdc-tse-i85.wsl.vmware.com --username root
```

You may also add a --password parameter. Otherwise, you get prompted for the password. If the operation is successful, no message is provided.

4. Set the target server to manage using vifptarget:

```
vi-admin@vma5:~> vifptarget --set wdc-tse-h56.wsl.vmware.com
vi-admin@vma5:~[wdc-tse-h56.wsl.vmware.com]>
```

Notice that the prompt now shows the name of the managed target host.

From this point on, the process is similar to that done via SSH or logged in locally to the host.

5. List the current setting of the /LVM/EnableResignature VSI node (see Listing 15.3).

Listing 15.3 Listing the Current EnableResignature Advanced System Setting

```
esxcli system settings advanced list --option /LVM/EnableResignature
   Path: /LVM/EnableResignature
   Type: integer
   Int Value: 0
   Default Int Value: 0
   Min Value: 0
```

```
Max Value: 1
String Value:
Default String Value:
Valid Characters:
Description: Enable Volume Resignaturing. This option will be deprecated
in future releases.
```

I highlighted the current value, which is 0. This means that the default ESXi host behavior is to not automatically resignature snapshot volumes.

Note that this parameter type is an integer. If you are logged in via SSH or locally on the ESXi host and you want to see the corresponding VSI node, you may run the command in Listing 15.4.

Listing 15.4   Listing EnableResignature VSI Node Content

```
vsish -e cat /config/LVM/intOpts/EnableResignature
Vmkernel Config Option {
    Default value:0
    Min value:0
    Max value:1
    Current value:0
    hidden config option:1
    Description:Enable Volume Resignaturing. This option will be deprecated
in future releases.
}
```

Note that because this is a configuration parameter, the root of its node is /config. Similarly, because the parameter type is integer, the VSI node is /config/LVM/intOpts/EnableResignature.

The highlighted text means Integer Options. If this node type were string, the node would have been /config/LVM/strOpts/<parameter> instead. LVM has no string type parameters. Also note from Listing 15.2 that the fields String Value and Default String Value are blank because the parameter type is Integer.

6. Change the value of the parameter from 0 to 1. This enables the host to automatically resignature snapshot datastores. To turn on the advanced setting /LVM/EnableResignature, you may run:

```
esxcli system settings advanced set -o /LVM/EnableResignature -i 1
```

Or you may use the verbose option:

```
esxcli system settings advanced set --option /LVM/EnableResignature
--int-value 1
```

7. The command does not return any messages if successful. To verify that the change took place, you may run

```
esxcli system settings advanced list -o /LVM/EnableResignature
```

See Listing 15.5 for the output.

Listing 15.5 Verifying the Outcome of Changing the `EnableResignature` Setting

```
esxcli system settings advanced list -o /LVM/EnableResignature
   Path: /LVM/EnableResignature
   Type: integer
   Int Value: 1
   Default Int Value: 0
   Min Value: 0
   Max Value: 1
   String Value:
   Default String Value:
   Valid Characters:
   Description: Enable Volume Resignaturing. This option will be deprecated
in future releases.
```

8. Rescan the host for datastore, which automatically resignatures the discovered snapshot datastores (see Listing 15.6).

Listing 15.6 Rescanning for Datastores

```
vmkfstools -V

Rescanning for new Vmfs on host

Successfully Rescanned for new Vmfs on host
```

9. Resignatured datastore should be mounted by now. To verify that, run

```
esxcli storage filesystem list |grep 'UUID\|---\|snap' |less -S
```

See Figure 15.6 for the output of this command.

Figure 15.6   Listing mounted snapshots

I truncated the output for readability. The missing columns are **Mount Point**, **Size,** and **Free**. If you compare the UUID to the original VMFS volume, you should notice the new one listed here.

To mount the snapshot LUNs on other hosts, repeat only Steps 4 and 8 if the other hosts share the same datastores you just resignatured.

Force Mount

Force-mounting a snapshot datastore is simply mounting it without modifying its signature. I reiterate that you must never do that on the same host that has the original datastore mounted.

The process for force-mounting a datastore snapshot is similar to the earlier procedure "Resignature a VMFS Datastore Using the UI" with the following differences:

1. In Step 7, select the **Keep the Existing Signature** radio button (see Figure 15.7).

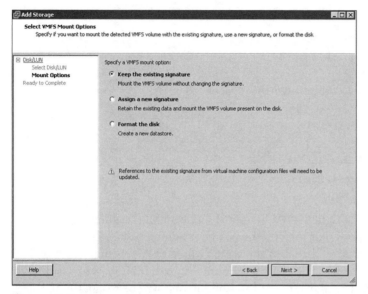

Figure 15.7 Force-mounting a snapshot

2. The VMFS datastore signature and name are retained.

Force-Mounting VMFS Snapshot Using ESXCLI

The process of force-mounting a VMFS snapshot using ESXCLI can be summarized as the following: obtain a list of datastores identified as snapshots (also referred to as *unresolved volumes*) and then mount each using the datastore name.

To do that, follow this procedure. You may adapt the sample script listed in the next section to automate the process.

1. Follow Steps 1–4 under the "Resignature VMFS Datastore Using ESXCLI" section earlier in this chapter.

2. To get a list of snapshot datastores, run

```
esxcli storage vmfs snapshot list
```

This returns a list of snapshot datastores (see Listing 15.7).

Listing 15.7   Listing Snapshot Datastores Using ESXCLI

```
esxcli storage vmfs snapshot list
4faeba13-6bf41bdd-6dd0-001f29e04d52
   Volume Name: LHN-LUN
   VMFS UUID: 4faeba13-6bf41bdd-6dd0-001f29e04d52
   Can mount: true
   Reason for un-mountability:
   Can resignature: true
   Reason for non-resignaturability:
   Unresolved Extent Count: 1
```

The output shows the original VMFS volume name and its original UUID (signature). It also shows that the volume can be mounted because there is no reason for un-mountability listed. In the same fashion, it shows that it can be resignatured because there is no reason for non-resignaturability. The last line in the output is the number of extents of this volume that will be resignatured.

If the original volume is still online, the volume will not be mounted until it is resignatured. Again, this is to safeguard the mounted datastore from corruption if the snapshot and the original datastore were both mounted.

To identify this case, you may run the previous command. Listing 15.8 shows the output of this command in this case.

Listing 15.8   Listing Reasons for Un-mountability

```
esxcli storage vmfs snapshot list
4faeba13-6bf41bdd-6dd0-001f29e04d52
   Volume Name: LHN-LUN
   VMFS UUID: 4faeba13-6bf41bdd-6dd0-001f29e04d52
   Can mount: false
   Reason for un-mountability: the original volume is still online
   Can resignature: true
   Reason for non-resignaturability:
   Unresolved Extent Count: 1
```

In this example, there is a reason for un-mountability, which is that the original volume is still online, and no reason for non-resignaturability.

Another case is where more than one snapshot of the original LUN extent or extents are presented to the same host. You would get the output in Listing 15.9.

Listing 15.9   Listing Duplicate Extent Case

```
4faeba13-6bf41bdd-6dd0-001f29e04d52
    Volume Name: LHN-LUN
    VMFS UUID: 4faeba13-6bf41bdd-6dd0-001f29e04d52
    Can mount: false
    Reason for un-mountability: duplicate extents found
    Can resignature: false
    Reason for non-resignaturability: duplicate extents found
    Unresolved Extent Count: 2
```

3. Mount each datastore identified in Step 2 using

   ```
   esxcli storage vmfs snapshot mount --volume-label=<volume-label>
   ```

   or the shorthand version:

   ```
   esxcli storage vmfs snapshot mount -l <volume-label>
   ```

   You may also use the datastore's UUID:

   ```
   esxcli storage vmfs snapshot mount --volume-uuid=<volume-UUID>
   ```

   or the shorthand version:

   ```
   esxcli storage vmfs snapshot mount -u <volume-UUID>
   ```

4. Verify that the datastores have been mounted by running

   ```
   esxcli storage filesystem list |less -S
   ```

Sample Script to Force-Mount All Snapshots on Hosts in a Cluster

The following script (Listing 15.10) is a sample PERL script that can be adapted to your environment to force-mount all snapshots on hosts that are members of a specific cluster. It was built based on examples shipped with vMA 5 appliance and are located in the /opt/vmware/vma/samples/perl directory. This script is usable on vMA 5.0 only. You must change the managed host to be the vCenter Server before running this script.

It does the following:

1. Takes in the cluster name as an argument.

2. Obtains the list of hosts in this cluster from vCenter Server.

3. On each host on the list from Step 2, runs `vmkfstools -V` to scan for VMFS datastores.

4. On each host on the list from Step 2, gets a list of snapshot of volumes using

   `esxcli storage vmfs snapshot list`

5. On each host on the list from Step 2, persistently mounts the datastores from the list in Step 4.

The syntax for using this script is

`mountAllsnapshots.pl --cluster <cluster-name>`

For example:

`mountAllsnapshots.pl --cluster BookCluster`

Listing 15.10   Sample PERL Script That Mounts All Snapshot Volumes on a List of Hosts in a Cluster

```
#!/usr/bin/perl -w

# mountAllsnapshots script
# Copyright © VMware, Inc. All rights reserved.
# You may modify this script as long as you maintain this
# copyright notice.
# This sample demonstrates how to get a list of all VMFS
# snapshots # on a set of hosts that are members of a vCenter
# cluster using "esxcli storage vmfs snapshot -l" command then
# mount them using "esxcli storage vmfs snapshot mount -l"
# command.
# Use at your own risk! Test it first and often.
# Make sure to not mount any VMFS volume and its snapshot on
# the same host.

use strict;
use warnings;
use VMware::VIRuntime;
use VMware::VILib;

my %opts = (
   cluster => {
      type => "=s",
      help => "Cluster name (case sensitive)",
```

```perl
      required => 1,
   },
);
Opts::add_options(%opts);

Opts::parse();
Opts::validate();
Util::connect();

# Obtain all inventory objects of the specified type
my @lines;
my $cluster = Opts::get_option('cluster');
my $clusters_view = Vim::find_entity_views(view_type => "ComputeResource");
my $found = 0;

foreach my $cluster_view (@$clusters_view) {
   # Process the findings and output to the console
   if ($cluster_view->name eq $cluster) {
      print "Cluster $cluster found!\n";
      my $hosts = Vim::find_entity_views(view_type => "HostSystem",
                                       begin_entity => $cluster_view);

      foreach my $host_view  (@$hosts) {
         my $host_name = $host_view->name;
         push(@lines, $host_name);
      }
      $found = 1;
   }
}

if ($found eq 0) {
   print STDERR "Cluster $cluster not found!\n";
   exit 1;
}

# Disconnect from the server
Util::disconnect();

if ((!defined $ENV{'LD_PRELOAD'}) ||
    ($ENV{'LD_PRELOAD'} !~ /\/opt\/vmware\/vma\/lib64\/libvircli.so/ )) {
```

```perl
    print STDERR "Error: Required libraries not loaded. \n";
    print STDERR "       Try mountAllsnapshots command after running ";
    print STDERR "\"vifptarget -s | --set <server>\"  command.\n";

    exit 1;
}

my $command;
my $err_out = "";
my @out;
my $TERM_MSG = "\nERROR:   Terminating\n\n";

foreach my $line (@lines){
    if($err_out eq $TERM_MSG) {
        print STDERR $err_out;
        last;
    }

    if($line) {
        print "Mounting all snapshot volumes on ". $line ."\n";

        #step1:  perform rescan
        $command = "vmkfstools";
        $command = $command . " --server " . $line . " " . "-V";
        $err_out = `$command 2>&1`;

        #step2:  list all snapshots
        $command = "esxcli";
        $command = $command . " --server " . $line . " " . "storage vmfs
snapshot -l";
        @out = `$command`;

        #step3: mount all listed snapshots.
        foreach my $ol (@out) {
            if ($ol =~ /([0-9a-f]{8}-[0-9a-f]{8}-[0-9a-f]{4}-[0-9a-f]{12})/) {
                $command = "esxcli";
                $command = $command . " --server " . $line . " " . "storage
vmfs snapshot mount -l $1";
                $err_out = `$command 2>&1`;
```

```
            }
        }

        if ($?) {
            if ( $! ) {
                print STDERR ": ".$!;
                $err_out = $TERM_MSG;
            } else {
                print STDERR $err_out."\n";
                if ($err_out =~ /Common VI options:/) {
                    $err_out = $TERM_MSG;
                }
            }
        } else {
            print STDOUT $err_out."\n";
        }
        print "\n";
    }
}

exit 0;
```

Summary

This chapter covered an overview of storage snapshots, replication, and mirroring. I explained the effect of these storage features on VMFS datastore signature and how vSphere handles them. I also included a sample PERL script to force-mount all snapshot datastores on hosts that are members of the same cluster.

## Chapter 16

VAAI

As vSphere 5 environments get larger and larger, the amount of data it handles gets even larger. This can have a negative effect on input/output (I/O) throughput and bandwidth as several operations done frequently by ESXi servers demand processing cycles and erode into valuable bandwidth. VMware designed a set of application programming interfaces (APIs) to offload most of the storage processing and bandwidth to the storage arrays, which frees up precious central processing unit (CPU) cycles and storage area network (SAN) /data local area network (LAN) bandwidth and allocates it to where it is needed.

This set of APIs is referred to VMware vStorage APIs for Array Integration (VAAI) . They utilize the T10 standard set of commands defined in SCSI Block Commands-3 (SBC-3).

What Is VAAI?

VAAI is a set of VMware vStorage APIs and new Small Computer System Interface (SCSI) commands designed to provide an efficient protocol between ESXi hosts and storage arrays that implement specific T10 standard commands. This is in addition to a set of fundamental storage operations (also known as primitives) that ESXi uses to speed up I/O operations that are more efficiently accomplished by the storage hardware. The ESXi host utilizes these primitives to improve performance of data transfer (also known as data mover) via standard T10 VAAI functions built in to the VMkernel and, for some primitives, via VAAI plug-ins installed on the ESXi host. The storage array must implement the VAAI T10 standard commands in its firmware in order to support some or all of the VAAI primitives.

In comparison, VAAI was implemented on ESX and ESXi 4.1 mainly via VAAI plug-ins built by VMware as well as some of the storage vendors that certified their arrays with that release for VAAI. Those that did not develop a plug-in were able to use the VMware-provided standard T10 plug-in named VMW_VAAIP_T10, which supported only the block zeroing primitive.

VAAI Primitives

vSphere 5 supports two groups of APIs: hardware acceleration and array thin provisioning APIs.

Hardware Acceleration APIs

Hardware acceleration APIs enable ESXi 5 hosts to offload the following primitives to the storage hardware:

- Block storage devices that support the following primitives:
  - Full Copy (also known as XCOPY)
  - Block zeroing (also known as WRITE_SAME)
  - Hardware assisted locking using Atomic Test and Set (ATS)

- NAS devices that support the following primitives:
  - Full file clone
  - Lazy file clone
  - Reserve space
  - Extended file statistics

More detail is provided later in this chapter.

Thin Provisioning APIs

Block devices have no visibility into the virtual machine file system (VMFS) structure or file allocation. For a VMFS volume that resides on a thin provisioned logical unit number (LUN), ESXi 5 has no way of identifying when the LUN is unable to grow on the storage array due to lack of disk space. In the reverse direction, the ESXi host has no way of informing the storage array of deleted blocks on the VMFS volume. This means that because the storage array is unaware of freed blocks on the thin LUN, it cannot reclaim them to make room for this or other LUNs' growth.

vSphere 5 introduced thin provisioning APIs to bridge the gap between the ESXi host and block device–based storage arrays.

These APIs provide the following primitives:

1. Dead space reclamation (also known as UNMAP)

2. Used space monitoring to avoid running out of space for LUN growth

More detail is provided later in this chapter.

Full Copy Primitive (XCOPY)

One of the most taxing operations on VMFS datastores is cloning or copying virtual disks. This is also known as *full clone*. It involves reading the virtual disks' blocks and then sending the copied blocks over the network (Fibre Channel (FC) Fabric, Internet Small Computer System Interface (iSCSI), or Fibre Channel over Ethernet (FCoE) network); then the array allocates the needed blocks and writes to them. This process, which uses the software DataMover, requires compute resources on the host, network bandwidth, as well as storage array port and LUN queues. DataMover is the VMkernel component that handles the block copy process in the absence of VAAI hardware acceleration.

The full copy primitive eliminates most of these operations by doing the following:

1. The host identifies the range of blocks to be copied and sends the block addresses to the array as part of the XCOPY command.

2. The array starts the copy process on its end.

3. When done, the array informs the host that the operation is done.

This offloads the processing to the storage array, which reduces the host's overhead as well as network traffic.

Figure 16.1 shows a storage array processor and total bandwidth utilization from an EMC CLARiiON without VAAI and with VAAI.

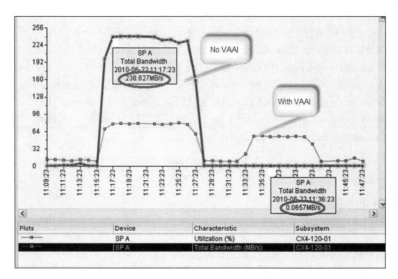

Figure 16.1   Comparing storage array performance with and without VAAI

It is clear from Figure 16.1 that the total bandwidth is significantly lower (close to zero) when VAAI is used. The storage processor utilization is slightly lower. The host CPU utilization overhead, which is not shown in this diagram, when VAAI is used is almost zero.

Block Zeroing Primitive (WRITE_SAME)

Zeroed thick is the default virtual disk format, which means that all the virtual disk blocks are preallocated but are not zeroed out at creation time. As the virtual machine (VM) writes to these blocks, zero pattern is written to them before writing the data. In the absence of VAAI, this process utilizes host CPU, storage processor, and bandwidth.

When you create an EagerZeroedThick virtual disk to avoid this, without VAAI it takes a long time for the file creation to complete. This is due to the fact that the host is writing zeros to all blocks. The larger the file, the longer it takes to complete the creation process. For additional details about virtual disk types, refer to Chapter 13, "Virtual Disks and RDMs."

Another example is the process of cloning a virtual disk and opting to use EagerZeroedThick as the target format. This operation is a combination of full clone and block zeroing. Without VAAI, the overhead is the combination of both operations.

With VAAI, the host sends the WRITE_SAME SCSI command to the array along with the range of blocks to be zeroed and the array writes the same pattern (zero) to all specified blocks. Some storage arrays have native features to accelerate this operation even more. Regardless, offloading the block zeroing operation to the storage array significantly reduces the host's CPU, memory, and network load from such operation.

Hardware Accelerated Locking Primitive (ATS)

The ATS primitive negates the need for SCSI-2 reservations during on-disk lock acquisition (see Chapter 14, "Distributed Locks"). The way ATS works is as follows:

1. The ESXi host needs to acquire an on-disk lock for a specific VMFS resource or resources.

2. It reads the block address on which it needs to write the lock record on the array.

3. If the lock is free, it atomically writes the lock record.

4. If the host receives an error—because another host may have beaten it to the lock—it retries the operation.

5. If the array returns an error, the host falls back to using a standard VMFS-locking mechanism using SCSI-2 reservations.

ATS Enhancements on VMFS5

When a VMFS5 volume is created on a LUN located on a storage array that supports ATS primitive, after an ATS operation is attempted successfully, the ATS Only attribute is written to the volume. From that point on, any host sharing this volume always uses ATS.

If, for whatever reason, the storage array no longer supports ATS—for example, firmware downgrade—all VMFS5 volumes configured with ATS Only will not be mounted and cannot be mounted. The only way to mount such volumes is either to upgrade the storage array firmware to a version that supports VAAI or disable the ATS Only attribute on the volume. To do the latter you may use the vmkfstools hidden option --configATSOnly.

```
vmkfstools --configATSOnly 0 /vmfs/devices/disks/<device-ID>:<Partition>
```

For example:

```
vmkfstools --configATSOnly 0 /vmfs/devices/disks/naa.6006016055711d00cff95e
65664ee011:1
```

You may re-enable the option by repeating this command using `1` instead of `0`. If you attempt to enable this on an upgraded VMFS5 volume, it fails with an error:

```
Only newly formatted VMFS-5 can be configured as ATS only
Error: Operation not supported
```

Thin Provisioned APIs

To better utilize thin provisioned block devices, vSphere 5 introduced vStorage APIs specific to such devices. These APIs are the UNMAP and Used Space Monitoring primitives:

- **UNMAP** — Deleted block reclamation primitive enables ESXi 5 hosts to report the list of deleted blocks on a VMFS datastore to the storage array. The latter can then reclaim these blocks from the thin provisioned LUN, which effectively reduces the thin LUN's used size to the actual used blocks.

- **Used Space Monitoring** — This primitive implements SCSI Additional Sense Code (ASC) and Additional Sense Code Qualifier (ASCQ) on the storage array's firmware that get sent to the hosts when a soft threshold and a hard threshold are reached. For example, the storage array is configured with a soft threshold of 20% of free space available for growing thin provisioned LUNs and a hard threshold of 10% of free space available. When the soft threshold is reached, the host receives a Check Condition with a sense key 0x6, an ASC of 0x38, and an ASCQ of 0x7. The host may then move the virtual disks to another datastore with sufficient space using storage DRS (Distributed Resource Scheduler). Otherwise, the host is allowed to continue to write to the LUN until the hard threshold is reached. This is reported to the host as a Check Condition with a sense key 0x7, an ASC 0x27, and an ASCQ 0x7. When that happens, the offending VM that wrote the last block that triggered the alarm is paused until free space is added or files moved out of the datastore.

- Used Space Monitoring enables the ESXi host to monitor the available space on which the thin provisioned LUN can grow. This is done in-band by receiving the status via the VAAI primitive. The host can then alert the administrator to plan to request adding space to the LUN or move files to another datastore before the LUN runs out of blocks on which the storage array can grow the thin provisioned LUN. Most storage vendors have opted to not use this primitive and instead use VASA-based reporting.

NAS VAAI Primitives

Another set of VAAI enhancements introduced in vSphere 5 are the Network Attach Storage (NAS) VAAI primitives. These primitives attempt to bring parity between NFS datastores and VMFS on block devices' VAAI capability.

The NAS VAAI primitives are Full file Clone and Reserve Space.

- **Full File Clone** — Equivalent to Block Device Clone Primitive (XCOPY). This allows offline virtual disks to be cloned by the NFS server.

- **Reserve Space** — This is equivalent to creating a thick virtual disk (preallocated) on NFS datastores. Typically, when you create a virtual disk on an NFS datastore, the NAS server determines the allocation policy. The default allocation policy on most NAS servers does not guarantee backing storage to the file. However, the reserve space operation can instruct the NAS device to use vendor-specific mechanisms to reserve space for a virtual disk of non-zero logical size.

If either of these two primitives fails, the host falls back to using the software DataMover as if VAAI is not supported. There is no ATS equivalent for NFS datastores.

- **Extended File Stats Primitive** —This allows the NAS filer to report accurate file stats to the host. This helps with reporting accurately thin provisioned virtual disks size as they grow.

Table 16.1 shows a comparison between NAS and block device primitives.

Table 16.1   Comparing NAS and Block Device Primitives

Use Case	NAS Primitives	Block Device Primitives
Create thick (pre-allocated) virtual disks	Reserve Space	No primitive is required. Native to the file system.
Hardware-assisted cloning (offline for NAS) of virtual disks (for example, cold migration, clone from a template)	Full File Clone	XCOPY and WRITE_SAME (full copy and block zeroing).
Hardware Accelerated Locking	N/A	ATS

Enabling and Disabling Primitives

Block VAAI primitives are enabled by default. However, you may need to disable one or more of the supported primitives as with the case of the UNMAP primitive. The latter was reported to have performance issues with implementation on some if not most of the supported storage arrays. As a result, VMware resorted to automatically disabling the UNMAP primitive upon installing ESXi 5 Patch 1 as well as Update 1.

NAS VAAI primitives are enabled by installing the vendor-specific NAS plug-ins. They are available as vSphere Installation Bundles (VIBs), which you can install using Update Manager or the following command on the ESXi host directly. To obtain the VIB, check the VMware HCL listing for the device, which includes a link to the storage vendor's download and installation instructions. (See the "Locating Supported VAAI-Capable NAS Devices" section for HCL (Hardware Compatibility List) details).

To install the VIB, first go through a dry run using the following:

```
esxcli software vib install -d /<path-vib-file>/<VIB-file-name> --dry-run
```

Example:

```
esxcli software vib install -d /vmfs/volumes/LHN-LUN/VMW-ESX-5.0.0-
NetAppNasPlugin-1.0-offline_bundle-710073.zip --dry-run
```

You may also use the verbose option `--depot` instead of `--d`.

This goes through the process of installing the VIB without actually installing it. I always prefer to do that to see if I run into any errors and to also identify if the host needs rebooting. The output of the dry run command is shown in Listing 16.1.

Listing 16.1   VIB Installation Dry Run

```
esxcli software vib install -d /vmfs/volumes/LHN-LUN/VMW-ESX-5.0.0-
NetAppNasPlugin-1.0-offline_bundle-710073.zip --dry-run
Installation Result
   Message: Dryrun only, host not changed. The following installers will be
applied: [BootBankInstaller]
   Reboot Required: true
   VIBs Installed: NetApp_bootbank_NetAppNasPlugin_1.0-018
   VIBs Removed:
   VIBs Skipped:
```

From this output, I can conclude that there are no errors and that the host requires rebooting. So, I have to plan a downtime for the installation.

When ready, run the same command without the `--dry-run` option to install the VIB (see Listing 16.2).

Listing 16.2   Installing the NAS VAAI Plug-in VIB

```
esxcli software vib install -d /vmfs/volumes/LHN-LUN/VMW-ESX-5.0.0-
NetAppNasPlugin-1.0-offline_bundle-710073.zip
Installation Result
   Message: The update completed successfully, but the system needs to be
rebooted for the changes to be effective.
   Reboot Required: true
   VIBs Installed: NetApp_bootbank_NetAppNasPlugin_1.0-018
   VIBs Removed:
   VIBs Skipped:
```

You can disable the block device primitives using the user interface (UI) or the command-line interface (CLI).

Disabling Block Device Primitives Using the UI

You can configure VAAI block device primitives' settings via the Advanced VMkernel Configuration option as follows:

1. Log on to vCenter Server as an Administrator or root user

2. In the inventory tree, select the ESXi host on which you will mount the datastore.

3. Click the **Configuration** tab.

4. Select Advanced Settings under the **Software** section.

5. Click the **VMFS3** node in the left pane. You should see the dialog in Figure 16.2.

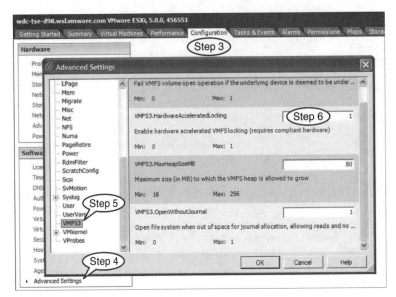

Figure 16.2   Modifying ATS VAAI primitives

6. Modify the value in the VMFS3.HardwareAcceleratedLocking field from 1 to 0.

7. Click the **DataMover** node in the left pane.

8. Modify the value of both listed fields from 1 to 0 and then click **OK**. (See Figure 16.3.)

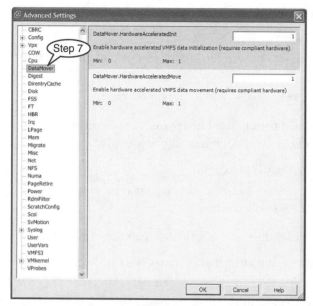

Figure 16.3   Modifying XCOPY and WRITE_SAME block device VAAI primitives

Disabling Block Device VAAI Primitives Using the CLI

If you have a large number of hosts you want to reconfigure to disable one or more of the VAAI block device primitives, you may use this procedure:

1. Log on to vMA appliance as vi-admin.

2. Run the `vifp listservers` command to verify that the ESXi hosts you want to modify were previously added to the managed targets list (see Listing 16.3).

Listing 16.3   Listing vMA 5 Managed Targets

```
vifp listservers


wdc-tse-d98.wsl.vmware.com        ESXi
prme-iox215.wsl.vmware.com        ESXi
wdc-tse-h56.wsl.vmware.com        ESXi
wdc-tse-i83.wsl.vmware.com        ESX
10.131.11.215                     vCenter
```

In this example, I have four ESXi hosts and one vCenter server registered on this vMA 5 appliance.

3. If the host you want to manage is not on the returned list, you may add it using the `vifp addserver` option:

```
vifp addserver wdc-tse-i85.wsl.vmware.com --username root
```

You may also add the `--password` parameter. Otherwise, you are prompted for the password. If the operation is successful, no message is provided.

4. Set the target server to manage using `vifptarget`:

```
vi-admin@vma5:~> vifptarget --set wdc-tse-h56.wsl.vmware.com
vi-admin@vma5:~[wdc-tse-h56.wsl.vmware.com] >
```

Notice that the prompt now shows the name of the managed target host.

From this point on, the process is similar to that done via SSH or logged in locally to the host.

5. List the current setting of the VAAI primitives' configuration (see Listing 16.4).

Listing 16.4 Listing Current VAAI Primitives Advanced System Setting

```
esxcli system settings advanced list -o /DataMover/HardwareAcceleratedMove
    Path: /DataMover/HardwareAcceleratedMove
    Type: integer
    Int Value: 1
    Default Int Value: 1
    Min Value: 0
    Max Value: 1
    String Value:
    Default String Value:
    Valid Characters:
    Description: Enable hardware accelerated VMFS data movement (requires
compliant hardware)


esxcli system settings advanced list -o /DataMover/HardwareAcceleratedInit
    Path: /DataMover/HardwareAcceleratedInit
    Type: integer
    Int Value: 1
    Default Int Value: 1
    Min Value: 0
    Max Value: 1
```

```
String Value:
Default String Value:
Valid Characters:
Description: Enable hardware accelerated VMFS data initialization
(requires compliant hardware)

esxcli system settings advanced list -o /VMFS3/HardwareAcceleratedLocking
    Path: /VMFS3/HardwareAcceleratedLocking
    Type: integer
    Int Value: 1
    Default Int Value: 1
    Min Value: 0
    Max Value: 1
    String Value:
    Default String Value:
    Valid Characters:
    Description: Enable hardware accelerated VMFS locking (requires
compliant hardware)
```

I highlighted the current value for each of the three primitives, which is 1.

Note that this parameter type is an integer (this is what int means).

6. Change the value of each of the parameters from 1 to 0 using the following command:

```
esxcli system settings advanced set -o /<node>/<parameter> -i 0
```

For example:

```
esxcli system settings advanced set -o /DataMover/
HardwareAcceleratedMove -i 0
```

```
esxcli system settings advanced set -o /DataMover/
HardwareAcceleratedinit -i 0
```

```
esxcli system settings advanced set -o /VMFS3/
HardwareAcceleratedLocking -i 0
```

This disables the corresponding primitive.

7. The command does not return any messages if successful. To verify that the change took place, repeat Step 5, which should return the value of 0 for each primitive.

8. Repeat Steps 4 –7 for each ESXi host.

Disabling the UNMAP Primitive Using the CLI

To disable the UNMAP primitive using the CLI, you may follow the previous procedure using this command in Step 5:

```
esxcli system settings advanced list -o /VMFS3/EnableBlockDelete
```

See Listing 16.5 for the output.

Listing 16.5   Verifying the Outcome of Changing the `EnableResignature` Setting

```
esxcli system settings advanced list -o /VMFS3/EnableBlockDelete
   Path: /VMFS3/EnableBlockDelete
   Type: integer
   Int Value: 1
   Default Int Value: 1
   Min Value: 0
   Max Value: 1
   String Value:
   Default String Value:
   Valid Characters:
   Description: Enable VMFS block delete
```

Replace Step 6 with this command:

```
esxcli system settings advanced set -o /VMFS3/EnableBlockDelete -i 0
```

You may also use the verbose version of this command as follows:

```
esxcli system settings advanced set --option /VMFS3/EnableBlockDelete
--int-value 0
```

Disabling NAS VAAI Primitives

NAS VAAI primitives cannot be disabled using specific configuration parameters like block device primitives do. The only way to disable them is by uninstalling the storage array vendor provided by VIB for the NAS primitives' support. You need to reboot the host to complete the removal process, so plan a downtime for that.

To uninstall a VIB, follow this procedure:

1. List the installed VIBs whose acceptance level is VMwareAccepted by using this command:

   ```
   esxcli software vib list |grep 'Name\|---\|Accepted'
   ```

Figure 16.4 shows a sample output.

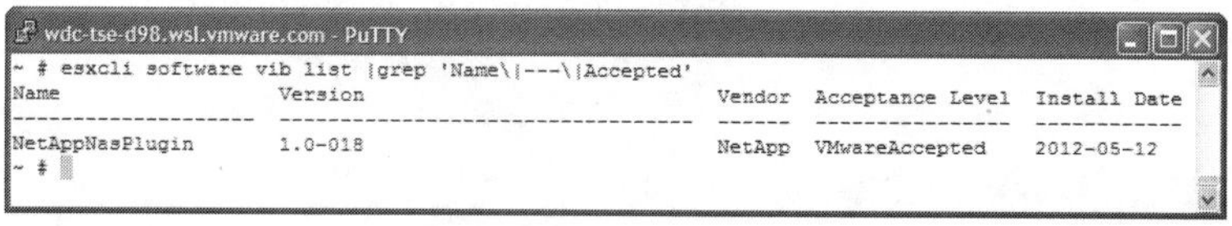

Figure 16.4   Listing installed partners' VIBs

2. If more than one VIB is listed in the output, identify which one is related to the NAS device (in this example, it is `NetAppNasPlugin`) and remove it using this command:

   ```
   esxcli software vib remove -n <VIB Name>
   ```

   Example:

   ```
   esxcli software vib remove -n NetAppNasPlugin
   ```

   It would be a good idea to try it first using the `--dry-run` option to determine what the removal results will be.

   The output of these commands is shown in Listing 16.6.

Listing 16.6   Removing NASS VAAI Plug-in VIB

```
esxcli software vib remove -n NetAppNasPlugin --dry-run
Removal Result
   Message: Dryrun only, host not changed. The following installers will be
applied: [BootBankInstaller]
   Reboot Required: true
   VIBs Installed:
   VIBs Removed: NetApp_bootbank_NetAppNasPlugin_1.0-018
   VIBs Skipped:


~ # esxcli software vib remove -n NetAppNasPlugin
Removal Result
   Message: The update completed successfully, but the system needs to be
rebooted for the changes to be effective.
   Reboot Required: true
   VIBs Installed:
   VIBs Removed: NetApp_bootbank_NetAppNasPlugin_1.0-018
   VIBs Skipped:
```

3. Reboot the host when done.

You may also use the verbose option `--vibname` instead of `-n` with this command.

VAAI Plug-ins and VAAI Filter

VAAI is handled on the host's end by PSA core plug-ins which are the following:

- **VAAI Filter**—VAAI Filter is a single plug-in installed by default on ESXi 5 hosts. It plugs into Pluggable Storage Architecture (PSA) framework side-by-side with Native Multipathing Plugins (NMP) and Multipathing Plugins (MPPs) (see Figure 16.5). All devices supporting VAAI get claimed first by the VAAI filter followed by VMkernel T10.

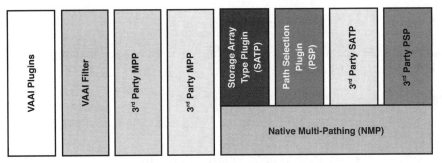

VMkernel Storage Stack
Pluggable Storage Architecture

Figure 16.5 PSA showing VAAI Plug-ins and Filter

- **VAAI plug-ins**—Storage arrays that do not fully implement the T10 standard commands can be supported with VAAI when the storage vendor creates and certifies a VAAI plug-in specific to their storage. Other storage arrays that support T10 do not require this plug-in because vmkernel in ESXi 5 integrates what used to be T10 Plugin in ESXi 4.1.

  These VAAI plug-ins sit along side the VAAI filter on top of a PSA framework. (See Figure 16.5.)

You may ask, how do I know if my storage array requires a VAAI plug-in?

This is easily answered by looking up the storage array on VMware HCL (also known as VMware Compatibility Guide or VCG), and the device details list the VAAI support status and whether or not plug-ins are required.

Locating Supported VAAI-Capable Block Devices

You may follow this procedure to look up the HCL:

1. Go to http://www.vmware.com/go/hcl.

2. Select **Storage/SAN** from the pull-down list in the **What Are You Looking For field.**

3. Select **ESXi 5.0** and/or **ESXi 5.0 U1** in the **Product Release Version field.**

4. Select **VAAI-Block** in the **Features Category** field.

5. Select the partner's name in the **Partner Name** field.

6. Click the **Update and View Results** button. (See Figure 16.6.)

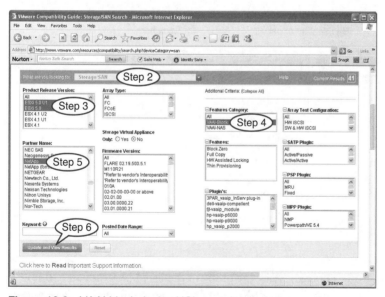

Figure 16.6   VAAI block device HCL search criteria

7. Scroll down to view the search results. Locate your storage array in the results and click the link with your ESXi release—for example, 5.0 or 5.0 U1 (see Figure 16.7).

Figure 16.7   Locating a certified VAAI-capable device on HCL

■ The array details are displayed. There you first click **View** under the Features column. This expands the array details to display the list of features including VAAI. Figure 16.8 shows a sample device that supports block zero, full copy, and HW assisted locking. However, the plug-in is blank. This means that the array implements T10 standard commands and does not require a special VAAI plug-in.

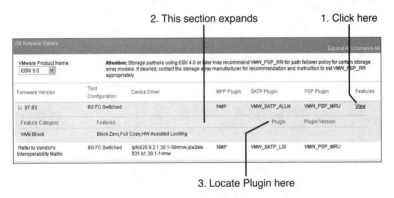

Figure 16.8   Displaying device details to locate VAAI plug-ins

■ If a VAAI plug-in were required, check the prefix of the listed plug-in name. If it is VMW, the plug-in is preinstalled on ESXi5 and no further configuration is required. (See Figure 16.9.) Otherwise, you may obtain the plug-in from the storage vendor and install it following the storage vendor's directions. In this example, 3PAR (now HP) storage arrays with 2.3.1 MU2 or higher firmware are certified for VAAI on vSphere 5.0 using the 3PAR_vaaip_inServ VAAI plug-in. The link to HP download portal is listed in the footnote. However, the same array with firmware version 3.1

does not require a specialized plug-in. This means that it supports T10 standard commands.

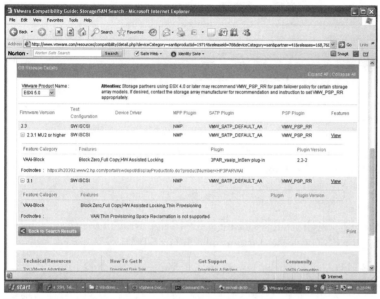

Figure 16.9   Listing device details showing no plug-in is required

Locating Supported VAAI-Capable NAS Devices

To locate a list of NAS devices that support NAS VAAI primitives, you may follow this procedure:

1. Go to http://www.vmware.com/go/hcl.

2. Select **Storage/SAN** from the pull-down list in the **What Are You Looking For field**.

3. Select **ESXi 5.0** and/or **ESXi 5.0 U1** in the **Product Release Version** field.

4. Select **VAAI-NAS** in the **Feature Category** field.

5. Select the partner's name in the **Partner Name** field.

6. Click the **Update and View Results** button. (See Figure 16.10.)

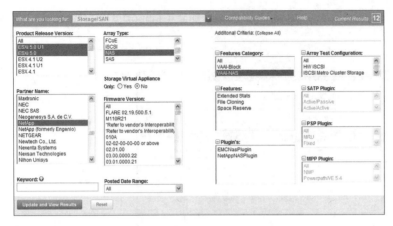

Figure 16.10   NAS VAAI HCL search criteria

7. Scroll down to view the search results. Locate your storage array in the results and click the link with your ESXi release (for example, 5.0 or 5.0 U1).

8. The array details are displayed. There, you first click **View** under the Features column. This expands the array details to display the list of features including VAAI. There you also find a footnote with instructions on how to obtain the plug-in VIB (see Figure 16.11).

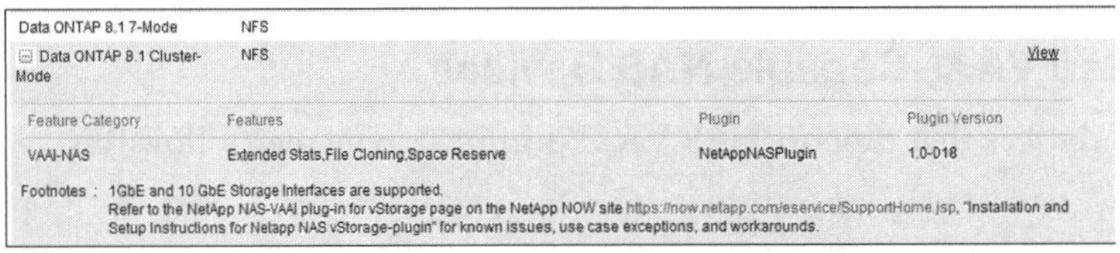

Data ONTAP 8.1 7-Mode	NFS		
⊟ Data ONTAP 8.1 Cluster-Mode	NFS		View

Feature Category	Features	Plugin	Plugin Version
VAAI-NAS	Extended Stats,File Cloning,Space Reserve	NetAppNASPlugin	1.0-016

Footnotes : 1GbE and 10 GbE Storage Interfaces are supported.
Refer to the NetApp NAS-VAAI plug-in for vStorage page on the NetApp NOW site https://now.netapp.com/eservice/SupportHome.jsp, "Installation and Setup Instructions for Netapp NAS vStorage-plugin" for known issues, use case exceptions, and workarounds.

Figure 16.11   Device details showing NAS plug-in HCL

After downloading the plug-in VIB, follow the vendor's directions for installing it. This may require a host reboot, so plan a downtime for doing that. See the "Enabling VAAI Primitives" section earlier in this chapter for an example.

Listing Registered Filter and VAAI Plug-ins

Preinstalled and newly installed VAAI Filter and VAAI plug-ins are actually vmkernel modules that get registered with the PSA framework. You may list the registered plug-ins using

```
esxcli storage core plugin registration list |grep 'Module\|---\|VAAI'
```

Figure 16.12 shows the output.

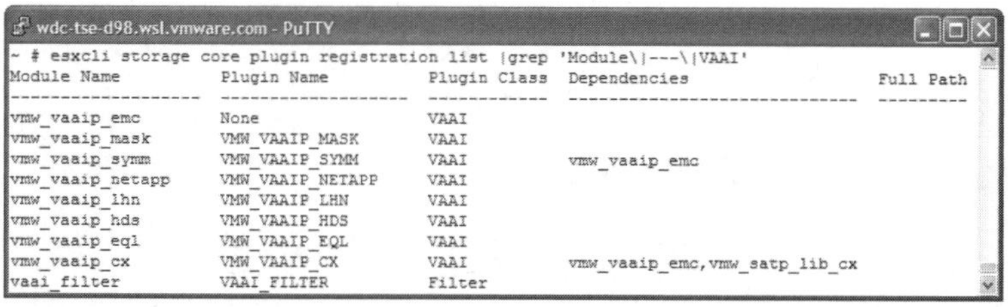

Figure 16.12   Listing VAAI plug-in registration

In this example, I have VAAI Filter registered along with VAAI plug-ins for symm, netapp, lhn, hds, eql, and cx. They are the plug-ins for EMC Symmetrix, NetApp, LeftHand Network (now HP), HDS, EQL (now Dell), and CLARiiON CX family, respectively. There is also vmw_vaaip_mask plug-in. This is used for masking devices from being claimed by VAAI. I discuss all these plug-ins in the next section.

NOTE

If you observe the Plugin Name column, you should notice that it is blank for the vmw_vaaip_emc module. The values in the Dependencies column show that the vmw_vaaip_symm module has a dependency on vmw_vaaip_emc. The same is true for vmw_vaaip_cx, which is also dependent on the vmw_satp_lib_cx library module.

In this example, the dependency is on a common library used by EMC storage–specific VAAI plug-ins. These types of libraries are installed by the VAAI plug-in installer or are already installed for VAAI plug-ins included with ESXi standard image.

Listing VAAI Filters and Plug-ins Configuration

For a device to be claimed by a VAAI plug-in, it must be first claimed by the VAAI Filter plug-in as shown in the output of

```
esxcli storage core claimrule list --claimrule-class=Filter
```

Or the shorthand version

```
esxcli storage core claimrule list -c Filter
```

The parameter `Filter` must use an uppercase *F*. Figure 16.13 shows the output of this command.

```
~ # esxcli storage core claimrule list -c Filter
Rule Class    Rule   Class    Type    Plugin        Matches
----------    -----  -------  ------  -----------   -----------------------------
Filter        65429  runtime  vendor  VAAI_FILTER   vendor=MSFT model=Virtual HD
Filter        65429  file     vendor  VAAI_FILTER   vendor=MSFT model=Virtual HD
Filter        65430  runtime  vendor  VAAI_FILTER   vendor=EMC model=SYMMETRIX
Filter        65430  file     vendor  VAAI_FILTER   vendor=EMC model=SYMMETRIX
Filter        65431  runtime  vendor  VAAI_FILTER   vendor=DGC model=*
Filter        65431  file     vendor  VAAI_FILTER   vendor=DGC model=*
Filter        65432  runtime  vendor  VAAI_FILTER   vendor=EQLOGIC model=*
Filter        65432  file     vendor  VAAI_FILTER   vendor=EQLOGIC model=*
Filter        65433  runtime  vendor  VAAI_FILTER   vendor=NETAPP model=*
Filter        65433  file     vendor  VAAI_FILTER   vendor=NETAPP model=*
Filter        65434  runtime  vendor  VAAI_FILTER   vendor=HITACHI model=*
Filter        65434  file     vendor  VAAI_FILTER   vendor=HITACHI model=*
Filter        65435  runtime  vendor  VAAI_FILTER   vendor=LEFTHAND model=*
Filter        65435  file     vendor  VAAI_FILTER   vendor=LEFTHAND model=*
~ #
```

Figure 16.13   Listing VAAI Filter claim rules

To verify if a VAAI plug-in has been installed, you can list the VAAI claim rules using this command:

```
esxcli storage core claimrule list --claimrule-class=VAAI
```

Or the shorthand version

```
esxcli storage core claimrule list -c VAAI
```

Note that the parameter `VAAI` must be all uppercase. Also, the long-hand version of the option `--claimrule-class` can be used with or without the equal sign. vSphere 4.1 required the equal sign. The shorthand version is documented without the equal sign. However, it accepts it if used. In other words, both the long-hand and shorthand versions of the command can be used with or without the equal sign.

Figure 16.14 show the output of this command.

```
wdc-tse-h56.wsl.vmware.com - PuTTY
~ # esxcli storage core claimrule list -c VAAI
Rule Class   Rule   Class    Type     Plugin             Matches
----------   -----  -------  ------   ----------------   --------------------------
VAAI         65429  runtime  vendor   VMW_VAAIP_MASK     vendor=MSFT model=Virtual
VAAI         65429  file     vendor   VMW_VAAIP_MASK     vendor=MSFT model=Virtual
VAAI         65430  runtime  vendor   VMW_VAAIP_SYMM     vendor=EMC model=SYMMETRIX
VAAI         65430  file     vendor   VMW_VAAIP_SYMM     vendor=EMC model=SYMMETRIX
VAAI         65431  runtime  vendor   VMW_VAAIP_CX       vendor=DGC model=*
VAAI         65431  file     vendor   VMW_VAAIP_CX       vendor=DGC model=*
VAAI         65432  runtime  vendor   VMW_VAAIP_EQL      vendor=EQLOGIC model=*
VAAI         65432  file     vendor   VMW_VAAIP_EQL      vendor=EQLOGIC model=*
VAAI         65433  runtime  vendor   VMW_VAAIP_NETAPP   vendor=NETAPP model=*
VAAI         65433  file     vendor   VMW_VAAIP_NETAPP   vendor=NETAPP model=*
VAAI         65434  runtime  vendor   VMW_VAAIP_HDS      vendor=HITACHI model=*
VAAI         65434  file     vendor   VMW_VAAIP_HDS      vendor=HITACHI model=*
VAAI         65435  runtime  vendor   VMW_VAAIP_LHN      vendor=LEFTHAND model=*
VAAI         65435  file     vendor   VMW_VAAIP_LHN      vendor=LEFTHAND model=*
~ #
```

Figure 16.14   Listing VAAI plug-in claim rules

In this example, only in-box plug-ins have been preinstalled on this host. The claim rules have a similar structure to the NMP claim rules discussed in Chapter 5, "VMware Pluggable Storage Architecture (PSA)," in the "MP Claim Rules" section. To recap, when a device is discovered by the PSA framework, the rule is matched to its corresponding VAAI plug-in by the Vendor and Model strings identified from the response to the INQUIRY command.

For example, in this output an HP P4000 is a LeftHand Network storage array that returns a Vendor string LEFTHAND and any model will be claimed by the VMW_VAAIP_LHN plug-in.

TIP

One of the plug-ins listed in Figure 16.14 is VMW_VAAIP_MASK. If you have a family of storage arrays that share the same Vendor and Model strings and you want to prevent the ESXi5 host from using VAAI with it, you may add a claim rule for VMW_VAAIP_MASK with a number smaller than 65429.

An example of adding a VAAI MASK claim rule is

```
esxcli storage core claimrule add --rule=65428 --type=vendor --plugin VMW_
VAAIP_MASK --vendor=EMC --claimrule-class=VAAI
```

Or the shorthand version:

```
esxcli storage core claimrule add -r 65428 -t vendor -P VMW_VAAIP_MASK -V
EMC -c VAAI
```

This adds a VAAI claim rule for the VMW_VAAIP_MASK plug-in to claim all devices whose Vendor string is EMC. Because that device already has a filter claim rule in place, you only need to add the VAAI claim rule.

The command does not return any feedback unless there is an error. To verify that the rule was added successfully, run this command:

```
esxcli storage core claimrule list -c VAAI
```

The output is shown in Figure 16.15.

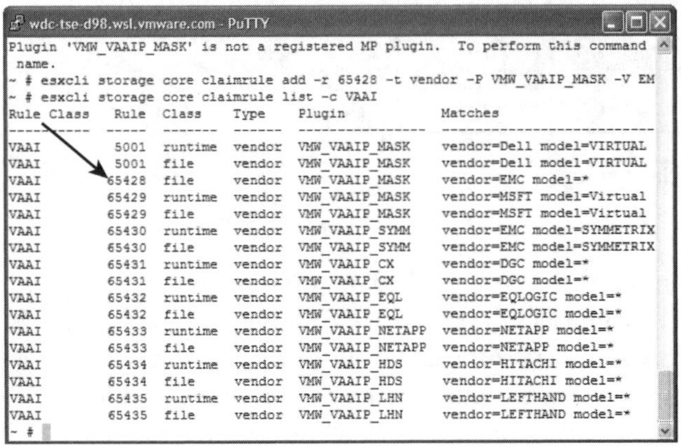

Figure 16.15   Result of adding a VAAIP_MASK claim rule

Because rule number 65428 is lower than the existing VAAI claim rule number 65430 for the EMC devices, the MASK claim rule claims all EMC devices instead of being claimed by the VMW_VAAIP_SYMM.

The only remaining step is to load the claim rule for it to take effect. To do that, run this command:

```
esxcli storage core claimrule load --claimrule-class=VAAI
```

Or you may use the shorthand version:

```
esxcli storage core claimrule load -c VAAI
```

The command does not return any feedback unless there is an error.

To verify the outcome, run:

```
esxcli storage core claimrule list -c VAAI
```

The output is shown in Figure 16.16.

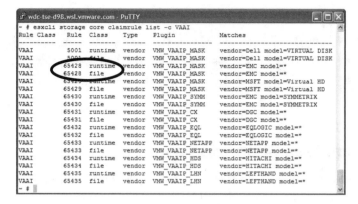

Figure 16.16   VAAI MASK claim rule loaded

Similar to MP claim rules, the class column of the output of loaded VAAI claim rules shows runtime as well as file.

Listing VAAI vmkernel Modules

As I mentioned earlier, VAAI plug-ins and the VAAI Filter plug-in are vmkernel modules. To list these modules you may run:

```
esxcli system module list |grep 'Name\|---\|vaaip'
```

Listing 16.7 shows the output.

Listing 16.7   Listing VAAI vmkernel Modules

```
esxcli system module list |grep 'Name\|---\|vaai'
Name                  Is Loaded  Is Enabled
-------------------   ---------  ----------
vaai_filter              true        true
vmw_vaaip_mask           true        true
vmw_vaaip_emc            true        true
vmw_vaaip_cx             true        true
vmw_vaaip_netapp         true        true
vmw_vaaip_lhn            true        true
```

> **NOTE**
>
> The output in Listing 16.7 shows only the modules related to devices connected to this ESXi host as well as the mask and filter plug-ins. In other words, the VAAI plug-in modules are loaded on demand.

Identifying VAAI Primitives Supported by a Device

When a device is first discovered, its support for VAAI primitives is ***unknown***. Periodically, the ESXi host checks the device for support of each VAAI primitive. If the device supports a given primitive, it is identified as **supported**. Otherwise, it is identified as **not supported**.

You may list the current VAAI support status of one or more devices using the CLI and the UI.

Listing Block Device VAAI Support Status Using the CLI

VAAI is one of the name spaces of ESXCLI, which is

```
esxcli storage core device vaai
```

The only available option for this command is `status` with a suboption of `get`.

So, the full command would be

```
esxcli storage core device vaai status get
```

Listing 16.8 shows the output of this command.

Listing 16.8   Listing VAAI Support Status

```
esxcli storage core device vaai status get

naa.60a98000572d54724a346a643979466f
    VAAI Plugin Name: VMW_VAAIP_NETAPP
    ATS Status: supported
    Clone Status: supported
    Zero Status: supported
    Delete Status: supported

mpx.vmhba1:C0:T0:L0
```

```
    VAAI Plugin Name:
    ATS Status: unsupported
    Clone Status: unsupported
    Zero Status: unsupported
    Delete Status: unsupported

naa.6001405497cd5c9b43f416e93da4a632
    VAAI Plugin Name:
    ATS Status: unsupported
    Clone Status: unsupported
    Zero Status: supported
    Delete Status: unsupported
```

If you want to limit the output to a single device, you may use the `--device` or `-d` option along with the device ID.

An example is shown in Listing 16.9.

Listing 16.9   Listing a Single-Device VAAI Support

```
esxcli storage core device vaai status get -d naa.60a98000572d5472
4a34695755335033
naa.60a98000572d54724a34695755335033
    VAAI Plugin Name: VMW_VAAIP_NETAPP
    ATS Status: supported
    Clone Status: supported
    Zero Status: supported
    Delete Status: supported
```

Listing 16.9 shows three devices:

1. Device ID `naa.60a98000572d54724a346a643979466f` was claimed by the VMW_VAAIP_NETAPP plug-in and shows that four VAAI primitives are supported, which are ATS, Clone, Zero, and Delete. These correspond to hardware assisted locking, full copy, block zeroing, and dead space reclamation, respectively.

2. Device ID `mpx.vmhba1:C0:T0:L0` was not claimed by a specific VAAI plug-in and shows none of the VAAI primitives as supported. This device is locally attached to the host, which is why its ID is prefixed with mpx. This means a Generic (X) Multipathing (MP).

3. Device ID naa.6001405497cd5c9b43f416e93da4a632 was not claimed by a
specific VAAI plug-in. However, it shows that it supports only the ATS primitive.
This simply means that the device supports hardware assisted locking, but it does not
have a specific VAAI plug-in installed on the host. How did the ATS support show
up then? The reason is that on ESXi 5, vmkernel already includes support for T10
VAAI standard commands. This used to be provided via the VMW_VAAIP_T10
plug-in on ESXi 4.1. When it attempted all primitives, only ATS was successful.

You can list individual device properties, which include VAAI-related information. Listing
16.10 shows an example.

Listing 16.10   Listing Device Properties

```
esxcli storage core device list -d naa.60a9800042574b6a372441582d6b5937

naa.60a9800042574b6a372441582d6b5937
    Display Name: NETAPP iSCSI Disk (naa.60a9800042574b6a372441582d6b5937)
    Has Settable Display Name: true
    Size: 10240
    Device Type: Direct-Access
    Multipath Plugin: NMP
    Devfs Path: /vmfs/devices/disks/naa.60a9800042574b6a372441582d6b5937
    Vendor: NETAPP
    Model: LUN
    Revision: 810a
    SCSI Level: 4
    Is Pseudo: false
    Status: degraded
    Is RDM Capable: true
    Is Local: false
    Is Removable: false
    Is SSD: false
    Is Offline: false
    Is Perennially Reserved: false
    Thin Provisioning Status: yes
    Attached Filters: VAAI_FILTER
    VAAI Status: supported
    Other UIDs: vml.020001000060a9800042574b6a372441582d6b59374c554e202020
```

The highlighted three lines show that the LUN is thin provisioned, VAAI Filter has claimed it, and that it supports VAAI, respectively. However, this does not show which primitives are supported.

Listing NAS Device VAAI Support Status

NAS devices, support for VAAI can be listed using this command:

```
esxcli storage nfs list
```

Figure 16.17 shows a sample output of this command.

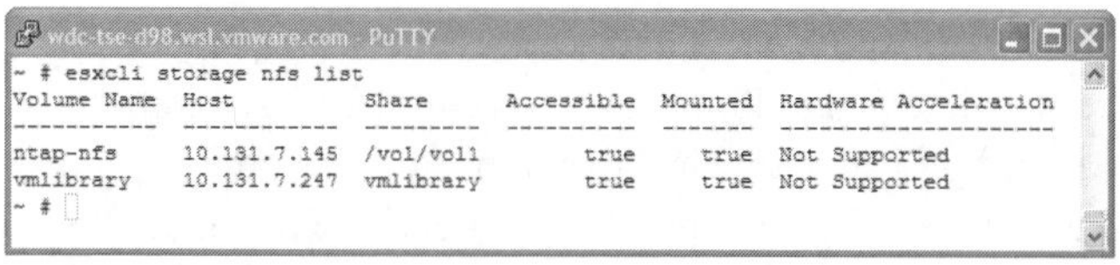

Figure 16.17   Listing NAS device VAAI support

In this output, the support status is listed under the hardware acceleration column.

Listing VAAI Support Status Using the UI

To list the devices, support status via the UI, use this procedure:

1. Log in to vCenter Server as an administrator user (for example, Administrator or root).

2. Navigate to and select the ESXi host in the inventory tree.

3. Select the **Configuration** tab and then select **Storage** under the Hardware pane.

4. If not already selected, click the **Datastores** button (see Figure 16.18).

Figure 16.18   Listing block and NAS devices, VAAI support

Figure 16.18 shows a combined list of NFS and VMFS datastores. The VAAI support status is listed under the Hardware Acceleration column. In this example, I have some devices showing status as Unknown and others showing Not Supported or Supported. If the block device on which VMFS datastore reside, supports all three of the block device VAAI primitives, the status is listed as Supported. Otherwise, if it supports fewer than the three block device primitives, it is listed as Unknown. If it supports none, it is listed as not supported. Table 16.2 shows a grid of support decisions.

If the NAS device exporting the NFS datastore supports VAAI and its corresponding plug-in is installed on the ESXi host, the Hardware Acceleration column would show a Supported status. Otherwise, it would show Not Supported.

> **NOTE**
>
> The Hardware Acceleration column is the last one in the list that would be outside the viewing pane in the resolution I used to take the screenshot of Figure 16.18. I moved it to the left by clicking on the column header and dragging it to the desired position.

Table 16.2   VAAI Support Status Decision

Support Status	ATS	Clone	Zero
Supported	Supported	Supported	Supported
Unknown	Not Supported	Supported	Supported
Unknown	Not Supported	Not Supported	Supported
Unknown	Supported	Not Supported	Supported
Not Supported	Not Supported	Not Supported	Not Supported

> **NOTE**
>
> I have not seen arrays that support ATS and/or Clone that do not support block zeroing. This is why I did not list the case where Zero is Not Supported other than in the last row where all three are not supported.

Displaying Block Device VAAI I/O Stats Using ESXTOP

To display I/O statistics, you may use esxtop directly on the ESXi host, via SSH, or using resxtop on vMA 5.0.

To display these stats, follow this procedure:

1. At the command prompt, type **esxtop**.

2. Press the letter **u**, which switches the view to Device Stats.

3. Press the letter **f**, which displays the list of column headers.

4. To toggle a column selection, press its corresponding letter (upper- or lowercase). When a column is selected, an asterisk (*) is displayed next to the column's letter. By default, A, B, F, G, and I are selected (see Listing 16.11).

Listing 16.11 Selecting Device I/O Stats Columns to Display in ESXTOP

```
Current Field order: ABcdeFGhIjklmnop

* A:   DEVICE = Device Name
* B:   ID = Path/World/Partition Id
  C:   NUM = Num of Objects
  D:   SHARES = Shares
  E:   BLKSZ = Block Size (bytes)
* F:   QSTATS = Queue Stats
* G:   IOSTATS = I/O Stats
  H:   RESVSTATS = Reserve Stats
* I:   LATSTATS/cmd = Overall Latency Stats (ms)
  J:   LATSTATS/rd = Read Latency Stats (ms)
  K:   LATSTATS/wr = Write Latency Stats (ms)
  L:   ERRSTATS/s = Error Stats
  M:   PAESTATS/s = PAE Stats
  N:   SPLTSTATS/s = SPLIT Stats
```

```
  O:   VAAISTATS= VAAI Stats
  P:   VAAILATSTATS/cmd = VAAI Latency Stats (ms)

Toggle fields with a-p, any other key to return:
```

5. Press the letters **B**, **F**, **G**, and **I** to deselect their corresponding columns (to save on display space).
6. Press the letter **O** to select the VAAI Stats column. If you want to display the latency stats, press the letter **P** as well. However, if your display is not wide enough for displaying all columns related to these two selections, I recommend selecting one at a time. So, for now, let's just select **O** only.
7. Press **Enter** to return to the stats display. Figure 16.19 shows the outcome.

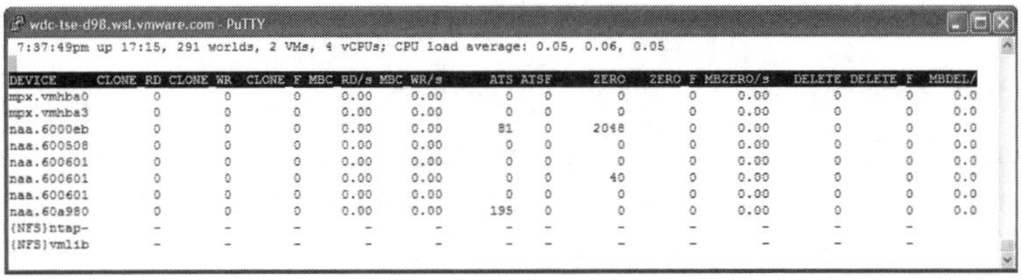
wdc-tse-d98.wsl.vmware.com - PuTTY

7:37:49pm up 17:15, 291 worlds, 2 VMs, 4 vCPUs; CPU load average: 0.05, 0.06, 0.05

DEVICE	CLONE RD	CLONE WR	CLONE F	MBC RD/s	MBC WR/s	ATS	ATSF	ZERO	ZERO F	MBZERO/s	DELETE	DELETE F	MBDEL/
mpx.vmhba0	0	0	0	0.00	0.00	0	0	0	0	0.00	0	0	0.0
mpx.vmhba3	0	0	0	0.00	0.00	0	0	0	0	0.00	0	0	0.0
naa.6000eb	0	0	0	0.00	0.00	81	0	2048	0	0.00	0	0	0.0
naa.600508	0	0	0	0.00	0.00	0	0	0	0	0.00	0	0	0.0
naa.600601	0	0	0	0.00	0.00	0	0	0	0	0.00	0	0	0.0
naa.600601	0	0	0	0.00	0.00	0	0	40	0	0.00	0	0	0.0
naa.600601	0	0	0	0.00	0.00	0	0	0	0	0.00	0	0	0.0
naa.60a980	0	0	0	0.00	0.00	195	0	0	0	0.00	0	0	0.0
{NFS}ntap-	-	-	-	-	-	-	-	-	-	-	-	-	
{NFS}vmlib	-	-	-	-	-	-	-	-	-	-	-	-	

Figure 16.19 Listing VAAI block device primitives stats in ESXTOP

> **NOTE**
>
> I had to reduce the device name column size to be able to display all the stats in the screenshot. I did that by entering **L** and then the size of the field. In this case, I set it to 10 characters. To reset it, repeat the same process using the size 0.

The columns listed in this view are

- **CLONE_RD**—Block clone (XCOPY) reads
- **CLONE_WR**—Block clone writes
- **CLONE_F**—Number of failed XCOPY commands
- **MBC_RD/s**—Megabytes of cloned data read per second
- **MBC_WR/s**—Megabytes of cloned data written per second

- **ATS**—Number of ATS successful commands

- **ATSF**—Number of failed ATS commands

- **ZERO**—Number of successful block zeroing (WRITE_SAME) commands

- **ZERO_F**—Number of failed block zeroing commands

- **MBZERO/s**—Megabytes zeroed per second

- **DELETE**—Number of successful deleted block reclamation commands

- **DELETE_F**—Number of failed deleted block reclamation commands

- **MBDEL/S**—Megabytes of deleted blocks reclaimed per second

If you had selected P in Step 6 to display the VAAI Latency Stats, the result would look similar to Figure 19.20.

```
 wdc-tse-d98.wsl.vmware.com - PuTTY
 7:41:28pm up 17:19, 300 worlds, 2 VMs, 4 vCPUs; CPU load average: 0.05, 0.05, 0.05

DEVICE                                  CAVG/suc    CAVG/f AAVG/suc  AAVG/f AVG/suc  ZAVG/f
mpx.vmhba0:C0:T0:L0                          0.00      0.00     0.00    0.00    0.00    0.00
mpx.vmhba32:C0:T0:L0                         0.00      0.00     0.00    0.00    0.00    0.00
naa.6000eb3ccb9840e9000000000000001d        0.00      0.00    11.19    0.00   33.16    0.00
naa.600508e000000000d4506d6dc4afad0d        0.00      0.00     0.00    0.00    0.00    0.00
naa.6006016047301a00eaed23f5884ee011        0.00      0.00     0.00    0.00    0.00    0.00
naa.6006016055711d00cef95e65664ee011        0.00      0.00     0.00    0.00    7.37    0.00
naa.6006016055711d00cff95e65664ee011        0.00      0.00     0.00    0.00    0.00    0.00
naa.60a9800042574b6a372441582d6b5937        0.00      0.00     0.93    0.00    0.00    0.00
{NFS}ntap-nfs                                  -         -        -       -       -       -
{NFS}vmlibrary                                 -         -        -       -       -       -
```

Figure 16.20   Listing block device VAAI latency in ESXTOP

The latency stats are self-explanatory. The following are the average times to complete a command measured in milliseconds:

- **CAVG/suc**—Successful clone average

- **CAVG/f**—Failed clone average

- **AAVG/suc**—Successful ATS average

- **AAVG/f**—Failed ATS average

- **AVG/suc**—This is actually ZAVG/suc, which is the latency of successful zero commands

- **ZAVG/f**—Failed zero command average

In general, you want a lower average for the successful commands (lower latency) and higher number of successful commands. Ideally, there should be no failed commands unless there is contention with a large number of hosts that can result in falling back to using software DataMover. If you see this scenario, you need to optimize your environment by spreading the load over more datastores—for example, using storage DRS with datastore clusters.

The VAAI T10 Standard Commands

I referenced VAAI T10 Standard SCSI commands throughout this chapter. If you would like to locate the T10 documentation, refer to the following links:

The ATS command (Atomic Compare and Write) is at

http://www.t10.org/cgi-bin/ac.pl?t=d&f=09-100r5.pdf

The Standard VAAI commands are specified in the SCSI Primary Commands-4 (SPC-4) document on T10 site at

http://www.t10.org/cgi-bin/ac.pl?t=f&f=spc4r35c.pdf

The remaining commands are OP-Codes (SCSI Operations Codes), which are in Table E.2 page 857 of the same SPC-4 document.

The WRITE_SAME op-code is 41h (0x41).

The UNMAP op-code is 42h (0x42).

A sample vmkernel log showing one of these commands is

```
cpu40:8232)ScsiDeviceIO: 2305: Cmd(0x41248092e240) 0x42, CmdSN 0x13bb23 to
dev "naa.60000970000292602427533030304536" failed H:0x0 D:0x2
```

The highlighted value represents the op-code, which means that the failed command was UNMAP.

Thin Provision Sense Codes appear in Table 56 in the SPC4 document (part 15 of 17).

These sense codes are for Out of Space (OOS) Warning and Out of Space (OOS) Error which are

- ASC 38h ASCQ 07h
- ASC 27h ASCQ 07h

respectively. (See the next section, "Troubleshooting VAAI Primitives," for some examples.)

This means thin provisioning soft threshold has been reached. This is the condition when a thin provisioned LUN on which a VMFS datastore resides reaches the preset soft threshold of available LUN expansion space on the array. The LUN may run out of space soon, and the vSphere administrator needs to take action to either free some space on the datastore and reclaim the deleted blocks or move some file to another datastore. This can be accomplished via storage DRS or manually via Storage vMotion.

Troubleshooting VAAI Primitives

One of the issues seen by the VMware Support Team is slow UNMAP performance.

Poor performance was reported to VMware when using the UNMAP primitive to reclaim deleted blocks. VMware identified that some implementation changes need to be done on most storage array vendors' firmware along with some changes on the ESXi side. Meanwhile, VMware released ESXi 5 Update 1 as well as Patch 1, which upon installation disables the UNMAP primitive. To reclaim the deleted blocks manually, you need to schedule a downtime to place the host in maintenance mode and then run this command:

```
cd/ vmfs/volume/<volume-name-to reclaim>
vmkfstools -y 70
```

This changes the current directory to the VMFS datastore on which you want to reclaim the deleted blocks. Then the `vmkfstools -y` command is run with the percentage of the deleted blocks you want to reclaim. In this example, I am reclaiming 70% of the deleted blocks. So, if I have 100GB of deleted block to reclaim, I reclaim 70GB of that space using the listed example.

This creates temporary files on the datastore and signals the storage array to reclaim the blocks. The temporary files get deleted after the operation is completed.

Sample Log Entries Related to VAAI

I mentioned the OOS warning in "Thin Provision APIs" section earlier in this chapter,.

An example /var/log/vmkernel.log message of an OOS warning is shown in Listing 16.12.

Listing 16.12 A Sample Log Entry Message of an Out of Space Warning

```
cpu4:2052)NMP: nmp_ThrottleLogForDevice:2318: Cmd 0x2a (0x41240079e0c0)
to dev "naa.6006016055711d00cff95e65664ee011" on path "vmhba35:C0:T24:L0"
Failed: H:0x0 D:0x2 P:0x0 Valid sense data: 0x6 0x38 0x7.Act:NONE
cpu4:2052)WARNING: ScsiDeviceIO: 2114: Space utilization on thin-
provisioned device naa.6006016055711d00cff95e65664ee011 exceeded configured
threshold
```

```
cpu4:2052)ScsiDeviceIO: 2304: Cmd(0x41240079e0c0) 0x2a, CmdSN 0x3724 to dev
"naa.6006016055711d00cff95e65664ee011" failed H:0x0 D:0x2 P:0x7 Possible
sense data: 0x6 0x38 0x7.
```

I highlighted the relevant entries, which are the following:

- **First Line reported by NMP**—A SCSI `WRITE` command (0x2a) failed with a check condition (D:0x2) and a sense key/ASC/ASCQ combination that means Out of Space Warning.

- **Second line reported by SCSI device I/O vmkernel component**—This line provides an explanation of the event, which is Space Utilization on the device exceeded the configure threshold.

- **Third line also reported by SCSI device I/O**—The `WRITE` command (0x2a) failed due to the same reason reported by NMP on the first line.

An example /var/log/vmkernel.log of an OOS error is shown in Listing 16.13.

Listing 16.13   Out of Space Error Sample Log Entries

```
cpu1:2049)NMP: nmp_ThrottleLogForDevice:2318: Cmd 0x2a (0x412400726c40)
to dev "naa.6006016055711d00cff95e65664ee011" on path "vmhba35:C0:T24:L0"
Failed: H:0x0 D:0x2 P:0x0 Valid sense data: 0x7 0x27 0x7.Act:NONE

cpu1:2049)ScsiDeviceIO: 2315: Cmd(0x412400726c40) 0x2a, CmdSN 0x8f6d to dev
"naa.6006016055711d00cff95e65664ee011" failed H:0x0 D:0x2 P:0x8 Possible
sense data: 0x7 0x27 0x7.

cpu7:37308)FS3DM: 1787: status No space left on device copying 1 extents
between two files, bytesTransferred = 0 extentsTransferred: 0
```

The messages in this log are related to an OOS error compared to a warning. It is reported when a VM using thin provisioned virtual disks attempts to write to a thin provisioned LUN that exceeds the hard threshold set by the array.

I highlighted the relevant entries, which are the following:

- **First line reported by NMP**—`WRITE` command (0x2a) failed with sense key and ASC/ASCQ combination that means Out of Space Error.

- **Second line reported by SCSI device I/O**—`WRITE` command (0x2a) failed with the same sense key and ASC/ASCQ combination.

- **Third line reported by VMFS3 DataMover (FS3DM)**—A copy operation failed between two files.

Summary

This chapter provided details about VAAI, which provides block device primitives, thin provision primitives, as well as NAS primitives. The latter two are new to vSphere 5. It also covered the details of how to enable and disable VAAI primitives as well as how to identify the various devices, support for each primitive.

Index

K-L

Q-R

U

V